From Whorf to Montague

From Whorf
to Montague

Explorations in the Theory of Language

PIETER A. M. SEUREN

OXFORD
UNIVERSITY PRESS

OXFORD

UNIVERSITY PRESS

Great Clarendon Street, Oxford, OX2 6DP,
United Kingdom

Oxford University Press is a department of the University of Oxford.
It furthers the University's objective of excellence in research, scholarship,
and education by publishing worldwide. Oxford is a registered trade mark of
Oxford University Press in the UK and in certain other countries

First Edition published 2013

Impression: 1

Published in the United States of America by Oxford University Press
198 Madison Avenue, New York, NY 10016, United States of America

British Library Cataloguing in Publication Data
Data available

ISBN 978-0-19-968219-5

As printed and bound by
CPI Group (UK) Ltd, Croydon, CRO 4YY

This book is dedicated to John Davey who has been my ever critical and helpful editor for forty years

Short contents

Contents

Preface

A year or so ago, I found myself with some four or five papers, on a variety of topics, that seemed to me to be deserving of a wider audience. It then occurred to me that these papers might well fit into a book spanning a spectrum of theoretical approaches that ranged from Whorf to Montague. No book critically covering such a wide range of topics exists and it might well be useful for students and teaching staff to face the fact that the field of linguistics comprises these extremes and anything in between. By placing these papers in a reasonable expository order, adding a chapter or two for the purpose of the book as a whole, I hope to have found a way to confront students and practitioners of linguistics and related subjects with at least a considerable part of the whole gamut of approaches and ideologies in the field of language studies and thus to help them define their own well-considered position. (This set-up has led to some overlap between the various chapters, but I hope the reader will find this helpful rather than disturbing.) At the same time, such a book would enable me to put forward and defend my own position, including my doubts and uncertainties, in this welter of opinions.

Besides two referees, who read the text on behalf of the publishers and provided many useful comments, a number of wonderful friends and colleagues have been of great help as I was composing the texts. I do not mention them here, as they are mentioned in the notes of the various chapters. But a blanket thank-you must go to the Max Planck Institute for Psycholinguistics at Nijmegen, which has enabled me for the past thirteen years to work there, mix with their people and thus be in the middle of things (without, I hope, being too much of a bother). All these have earned a lasting vote of gratitude.

P.A.M.S.
Nijmegen 2012

Abbreviations and symbols

AAPL	Aristotelian-Abelardian predicate logic
ABPL	Aristotelian-Boethian predicate logic
AUX	Auxiliary
BNPL	Basic-Natural Predicate Logic
Ent	Totality of all entities
GLH	Generalized Logical Hierarchy
IDAP	Internal Definite Anaphora Principle
KK	Katukina-Kanamari
LOCA	Leaking O-Corner Analysis
LOW	Operator Lowering
MAPP	Monomorphemic Alternative Priority Principle
NP	noun phrase
NR	Negative Raising
NST	Natural set theory
OI	Object Incorporation
OP	operator
OR	Object Raising
PAH	Predicate-Argument Hierarchy
PPP	peripheral prepositional phrase
PR	Predicate Raising
PWS	Possible World Semantics
RAH	Relative Accessibility Hierarchy
RBS	Right-Branching Switch
SA	Semantic Analysis
SD	Subject Deletion
SMPL	Standard Modern predicate logic
SMST	Standard mathematical set theory
SOC	Scope-Ordering Constraint
SOV	Subject–Object–Verb
SR	Subject Raising
SSV	substitution salva veritate

SVO	Subject–Verb–Object
TBP	True Binarity Principle
UEI	Undue existential import
UG	Universal Grammar
Un	Universe of possible situations
UPG	Universal Principles of Grammar
UPL	Universal Principles of the Lexicon
V	verb
VR	Verb Raising
VS	Valuation Space
VSO	Verb–Subject–Object
W	the set of all possible worlds
>|<	contradiction
><	contrariety
⊢	entailment
≡	equivalence
≥<	subcontrariety

Introduction

It has become customary, these days, to take a high view of language and talk about it in the global terms used by CEOs of large multinationals, for whom the lowest number worth mentioning needs at least nine digits to be written down in longhand. One hears and reads about overall 'design features' of language or of the mind, 'engineering solutions', long-term evolutionary traits, overall learnability conditions, rough similarities with physiological brain processes and so on, and I have no doubt that it is useful to look at language and cognition in that sort of way from time to time. But I can't help noticing that the linguists, psychologists, biologists and what not who propose their arguments in such visionary terms usually fail to realize how complex language is and how great the risk of fatally flawed perspective-taking. This risk is very real, especially because, other than competent CEOs, linguists and others involved still do not fly high enough to have an adequate overall view of how their object of enquiry is organized. There still is much unclarity as regards the main parameters of language, such as the nature of meaning, the nature of linguistic competence, the relation between linguistic form and linguistic meaning, the relation between linguistic meaning and cognition, to mention just a few. Familiarity with the complexities of language would certainly dampen the enthusiasm for such Olympian views. In the study of language, great visions spanning billions of years and thousands of languages and treating cognition as if it were already in the bag are as yet premature, to say the least. Neither language nor cognition nor evolution is in the bag as yet, not by a long shot. Therefore, happily back from our Olympian holiday, we had better turn to the daily grind again.

This book is about the daily grind. Its purpose is twofold. First, it aims to show that the closer one looks at language, the more pragmatic and cognitivist principles fade away as possible explanations. Secondly, it argues that the use of the standard mathematical logic, with all its formal appendages, is inappropriate for the study of language, as nature has found its own, functionally advantageous, way in the maze of possibilities afforded by logical space. It is a collection of more or less autonomous chapters all centred around the ancient theme of the relation between language, the mind and the world (with the 'collective mind' of any language community playing an important background role). With one exception, all chapters were written in 2010 or 2011, that is, after the publication of my latest two-volume book *Language from Within*. Chapter 7, on reflexivity and identity, is a reworking of a festschrift contribution I wrote in 1989. The first three chapters look at language from an informal point of view, focusing on the social reality of language (Chapter 1), the perennial question of the primacy of language or thought (Chapter 2) and the age-old question of the relation between universal and language-specific features of human language(s) (Chapter 3). There then follow three mildly introductory chapters on the formal properties of language. Chapter 4 is about the relation between language, logic and mathematics—a topic that even formal semanticists and mathematical linguists are not clear about. Chapter 5 is entirely data-oriented, trying to show that the facts of language are of such complexity that it is wholly unrealistic to hope that a theory without 'abstract' principles and rule systems could possibly do the job. Chapter 6 argues that a grammar is a rule system mediating between propositionally structured thoughts and phonologically organized recipes for pronunciation or other systems of utterance production. The argument is directed against the still widespread (Chomskyan) idea that grammars are autonomous and independent of meaning— that is, algorithmic rule systems generating (preferably infinite) sets of output strings. This random generator view of grammars is rejected on the grounds of being *absurd* in any realistic sense and theoretically *perverse* when taken as a mere instrumentalist way of marshalling the facts. In contrast, the view is favoured that sees grammars as ancillary algorithmic rule systems mediating between thought and sound. Consequently, what has become known as the Chomsky hierarchy of formal grammars must be deemed irrelevant to the study of natural language. Chapter 7 aims at showing that reflexivity is much more than a mere coreference relation between a subject term and a term further down the Matrix sentence. In fact, if it is assumed that reflexivity is deeply embedded in cognition, some highly problematic facts, exceeding even the explanatory powers of pragmaticists, will have found a safe haven—though much remains to be done to work out the details. The last two chapters look into the future, in that they present new insights and new avenues of research, especially in semantics and the natural logic of mankind and its language. Part of this process is a fairly radical rephrasing of the basic principles of logic, which is reconnected with cognition and language, and an all-out rejection of what has become known as possible-world semantics.

With one exception, a prominent theme in all this is the status of what some are fond of calling 'abstract' rule systems underlying speech, the actual use of language, and in a direct link with this, the question of how much computational power, general or purpose-specific, is to be attributed to the human mind. My own experience has taught me that one should never underestimate the powers of the mind, whether human or animal. In fact, I am prepared to see the mind accredited with unlimited powers as long as I see no evidence to the contrary, especially when no other explanation than a powerful mind seems to be available to account for the facts observed.

This is true in particular for the syntax of human languages. The essentially Romanticist view that syntax is nothing but the free or 'creative' putting together of words in sentences, following the associative 'movements of thought', reigned supreme in linguistics until well into the twentieth century. We now know better, of course, or at least we ought to know better, but the view that syntax is a matter of freely stringing together words into sentences and thus belongs to the study of performance—or to stylistics with all its literary implications—persisted for a long time. It was common during the nineteenth century and even later authors like De Saussure (1916) and Gardiner (1932) still held the view that syntax was a question of 'parole' or, in Gardiner's words, 'speech', not of 'langue' or the language system.[1] Not until American structuralism and, in particular, generative grammar developed the notion of syntax as a system of structures put together by combinatory rules (Harris 1951), could the linguistic world be convinced that syntax is a formal rule system non-declaratively present in the mind of competent speakers and part of their linguistic competence. It is one of the purposes of this book to help reinforce and further refine the view that syntax is a universally constrained, non-declarative formal rule system converting thought-produced propositional structures into the well-formed surface structures of any given language or language variety.

That this point of view has to be vindicated is clear when one realizes that these days linguists tend to write formal syntax out of the script of theoretical linguistics. It is said that the notion of syntax as a set of rules is an academic fiction and that linguistic production is governed by 'habits' arising from statistically dominant patterns of speaking on the one hand and 'creative' thought processes on the other. Those who support that view revive the old and, we thought, decisively discredited view that utterances are produced and structured mostly according to statistical frequency measures and, to the extent that they are not, according to 'creative' patterns of cognitive and perhaps emotional 'thought' of whatever kind. This 'cognitivist' school thus attempts to unite the information technology view current in the period immediately following Word War II with the view current in the late nineteenth and the early twentieth centuries that syntax is a matter of free creation, whereby speakers follow the (totally undefined) 'movements' of their (equally undefined) 'thoughts'. Needless to say, this brand of 'cognitivism', manifesting itself, in various guises, as so-called *cognitive* or *usage-based grammar* (Langacker 1987, 1991, 2003; Goldberg 1995, 2006; Tomasello 2003; Croft 1991, 2001), is rejected, if only because it simply ignores the masses of empirical evidence and theoretical arguments accumulated over the past half century that make it untenable. Whoever wishes to discard or discredit this accumulated wisdom should at least address the issues, but

---

[1] During the 1930s, the Dutchman Gerrit Overdiep published a 'stylistic grammar' of Dutch (Overdiep 1937), gathering a fairly large circle of followers.

the newfangled cognitivists don't do that. They just ignore them, thereby depriving their students of what they are entitled to, adequate knowledge of the state of the art.

A similar inability to come to terms with the cognitive powers of the human mind is manifest in modern mathematical logic and in particular in Montagovian possible-world semantics—the topic of the last two chapters. In Chapter 8, I make an attempt at fleshing out the notion, defended and developed in earlier publications (especially Seuren 2010), that there is a logic inherent in the human mind and thus in the meanings of the operator words defining that logic, which differs in crucial details from standard modern logic. This *natural logic* is not only impeccably sound, it is also a great deal richer, more powerful and more functional than standard modern logic.

That being so, the bottom falls out of Gricean pragmatics, which was set up, during the 1970s, expressly to bridge the gap between the allegedly unique and inviolate system of modern mathematical logic on the one hand and, on the other, human language thought to be sloppy, ambiguous, vague and generally unreliable. In Chapter 7, I single out one particular class of phenomena, all to do with reflexivity in language and cognition. These phenomena are clearly in the intended remit of Gricean pragmatics, but Gricean pragmatics is unable to account for them. It is shown that one simple logico-semantic restriction, the *True Binarity Principle*, provides an immediate and generally valid explanation for a wide variety of linguistic facts to do with reflexivity. Thus, to mention only three examples, it makes clear why a sentence like *All the girls in her class envy Trisha* does not imply that Trisha envies herself, even though Trisha is a girl in her class, or why the question *Are you your father's son?* is silly in a way that the question *Are you Jacob's son?* is not, even though Jacob is the addressee's father, or why *I didn't educate me* does not mean what *I didn't educate myself* means (both with contrastive accent on the subject term *I*). Current semantic theory, of whatever persuasion, has no provision for these obvious facts. Nor does pragmatic theory.

Chapter 8 goes further. It shows that the triadic predicate logic proposed in Hamilton (1866), though considered inferior by modern logicians, is in fact the basis for a generalized logical hierarchy which also produces the classic Square of Opposition and standard modern predicate logic—though the latter turns out to be extremely impoverished compared to the other two systems. The chapter also shows how natural logic is seen to follow a pattern of three contraries complemented by three subcontraries, a pattern that is gradually beginning to appear to be of a more general cognitive nature. How far this three-plus-three pattern goes in cognition in a general sense is still beyond the horizon, but that there is a striking parallel between natural logic on the one hand and the way humans perceive colours on the other, seems certain. (The colour parallel was discovered and has been elaborated by Dany Jaspers in his recent work about colour perception; see Jaspers 2010, 2011.) All this has come to the fore as a result of a fresh and novel way of looking at logic.

It thus appears that the generally accepted view that the human mind and, with it, human language are logically incompetent is as misguided and misinformed as the once popular view that syntax reflects the whimsical movements of associative thought. There is a parallel in that both views are essentially Romanticist, resulting from the general desire that arose during the eighteenth and prevailed during the nineteenth century to let feelings prevail over reason (to put it simply). Perhaps the time has come now to call the old view into question and to investigate whether human nature has not been undervalued with regard to logical thinking. It is now beginning to transpire that human nature, far from being logically incompetent, is far wiser and shrewder in logical matters than logicians have been prepared to give it credit for.

I must emphasize, in this context, that what I try to undermine is not the *validity* of modern logic, in the accepted sense of the term 'validity' as 'true in virtue of meaning' or 'analytically true'. Rather, what I am attacking is the notion that modern logic is the only repository of validity. In fact, I argue that there are many more valid systems of logic than the average modern logician is prepared to allow for and that natural human logic is to be found outside the area recognized and explored by standard modern logic.

In order to shore up my argument I have had to delve into the foundations of logic in general and of standard modern logic in particular. And as I did that, I found the existing foundations highly incomplete, inadequate and clearly bearing the imprint of the kind of neopositivism that was current during the mid-twentieth century, which makes them unfit to carry the weight of the human factor and, in particular, of cognition. The same goes for possible-world semantics which, being overformalized, obviously misses the link with cognition and, in addition, runs foul of severe empirical obstacles that do not look as if they can be overcome without giving up the entire paradigm.

This book is thus explicitly meant to be controversial—not unexpectedly to those who are familiar with my writings. Yet what I am advocating is not extremist but, on the contrary, moderate in all possible ways. I sustain that, in general, the serious study of language is typically a matter of steering a middle course between various kinds of Scylla and Charybdis—between formalization and nonformal or partially formal analyses, between modularity and open access to general knowledge, between non-declarative and declarative knowledge, between minute analyses and overall model building, between physical and psychological facts, and, in a general sense, between forging ahead and leaving questions undecided. And in the middle of it all, I propose that we should always realize how important it is to cling to the little we have sufficient reason to say we actually know. If this is controversial, then we have reason to reflect upon the present state of language studies, which is precisely what the book before you is meant to bring about.

1

The settling of a language

1.1 A language as part of social reality

This chapter is of a preliminary nature. It is needed not only because settling is a recurrent feature in most of the following chapters but also, in a wider context, because it has a certain explanatory power that has not so far been recognized in theoretical linguistics. Although the term *settling* is based on notions that have for the most part been well-known in sections of linguistics for quite some time, the significance and, I dare say, central role of settling in the coming about and the identity of each specific language and thus the consequences of settling as a factor in the acquisition, the use and the change of any specific language have so far been, if not unknown, in any case underemphasized in the study of language. The reader will understand that, given the new perspective given to this notion, a great deal of further thinking and empirical support is necessary to give it more muscle and clout in linguistic theorizing and linguistic practice alike.

Modern notions like grammaticalization, degrammaticalization, reanalysis, functionality-driven change, and many more, have become legal tender in linguistics, but it is seldom realized that all such processes come to nothing if they are not initiated in and subsequently accepted by any given language community, which reigns supreme in questions regarding the specific form and identity of any given language or language variety. Writing about language and language change without taking settling into account is like writing about law and legislation without taking into account the role of the legislator.

In general terms, settling is the process whereby norms become accepted in a society. Some such norms are linguistic. Linguistic settling occurs when certain ways of speaking 'catch on' in a society or community or a subgroup thereof. Settling phenomena are historical processes of a social nature. They are an indispensable element in sociopsychological processes whereby some attitude, norm or behavioural manifestation gets viewed as 'standard' or 'the thing to do'. It does not look as if social psychology has much to say about the highly elusive turning point in social reality (called 'catastrophe' in the mathematics of dynamical systems), when an innovation becomes accepted as 'standard' for any given group or subgroup. Power relations, fascination and group solidarity seem to be important factors guiding any settling processes, but precisely how and to what extent remains to be sorted out.[1]

Lewis (1969) is an early harbinger of the notion of social reality, but it still misses the point. It considers it to be 'a platitude that language is ruled by convention' (p. 1) and speaks of *conventions* as getting established on the basis of mutual practical *interest* (and tries to capture this notion in the mathematical terms of game theory). But it fails to recognize the philosophically important fact that social reality can make utterances true or false (which is why it is a form of reality): sentences like *Rockefeller was rich* or *'She told me the news' is ungrammatical in English* are true on account of facts in the realm of social reality. Moreover, by putting up each individual's practical interest as the main criterion and *raison d'être* for conventions, it misses the point that members of a society conform to the norms and conventions set by their society out of a deeply ingrained psychological need to 'belong', to have a social identity, and that, conversely, a flouting of one or more norms of the society one belongs to signifies an attitude of rejection or at least a wish to be different in some respect, even if that is definitely *not* in one's interest.

The following passage is illustrative (Lewis 1969: 118–19):

Sometimes people copy each other's actions—say, mannerisms—more or less unaware that they are doing so. Given a group composed entirely of such people, a mannerism can spread and persist by mutual imitation. But there is no preference involved on anyone's part (unless we count every inclination as a transient preference). Each simply does something, not caring and scarcely knowing whether he does it or not. So *a fortiori* his action does not answer to any interest in so acting if the others do. The regularity produced is not a convention.

Lewis is still unaware of the sociopsychological fact that, in following or not following a 'mannerism', there clearly is a 'preference involved', namely that of wishing or not wishing to belong to a group—a key factor in the coming about of a language. Lewis may prefer not to call 'mannerisms' of the kind intended *conventions*. Yet they do, if adopted by a (sub)group, take part in the making up of a language or language variety. The real question is: how and when does some form of behaviour become generally or partially accepted in a (sub)group, that is, settled? Lewis's game-theoretical mathematics falls far short of providing an answer. In fact, no answer has been given to that question yet.

Searle (1995) is the first philosophical publication, to my knowledge, that recognizes the ontological autonomy of social reality. As such it marks an important

---

[1] Sherif and Sherif (1966) (referred to in Eibl-Eibesfeldt 1989: 290) investigated experimentally-induced group formation among initially unacquainted 11- and 12-year-old boys in a holiday camp. It was found that within two to three days small groups of three to four boys had formed naturally, on the basis of personal preferences. The authors then assigned the boys to two new groups, intentionally separating friends. Each new group was assigned a variety of camp tasks. Within days, new group habits, attitudes and working methods developed, along with a strong sense of group pride and solidarity. Interestingly, besides secrets and jokes, a group-specific jargon developed in each of the two new groups, which goes to show how closely linguistic settling phenomena are correlated with feelings of group identity.

passage in philosophical thinking. Unfortunately, for what seem to be autocentric reasons, Searle's analysis of the concept of social reality is unduly fixed upon speech acts, in that, for him, social reality comes about exclusively as a result of speech acts— a concept that he extends to cover 'implicit' speech acts, whatever that may mean.

Settling has occurred the moment individuals feel collectively that they follow the (old or new) group standard when thinking or behaving in a particular way. Linguistic settling phenomena define what speakers see as the *identity* of their language or language variety, in line with their social identity or identities. All socially valid linguistic norms are the result of settling processes. Sometimes they are, perhaps distantly, correlated with some cultural alignment with regard to cognitive categories, but such cultural alignment is itself again the result of settling. Mostly, however, linguistic settling is the result of the wish of groups of speakers to manifest themselves linguistically to other members of the community and to outsiders in a specific way, just as there are socially driven alignments for dress or good manners. This is obviously so for pronunciation but it also holds for lexical meanings, idioms and even rules of grammar. All historical changes in languages are the result of settling, perhaps motivated by functionality or a wish to be different from other groups, but no innovation becomes part of the language or dialect unless it is sanctioned by group agreement. Dialects develop at least in part as a result of speakers wishing to manifest their regional identity in the vernacular spoken.[2] This is also the case for sociolects and the corresponding socio-cultural identity or identities, and for interactional varieties, set out on a scale ranging from informal to formal, with sometimes specific niches for certain interactional settings, as, for example, the so-called 'mother-in-law' language in the Australian language Dyirbal discussed in Dixon (1972: 32–4, 292–6) (see section 3.3). Any language spoken by a community with internal social divisions will have an amount of dialectal, sociolectal and interactional variation, much or most of which forms part of the linguistic competence of its speakers. Linguistic competence is thus virtually always internally complex in that speakers have active, and above all passive, command of a large number of internal variants, each marked for a value on geographic, social and interactional parameters. Any adequate description of a language will, therefore, have to specify such internal variability of linguistic competence (see Seuren 1982 for an extensive discussion).

In exceptional cases, especially when a language comes into being under forced conditions, settling can take place on a massive scale and at high speed, so that a new language is defined possibly within the time span of one generation (as in the case of

---

[2] It is not surprising to see that languages of nations with a strong and historically ingrained sense of unified national identity and a corresponding weak sense of regional identity show relatively little dialect variation and change relatively little over time. This is typically so for Turkish, spoken by a nation with a long tradition of strong nationalism. Although Turkey's geography meets all conditions for great dialectal variation (large distances through thinly populated areas, great regional isolation), dialectal variation within Turkish as a national language is minimal compared with other nations.

Creole languages, discussed in section 1.3), but once a language has settled and has acquired its social identity, further settling is, for the most part, a slow process, affecting only some elements of the language at a time and doing so in a way that is largely imperceptible to its speakers.

The closest modern linguistic theorizing comes to the notion of settling is in *speech accommodation theory*, first broached in Giles (1973) and meanwhile integrated as an aspect of sociolinguistics and dialectology (see, for example, Giles, Coupland and Coupland 1991). In Giles (1973) it is shown that in speech occurring in binary face-to-face interaction, depending on each interlocutor's desire to be accepted or positively looked upon by the other, class and dialect differences in pronunciation and even in syntax tend to get reduced, whereas they tend to get accentuated when an interlocutor has the conscious or unconscious wish not to be associated with the other, for whatever reason—all without the interlocutors being in the least aware of their behaviour. When extended to groups of speakers and their mutual attitudes, often following institutionalized power relations, such accommodation or dissociation processes take on a social dimension and may thus reach that elusive turning point at which the results 'catch on'—that is, become settled (Auer and Hinskens 2005: 336). Unfortunately, the theoretical consequences of this and similar insights have hardly been explored to the extent they deserve to be. Auer and Hinskens (2005) and Kristiansen and Jørgensen (2005) are exceptions. Auer and Hinskens (2005) still fails to break away from the accepted but false notion that accommodation phenomena are the automatic result of mere frequency of occurrence conditions. By contrast, Kristiansen and Jørgensen (2005), and also Kammacher, Stöhr and Jørgensen (2011), are the only publications I have been able to trace in which the view is defended that large scale *subjective acceptance* is the crucial factor in language (or dialect or sociolect) change. Settling theory is in agreement with this point of view and seeks to develop it further, integrating it into the general theory of language.

Frequency of occurrence clearly plays some role, but, it seems, much less in settling processes than in the stable use of fully settled language systems, where frequency of use leads to ingrained routines and thus contributes to the stability and fluent command of the system. In settling, however, the crucial, though so far elusive, factor seems to be the 'feeling' among a group of speakers that this or that is the 'thing to do' when you want to make manifest that you belong to a certain group with a certain status and mentality. For this 'feeling' to come about, frequency is of minor importance: a handful of occurrences often suffices for an innovation to 'catch on'. Much more important is the evaluation associated with the phenomenon in question. When that evaluation is positive, it *causes* frequency, rather than the other way round. Attributing that 'feeling' to frequency measures is an aberration that is typical for the in many respects destructive influence of neopositivism in the human sciences. Neopositivism tried to reduce the human mind to a passive receptacle of external influences, but it is now finally, and too slowly, beginning to be recognized that the human mind is a highly active processing system that takes sense data as input and delivers specific conceptualizations, mental representations, memories, theories, tendencies and, in the end, forms of behaviour, owing to its own internal causal powers.

During the 1960s, if one wanted to be seen as sympathizing with, or belonging to, the new hippy movement in the English-speaking world, one used certain marked hippy-flavoured expressions, such as *suss out* (for 'figure out') or the now hopelessly dated *groovy* (called 'cool' in our day), or the now generally accepted *album* (originally for one or more long-play pop-music records forming a set and packed in a fancy cover, now currently used for a CD with pop music). This 'feeling', which may arise even under conditions of low frequency of use, is the determining factor of what I call 'settling'. I thus fully endorse Niedzielsky and Giles (1996: 338), quoted in Auer and Hinskens (2005: 335): 'accommodation theory should be one of the major frameworks to which researchers in language change should turn.'

Unfortunately from a theorist's point of view, speech accommodation theory has concentrated mainly on practical applications (medical and care settings, legal discourse, selection and training of radio and TV speakers, second language learning, language switching in bilingual communities, etc.). Giles et al. write in their introductory chapter (1991: 3):

It is, in fact, the *applied* perspective that predominates in the following chapters and in accommodation theory as a whole. As the title of the volume implies, we present accommodation theory here less as a theoretical edifice and more as a basis for sociolinguistic explanation. The book as a whole seeks to demonstrate how the core concepts and relationships invoked by accommodation theory are available for addressing altogether pragmatic concerns [...].

The present chapter is meant to contribute to a better understanding of the *theoretical* aspects of speech accommodation theory and its more comprehensive partner, settling theory.

A few examples taken from the history of modern linguistics may illustrate how settling theory fills a much neglected gap. The, at the time heated and often fruitless, debates around the Young Grammarians' notion of exceptionless sound laws would have been much more orderly and sedate, Schleicher's (1861/2) *Stammbaum theory* and Schmidt's (1872) *wave theory* of language change would have been easily reconciled, and the Saussurean-Chomskyan notion of linguistic competence would have been much richer and more adequate, had the notion of settling, and thus of internally structured social reality, been taken into account in a proper manner.[3]

And as regards modern times, the recent study by the seasoned and highly respected sociolinguist Peter Trudgill (Trudgill 2011), which deals with 'social

---

[3] For a more complete discussion of nineteenth-century concepts of convergence and divergence of dialects and sociolects, see Hinskens et al. (2005: 2–5). Their discussion makes it clear how much a proper notion of sociolinguistic settling is needed.

determinants of linguistic complexity', as its subtitle says, and discusses the entire modern relevant literature, fails to present settling as an explanatory factor in language change, in particular as regards the rate, the magnitude and the direction of change. Trudgill does point, for example, at the correlation between linguistic conservatism and the geographical isolation of small communities of expatriates, such as the small and relatively isolated communities of Dutch speakers in the United States (or Brazil, for that matter), who are keen to stress and preserve their original character and thus put a damper on both change and variability (apart from adstrate influence from the surrounding standard language), but the sociopsychological factor of settling remains implicit.[4] Owing to the overall neglect of the settling factor in the sociolinguistic literature, sociopsychological processes related with status, group identity and similar phenomena, and the role of in-built social regulatory mechanisms have remained underexposed.

Settling phenomena constitute what has to be *learned and memorized* in the process of language acquisition: they form the load of linguistic (lexical) memory in the language acquisition process. This applies in particular to idiomatic expressions and ways of speaking, which makes it harder to acquire full command of a (foreign) language but also makes for greater predictability of what speakers will actually say in given contexts, given a fully competent listener. Even so, however, settling phenomena are subject to whatever universal constraints there are on how languages can develop (see Chapter 3), and also to existing grammatical and semantic rules and patterns. Cases where existing rules and even rule systems are put aside are relatively rare but they do occur and may lead to a structural or semantic change in the language concerned. For example, for decades, American journalists used a manneristic locution of the type *Says Dr. Mortimer: 'Blablabla.'* This is ungrammatical in normal English, yet it became accepted in newspaper and magazine reports. Had it acquired enough prestige and become generally accepted in the language community as a whole, and had it been extended to sentence structure generally, it would have meant a structural change of the language: English might have become a verb-first language. It hasn't (in fact, the mannerism seems to have petered out), but it could have happened.

The settling of a language thus comprises sociolinguistic processes in virtue of which certain ways of speaking, whether at the phonetic, phonological, morphological, syntactic, semantic, lexical or idiomatic level, become socially aligned or accepted, on grounds of group identity, mostly just by mere chance, but always

---

[4] Interestingly, the German-Austrian linguist Hugo Schuchardt (1842–1927), already stressed the sociopsychological factor as a determinant of phonological and other forms of language change. In his little pamphlet against the Young Grammarians (Schuchardt 1885), he uses the concept of *fashion* (German *Mode*) to show that sound laws are far from exception-free. As with most of Schuchardt's other important contributions to linguistic theory, this insight was ignored in mainstream linguistics.

within the bounds of what is permitted or possible in natural language and of comprehensibility criteria set by the language as it was before the particular settling process set in. Such settling is a direct consequence of the fact that each specific language or (dialectal or sociolinguistic) language variety, as opposed to what we call 'language' in general, is a piece of *social reality*. The ontological status of a specific language or language variety is not that of the material world (languages are not sets of utterances), nor that of the mental world of imaginations or abstractions (languages are not sets of sentences), but that of the social world. In general, social reality is epiphenomenal upon mental reality and emerges as soon as there is a community of humans functioning as a social group. Social reality comprises the body of all conventions, norms and values internalized by the members of any given social group or society. Any community's *culture* is thus closely interwoven with its social reality, a culture being considered to be the sum of all abilities, traditions, beliefs, knowledge, learning, and the tangible products thereof, developed and produced within a community and thus accessible to its members.

To see how *real* social reality is, one only has to consider the fact that the notions of wealth or poverty, though expressed in material terms, result from socially valid conventions and norms. And likewise for such apparently trivial properties as having a name,[5] being employed or married, having rights and duties, and so on. Any given language L is clearly part of social reality, in that L has been adopted by, or in, a particular community or society as a conventional system for the expression of *intents*—that is, speech acts that socially commit the speaker with regard to any given proposition (see Chapter 4 in Seuren 2009a).

Since the mid-1960s, it has been customary, in the wake of Chomsky (1964; 1965), to equate the concept of 'specific language' with that of 'linguistic competence'—that is, with what any individual competent speaker has internalized in the way of, largely tacit, knowledge (or command) of any specific language L. This, however, is only part of the picture. If it were the whole picture, as was already stressed by De Saussure (1916),[6] it would be impossible for an individual speaker to discover, say, a new word in L, since the speaker, being competent in L, should already know the word. Yet speakers do discover new words in their language all the time. The reason is that if

---

[5] Kripke's (1972; 1980) philosophical, so-called 'causal', theory of proper names, for example, no matter how influential, is invalid for a number of reasons, one of them being the fact that that author seems totally unaware of the notion of social reality. Being called 'Paul' is a socially defined property of the person concerned—not, of course, a physical property—and can thus be used for referential identification like any other property, physical or social, adhering to individual entities. See Seuren (1998: 378–81; 2009a: 130, 191–2) for further discussion.

[6] De Saussure wrote (1916: 30), confusing language in general with each specific language (translation mine):

Language ['la langue'] [...] is a grammatical system virtually existing in each brain, or, more precisely, in the brains of a totality of individuals; for language is not complete in any single brain, it exists perfectly only in the mass of speakers.

L is the language of a complex language community, it will be practically impossible for any speaker to have a full command of the entire lexicon and of all varieties of L current in the community in question. That being so, it will be the rule for any speaker to have no more than a partial command of L, so that there is plenty of room to find out about parts of L beyond the speaker's own mastery, just as one may find out new facts about customs, norms or values within the same overall community one is a member of, but beyond or outside the section one happens to be part of or familiar with.

De Saussure already saw, to some extent at least, the importance of the social parameter in the study of language. For him, language, or rather any specific language, is a social fact. We read, for example (De Saussure 1916: 25) (translation mine):

Language ['la langue'] [. . .] is at the same time a social product of the language faculty ['faculté du langage'] and an ensemble of necessary conventions adopted by the social body to make possible the use of this language faculty by individual speakers.

But he does not elaborate this notion in any depth. Yet De Saussure's analysis was more advanced than Chomsky's, whose notion of 'competence' fails entirely to take the social parameter into account.

Settling is not an option; it is a necessity. Not only do speakers have to settle on phonological form, they also need to consider their language to be part of their social identity. And their social identity is many-layered. Every individual is, first of all, a member of one wide group as opposed to other comparable wide groups. But then, within the wide group, there are many subdivisions, according to socio-economic status, authority, profession, political preference, hobby, or otherwise.[7] Depending on the kind of interaction, speakers will wish to emphasize or de-emphasize their specific social status, whether high or low, and often also their socio-political ideology, whether left or right, or whatever. This makes it necessary for the language common to the community in the wide sense to incorporate masses of, usually minute, distinctions indicative of specific social groups and specific interactional situations. This is achieved by means of mostly inscrutable processes of social alignment resulting in sociolinguistically marked features of the language in question—that is, settling.

As a matter of method, to attribute real or apparent whims of any given language to mere arbitrary settling is a last-resort measure. That is, one has to investigate first whether there is any reasonable way of attributing a particular seemingly unruly feature of a language to some systematic factor or feature in language in general or in the language or language group at issue in particular. If there is, that rule system or general principle is the main explanatory factor. Of course, that rule or rule system is

---

[7] See, notably, Labov (1966), Seuren and Hamans (2010) and some comments made in Seuren (2009a: 148) for the importance of social stratification as a factor in language change.

itself the result of settling, but the linguist must try first of all to formulate the rule or rule system in such a way that exceptions are minimized. Only when there seems no way of reducing an apparent irregularity to any general principle, is one entitled to consider the possibility that it is due to mere arbitrary settling, the whimsical 'will of the people'.

For example, Italian has the words *chiunque* ('whoever'), *qualunque* ('whichever'), *dovunque* ('wherever'), *comunque* ('however', in the literal sense of 'no matter how'),[8] but *quandunque* ('whenever'), though current in older forms of the language, has lost favour with 'the people' and is now obsolete, and **cheunque* (for 'whatever') has never existed. No alleged universal scale seems to be involved in this selection, nor does there seem to be any general principle in language, cognition or social reality that would predict this precise selection, which does appear to be fully arbitrary. Or take the Portuguese word *erro* ('error'), from Latin *error*. All other words belonging to this class, derived from Latin third declension masculine nouns ending in *-or* (*terror, amor*, etc.), have ended up in modern Portuguese with the final accented syllable *-or*, based on the Latin accusative singular. And analogously in most other Romance languages. The form *erro* is unique, in that it has accent on the first syllable and lacks the final *-r*, suggesting that it stems from the Latin nominative singular form. Why this exception to the rule should have come about is unknown. It certainly violates the Young Grammarian principles of absolutely regular linguistic change. All we can do is fall back on settling as a last-resort measure, invoking the whimsical 'will of the people'.

Clearly, if in future any general principle were to be unearthed predicting the particular selection in Italian *-unque* words described above, or the unique form *erro* in Portuguese, the 'mere settling' label must give place to a more detailed and more explanatory label, which will, however, still include 'settling' as a final seal of approval by the language community in question. The general point is that irreducible arbitrary settling phenomena resulting from arbitrary social alignment processes do occur in natural languages and this fact has not been sufficiently taken into account as an ultimate explanatory principle to fall back on in theories of language and language change.

1.2 Languages 'go their own way'

The study of settling phenomena corresponds with the study of what is arbitrary, or a matter of free variation, in any specific language, as opposed to what is necessary or preferred on grounds of conceptual structure or the physical, physiological and mental ecology of language in general, and no doubt also of universal, specifically

---

[8] Note that the current modern meaning of English *however* is a case of semantic bleaching as discussed in section 1.2.2.

linguistic constraints beyond those imposed by the ecology of language. Given that a language is by definition the property of a language community and thus belongs in the realm of social reality, the question is: how far does the arbitrariness of any specific language go? To what extent is a community of speakers free to settle on the expressive means of their choice? Do speakers have unrestricted freedom or are they subject to universal restrictions dictated by the necessities or the functionality of ecological criteria of cognitive structure, brain structure, the physics and physiology of sound production and perception and of specifically linguistic universal constraints? The question is an old one, but the role of settling—that is, of being part of social reality—has been underemphasized in the literature. Yet it has a direct bearing on certain wide-ranging current debates in linguistics, such as the debate between Whorfians and non-Whorfians (see Chapter 2), or between universalists and relativists (see Chapter 3).

1.2.1 *The arbitrary extension of semantic categories*

Settling is evident, for example, in the extension from natural to arbitrary nominal gender. In Greek, Latin, German and many other languages with triple nominal gender, it is obvious that masculine and feminine gender are somehow related to the natural genders male and female, respectively: nouns denoting males are typically masculine and likewise for females and feminine gender, neuter gender being reserved for genderless objects. Yet apart from these 'grounding' cases, so to speak, the three genders are distributed over the nouns of these languages in what can only be described as arbitrary ways (see Köpcke and Zubin 1996 for the vagaries of nominal gender assignment in German). Thus, to take just a couple of examples, Latin feminine *mensa* ('table') corresponds to German masculine *Tisch*. Yet there was never anything feminine about a table in Roman culture, nor anything masculine about it in German culture. Or take the class of words in the Romance languages ending in the various equivalents of the Latin suffix *-aticum* ('having to do with'), as in French *courage*, *voyage*, *paysage*, or Italian *coraggio*, *viaggio*, *paesaggio*. All such words are masculine in French and Italian, which is understandable since they derive from Latin neuter forms in *-aticum*. Yet in Portuguese, the corresponding words, such as *coragem*, *viagem*, *paisagem*, are feminine. Why? No other reason can be given than that it has been the 'will of the people' to make these words feminine.

Allegory is remarkable in this regard. In allegory, there is, surprisingly perhaps, some reverse influence, from arbitrary grammatical gender back to cognition. For example, the Ancient Greek playwright Sophocles, in his play *Electra* (c. 405 BCE), lines 75–6, writes: 'For the Right Moment has come, he who is the highest ruler over all human enterprise.' The masculine Greek noun *kairós* ('the right moment') requires the male allegorical *epistátēs* ('ruler') in Greek, and not its possible female (allegorical) counterpart *epistátria* (the word is not attested in Ancient Greek but means 'female ruler' in Modern Greek). English allows for *he* and *ruler* as it has no nominal gender distinction between masculine and feminine, but in German, which has feminine, masculine and neuter nominal gender, *kairós* may be translated as the feminine *die richtige Zeit*, which requires the feminine forms *sie* ('she') and *Herrscherin* ('female ruler') for the allegory: 'Denn jetzt ist die richtige Zeit da, sie, die übermächtige Herrscherin über jedes Menschenwerk.' But *kairós* can also be translated as the (masculine) *Zeitpunkt*, in which case the translation has to be 'Denn jetzt ist der richtige Zeitpunkt da, er, der übermächtige Herrscher über jedes Menschenwerk.' One could not possibly use *Herrscherin* in the latter or *Herrscher* in the former translation. The same goes for the motto of the following chapter 'Lingua ancilla mentis' ('Language is the mind's handmaiden'). It would be impossible to say in Latin *!'Lingua famulus mentis' ('Language is the mind's (male) servant'), the reason being that *lingua* has feminine gender and thus requires a female allegorical personification. This interesting phenomenon has not so far been explored to any extent.

1.2.2 *Semantic bleaching*

Settling processes, especially when they are instances of grammaticalization (the common process whereby an independent lexical word becomes incorporated into the morphology or a strictly regulated separate subpart of the syntax of a language), often imply what is known as 'semantic bleaching', a process whereby words, expressions or constructions lose elements of their original truth-conditional, emotive or attitudinal meaning and become standardized as expressive means for less idiosyncratic semantic categories. For example, the English expression *be going to* lost its original meaning of 'be moving in the direction of' to become a semi-auxiliary verb denoting expected proximate future, often assuming the phonologically contracted form *gonna* in the process.

The English future auxiliaries *shall* and *will* are clear cases of semantic bleaching. *Shall* derives from a Germanic verb meaning 'owe, be indebted' (related to the German word *Schuld* 'debt, fault'); *will* from a Germanic verb meaning 'want, wish, choose'. The Modern Greek particle of futurity *tha* derives (with a great deal of phonological wear) from the stem *thel-* of the verb *thélein* ('want', 'wish') followed by the particle *na* ('that'). Likewise for the future tenses in the Romance languages, all derived from a verbal infinitive plus the Latin verb *habere* ('have'), bleached to the sense of mere futurity via an implicitly suppleted object term 'have the intention/ task to....'. Many languages have a comparative construction with a preposition meaning 'from' as the comparative particle: 'John is taller 'from' Harry' (Stassen 1985). Here, the comparative is seen as a parameter on which John's value is high, reckoned 'from' Harry's value. All these are clear cases of semantic bleaching, and many more such cases could be quoted.

And why did these innovations take place? Partly, as in the case of futuricity in Greek and the Romance languages, because the old, often irregular, morphological paradigms had become too complex to acquire for young learners, whose vernacular was often a non-Greek or non-Latin language, and partly, as in the case of English, because the old paradigms had become too closely associated with a (pre-Norman-Conquest) past that was better forgotten. In all cases, new generations settled on new forms to express futuricity, and these new forms show, besides conspicuous parallels and analogies, also considerable variety.

The lexicon is replete with bleached meanings. The German verb *scheinen* and the Dutch verb *schijnen* (both in the meaning 'seem') are cases in point. They were bleached from an original verb meaning 'shine' and consequently adapted to their present verb-argument structure and corresponding syntax. Or consider German *stehen* or Dutch *staan*, both with the literal meaning 'stand' but bleached to the meaning 'occur in a book, text or image', for which English uses the verb *be*. Again, such cases are ubiquitous.

Metaphor plays an important role in this respect. One only has to think of the countless bleached (and thus conventionalized) metaphors in all languages of the world, whose origins sometimes lie in a forgotten past. Most such metaphors have become entirely opaque, in the sense that speakers no longer realize the original meaning transfer. Thus, English speakers not belonging to the exclusive class of those trained in etymology will not or hardly think of a hand when using the expression *handed down through the ages*, or of a raising process when using the expression *raise an objection*—even though there may be imperceptible stirrings of the original items (*hand, raise*) that are picked up by brain scanners but do not enter the stream of active or passive speech processing. Consequently, what has been handed down through the ages cannot be said to be *handed up* to the future, nor can an objection said to have been raised be said to be *lowered* again: idiosyncratic settling has broken the opposition relations concerned. Likewise, a sentence like *John was given the sack* is not processed in terms involving an actual sack, nor will speakers be able to refer to the sack said to have been given to John by means of the anaphoric pronoun *it*: we cannot say *!John was given the sack but he gave it back*.

Some bleached metaphors, however, have been less integrated into the language at hand and have retained some semantic transparency. When we use the expression *The penny dropped*, some notion of a penny seems to be still there, since we can say, for example, *At that moment, the penny was supposed to drop, but it didn't*, where the anaphoric *it* refers back to the metaphorical penny. Likewise with the expression *ring a bell*, as in *His mention of Ann Lipmore rang a bell, but the bell was never answered*. All such facts and distinctions must be memorized and classified in the proper manner, due to the whims of 'the people', who settle for certain ways of speaking and reject others, in terms of a given overall system about which we still know relatively little.

1.2.3 *Auxiliation*

In what probably amounts to most cases, settling is arbitrary only within preset limits and follows preset tendencies found in language after language. One such tendency is *auxiliation* (Seuren 1996; Kuteva 2001), the well-known process whereby standard frame-setting predicates, such as predicates for the time-setting, modality, or source-of-information category (evidentiality) of the proposition as such, acquire a special 'auxiliary' status, implying that such predicates tend to become morphologized as affixes integrated into finite-verb morphology or as particles forming part of a verbal cluster (as in most Creole languages); or, when they maintain predicate status, they are incorporated into verbal clusters in particular ways and thus reduced to a restricted paradigm allowing only for finite verb forms (as with the English modal auxiliaries).[9]

Auxiliation processes clearly follow a common pattern, yet languages differ as to the details, including the extent to which they let the candidate predicates follow the pattern. A striking example is offered by the Dutch and German verbs for *futuricity* (it is well-known that futuricity is not a tense but a modality or source-of-information category). The Dutch verb for futuricity is *zullen*; the German equivalent is *werden*. A typical feature of auxiliation is the lack of infinitives and participles. In this light, one observes that Dutch *zullen* has not (yet) undergone auxiliation, whereas German *werden* has, as appears from the fact that (1.1a) is good grammatical Dutch, whereas (1.1b) is ungrammatical in German. The reason we are entitled to say this is that Dutch still allows for the infinitival form *zullen*, whereas German has already reached the auxiliation stage where the infinitival *werden* is excluded (see also the examples (2.1) to (2.4), and note 13 in section 2.3.8):

(1.1)   a.   Het had niet zullen regenen vandaag.
         b.   *Es hätte nicht regnen werden heute.

Both sentences mean 'the prediction was that it would not rain today', and the grammatical analysis of both sentences is largely parallel (but for the fact that the Dutch infinitival cluster *zullen regenen* is right-branching, whereas its German counterpart *regnen werden* is left-branching; see section 5.3.1). Yet (1.1a) is fully grammatical but (1.1b) is fully ungrammatical. This curious contrast between German and Dutch has not only remained largely unobserved in the literature, it is also crucial to show that languages vary in the extent to which they 'allow' their

---

[9] For at least the European languages, the restricted paradigm of auxiliarized predicates is explained by the assumption that they are re-assigned a position, in the underlying semantic analysis (SA) of sentences, between the two tenses *present/past* and *simultaneous/preceding* (Seuren 1996). Typically, causative and permissive predicates do not undergo grammatical auxiliation but are prone to a lexical process whereby they are turned into lexicalized morphemes (see section 3.7.2.3). In this respect, the 'will of the people' clearly appears to be constrained by general principles.

modal verbs to auxiliate. Dutch and German have hardly started to auxiliate their modals, but the case of *zullen/werden* shows that the tendency is there. The determining factor here can only be, it seems, the inscrutable 'will of the people'— that is, settling—but constrained by principles that transcend specific language communities.

As regards the English modals, it is well-known (see, for example, Van Kemenade 1992) that in Old English they were more like other verbs, with a less restricted paradigm—though there seem to have been some restrictions with regard to 'ordinary' lexical verbs. Van Kemenade quotes Old English (1.2), with the infinitive form *cunnen* ('to be able'), which shows that, at the period concerned, auxiliation of *can* had not been completed (Van Kemenade 1992: 159):

(1.2)   ...þatt   I   shall   cunnen   cwemenn   Godd
         ...that   I   shall   can   please   God
         '...that I will be able to please God'

The gradual disappearing of the verb-clustering process from English syntax (probably under the influence of Norman French syntax) during the Middle Ages may have rendered such constructions less popular and may have speeded up the auxiliation process. Be that as it may, no account will be viable unless it takes 'the will of the people' as an integral part of the story, whereby it is accepted that one change in the grammar may precipitate other changes, in that it will predispose the community of speakers to incorporate further changes that now 'feel' more natural as they follow the same grammatical pattern. It thus seems that the notion of settling, introducing as it does the factor of social psychology, makes for a more complete understanding of processes of historical change of languages. Yet it does not exhaust the explanation, since there is clearly a common development, most developed in English, less in German and even less in Dutch, in which the process of *auxiliation* leads to the loss of non-finite verb forms. Sociolinguistic settling cannot be invoked here, since during the period in which these processes took place in the languages mentioned, there was no social interaction to speak of between the communities concerned.

Other striking examples of the fact that settling is not arbitrary but subject to rules and principles of language-specific and universal grammar are the English verbs *need* and *dare*. These two verbs have only partially undergone auxiliation. Normally, English auxiliation takes away the final -*s* of the present tense third-person singular and makes the following infinitive come without the usual particle *to*. *Dare* and *need* can only (optionally) occur as auxiliaries in a so-called 'negative context'—that is, under a commanding negation or in a question or conditional context (*if*-clauses or restrictive relative or participial clauses under an *any*-antecedent). Auxiliary *dare* and *need* are thus classic *negative polarity items*. When these conditions are not met, *dare* and *need* must be used as ordinary main verbs (with the third-person singular -*s* and with the particle *to* for the following infinitive). This is a typical settling phenomenon, in that the community of English speakers at some time in the past decided to allow the original main verbs *need* and *dare* to enter the path of auxiliation—taken by other 'supporting' verbs before—but only as negative polarity items. This development, whilst subject to 'the will of the people', is not totally arbitrary, since both auxiliation and negative polarity are firmly lodged in the universal principles of human language. This explains why learners of English, once they have mastered the auxiliary (negative polarity) use of *need* and *dare*, automatically—that is, without explicit instruction—allow for a sentence like *Anyone who dare lay hands on her will regret that*, but will reject its thinkable equivalent **Anyone daring lay hands on her will regret that*, the reason being that, once *dare* is used as an auxiliary, its present participle *daring* is excluded—despite the general rule allowing relative clauses to be replaced with participles and despite the frequent and grammatical occurrence of the word *daring* as an adjective, a noun or as the present participle of the non-auxiliary main verb *dare*. By contrast, the English verb *help*, which has not undergone auxiliation but happens to take an optional *to* for its infinitival complement, shows a different behaviour, as one can say both *Anyone who helps find the thief will be rewarded* and *Anyone helping find the thief will be rewarded*. (It does not look as if any statistics-based or 'usage-based' theory of grammar or language acquisition will be able to account for such facts.)

1.2.4 *Perfective auxiliaries:* have *or* be

Another conspicuous case where language takes liberties with regard to semantic categories is provided by the selection of perfective auxiliaries—the equivalents of *have* and *be* in the various European languages that make the distinction. There seems to be a rough general principle to the effect that *have* is used for the perfective tenses of action verbs, while *be* is selected for stative verbs and for verbs indicating movement or change of state. But, apart from the fact that this general principle fails to cover all cases, there are so many exceptions—different exceptions for each language concerned—clearly contradicting it, that no general, leak-proof principle has been found so far, whether for each specific language or for all languages concerned. The question is, in fact, a well-known red herring in the study of European languages. It seems that the assumption of settling processes, interfering with the general semantic principle and thus making this principle harder to detect, will be helpful towards finding a well-founded, satisfactory albeit last-resort, solution to this old problem.

It will then be necessary to explain how the underlying semantic principle, though overridden in many instances, is still felt to guide and direct interpretation. For example, every Dutch speaker will immediately catch on to the difference between, on the one hand, *Ik* ʙᴇɴ *in de boom geklommen* ('I climbed into the tree'), with the perfective auxiliary *zijn* ('be'), and *Ik* HEB *in de boom geklommen* ('I have been climbing in the tree'), with the perfective auxiliary *hebben* ('have'), on the other. The latter denotes an activity within a certain area (the tree); the former denotes a movement from one place to another. Dutch speakers are not taught that difference, yet they immediately see the point of the observation and accept it. When confronted with novel cases, speakers and hearers will fall back on the original underlying semantic principle. The mechanics of processes of this nature is still opaque, yet to find out one first has to formulate the settling principle, something which has not been done so far.

1.2.5 *Subtle near-synonyms:* use *conditions versus* truth *conditions*

The settling of a language also extends to the many cases where the use of near-synonyms is governed by minute and subtle cognitive distinctions that are not truth-conditional (though obviously at the command of speakers), where linguists have, in many such cases, not or only imperfectly been able to identify them and make them explicit. This is not to say that settling is always without truth-conditional implications. Semantic bleaching and semantic specialization as historical processes necessarily involve truth conditional changes. Yet the combined result of bleaching and specialization may result in a situation where 'category mistakes' are not truth-conditional but are merely errors of usage. The Dutch sentences, discussed a few lines above, *Ik ben in de boom geklommen* and *Ik heb in de boom geklommen* differ truth-conditionally precisely because Dutch speakers have settled on the use of the perfective auxiliary *zijn* ('be') for intransitive verbs of movement and on *hebben* ('have') for verbs of activity. If a verb, such as *klimmen* ('climb'), can be used both as a verb of movement and as an activity verb, the choice of *zijn* or *hebben* as a perfective auxiliary triggers a truth-conditional difference. Likewise, as observed by a referee, in English you go some place *in* a taxi but *on* a bus, the generalization being that *on* is used with scheduled means of transportation. Now, when someone speaks of going to the moon *in* a rocket this is not the same as speaking of going to the moon *on* a rocket: the latter implies a regular rocket service to the moon (unless one thinks of a person riding a rocket to the moon, as in a children's story). But let us focus here on non-truth-conditional cases of settling.

Consider the case of Dutch verbs of 'being located'. They are spread over a number of near-synonyms—all the result of semantic bleaching—including *staan* ('stand'), *liggen* ('lie'), *zitten* ('sit'). Dutch speakers say that plates 'stand in' the cupboard, money 'stands on' a bank or a word 'stands in' a text. The Dutch sentence *Bob staat op de foto* is ambiguous between 'Bob is in the picture' and 'Bob is standing on the picture', but *Bob zit op de foto* can only mean 'Bob is sitting on the picture'. Napkins 'lie in' the cupboard and money 'lies in' the drawer, while wine 'sits in' the bottle and John 'sits in' prison or as a student 'at' a school, with the preposition *op* ('on'), but at a university only as a staff member, with the preposition *aan* ('at'). (In the nineteenth century, an elementary school teacher 'stood at' (*aan*) a school.) When a Dutch speaker says that the plates *sit* in the cupboard, when they are in fact there, what is said is not false but merely ill-expressed. The exact cognitive conditions for the proper use of these and similar variants are thus not of a truth-conditional nature but merely a matter of conventionalized proper usage and thus of linguistic settling.

Likewise as regards the corresponding causatives, in the sense of 'cause to be located', which are spread over a handful of near-synonyms, such as *zetten* ('set'), *leggen* ('lay'), *stoppen* ('put away'), *doen* ('do'). Typical examples of proper uses of these verbs are the following, though there are overlaps, mostly with subtle semantic distinctions: *zetten* is typically used, for example, for putting a car in a garage, flowers in a vase, books on a shelf or plates in a cupboard; *leggen* is used, for example, for putting napkins in a drawer, soap in the bathroom or books on a table (horizontally); *stoppen* is used, for example, for putting money in your pocket, a man in prison or a bribe into a policeman's hand (the general principle being that the object of this verb is somehow 'put away'). *Doen* is used, for example, for putting milk in your coffee, children in a school or a scarf around your neck. Such terminological distributions are highly problematic for descriptive linguists, and also for both foreign and native learners of Dutch (my seven-year-old granddaughter still hasn't mastered all the nuances), who naturally look for cognitive features or categories crucial for the proper use of each of the verbs in question. I have only been able to give some examples, but it makes sense to look for valid generalizations in terms of cognitive features, or else Dutch speakers would not be able to make the right selection on each new occasion. Yet searches for such cognitive-semantic generalizations have so far been only partially successful, as one invariably comes across cases that do not fit the generalizations tested out so far (see section 3.7.2.3 for more discussion).

Such *ad hoc* cognitive categories are culturally and cognitively irrelevant, pre-existing, probably universal, cognitive features or distinctions that are frequently activated simultaneously and then bundled, not as truth-conditionally defined concepts but as ready-to-hand criteria at a non-conscious level, as part of the automated language routine. (The rapid and automatic processing of such feature bundles as cognitive-semantic criteria for appropriate use is more easily understood if one accepts that mental representations—as opposed to the analytic semantic representations that are the direct input to the grammar module—are given in terms of *situational configurations*, as proposed in section 7.6.) These bundles (together with their idiosyncratic quirks) can then be called upon to regulate the *appropriate use* of certain words or combinations of words without any consequences for the truth or falsity of what is being said. We are dealing here with *use conditions*, not *truth conditions*—a fact totally overlooked in formal model-theoretic semantics (see Chapter 9). Nor are there any implications with regard to culture-bound thinking. It would be absurd to say that Dutch culture differs from the culture(s) of speakers of

English in that it is important for the Dutch, in their daily dealings, to distinguish between different ways of being located or being caused to be located.

One detects such secondary settling effects all over all languages. In English, one travels *by sea*, but in Dutch *over zee*, in Italian *per mare* and in Greek *dhià thálassa* (Italian *per* and Greek *dhià* meaning 'through'). In German, one is *verliebt in* ('in love in'), in Dutch, one is *verliefd op* ('in love on'), and in English, one is *in love with* someone. When I say *The fly is at the ceiling*, what I say is not false when the fly is on the ceiling, but true though ill-expressed. Likewise, when I say *Tom is married with Kate* in a situation where Tom and Kate are married, what I say is not false but true, though ill-expressed. The way English has settled requires the preposition *to* with the verb *marry* when reference is made to a spouse and the preposition *with* when reference is made to the number of children born in a marriage. We say *Tom is married WITH two children* (but note that when the two children are called Bob and Suzy, one cannot say *Tom is married with Bob and Suzy*).[10] This is not to do with any cognitive categorization of our world but with linguistic competence, which requires a command of all settling results in the language. The *concept* underlying the word *with*, though truth-conditionally covering the relation between spouses, is, idiosyncratically, not expressed as *with* in English but as *to* when applied to married partners. This has nothing to do with any presumed cultural or cognitive differences between English-speaking and non-English-speaking people.[11]

Likewise, in English, we *mow the lawn* but we *cut the grass*, or we *still our hunger* but *quench our thirst*, or we *rehearse* in a group but we *practise* alone (except in the case of choir practice, or when one rehearses French words).[12] But when I say that I cut the lawn or mowed the grass, or that I quenched my hunger or stilled my thirst, or that I rehearsed a Mozart sonata in my attic room, my lexical error does not affect the truth or falsity of what I am saying. And there is no question of my having the wrong concept in mind when I commit such errors. Nor does it make sense to say that such distinctions point to cultural differences between English-speaking and other speech communities. They are merely the largely arbitrary result of the 'will of the people'.

---

[10] This has the awkward consequence that, in this case, the generally valid logical procedure of *existential instantiation*—that is, the inference from *some F* to an assumed particular *F*, for some predicate *F* (Barwise and Etchemendy 1999: 322–3)—suddenly ceases to apply.

[11] A referee interestingly observed *inter alia* that English *married to* is matched by *engaged to, betrothed to, wedded to, related to* and a few other similar cases, which gives rise to the question of whether settling isn't too simple a solution. Possibly, the answer lies in the assumption that settling idiosyncrasies of the lexical kind may extend over categories, as in the case of perfective auxiliaries discussed above. Perhaps also, other factors than mere settling are at play. In defence of my uncertainty, I may point to what is said in the opening paragraph of this chapter about the need for further thinking and further empirical research to give more precision, depth and explanatory power to the notion of settling.

[12] There are other differences between *rehearse* and *practise*. In particular, one *rehearses* for a (group) performance but one *practises* to improve one's skill.

The question often arises, in this connection, whether alternative surface structure realizations reflect a single meaning and are thus mere synonyms or whether there is a hitherto unobserved subtle semantic difference. One may wonder, for example, whether the English pair *He continued playing* and *He continued to play* are just stylistic variants (as opposed to, for example, *he stopped listening* and *he stopped to listen*) or whether there is, after all, some hitherto undetected subtle semantic distinction. If there is such a distinction, in this or similar cases, it has nothing to do with cognitive categorization processes and everything with settling—the way speakers are, in total unawareness, in alignment with regard to their ways of expression, without any cognitive or cultural implications.

1.3 Creolization: the case of Sranan

Creole languages (Holm 1988/9), which mostly arose as a result of mixed slave populations having to communicate with white plantation owners and their overseers, are test tube instances of fast settling. Their documentation shows how lexical items, paradigms, tense-modality-aspect systems, phonological and syntactic rules, and idioms come into being as soon as the language in question becomes the native language of young children and the (officially or unofficially) recognized medium in a community. From there on, the language gradually develops further, steadily narrowing down or changing the norms of acceptability.

The clearest and best documented case in point is *Sranan*, the Creole language of Surinam, on the north coast of South America. Surinam was established in 1651 as an English plantation colony. The slaves that were imported from West Africa came into intensive contact with English on the plantations in Surinam, where they had to communicate with the overseers. In 1667, after a peace agreement between the Dutch and the English, the Dutch colony New Amsterdam, renamed New York, was swapped for the then more profitable sugar producing English-owned colony Surinam. The Dutch thus began to take over from the English in Surinam in 1667. By 1680 all original English plantation owners had left and Dutch owners had taken over (Voorhoeve and Lichtveld 1975: 275). In 1975, Surinam gained its independence from the Netherlands but the national language of the country still is the English-based Creole which apparently settled during those few decades in the late seventeenth century. There are written records of the language as from c. 1700, which show clearly what it was like in the early eighteenth century and how it developed over the subsequent years (Schuchardt 1914: iii–xxxv; Voorhoeve and Lichtveld 1975: 273–84). Despite the presence of the Dutch for about 350 years, the influence of Dutch on Sranan has remained minimal, restricted to a few lexical borrowings. Schuchardt writes, with regard to the earliest records of the language: 'Die Übereinstimmung der Sprache mit der heutigen ist sehr gross, fast befremdend' ('The similarity of the [original; PAMS] language with that of today is very great, almost astonishing')

(Schuchardt 1914: xix). This shows better than anything else how a language can come into being and 'settle' within a very short period of time, after which it more or less stays put, developing only at a much slower rate, the way normal, well-settled, languages do. The case of Sranan is unique in that there is no other language, Creole or non-Creole, that is so well-documented right from the start. Sranan is thus, so to speak, a laboratory case showing how a language can settle in the course of little over one generation.

1.4 The heteromorphy problem

In virtue of the highly arbitrary nature of secondary settling, much of it—and thus much of language—breaks in on any possible pre-existing one-to-one correlation between linguistic and conceptual categories and structures (see section 3.8.1). This touches on an ancient problem, which, surprisingly, has not been provided with a standard name, but which I call the *heteromorphy problem*.[13] It is posed by the question *why* natural languages do not differ merely as regards the phonological form of their morphemes but also in the coverage of their lexical items and in their grammars and the resulting surface structures. As regards the grammatical, rather than the lexical, aspect of things, this question is as old as the distinction made by philosophers and linguists between semantically irregular and often ambiguous surface structures on the one hand and 'regimented', semantically regular, unambiguous and explicit semantic analyses (SAs) on the other. That languages differ phonologically is unavoidable, since there is, in general, no intrinsic necessity for the choice of one particular form over another for the expression of a lexical meaning. This is De Saussure's celebrated 'arbitrariness of the linguistic sign'. But why do all humans not have the same grammar, the grammar of the conceptual structures we call SAs? Why do SA-structures have to be modified by the grammar rules of each specific language into surface structures that vary widely across the languages of the world?

Part of the answer may be that SA-structures are hard to process for listeners, since sound is mainly serial and is less appropriate for the expression of semantic scope and dominance hierarchies, whereas SA-structure is essentially a question of scope and dominance relations. Consequently, serially presented surface structure must contain sufficient clues as regards the underlying semantic scope and dominance relations—which requires a mapping procedure from hierarchical tree structures onto merely linear surface structures. As is argued in section 3.7.2.2, this requirement

---

[13] Chomsky (1995) calls it the *displacement property* of natural language(s). This term, however, is badly inadequate, as the differences between the semantic form of SAs (Chomsky's 'logical form') on the one hand and linguistic surface structures on the other involve so much more than just 'displacement' of elements—in fact, they constitute the totality of the grammar of a language—that this term must be regarded as inappropriate.

is met partly by the *Scope-Ordering Constraint* (SOC), which *grosso modo* maps scope hierarchies onto left-to-right ordering in surface structure.

A further factor may lie in a natural tendency to minimize the occurrence of bound variables, resulting from the universal tendency called *Matrix Greed* (see the definition in (3.32) of section 3.8.1). Given the best of the modern formal languages of logical analysis available to date, a sentence like (1.3a) is taken to be the grammatical product of the Russellian formula (1.3b) or, if one prefers, of the Generalized Quantification formula (1.3c):

(1.3)   a.   All flags are green.

       b. $\forall_x[\text{Flag}(x) \rightarrow \text{Green}(x)]$
          'for all x, if x is a flag then x is green'

       c. $\forall_x[\text{Flag}(x), \text{Green}(x)]$
          'the set of flags is included in the set of green things'

In both (1.3b) and (1.3c), the variable *x* occurs twice, in all cases bound by the universal quantifier $\forall$ (whose subscript *x* signals the fact that it binds the bound variable *x*). In (1.3a), however, no variable occurs, owing to the grammar of English, which accounts for the incorporation of the quantifier into the matrix subject term, resulting in *all flags*, and the subsequent disappearance of the variable from the matrix predicate *green*. All languages have some similar procedure, whereby the quantifier is incorporated into the term bound by it.

This does not mean that surface structures never contain bound variables. They do, as appears from cases like (1.4), where the logico-semantic analysis contains multiple occurrences of the same bound variable:

(1.4)   Some parents not caring about *their* children are blamed by *their* neighbours.

Here, *their children* and *their neighbours* represent underlying 'children of *x*' and 'neighbours of *x*', respectively, the variable *x* being bound by the noun phrase *some parents*. It is thus not so that natural languages make bound variables disappear altogether, but they do minimize their occurrence through Matrix Greed.

Apart from this, however, I submit that part of the answer may also be found in the need of each language community to distinguish itself from other language communities. Whatever abstract, formal language is taken to represent semantic structures, and thus to underlie surface structures, leaves too little room for language-specific variation. Matrix Greed does provide that room in that there are many different rule-governed procedures in virtue of which rigid, hierarchically organized SA-structures can be 'flattened' to largely one-dimensional serial sound sequences, whose only escape into a second dimension is provided by prosodic modulation. This opens up a much-needed treasure trove of new settling possibilities, happily grabbed from by each language community.

Settling may thus result in a sometimes severe denting of the direct correlation between linguistic and conceptual structures and categories. It diminishes semantic transparency and enhances semantic opacity. But it is a powerful factor in the process whereby both a language and the community speaking it acquire their own specific, culturally delimited, identity. In fact, the theory of settling is, ultimately, the theory of semantic opacity in language.

2

The Whorf hypothesis

Lingua ancilla mentis
(Language is the mind's handmaiden)

2.1 Introduction*

Over the past few decades, what has become known as the 'Whorf hypothesis', called after the American chemical engineer and amateur linguist Benjamin Lee Whorf (1897–1941), has been playing an increasingly dominant role in the study of language. In general terms, the hypothesis, or thesis, says that *language influences or determines thought and because any natural language is a shared property of a speech community, language influences or determines culturally bound ways of thinking with all the consequences thereof.* Those who believe that language *influences* thought represent the so-called 'weak' version of the hypothesis; those who say that language *determines* thought represent the 'strong' version. The 'strong' version is easier to deal with, as it is clear in its nongradability—apart from the inherent vagueness still shrouding the concept of *language* (often confused with *speech*) and the extreme complexity of the machinery caught under the umbrella term *thought*. By contrast, the more popular 'weak' version immediately begs the question of how far the alleged influence goes, which in turn requires an analysis of both language and thought into articulated elements. In other words, the weak version requires, more than the strong version does, adequate analytical knowledge of both language and thought.

The unclarity regarding the notion of thought, which means different things to different debaters, has been particularly harmful. There is still no generally accepted overall architecture showing the structure of thought processes. In order to bring some clarity in this respect, I propose here, in provisional and approximate terms, a double distinction between, on the one hand, *central* and *peripheral* thought and, on the other, between *dormant* and *frequent* thought processes. By central thought

---

* I am indebted to Gunter Senft and Peter Hagoort of the Max Planck Institute for Psycholinguistics at Nijmegen, to Andrea Bender of the University of Freiburg, to the late Melissa Bowerman, and in particular to Pim Levelt, for their generous but critical attention and their corrections, suggestions and references.

I mean the largely conscious cognitive activity whereby humans attempt to gain conceptual and logical clarity, precision and consistency in their world representations. Peripheral thought, by contrast, takes the products of central thought and processes them for further, practical applications, such as speech. Other than central thought, peripheral thought is largely nonconscious and mechanical, accompanying what is known as routine behaviour. The second distinction, that between dormancy and frequency, rests on memory, in that frequent use of thought patterns facilitates cognitive access, whereas dormancy, or the result of a long period of non-use, makes cognitive access harder. (The metaphor of 'depth', often used by Whorfians, is of little use in this context, as it may apply to a 'deep' embedding in the nonconscious or routine machinery of the mind or to a 'deep' insight into the complexity of the issues thought about.)

In the following, I argue that the one-to-one correlation between the categories of language and those of thought, postulated by Whorf, is largely mythical. What seems to be the case—apart from the fact that *settling*, discussed in the previous chapter, massively cuts through regular mappings of cognitive categories onto language and thus makes for massive semantic opacity—is that there is a marginal but measurable influence of language on those areas of peripheral thought that come into action when speakers are preparing for speech. As far as language is concerned, peripheral thought channels central thought content into the semantic categories afforded by the language. It is the level of language-specific thinking identified as 'thinking-for-speaking' (Slobin 1987) or 'microplanning' (Levelt 1989: 144–57; 1996: 77).

Recent experiments, about which more in section 2.4, strongly suggest that peripheral 'thinking-for-speaking' is more than just an interface between thought and language. It forms a structured level of processing on its own, largely as a result of habitual lexical selections and the grammatical consequences thereof. The recently gained evidence shows that, in the border area of thought and language, where Slobin's 'thinking-for-speaking', or Levelt's 'microplanning', takes place, the packaging of central thought content for linguistic expression and the unpacking of incoming linguistic goods for delivery to central thought is quite an industry.[1]

All theories agree that no matter how far language may be taken to 'seep' into nonconscious thought, there is always a universal, species-specific, residue of central cognition *not* affected by language. The position favoured here is that there is a relation between frequency and peripherality, in that the use of a language creates cognitive activation patterns which, when frequent, become routines and thus no longer need the meticulous attention of central thought processes. Such activation

---

[1] As a historical curiosity it may be observed that the French counterrevolutionary political philosopher and 'généraliste' Viscount Louis-Gabriël-Ambroise de Bonald (1754–1840) was known for his thesis that 'man thinks his speech before speaking his thought', thus anticipating Slobin and Levelt by a century and a half (see Joseph 2012: 289).

effects are strongest at the periphery, getting weaker as they affect more central thought. This relation is shown in Figure 2.1, which allows both for frequent but central activation, as in the case of scientific thinking by specialists who have to rethink issues time and again, and for peripheral but infrequent (dormant) activation, as with the occasional use of the mother tongue by longtime emigrants. In Figure 2.1, the two axes have been given equal weight, for lack of evidence to the contrary. Further evidence may, of course, change the weighting.

In this provisional and hypothetical perspective, which is, of course, subject to further theorizing, experimenting and correcting, frequency is likely to cause routine formation, saving, so to speak, the speaker a trip to central thought (just like frequent use of phonologically complex words in the same discourse leads to phonetic 'wear', short-cutting full phonological processing). Combined high frequency and peripherality—that is, a high routine rating—is likely to be conducive to reducing the strength of activation effects, which, so to speak, 'spill over' into language. Everything happening in the high-frequency high-peripherality area of the mind is taken to be well below any threshold of possible awareness: routines are by definition automatic. The reason why language 'seeps' into the peripheral areas of the non-conscious part of the human mind could well be that language is an important, perhaps the most important, source of activation frequency.

The general picture is that the thinking mind needs peripherality and thus routine formation to reduce attentional effort for less essential elements in the message to be transferred, and thus to facilitate frequent specialized interaction with the world. Yet it is a likely thought that the mind can only take so much of routine formation. Hence the spill-over into a separate language module (settling). I must stress, however, that

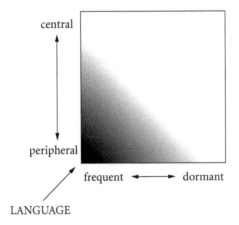

FIGURE 2.1 Decreasing strength of activation effects and corresponding increase of routine processing: the whiter, the more central and/or the more dormant and the greater the attentional effort

all this is no more than a perspective. It is mentioned here because, in the present chapter, this perspective is used to give the phenomena their place and thus create greater clarity. As a potential theory, it is obviously in need of further elaboration and empirical testing, and probably also of correction. But it is the best I can do, given the total absence of any theory providing an overall architecture of human cognition.

Apart from this, however, one aspect of the Whorf hypothesis that cannot be neglected is the fact that it has become part of a wider *ideological, anti-formalist complex*. Besides other influences, this complex bears the hallmark of the neopositivist movement rife in the American world during much of the twentieth century and rejecting any assumption of underlying causal mechanisms to explain the observed phenomena (but without the behaviourist rejection of concepts to do with mind and thought), and laced with a good shot of the eighteenth-century Romanticist *Noble Savage* philosophy, which saw 'savages' as unspoiled by Western civilization and morally superior in their innocence (see section 3.2 for more comment). Part of the anti-formalist ideology is the conviction, not open to discussion, that languages differ from each other at all levels and without restrictions, here called *linguistic relativism* (for the use of this term, see section 3.1.1).

Linguistic relativism, in the sense just defined, is usually equated with Whorfianism. The two, however, are not identical, in fact, they are logically independent (see the sections 3.1.1 and 3.4), since one can be a relativist without being a Whorfian (no influence of language on thought but unrestricted linguistic diversity) and one can also be a universalist while being a Whorfian (human language is highly unified and this has had far-reaching effects on the mind). Relativism is opposed to universalism; Whorfianism is opposed to the traditional view of language as a willing expressor of thoughts. The classic definition of linguistic relativism, though without the term, is given in Sapir (1921: 2): 'Speech [for Sapir, this meant 'language'; PAMS] is a human activity that varies without assignable limit as we pass from social group to social group.' Lyons (1977: 245) defines relativism correctly: '[T]he actualization of particular phonological, grammatical and semantic distinctions in different language-systems is completely arbitrary. This can be referred to as the doctrine of linguistic relativity.' Yet he immediately goes on to say: 'Since its best known proponent, in recent times, was Whorf (1956), it is commonly known as Whorfianism, or the Whorfian hypothesis', thereby confounding two distinct notions. I take the term *linguistic relativism* to refer to the thesis proposed in Evans and Levinson (2009: 429):

[L]anguages differ so fundamentally from one another at every level of description (sound, grammar, lexicon, meaning) that it is very hard to find any single structural property they share. The claims of Universal Grammar [...] are either empirically false, unfalsifiable, or misleading in that they refer to tendencies rather than strict universals.

Chapter 3 aims to refute this claim.

A notable neopositivist element in modern forms of Whorfianism is the rejection of any postulated automated formal cognitive machinery, often called 'abstract', underlying the utterances in a language and defining each specific language. For the followers of this ideology, what they call 'real language' is only found in actual usage and it is only on the basis of usage observations that any theories about language can be formulated.[2] This, of course, amounts to a fatal confusion of language as a system of rules and principles on the one hand, and the use of language, usually called 'speech', on the other. Whorf himself did not share this extremely naïve idea—which is like saying that there are no traffic rules but only actual traffic taking place—but it has become a stock element in the ideology of modern Whorfians and linguistic relativists. Chapter 5 aims at showing that this article of faith is not only empirically untenable but also, in fact, absurd.

The recent rise of the anti-formalist ideology may well be seen as a reaction to the opposing formalist ideology, manifest in Chomskyan linguistics and to an even higher degree in the excessively formalist development of Montagovian possible-world semantics (criticized in Chapter 9). I defend the moderate position (argued for in detail in Chapter 1 of Seuren 2009a), that one should avoid ideologies and pursue the ideals of good science, that is, the development of explanatory theories that are based on serious facts, proper analysis and sound thinking, formalizing where that seems useful but proceeding without formalization when the factors involved are so manifold or so undisciplined or so little understood that formalization is bound to miss the point.

2.2 Some history

2.2.1 *The Whorf hypothesis in North America*

The Whorf hypothesis was not Whorf's original product. It had a history, going back directly to the American anthropologist-linguist *Edward Sapir* (1884–1939), and via

---

[2] This is how the study of linguistics at the Radboud University in Nijmegen (Netherlands) is characterized on the linguistics department's website (my translation):

Study REAL language! If you study linguistics in Nijmegen, you will study the concrete, spontaneous use of language as it occurs in real life. In science, this is called the *empirical approach*. Empirical science aims at understanding and explaining the world by first collecting and describing the facts. It thus stands in contrast with a more theoretical approach where scientists first think up theories and then confront them with reality. As an empirical linguist you look at linguistic behaviour and usage in various situations of language use. When you do that you are automatically faced with two important functions of language: communication and information transfer. These two functions occupy a central place in the linguistics curriculum at Nijmegen University.

I would not have quoted this text if the attitude it expresses were unique. It is sad and shameful to see such a primitive and uninformed, in fact populist, notion of what constitutes empirical science and scientific theory being imparted to students at university level. Chapter 5 of the present book gives an idea of how complex the facts of language are and what sort of theoretical, methodological and descriptive challenges they really pose.

Sapir to the father of American anthropology *Franz Boas* (1858–1942), whose Introduction to the *Handbook of American Indian Languages* of 1911 explores, among other alternatives, the possible viability of the idea underlying the Whorf hypothesis. The history goes even further, extending to the highly influential German *savant* and linguistic philosopher *Wilhelm von Humboldt* (1767–1835), who presented his general ideas about language in the separately published Introduction to his work on the Kawi language (Von Humboldt 1836). Von Humboldt, in turn, came to his Whorfian ideas under the influence of the eighteenth-century French philosopher *Étienne Bonnot de Condillac* (1714–1780), with whose ideas he became acquainted during his stay in Paris from 1797 till 1801, and of the German Romantic poet-philosopher-clergyman *Johann Gottfried Herder* (1744–1803), whose *Abhandlung über den Ursprung der Sprache* ('Treatise on the Origin of Language') of 1772, though consisting largely of Romantic rhetoric without any proper argument, had a great influence on later ways of thinking about language. Consequently, the hypothesis is often called the *Humboldt-Sapir-Whorf hypothesis*. I will refrain from a discussion of how de Condillac, Herder, von Humboldt and others contributed to the Whorfian paradigm, mainly because these authors are too remote for the present purpose.[3] But I will look in some detail at the views expressed by Whorf's immediate predecessors, Boas and Sapir.

Boas, a level-headed analytical thinker, called attention to the now generally accepted fact that different cultures call for different lexical and perhaps also grammatical distinctions: he presented the now almost legendary case of three words for snow in Eskimo (Boas 1911: 21–2) (later inflated by others to thirty plus; see Pullum 1991). He thus prepared the ground for the insight that universals are not ready for the taking. He discusses at length all kinds of possible relations between language, culture and race, constantly warning against premature conclusions and stressing the necessity of empirical proof or at least support. It is thus not surprising that he never actually proposes anything like the Whorf hypothesis. On the contrary, he consistently writes in terms of the paradigm according to which language *expresses* thought—unlike Whorf, for whom language *influences* thought. The closest he comes to the Whorf hypothesis is where he discusses the relation between language and thought (Boas 1911: 60):

First of all, it may be well to discuss the relation between language and thought. It has been claimed that the conciseness and clearness of thought of a people depend to a great extent upon their language. The ease with which in our modern European languages we express wide abstract ideas by a single term, and the facility with which wide generalizations are cast into the frame of a simple sentence, have been claimed to be one of the fundamental conditions of the clearness of our concepts, the logical force of our thought, and the precision with which we eliminate in our thoughts irrelevant details. Apparently, this view has much in its favor.

---

[3] For a survey of the historical origins of the Whorf hypothesis, see Koerner (2000).

Yet he immediately goes on to stress that American Indians are easily taught the European 'wide generalizations' against habitual manners of speaking in their own language but without any change in its lexical or grammatical system, concluding that, 'it seems very questionable in how far the restriction of the use of certain grammatical forms can really be conceived as a hindrance in the formulation of generalized ideas' (Boas 1911: 60). It thus appears that Boas, by cautiously discussing it, helped prepare the ground for the Whorf hypothesis as it is known today, but he did not subscribe to it.[4]

Sapir is a different matter. He comes much closer to Whorf than any other linguist of note of the period. Like Boas and many others, Sapir was intrigued by the relation between language and culture seen as socially construed reality. He was, on the whole, cautious as regards the question of what influences what, but in a few passages he comes close to the Whorf hypothesis, though he stops short of actually formulating it. I will quote two passages. The first is quite famous (Sapir 1929: 210):

Language is a guide to 'social reality'. Though language is not ordinarily thought of as of essential interest to the students of social science, *it powerfully conditions all our thinking about social problems and processes* [italics mine; PAMS]. Human beings do not live in the objective world alone, nor alone in the world of social activity as ordinarily understood, but are very much at the mercy of the particular language which has become the medium of expression for their society. It is quite an illusion to imagine that one adjusts to reality essentially without the use of language and that language is merely an incidental means of solving specific problems of communication or reflection. The fact of the matter is that *the 'real world' is to a large extent unconsciously built up on the language habits of the group* [italics mine; PAMS]. No two languages are ever sufficiently similar to be considered as representing the same social reality. The worlds in which different societies live are distinct worlds, not merely the same world with different labels attached.

The second, less known, passage (Sapir 1931: 578) is:

Such categories as number, gender, case, tense, mode, voice, "aspect" and a host of others, many of which are not recognized systematically in our Indo-European languages, are, of

---

[4] Nor did Leonard Bloomfield (1887–1949), who criticized the Whorf hypothesis *avant la lettre* in his early book on linguistic theory (Bloomfield 1914: 85):

In Malay the experiences which may be logically defined by us as 'offspring of the same parents' are classed together, and for such an experience is used the word *sudara*. In English we form no such class; we form two classes, according to the sex, and speak of a *brother* or a *sister*. Now, it would be manifestly absurd to say that a Malay does not know his brother from his sister; it would be no less absurd, however, to say that English-speaking people are unable to form the general idea conveyed by the Malay word. Both languages can express the experiences for which no single designation exists by a compound expression which analyzes them,—the Malay by saying *sudara lakilaki* and *sudara perampuwan*, where the added modifying words resemble our terms 'male' and 'female'; and the English by saying *brother or sister* or *child of the same parents*.

It is easy to see why Sapir and Bloomfield did not see eye to eye in matters academic.

course, derivative of experience at last analysis, but, once abstracted from experience, they are systematically elaborated in language and are not so much discovered in experience as imposed upon it because of the tyrannical hold that linguistic form has upon our orientation in the world.

Here, Sapir is more Whorfian than ever, though still *avant la lettre*. While it is not clear what he may have meant by categories being 'systematically elaborated in language', one may concur when he speaks of categories that are 'abstracted from experience': one often sees that lexical categories, such as nominal gender, have a natural origin but are subsequently extended arbitrarily beyond their natural range as a result of the process I have called *settling* (Chapter 1). Given a natural origin for lexical categories, *purely sociolinguistic processes often take over*, so to speak, whereby the link with the original cognitive or cultural conceptualizations is gradually lost. One may even see what he means when he speaks of the 'tyrannical hold' that language is said to have 'upon our orientation in the world', as the semantics of a language forces its speakers to activate certain cognitive features while neglecting others and this much repeated activation may well leave habitual 'grooves' in one's thinking (see section 2.4.1.2 below on absolute orientation), though to speak of a 'tyrannical hold' is clearly over the top. What tripped him was the failure to make the distinction between central and peripheral ('border-area') thought and to see the cross-cutting, cognitively dulling, effects of language settling processes.[5]

It is clear that Sapir and his (adult) student Whorf were, generally speaking, on the same wavelength. Yet for Sapir the question of the causal direction from language to culture and thought was not a central concern, whereas for Whorf it was.

The Whorf hypothesis was, of course, presented in North America and that is where it flourished, faded and reflourished during the second half of the twentieth century. Significantly, it flourished among anthropological linguists, who had learned to value non-Western cultures with their traditions and their systems of norms and values. There was a vivid awareness among anthropological linguists of the fact that it is mainly through the vernacular that the identity, the traditions and the specific values of each non-Western community are taught, maintained and propagated. This insight naturally led to the idea that it was also actually the vernacular that had brought about the culture complete with its world view and value system.

---

[5] Sapir, who had no clear idea of what the settling of a language amounts to, somewhat surprisingly wrote (1921: 233): 'Nor can I believe that culture and language are in any true sense causally related. Culture may be defined as *what* a society does and thinks. Language is a particular *how* of thought.' This is probably true as long as one leaves the lexicon out of account, as Sapir explicitly did (on page 234), and, more to the point in the present context, as long as language and culture are considered in the light of central thought processes. But it seems less tenable with regard to settling phenomena, which not only show an omnipresent, persistent influence, at all levels, of societal pressure upon each specific language, dialect or sociolect but also often incorporate culturally relevant metaphors or other semantic transfers into the automated language machinery.

2.2.2 *European 'Whorfianism': Leo Weisgerber*[6]

Although Whorfianism as we know it is an American phenomenon, Europe had its own version independently of what was happening in North America. European 'Whorfianism' likewise had its roots in Herder (1772) and Humboldt (1836) and German Idealism in general. But in Europe, other than in America, this cultural trend led to strong feelings of national identity and, as so often, of national superiority. Feelings that in America were channelled to the non-Western cultures studied, leading to vicarious pride and sympathy, were to a large extent fixated upon the scholars' own culture in Europe, resulting in undue nationalism. After 1920, the nationalist streak, already present in German culture, was boosted to much greater heights by the humiliation suffered as a result of the German defeat in the First World War. As we know, this nationalism, grown into violent right-wing populism, in the end destroyed the democratic Weimar Republic and led to a Nazi dictatorship and the disastrous Second World War.

During the interbellum, which lasted from 1919 till 1939, nationalism was rife in Germany and, because of Germany's leading cultural role in Europe, in many other European countries as well. In this context we meet the figure of the German linguist Leo Weisgerber (1899–1985), born in Lorraine, which was lost to France under the terms of the Treaty of Versailles of 1919—a further insult to German nationalism. Apart from being a great stimulator of proper teaching of German in the school curricula, Weisgerber, originally a Celtic scholar, was well read in international, including American, linguistics, with a particular preference for the anthropological angle. Like so many other German intellectuals of the period, he was not a Nazi but ready to collaborate with them. After World War II he was officially cleared but some opprobrium stuck to him ever after. As a result, little reference was made to his work after 1945 and he slid into gradual and inglorious oblivion.

The work by which he is mostly known revolves around the notion of *Muttersprache* ('mother tongue'), his book *Muttersprache und Geistesbildung* ('Mother tongue and education of mind')[7] of 1929 being the most notable instance. Here we read (Weisgerber 1929: 44–5) (all translations are mine):

---

[6] Pim Levelt drew my attention to the relevance, in this context, of the now almost forgotten Weisgerber.

[7] The German word *Geistesbildung* is untranslatable, going back to Wolfgang Goethe (1749–1832). *Bildung* stands for 'formation, education, erudition', and *Geist* for 'mind', but with strong components of 'ghost' and 'spirit'. The compound *Geistesbildung*, once opposed to the now obsolete *Herzensbildung* ('education of the heart, emotional education', implying the teaching of tact and empathy), stands for the more intellectual aspects of the educational moulding of individuals into a state of mind that will make them properly educated erudite citizens with a well-developed sense of cultural identity. The notion is, of course, immediately recognizable but English has no accepted term for it. Perhaps 'intellectual, moral, cultural and civic education' comes closest.

The mother tongue is for all humans the language of their speech community. No human being has his own individual language, no human being is without a mother tongue. Therefore, to understand the role of language in human life it is necessary to have a more precise knowledge of the essence and of the *effects* of a language in the life of a speech community. [italics mine; PAMS]

Then he mentions the problem of adequate translation (Weisgerber 1929: 72):

It is expected of anyone who has a real command of a foreign language that they think in the terms of that language. What makes translating from one language into another a hazardous art is, again, not the different sounds but has to do with the content, which cannot, or only with difficulty, be cast from the modes of thinking of the one language into those of the other without the translation becoming a falsification.

A little further down, the 'Whorfian' element crops up explicitly (Weisgerber 1929: 75):

When we look beyond our small circle of closely related languages, we see in how many ways other languages deviate contentwise, *which, naturally, has as a consequence that those who belong to different language groups and languages think differently*—a fact that every unprejudiced observer must admit. [italics mine; PAMS]

He goes on to show his disapproval of the logical approach to language, which, remarkably, he shares with his American counterparts (Weisgerber 1929: 75–6):

Precisely in this respect, the comparative linguist must raise the strongest possible objection against the view, often expressed especially by logicians (Marty, Drews and others), that humans think in basically identical ways, that the differences between languages, in so far as the content is concerned, are relatively unimportant. It is because of this view that the problems of inner language form ['innere Sprachform'] are inaccessible to men like Marty and Funke. Totally incomprehensible is the statement by Drews (1928: 68):

In the end, there are different languages and many different grammars, but only one logic. One and the same intellect expresses itself in the most different sounds in different nations and individuals, according to their bodily structure, their environment, their culture, but always in such a way that it is possible to translate any language, no matter how deviant its structure, into any other.

Yet even those who translate closely related languages into each other already complain that an adequate translation is impossible and a certain measure of falsification unavoidable. Even a single German sentence cannot be translated into a language outside the sphere of European culture without a complete rethinking of its contents. One cannot push logical analysis to the point that 'thinking about the same state of affairs' and 'having the same thought' are equated, whereby the difference is swept aside as being unimportant. What, in the end, a logic will look like that has arisen from a different, non-Indo-European language can only be judged when such a logic is available. It is highly unlikely that, in such an event, the logic we know will remain the only one.

The question of the uniqueness of logic is, of course, an important one, even if its treatment by Weisgerber shows a basic lack of expertise. I defend the view (Seuren 2010) that a logic is defined, apart from its axioms and the ranges of its variables (its ontology), by the lexical meanings of its operators. If these lexical meanings show the same versatility and variability as so many other lexical items across different languages, then, indeed, one would expect large numbers of culture-sensitive logical systems. Such logical relativism, however, is highly unlikely, given the fact that logical systems are developed by their makers in the closest possible relation to the highest level of central thought, which, as is generally agreed, is species-specific—that is, universal—for mankind.

From here on, Weisgerber expatiates on kinship terminology, colour terms, verbs of location and movement and, finally on subtle cross-linguistic differences in the use conditions of prepositions and verbal tenses (imperfect, punctual past, perfect), putting settling phenomena such as those described in Chapter 1 and culturally or cognitively significant phenomena into one basket. The following passage, reminiscent of Herder (1772: 149–50), shows how strongly Weisgerber was impressed by the diversity of languages and hence by what, for him, were the different ways of thinking in different cultures (Weisgerber 1929: 85):

No less different are languages in their *relation systems*. One has to think only of the difficulties experienced by Germans in acquiring a 'feel' for the proper use of prepositions in a foreign language, of the imperfect and historical perfect in French, of the active and medium moods in Greek, of perfective and imperfective verbs in the Slavonic languages, etc. This shows, one would say, that the beginning learner has no inner feeling for such foreign conceptions. He has not developed the habit of being alert to distinctions that are made in the foreign languages but are not or much less observed in his native language. Such phenomena are found specifically in the more finely tuned peculiarities of languages, where even scientific research has not or only very partially been able to capture the specific frame of mind proper to the different languages.

Weisgerber then goes on to say that what is essential about linguistic diversity is not so much the different forms as the different semantic content, the *inner language form* stored in each language's grammar and lexicon, falling back on Humboldt's notion of 'innere Sprachform'. The passage ends as follows (Weisgerber 1929: 86):

Here we capture what is essential about language. With and in each language is defined a specific way of seeing the world and its phenomena. Thus one can say that *a language hosts a specific world view* in its inner form. Every human growing up into a specific language must integrate its way of understanding the world of phenomena as presented to the mind. This way, *all members of a speech community process their experiences in conformity with the inner form of their mother tongue and think and act accordingly.* [italics mine; PAMS]

The similarities with basic Whorfianism will be obvious. It will also be clear why, in a chapter on the Whorf hypothesis, mention of Weisgerber is appropriate, even if, owing to the vicissitudes of history, the man has been virtually forgotten in our day.

The question of why and how these two very different persons, Whorf and Weisgerber, came to have the same ideas during the same years but in very different cultural contexts, is one that I am happy to leave to historians.

2.3 Whorf

2.3.1 *The hypothesis analysed*

Neither Whorf nor Whorfianism has ever had my sympathy. When I read Whorf (1956), the posthumous collection of his most seminal papers, in my early days and again recently from beginning to end, what I found, on both readings, was, besides a somewhat exalted tone, a great deal of uncontrolled, and sometimes even mystic and occult, thought—the work of an unprofessional, who, towards the end of his life, sounded more like a preacher than like an academic investigator.[8] I resented the enormous influence of the Whorf hypothesis in anthropological linguistics and psycholinguistics until, in the course of writing the present chapter, fruitful discussions with friends and colleagues and the renewed scrutiny of my own premisses made me realize that the Whorfian turn has led to important new insights which, though not confirming the Whorfian outlook, would probably not have come about had it not been for the sustained efforts of Whorfian-minded linguists and psychologists.

Initially, following Whorf's premature death in 1941, the Whorf hypothesis spread like wildfire among anthropologically inspired linguists, though it met with staunch resistance on the part of the theoretical linguists, especially the structuralists and then those siding with Chomskyan generative grammar. Since the Chomskyan paradigm began to decline, a few decades ago, Whorfianism has come back with a vengeance. Nowadays it is again adhered to by tribes of anthropologists, anthropologically oriented linguists and even psychologists.

Whorf did not present what we now call his 'hypothesis' as such, but rather as a statement of fact, necessarily following from his analyses. Only later was it recognized that his logic was not as compelling as he thought it was and did one start to speak of the Whorf *hypothesis*. For Whorf it was a *thesis* (or perhaps rather a *dogma*). He describes his thesis in succint terms by saying that '[w]e dissect nature along lines laid down by our native languages', which means that '[t]he categories and types that we isolate from the world of phenomena [... are] to be organized by our minds—and this means largely by the linguistic systems in our minds' (Whorf 1956: 213). Apart

---

[8] Whorfians are usually reticent about the fact that Whorf was a practising theosophist, steeped in oriental mysticism. The last essay in Whorf (1956), 'Language, mind, and reality', written just before his death and published posthumously in a theosophical journal brought out in Madras, is so far removed from normal academic writing that it would be cruel to subject it to rational criticism. It should also be remembered that Whorf had a lifelong admiration for the French esoteric occultist Antoine Fabre d'Olivet (1768–1825), who saw sublime abstract meanings in Hebrew letter signs.

from the fact that the escape hatch built into the thesis by means of the word 'largely' (the 'weak' version of the thesis) makes this statement hard to test, one sees that the tendency in the Whorfian thesis is to diminish the role, in human life, of autonomous creative thought and to enhance the role of physically observable language or speech in explaining the functioning of human beings, whereby the emphasis is continuously on how languages *differ*, not on what ties them together.

This places the thesis in the context of neopositivist and behaviourist thinking, the extreme modern version of empiricism, which (unsuccessfully) aims at reducing man to an idiosyncratic result of physical factors. Yet Whorf himself was not a behaviourist, though he was not in principle averse to behaviourism. But Whorfianism and behaviourism do not go together (Whorf 1956: 41). In fact, Whorf's terminology forces the interpretation that the 'dissecting' of nature 'along lines laid down by our native languages' is meant to refer to what is more commonly known as *concept formation*, which is indeed the term used by later scholars, both Whorfian and non-Whorfian. Since the notion of concept, as generally accepted, involves at least the conditions to be satisfied by the entities falling under a concept C for the attainment of truth when it is said of an entity e that e *is* C—that is, since concepts necessarily involve truth conditions—it follows that the strong version of the Whorf hypothesis implies that language determines in any case the truth-conditionally defined satisfaction conditions of the concepts used in the (true or false) mental propositions we form about the real or any imagined world.

This being too tall an order, modern researchers who wish to prove Whorf right tend to relax this criterion and speak of different concepts in cases where there is no question of different conditions for truth or falsity but merely for the proper use of words as a result of settling processes (see section 1.2.5). But this relaxing of the notion of concept undermines the connection with the Whorf hypothesis, which is primarily about truth-conditional aspects of meaning (Whorf's 'dissecting' of nature). Outside these truth-conditional aspects, it is hard to decide whether conceptual differences are involved or merely different conditions of use. Harking back to the use, in English, of the preposition *to* with the verb *marry* when reference is made to a partner in marriage, discussed in section 1.2.5, it seems hard to maintain that for speakers of English the concepts of 'with-ness' and/or of 'marriage' differ from the corresponding concepts that speakers of other languages operate with, where one is normally said to be married *with* a spouse. And it would be even harder to suggest that this reflects a difference in culture between speakers of English and those of other languages.

To the extent that such language-specific, non-truth-conditional conditions on the proper use of words and other expressive means are at issue, the Whorf-hypothesis must be taken to be irrelevant. Yet, as we will see in Section 2.4, some modern researchers focus on precisely such cases in an effort to support that hypothesis. The success of their experiments, however, does not support the Whorf hypothesis but, rather, the hypothesis that frequency effects may establish peripheral cognitive 'grooves', following the pattern shown in Figure 2.1.

2.3.2 *The perennial problem: the direction of causality*

One main problem with the Whorf hypothesis—besides many others—is that the entire Whorfian point of view hangs on a missing link in its basic argument. Apart from the fact that Whorf's use of the terms *thought* and *language* is far too flexible and unforgivably vague, there is no answer to the question *why* one should think that the categories of language cause or determine or influence those of thought and not the other way round. Nor does one find a comprehensible answer—settling phenomena being left totally out of account—to the question *how* language should be thought to have acquired its categorizations in the first place if it was not through human cognition expressing itself in it.

This question is briefly discussed in Whorf (1956: 156):

How does such a network of language, culture, and behavior come about historically? Which was first: the language patterns or the cultural norms? In main they have grown up together, constantly influencing each other. But in this partnership the nature of the language is the factor that limits free plasticity and rigidifies channels of development in the more auto-cratic way. This is so because a language is a system, not just an assemblage of norms. Large systematic outlines can change to something really new only very slowly, while many other cultural innovations are made with comparative quickness. Language thus represents the mass mind; it is affected by inventions and innovations, but affected little and slowly, whereas TO inventors and innovators it legislates with the decree immediate.

This, however, is not a very convincing answer. Why should language be a 'rigidify-ing' system and why should cognition not be? How can language 'represent the mass mind' and at the same time be the main factor behind its categorizations, which would make the mass mind represent language? How can language be 'affected by inventions and innovations' without these inventions and innovations having first passed through the minds of its speakers? A benevolent answer would be that Whorf is intuiting something like what I have called, in Chapter 1, the social settling processes taking place in all languages and indeed affecting them 'little and slowly'. But if that is his argument, it undermines his own thesis because settling processes do not, on the whole, have an impact on concept formation, on the ways we 'dissect nature'.

Whorf's position, in whatever interpretation, thus crucially depends on the *direction of causality* postulated. Whorf himself posited that the direction is from language to thought, but he gave no serious argument why one should accept that. This was quickly seen, not only by sceptics, such as, notably, Lenneberg (1953) or Brown and Lenneberg (1954), but also by many of his followers, who approached the Whorf hypothesis in a more professional manner than was done by Whorf himself and produced valid evidence for linguistic effects not so much on central as on peripheral thought. But such effects are precisely non-Whorfian because (a) they mostly involve the results of settling processes, which fall outside the Whorfian frame, and (b) they do not involve central thought, which is what the Whorf hypothesis is about, but only peripheral thought processes taking place in the border area where thought and language meet.

2.3.3 *Confusing the* HOW *and the* WHAT

Let us look at Whorf's texts in some detail so that we see how he jumps from an alleged *correlation* between language and culturally fixed patterns of thought to a *causal determination* of thought patterns by language, yet all the time recoiling from a full statement of this point of view and leaving room for other factors that remain largely unspecified. We start on p. 134 of Whorf (1956):

> There will probably be general assent to the proposition that an accepted pattern of using words is often prior to certain lines of thinking and forms of behavior, but he who assents often sees in such a statement nothing more than a platitudinous recognition of the hypnotic power of philosophical and learned terminology on the one hand or of catchwords, slogans, and rallying cries on the other.

It is a truism that people can be informed or persuaded by the use of words: education takes place largely through words; historical events are often brought about by rhetoric; sales techniques live by it. But this has nothing to do with Whorf's thesis, which is about grammatical and lexical patterns in a language influencing cognitive sortal categorizations or world construals. Whorf here resorts to a rhetorical ploy by confusing *actual thought content* (in particular evaluative judgements) and *language use* on the one hand with the merely instrumental *cognitive categorizations* and *languages as socially fixed systems* on the other. As Sapir said (1921: 233; see note 5), one should not confuse the WHAT and the HOW in the use of language. A confusion of the two would allow one to say, for example, that the Russian Revolution of 1917 was caused by the Russian language. Possibly, reading the present chapter will make you look at the Whorf hypothesis in a different way from before—because of the words used in it, if you like. But does this confirm the Whorf hypothesis? Of course not. It is because of the vagueness and lack of specificity of his terminology that Whorf managed to get away with this 'argument'.

This mistake of confusing the HOW and the WHAT (see also Lenneberg 1953: 467), the machinery and the specific uses made of it, is often made by Whorfians. And for an obvious reason: since it is a truism to claim that the use of language 'can cause a cognitive structure' (Brown and Lenneberg 1954: 457)—the WHAT function, which is the *raison d'être* of language—it is seductive to use this truism to support much more doubtful claims about the HOW of language, the machinery relating thought structures and linguistic structures.

A recent example of such illegitimate transfer from the WHAT to the HOW is found in Enfield (2000), where the position of 'linguocentrism' is defended, meaning that (in the study of culture, one presumes), 'language' and 'nonlanguage' are so closely bound up with each other that they cannot be separated. And why? Because (Enfield 2000: 126):

[T]he achievement of culture involves semiotic processes which allow us to create and maintain the 'shared-ness' of ideas and significances which culture entails. And language is overwhelmingly the dominant semiotic system for humans in the process of creation and maintenance of the social alignment of ideas which we call culture.

Note that the entire quote can stand unchanged if we apply it to a subpart of culture, say religion, simply reading *religion* for *culture*. Does the fact that religion crucially involves the use of language now mean that we cannot separate language from religion, that religious 'conceptualization is essentially linguistic in nature' (Enfield 2000: 130)? Or that the linguistic system of a community either determines or influences its religion? Again, of course not. All that follows is that the *use of language* is indispensable, not only for the achievement of culture but for the achievement of a whole lot of other things as well. Language is an indispensable, or at least very useful, *tool* for the bringing about of ideas, views, attitudes in other people's minds, but it is, obviously one would say, not the *cause* of such processes.

It is sometimes said, in defence of the Whorf hypothesis, that tools may influence achievement: the better the tool the better the product. This is no doubt so. New musical instruments have given rise to new and more sophisticated techniques, musical styles and genres. And many more such examples could be given. But does this really support the Whorf hypothesis? It seems not. For if this argument is raised in support of the Whorf hypothesis, it shows again a confusion of the WHAT and the HOW. We may accept that the settling processes a language goes through in its development will contribute to an increased subtlety of expression and to more finely tuned calibrations of the expressive means employed. We may likewise accept that the subtler use of language made possible by settling processes makes a heavier demand on cognition, which is made to work harder as it prepares for speaking—the 'thinking-for-speaking', as in Slobin (1987)—thus honing the cognitive faculties involved in the preparation of utterances. But all this is more a question of WHAT is expressed, of the specific use made of the machinery in each particular case, than of the central cognitive machinery itself, which is what the Whorf hypothesis is meant to be about.

2.3.4 *The alleged primacy of language over cognition*

Whorf repeatedly emphasizes the overall importance of language, in particular specific languages or language groups. Let us consider some quotes. Speaking of the notion of time (an often recurring theme in Whorf's writings, about which more is said below) and of its importance in all aspects of life, he says (Whorf 1956: 153–4):

No doubt this vast system, once built, would continue to run under any sort of linguistic treatment of time, but that it should have been built at all, reaching the magnitude and particular form it has in the Western world, is a fact decidedly in consonance with the patterns of the SAE [= Standard Average European; PAMS] languages. [...] Thus our *linguistically determined thought world* [italics mine; PAMS] not only collaborates with our cultural idols and ideals, but engages even our unconscious personal reactions in its patterns and gives them certain typical characters.

Speaking about European art (whatever that might be), he concludes (Whorf 1956: 156):

It may be that in this way our metaphorical language that is in some sense a confusion of thought is producing, through art, a result of far-reaching value—a deeper esthetic sense leading toward a more direct apprehension of underlying unity behind the phenomena so variously reported by our sense channels.

And again on p. 214:

[N]o individual is free to describe nature with absolute impartiality but [everyone; PAMS] is constrained to certain modes of interpretation even while he thinks himself most free. The person most nearly free in such respects would be a linguist familiar with very many widely different linguistic systems. As yet no linguist is in any such position. We are thus introduced to a new principle of relativity, which holds that all observers are not led by the same physical evidence to the same picture of the universe, unless their linguistic backgrounds are similar, or can in some way be calibrated.

How depressing for Chinese and Japanese scientists!
   A veritable eulogy on language is found on pp. 220–1:

I say new ways of THINKING about facts, but a more nearly adequate statement would say new ways of TALKING about facts. It is this USE OF LANGUAGE UPON DATA that is central to scientific progress. Of course, we have to free ourselves from that vague innuendo of inferiority which clings about the word 'talk', as in the phrase 'just talk'; that false opposition which the English-speaking world likes to fancy between talk and action. There is no need to apologize for speech, the most human of all actions. The beasts may think, but they do not talk. 'Talk' OUGHT TO BE A more noble and dignified word than 'think'. Also we must face the fact that science begins and ends in talk; this is the reverse of anything ignoble.

Apart from the empty rhetoric of this passage, which exemplifies the old saying that one should think before one speaks, and despite the confusion of the HOW and the WHAT in the last sentence, one wonders how Whorf imagines, in the terms of his own (hypo)thesis, that 'the beasts may think' without the input of any form of language!
   At times, Whorf himself shrinks back from the consequences of his position, as we see on p. 221:

Thus the world view of modern science arises by higher specialization of the basic grammar of the Western Indo-European languages. *Science, of course, was not* CAUSED *by this grammar; it was simply colored by it.* (italics mine; PAMS)

As so often when it is used, one wonders about the word *simply*!

2.3.5 *Grammar as a formally definable system*

For Whorf, grammar is, perhaps surprisingly, taken to be a *formally definable system*, not a haphazard, more or less iconic, improvisation (Whorf 1956: 156):

But in this partnership [of language and culture; PAMS] the nature of the language is the factor that limits free plasticity and rigidifies channels of development in the more autocratic way. This is so because a language is a system, not just an assemblage of norms.

And again on p. 230:

The exactness of this formula [of phonotactics; PAMS], typical of hundreds of others, shows that, while linguistic formulations are not those of mathematics, they are nevertheless precise.

And most strongly on pp. 244–5, where he quotes the American philosopher Harold N. Lee (1899–1990), who appears here as an early harbinger of the formalization of the human sciences:

In a valuable paper, 'Modern logic and the task of the natural sciences', Harold N. Lee says:

Those sciences whose data are subject to quantitative measurement have been most successfully developed because we know so little about order systems other than those exemplified in mathematics. We can say with certainty, however, that there are other kinds, for the advance of logic in the last half century has clearly indicated it. We may look for advances in many lines in sciences at present well founded if the advance of logic furnishes adequate knowledge of other order types. We may also look for many subjects of inquiry whose methods are not strictly scientific at the present time to become so when new order systems are available. (*Sigma Xi Quart.*, 28: 125 (Autumn 1940)).

To which may be added that an important field for the working out of new order systems, akin to, yet not identical with, present mathematics, lies in more penetrating investigation than has yet been made of languages remote in type from our own.

Apparently, Whorf takes languages to be precisely or formally defined systems, as opposed to cognition, which is not, and, apparently, it is because of that difference that language is believed to influence cognition or at least to make cognitive categorizations more precise. Yet when we look at what is known about cognition and language, we see that cognition has, so far, beaten language as regards precision, even to the point of becoming frustratingly elusive (think, for example, of the elusive concept of polysemy). As has been shown in Chapter 1, cognition is capable of applying the most finely tuned distinctions, some of which may be selected for the purpose of lexical distinctions in some language while others remain idle. Cognition has its own, still largely undisclosed laws and principles. In general, whatever system there is in the semantics of language is to be found in the workings of cognition, language being merely an observable outlet of cognition, the mind's visible handmaiden.

2.3.6 *Whorf's attitude towards mathematics and the sciences*

Like many of his contemporaries, including Leonard Bloomfield, Whorf looked up with awe to the newly flourishing disciplines of formal logic and mathematics, which had known a foundational renaissance since the mid-nineteenth century. Yet, like Bloomfield, he had no inside knowledge of these subjects. From his layman's point of view, Whorf looked forward to a formal science of semantics (which he confused with grammar). He differed, however, from modern formal linguistics and semantics in that he wanted or expected the grammars/semantics of each language to be radically different, envisaging a different 'mathematics' or 'logic' for each specific language, whereas modern formal theories of grammar or semantics seek to maximize unity, aiming to keep the same underlying formal system for all languages. Present-day Whorfians do not, on the whole, follow Whorf with regard to the formal character of grammar or semantics. In their general outlook, any notion of formal grammar or semantics, in whatever sense, is to be rejected, as they see each language as an idiosyncratic, largely arbitrary improvisation arising from communicative strategies.

Whorf's relativism explicitly extended to science. Many quotes could be given showing this, but perhaps the most telling is the following (Whorf 1956: 246–7):

What we call "scientific thought" is a specialization of the western Indo-European type of language, which has developed not only a set of different dialectics, but actually a set of different dialects. THESE DIALECTS ARE NOW BECOMING MUTUALLY UNINTELLIGIBLE. The term "space", for instance, does not and CANNOT mean the same thing to a psychologist as to a physicist. Even if psychologists should firmly resolve, come hell or high water, to use "space" only with the physicist's meaning, they could not do so, any more than Englishmen could use in English the word 'sentiment' in the meanings which the similarly spelled but functionally different French utterance *le sentiment* has in its native French.

How, then, can science escape from this Whorfian relativism and gain the universal validity it obviously has? The answer given is the following (Whorf 1956: 247):

For certain linguistic patterns rigidified in the dialectics of the sciences—often also embedded in the matrix of European culture from which those sciences have sprung, and long wor-shipped as pure Reason per se—have been worked to death. Even science senses that they are somehow out of focus for observing what may be very significant aspects of reality, upon the due observation of which all further progress in understanding the universe may hinge.

Again, Whorf fobs his readers off with an evasive answer. For the escape clause that linguistic patterns can be 'rigidified' and 'worked to death' so that they lose their impact on cognitive structures can be used any time the thesis is in danger of being falsified. This way no workable thesis or hypothesis remains. The real answer, of course, is that science is not language-relative precisely because it appeals to the highest levels of central thought, forging its own terminology whenever necessary.

2.3.7 *Levels of thinking*

For Whorf, our thinking ('largely') proceeds along lines set out by the language we happen to be born into, whereby this language is a formally definable system governing the structure and the meaning of our utterances. But then we are taken by surprise when we read (Whorf 1956: 149):

Consciousness itself is aware of work, of the feel of effort and energy, in desire and thinking. Experience *more basic than language* [italics mine; PAMS] tells us that, if energy is expended, effects are produced.

And again (Whorf 1956: 239):

[T]he tremendous importance of language cannot, in my opinion, be taken to mean necessarily that nothing is back of it of the nature of what has traditionally been called "mind." My own studies suggest, to me, that language, for all its kingly role, is in some sense a superficial embroidery upon deeper processes of consciousness, which are necessary before any communication, signaling, or symbolism whatsoever can occur, and which also can, at a pinch, effect communication (though not true AGREEMENT) without language's and without symbolism's aid.

Whorf seems to be groping here for the distinction between central and peripheral thought but he does not see his way through. He vaguely envisages a 'mind' that is subdivided into various parts or levels but does not quite know what to do with it. He obviously felt ill at ease with the notion 'mind', something he had in common with many of his contemporaries, especially the behaviourists. The term *consciousness* is used with less discomfort. Apparently, consciousness is a part of the mind that is not influenced by language. There is also the postulated non-conscious *mechanism* of grammar or semantics. But for Whorf, the 'dissecting of nature', the 'categories and types that we isolate from the world of phenomena' (Whorf 1956: 213) belong to those parts of the mind that depend on the categorizations made by the language spoken by the subject in question. However, the question of how consciousness, taken to precede language and thus independent of it, can possibly be thought to function without the 'categories and types that we isolate from the world of phenomena' remains unanswered. The 'beasts' are said probably to be able to think (p. 220), but how they can think without any 'categories and types that we isolate from the world of phenomena' is not clarified. It very much looks as if, for Whorf, language usurped its 'kingly role' from 'deeper processes of consciousness, which are necessary before any communication'. But how language and those 'deeper processes of conscious-ness', 'traditionally called "mind"', relate to each other, how this awareness, this 'experience more basic than language' categorizes its experiences as it 'dissects nature', is far from clear. Whorf obviously had no idea of what I have called (section 2.1) the 'architecture' of thought processes. Nor, for that matter, do we.

On the same page 239, a few lines down from the last quote given, Whorf's linguistic relativism even makes him call into question the validity of the general term *language*:

It may even be in the cards that there is no such thing as "Language" (with a capital L) at all! The statement that "thinking is a matter of LANGUAGE" is an incorrect generalization of the more nearly correct idea that "thinking is a matter of different tongues." The different tongues are the real phenomena and may generalize down not to any such universal as "Language," but to something better—called "sublinguistic" or "superlinguistic"—and NOT ALTOGETHER unlike, even if much unlike, what we now call "mental."

Did he encounter a language without a word for 'language'? Is our use of the general term *language* due to us being speakers of an Indo-European language? Probably not, yet the quote shows that Whorf went for linguistic, cognitive and cultural relativism in a big way.[9]

2.3.8 *Whorf's arguments: Hopi time and tense, Shawnee sentence types*

But did he have arguments? Whorf certainly thought he did. An important argu-ment, one that he repeatedly falls back on, is to do with the Hopi tense system (Hopi is an American Indian language of the Uto-Aztecan language family, spoken in the Navajo reservation in Arizona). The description of this system in Whorf (1956) is terminologically confusing. On p. 103 it is said that 'there are three tenses: past (i.e. past up to and including present), future and generalized (that which is generally, universally, or timelessly true), all of which are mutually exclusive'. On p. 144 one reads that 'verbs have no "tenses" like ours, but have validity-forms ("assertions"), aspects, and clause-linkage forms (modes), that yield even greater precision of speech'. Sometimes one wonders if a category of evidentiality is implied: 'Hopi verbs have three assertions: REPORTIVE (zero form), EXPECTIVE (suffix -*ni*), NOMIC

---

[9] Evans and Levinson (2009: 435) criticizes Fodor (1975), Pinker (1994) and Li and Gleitman (2002) for holding that thought content expressed in language is universal. The two authors do accept that, when utterances are produced, thought content is expressed in linguistic form. But, according to them, the thought content is not universal but specific for each language. It seems to me that a decision on the latter position must lie in a further analysis of what is meant by 'thought'. A sensible view holds that 'thought' takes place at different levels (see section 2.1). According to this view, there are at least two, but quite possibly more than two, levels of thought. There is at least a central level of thought, operating with, probably species-specific (universal), cognitive categories, and a level of 'thinking for speaking' (Slobin 1987) or 'microplanning' (Levelt 1989: 144–57) where the message is planned, in relation to given context and situation, and where lexical items are accessed that come closest to the not yet lexical 'deeper' level of thinking. If this is correct, the relativist and the universalist view are mutually consistent and can thus both be right, depending on what thought level is taken as a reference point.

(suffix -+^{w}i).[10] These translate, more or less, the English tenses' (p. 113). But there is no systematic analysis of either the grammar or the semantics of the Hopi tense system. We thus must do with the little Whorf gives us.

Apart from the fact that no argument is given that would show (a) that the Hopi have a notion of time that differs from ours, and (b) that, if so, it is their language that shapes their thinking about time and not the other way round, whatever little he tells us about the Hopi tense system is, in fact, not at all surprising or outlandish.[11] Many Indo-European languages have a gnomic tense, often homomorphic with the present tense but sometimes, as in ancient Greek, with the *aorist* (the term means 'unlimited'), which is also, and much more frequently, used for past point events. The collapsing of past and present into one factual tense is easily understood: Aristotle, a representative of Western culture if ever there was one, defined his bivalent theory of truth on the present and the past. The future, however, was, for Aristotle, of a different order where ordinary bivalence does not apply, as he argues in the famous passage of the sea battle in his *On Interpretation* (see Seuren 2009a: 223).

The treatment of the future as a modality, which is in essence how Whorf describes the Hopi future tense, is common to all European languages, whether or not of Indo-European stock. English and other Germanic languages are a clear case in point, in that they express futuricity by means of a modal auxiliary that behaves like other modals (see section 1.2.3). In English and German, the modal auxiliary verb for futuricity is characterized by the famous defective paradigm that robs auxiliarized modal verbs, such as English *may, can, will, must,* of infinitives and participles, and thus of compound perfective tenses, leaving them only the simple present and the simple past tense, but allowing for subordinate perfective infinitivals.[12] Examples (2.1a,b) are thus grammatical in English and German, respectively, but (2.2a,b) are ungrammatical in these languages (the German forms *würde* and *hätte* are in the past subjunctive rather than the past indicative, as the combination of past and future is normally used for counterfactuals, which require the subjunctive mood):

---

[10] Whorf seemed unaware that *nomic* is not an English word. He probably meant *gnomic,* the usual term for the generic tense, derived from Greek *gnōmē,* in the sense of 'generally accepted truth, aphorism'.

[11] In fact, Malotki (1983)—a book of 677 pages—contains a crushing amount of data showing that Whorf's statement (Whorf 1956 : 57–8) 'After long and careful study and analysis, the Hopi language is seen to contain no words, grammatical forms, constructions or expressions that refer directly to what we call 'time' [...]. Hence, the Hopi language contains no reference to 'time', either explicit or implicit', was in fact not based on very 'long and careful study and analysis'. It took the really long and careful study and analysis carried out by Malotki to show that, in this respect, Hopi is in no way exceptional among the languages of the world, including the 'standard average European' or SAE languages, so begrudged by Whorf for their dominant status in the modern world. Unfortunately, Malotki's study, for all its length, says nothing about grammatical tense in Hopi. One inevitably suspects, however, that, had it dealt with grammatical tense as well, it would have equally exposed Whorf's lack of expertise.

[12] That German appears to have an infinitive (but no participle) for the futuricity auxiliary *werden* is explained by the fact that *werden* has other meanings as well: it also means 'become' and it is the passive auxiliary 'be'; both allow for infinitives (and marginally for participles).

(2.1) a. He [will/would] [eat/have eaten].

      b. Er [wird/würde] [essen/gegessen haben].

(2.2) a. *He [has/had] would$_{\text{past participle}}$ [eat/have eaten].

      b. *Er [hat/hätte] [essen/gegessen haben] werden.[13]

This defective paradigm is due to the process of AUXILIATION, whereby would-be auxiliaries lose their status of full lexical verb and are typically incorporated, at the level of semantic analysis, between the higher simple tense option PRESENT/PAST and the lower perfective tense option SIMULTANEOUS/PRECEDING, which accounts for the perfect tenses (see Seuren 1996: 80–4).[14]

But even in those European languages where the future appears as a *morphological* tense category, as in the Romance or the Slavonic languages, the same restrictions apply. Thus, the French sentences (2.3a), where the present or past future tense takes a subordinate simultaneous verb (*manger* 'eat'), and (2.3b), where the present or past future tense takes a subordinate perfective verb (*avoir mangé* 'have eaten') are fully grammatical:

(2.3) a. Il [mangera/mangerait].

        'He [will/would] eat.'

      b. Il [aura/aurait] mangé.

        'He [will/would] have eaten.'

But French, or any other language with a morphological future tense, has no literal equivalent of (2.2a,b), or of the grammatical Dutch sentence (2.4) (see note 14):

(2.4) Hij [heeft/had] zullen eten./Hij [heeft/had] gegeten zullen hebben.

      'He [has/had] would$_{\text{past participle}}$ [eat/have eaten].'

There are thus good grounds for the generalization that the morphological future tense found in, for example, the Romance languages is a morphologization of what at the semantic level is a modal predicate (just as, for example, Turkish has turned all its modal predicates into bound morphemes).

Against this background, there is nothing surprising about the fact that Hopi expresses present and past as factual tenses but futuricity as a modal auxiliary. This

---

[13] Contrast this with, for example, the fully grammatical:

(i) Er hätte essen sollen.

   'He should have eaten.'

with the verb *sollen* ('must'), which, like Dutch *zullen*, has not (yet?) undergone auxiliation.

[14] Interestingly, the Dutch equivalent *zullen* of English *will* or its German counterpart *werden* has not so far undergone auxiliation and still functions as a full lexical verb. Thus the Dutch analogs of the sentences condensed into (2.2b) are fully grammatical: *Hij [heeft/had] zullen eten; Hij [heeft/had] gegeten zullen hebben* (as in example (2.4) in the text).

treatment reflects the ordinary, and probably universal, human way of dealing with past, present and future. Whorf's dreams about the gnarled-faced Hopis possessing a superior timeless wisdom that is alien to us, superficial Indo-Europeans, thus amount to nothing.

Moreover, tense/aspect systems in languages have not been found to correspond crucially with cognitive structures, cognitive processing or cultural notions. The Chinese, who have a rudimentary tense system in their language, are not known for any impediment in dealing with their rich historical past, whereas Hindus, whose Sanskrit has a rich tense system, actually prefer timeless being to historical dating.

The weakness of the Whorf hypothesis is perhaps most easily shown by means of parallels from our own well-known European languages. Consider the peculiar fact that Dutch uses locative terms for inanimate (and colloquially also animate) relatives, interrogatives, demonstratives and quantified pronominals in combination with prepositions. Thus, Dutch naturally uses locatives in cases like the following (the locative expressions are printed in italics):

(2.5)   a. het boek *waar*over ik je vertelde
          'the book about which (lit. 'about where') I told you'

   b. *Waar*mee heb je de deur geopend?
      'With what (lit. 'with where') did you open the door?'

   c. *Daar*mee heb ik de deur geopend.
      'With that (lit. 'with there') I opened the door.'

   d. Dat heeft *overal* mee te maken.
      'That has to do with everything (lit. 'with everywhere').'

   e. Hij zit *ergens* mee.
      'He is troubled about something (lit. 'about somewhere').'

   f. Dat verhaal gaat *nergens* over.
      'That story is about nothing (lit. 'about nowhere').'

German has the same phenomenon but to a lesser extent: it disallows locative pronominals for animate (antecedent) nouns and in adverbials. It thus has locative equivalents for (2.5a–c), but not for (2.5d–f). Consider, for example, Wittgenstein's famous last sentence of his *Tractatus Logico-Philosophicus*:

(2.6)   *Wo*von man nicht sprechen kann, *dar*über muß man schweigen.
          'Of what (lit. 'of where') one cannot speak, about that (lit. 'about there') one can only remain silent.'

In English, remnants of the same phenomenon are found in expressions like *whereupon, thereupon, thereof, thereto, thereafter, whereto, wherewithal*, etc.

Now suppose Hopi had been a world language and Whorf a Hopi researcher investigating the exotic European languages Dutch, German and English. Being

Whorf, he would then no doubt have concluded that the Dutch, the Germans and the Brits (and the Americans as well) have a special preoccupation with space and that they are unable to conceive of (inanimate) objects, whether concrete or abstract, in their own right but have to see them all in terms of some literal or metaphorical space occupied by them. Such a conclusion would, of course, lack any foundation, but isn't that exactly what Whorf, a speaker of English, does with regard to Hopi and all those other American Indian languages he cast his eye on?[15]

Another such parallel: in a somewhat triumphant tone, Whorf vaunts the fact that the American Indian language Shawnee has pairs of sentences that are structurally parallel but translate into very different structures in, say, English (Whorf 1956: 233–4)—a fact that should show that Shawnee Indians 'think' very differently from Europeans or white Americans and that this difference in thinking is caused by the differences in the two languages. Neither is true, I contend, but this is how Whorf wants it to be.

His main example is the following. The Shawnee sentence *Ni-l'θawa-'ko-n-a* translates as 'I pull the branch aside', whereas the structurally parallel sentence *Ni-l'θawa-'ko-θite* is translated first (p. 233), at the very outset of the section, as 'I have an extra toe on my foot', making one think of a foot with six toes in line—a rarely occurring variant in otherwise normal human beings. Yet at the bottom of the next page it transpires that this is not what the second sentence means. Here the second sentence is translated as 'I have an extra toe forking out like a branch from a normal toe'—a known effect of inbreeding. The common element, according to Whorf, is the 'forking out' of branches on the one hand and sprouting toes on the other. Of course, if Whorf had provided the latter translation right at the beginning, his text would not have had the stunning effect intended by him, since then any reader would have caught on immediately to the semantic similarity between the two sentences.

But apart from this salesman's ploy, it is quite common to find pairs of sentences that are structurally analogous in one language but require structurally very different translations in another, without the difference having any further nonlinguistic significance (they just drive developers of machine translation programmes to despair). Consider the German sentences (2.7a,b), which are close parallels, not only semantically but also structurally:

(2.7)   a. Er schwimmt gerne.
      b. Er schwimmt oft.

[15] We know, of course, that there is a universal tendency to express temporal notions by means of spatial terms—an instance of the overall 'primacy of spatial organization for human cognition' (Miller and Johnson-Laird 1976: 375). This fact is in principle explained by the greater abstractness of time compared to space and by the partial isomorphy of temporal and spatial parameters—a constellation that is conducive to a metaphorical transfer from space to time. Yet this is not Whorf's reasoning with regard to the Hopi tense system.

Now consider their English translations (2.8a) and (2.8b), respectively, which are structurally very different from each other:

(2.8)   a. He likes to swim.
        b. He swims often.

Or consider the German pair (2.9a,b) and their English translations (2.10a,b):

(2.9)   a. Mord verjährt nicht.
        b. Gold rostet nicht.

(2.10) a. There is no statutory limitation on murder.
        b. Gold doesn't rust.

Again, (2.9a,b) are structurally analogous, whereas (2.10a,b) have very different structures. All this means is that the concept 'with pleasure' is expressible in German by means of the adverb *gerne*, whereas English requires a lexical verb such as *like*, followed by an infinitival or a participial, or that the concept 'acquiring impunity', applied to a crime discovered after a certain amount of time, has the corresponding verb *verjähren* (something like 'superannuate') in German but is expressed in English by means of the legal nominal phrase *statutory limitation*, with obvious syntactic consequences for the rest of the sentence.[16]

A further example of this nature is the following. English has sentences like:

(2.11) a. The man is reportedly dead.
        b. The man is admittedly dead.
        c. The man is probably dead.

Their German equivalents are the following:

(2.12) a. Man sagt, daß der Mann tot ist.
           'One says that the man is dead.'

        b. Ich gebe zu, daß der Mann tot ist.
           'I admit that the man is dead.'

        c. Der Mann ist wahrscheinlich tot.
           'The man is probably dead.'

The English sentences are structurally analogous, but the German sentences are not: (2.12a) and (2.12b) require a periphrastic construction with a commanding verb,

---

[16] Thus, one could say in German:

(i)   Mord verjährt nicht, genau so wie Gold nicht rostet.
      (There is no statutory limitation on murder, just as gold doesn't rust.)

But the English translation would lose the stylistic effect the German sentence has.

whereby (2.12a) requires the impersonal *man* ('one') as subject term but (2.12b) the first person singular pronoun *ich* in subject position. Only (2.12c) is structurally parallel to its English counterpart. There is, of course, no evidence at all that the more liberal use of sentence adverbials in English compared with most other languages either reflects or causes any cognitive or cultural category or way of thinking, as such phenomena are purely linguistic idiosyncrasies. Yet what Whorf does with his Shawnee example is precisely that: assign cognitive and/or cultural significance to what is, to the best of our knowledge, nothing but idiosyncratic linguistic chance, the result of settling processes.

I could go on like this and take every single example presented by Whorf to pieces, but the fact of the matter is that there isn't a single forcible *argument* in Whorf's writings demonstrating that language either *determines* thought (the 'strong' version of his thesis) or *influences* it (the 'weak' version).

2.3.9 *Language expresses thought: arguments against Whorf*

But how about the opposite? Is there evidence that language *reflects* or *expresses* 'thought', in some sufficiently clear sense? In fact, there is plenty. Even without any experiments it stares one in the face. In many cases it is so trite that it stays unnoticed. In a general sense, one can adduce the many instances of, sometimes great, linguistic diversity within the same culture, or of linguistic constancy through, sometimes great, cultural upheaval (as in the case of the Russian Revolution of 1917).[17] Such instances show at any rate that one should not posit too close a correlation between the grammar and lexicon of any given language on the one hand and culture-bound conceptualizations on the other.

Most of grammar and much of the lexicon results from settling within the terms of a modular—that is, fully automatic and autonomous—system of items and rules converting propositional thought content into linguistic surface structures, with only a small number of interfaces with the conscious mind (Seuren 2004a: 82; 2009a: 253–4). Linguists, in their daily practice of finding principles and regularities, are, on the whole, unaffected by any Whorfian considerations, simply because the categories and regularities they discover are too clearly detached from culturally or cognitively bound ways of thinking. No one bothers about Whorf when it is found, for example, that the choice between *de* and *à* in French infinitival complements is not entirely idiosyncratic, in that most, but not all, verbs that take a direct object, such as *engager*

---

[17] The birth of the Romance languages after the fall of the Roman Empire is another case in point. The new Romance vernaculars came into being as recognized and standardized languages a long time after the collapse of the Roman Empire and the reason why they came into being was mainly the fact that the socio-cultural regulatory and norm-setting systems for the old Latin language, giving it its identity, had fallen away and had been replaced with new cultural identities and new local regulatory and normative social machineries. The languages thus followed the socio-cultural and political events, not the other way round.

('engage'), *contraindre* ('force'), *inviter* ('invite'), *obliger* ('oblige'), *encourager* ('encourage'), select *à* (though their passives sometimes select *de*), whereas intransitive verbs that take an indirect object, such as *conseiller* ('advise') or *promettre* ('promise'), always select *de* (perhaps in order to avoid two *à*-complements).[18] These are fully modularized aspects of human languages and they form the bulk of the material linguists work with.

The particular way in which the central thought system—in the sense of a specifically human, innate system enabling humans to shape categories and concepts and form propositional thoughts in which a property is assigned to an entity—is put to work in a socially united group is no doubt a main contributing factor in the coming about, over many generations, of a world view and a culture. If the group in question is still without a language, some language will emerge—though few pure instances are known. All we have is evidence from communities forcibly composed of speakers of mutually unintelligible languages, as in plantation colonies established from the seventeenth century onward (see section 1.3), or from communities of young congenitally deaf children placed together in an institution. In all such cases a new language has been seen to arise: Creole languages in plantation colonies; gestural languages in institutions for the deaf (Tervoort 1953; Senghas et al. 2004). The possession of a language will, in turn, be an enormous boost to further cultural and intellectual development, but only because of the WHAT, not because of the HOW. The vastly increased CONTENT of culturally shared thought will then again call for further development and refinement of the linguistic tools needed. There is no reason to assume that a 'primitive' language somehow mysteriously refines and develops itself and thus calls for greater cultural and intellectual development.

Then, lexicons, being as large and as many as they are, are inexhaustible sources of instances that disprove the Whorfian point of view.[19] There is, first, the widespread phenomenon of new words arising. Peter Hagoort suggested to me the example of the new Dutch word *weigerambtenaar*, literally a civil servant ('ambtenaar') who refuses ('weiger'). The word is used specifically for civil servants in town halls who refuse to marry gay couples on conscientious grounds. To suggest that the word was there first and that it gave rise to the phenomenon of civil servants refusing to marry gay couples is, of course, absurd. Ubiquitous and common sense evidence of this nature has never been addressed in a serious way in the Whorfian tradition, which is why so many have raised their eyebrows in wonder ever since this tradition made its appearance.

---

[18] Attempts to detect some pristine meaning in infinitival particles, such as 'purposiveness' in the French infinitival particle *à* (Haspelmath 1989), lack factual support and are thus open to doubt (in fact, an original locative meaning for French *à*, German *zu*, Dutch *te*, English *to* seems equally, if not more, plausible). No such semantic origin has ever been proposed for the French particle *de*, probably because the genitive is a jack-of-all-trades (see below).

[19] For some interesting and telling examples, see Clark (1996).

Examples abound in the area of *semantic change* or *semantic transfer*. The English word *meat* originally meant 'food'. What other cause can there have been for this semantic change than that, in England, meat was the *pièce de résistance* of a meal, so that speakers began to associate the notion of food with, specifically, meat? The word *meal* originally meant 'fixed mark/place/time' (German *mahl*, as in *Mahlzeit* 'meal', or *mal*, as in *Denkmal* 'monument'). Again, how can this word have been narrowed down to the meaning 'meal' other than because meals were the most salient events dividing a day?

The Dutch word *winkel* ('shop') originally meant 'corner', as still found in *winkelhaak* (ambiguous between 'rectangular tear in a fabric' and 'carpenter's square'). The reason for this semantic change is obvious: shops used to be found predominantly at street corners, where they would be most visible and attract most buyers. According to Whorf, it would have been because of the Dutch language that Dutch shops were mainly found at street corners: the language would, at one point, have identified street corners with shops! Any explanation that would seek the source of such semantic changes in the language and not in cognition would amount to an allegorization of language and thus be not only circular but actually bizarre. This conclusion is hard and direct, but it stands, and it is not a caricature, as Whorfians have suggested.[20] For if Whorf left room for facts of the world to influence the way we refer to things in it—a causal path that can only go via cognition, so that it is cognition that influences language, not the other way round—he never said so. Nor did he, or any of his followers, specify how Whorfian theory is to be reconciled with ubiquitous facts of this nature.

I can only give a few examples from the ocean of similar facts. The English word *heart* is primarily used to refer to the organ that pumps blood around the body. But it is also used for *courage*: *I didn't have the heart to go into the house*. In fact, the very word *courage* derives from Latin *cor* ('heart') plus the suffix *-aticum* ('something to do with', as in the word *language*: 'something to do with *lingua*, the tongue'). How could this specific, lexically recorded, use have come about other than via a *cognitive* connection, in that it is commonly *thought* that the heart is the seat of courage? There is nothing in the *language* that would make the connection. And no one will hopefully suggest that, because of this double use of the word *heart*, English speakers don't know the difference between someone's heart and someone's courage.[21]

---

[20] Chris Swoyer, a staunch Whorfian who is unlikely to wish to make a caricature of Whorfianism, writes in his 2003 article 'The linguistic relativity hypothesis' for the *Stanford Encyclopedia of Philosophy*: 'the Babylonians didn't have a counterpart of the word 'telephone', so they didn't think of telephones.' Yet the Dutch had no word for 'shop' but they did think of shops, and having no word for it they took an existing word and changed its meaning—a perfectly normal procedure.

[21] One may also think of cases like the now obsolete use, in medieval Arabic and Spanish, of the word *algebrist* for both mathematicians and medical doctors. This in itself surprising unification of two professions into one word was due to the fact that, during a certain period, doctors used to be also

Words for air, breath or smoke are often used to denote the less tangible phenomena of mind or soul. Greek *thýmos* ('mind, mood') is cognate with Latin *fumus* ('smoke'); Greek *ánemos* ('wind') is cognate with the two Latin words *animus* ('mind, mood') and *anima* ('soul'); Greek *psychḗ* ('soul', originally 'cold breath') is cognate with Greek *psychrós* ('blown cold') and *psýchein* ('blow cold'). Romanian *suflet* 'soul' derives from Latin *subflatum* 'softly blown', the past participle of the verb *subflare* ('blow softly'). (Note that *suflet* is the exact phonological counterpart of French *soufflé*, which, of course, has a much more mundane meaning.)

The English word *bald*, meaning 'devoid of usual covering' and applied specifically to heads or skin (and by extension to humans lacking hair on their scalp), is also applied to tyres, rocks and textiles whose pile has worn off. Clearly, this specific applicational restriction of the word *bald* in no way imposes the idea on English speakers that heads, skin, tyres, rocks and piled textiles form one cognitive category. Nor does anything similar happen to speakers of German, where the word *kahl* comprises not only the cases where English speakers use *bald* but also those where they use *bare*, as in *a bare wall*, *a bare tree*, etc.[22] These are applicational restrictions that *use* existing cognitive distinctions but do not necessarily *unify* them into one cognitive category or concept. How such restrictions come into being is largely a matter of fine-grained sociolinguistic alignment or settling processes whose precise details have mostly been lost in the mists of time.

A further, specific, argument against the Whorf hypothesis, never noted in the literature, is the following. Dutch has the words *neef* ('nephew' or 'male cousin') and *nicht* ('niece' or 'female cousin'); Italian has the word *nipote* ('nephew/niece' or 'grandchild'). Dutch also has the words *oom* and *tante* and Italian has *zio* and *zia* for 'uncle' and 'aunt', respectively, just as in English. Remarkably, however, when one asks a Dutch speaker, of the right age but out of context, how many *neven* or *nichten* he or she has, the answer will be that the question needs clarification: what kind of *neef* or *nicht* do you mean? And analogously in Italian. Ask an Italian speaker, of the right age but out of context, how many *nipoti* he or she has, the answer will again be: what kind of *nipote* do you mean? But when asked how many *uncles* or *aunts* they have, Dutch and Italian speakers alike will answer the way speakers of English will, not making any distinction between the many kinds of uncle or aunt there are: father's or mother's sibling or sibling's husband or wife. Yet in many languages these different kinds of uncle and aunt are strictly distinguished by different words. This raises a serious problem for Whorfians. For if language influences or determines

---

mathematicians. But there is, of course, no implication that Arabic or Spanish speakers of the period in question were unaware of the difference between a doctor and a mathematician.

[22] This shows the limited validity of George Lakoff's thesis, defended in Lakoff (1987), that linguistic categories reflect cognitive categories: they sometimes do, but often don't. The precise criteria are more intuited than actually known. It's like the difference between polysemy and ambiguity: despite many efforts, lexicology has not so far yielded a precise and adequate set of criteria for the distinction.

categories of thought, then why should Dutch or Italian speakers have the need for clarification when asked about their cousins, nephews, nieces or grandchildren? Apparently, we have to do here with a lexical field, kinship terminology, where *language underdetermines cognition* in that linguistically unexpressed cognitive and cultural distinctions sometimes do and sometimes do not result in lexical ambiguity—something the original Whorf hypothesis makes no allowance for.[23]

'Neo-Whorfianism', such as presented in Levinson (2003), recognizes this fact: 'thought is richer than language', says Levinson (2003: 292) on the grounds of recent experimental findings. But if so, it is not clear why the predicate *Whorfian* is still used, whether or not prefixed by *neo-*. For the essence of the Whorf hypothesis is denied and the new 'neo-Whorfian' insights are in full agreement with non-Whorfian, and even anti-Whorfian, theories. What is really at issue is the (very fruitful) investigation and exploration of the border area between language and thought, where it is to be expected that the 'packing' of propositional thoughts for linguistic expression and the 'unpacking' of incoming linguistic signals gives rise to non-central, convenience-based, storing systems that are adapted to any specific language in question. The examples (2.7) to (2.12) presented above are live demonstrations of the traffic that goes on in that border area. There is no need to dig in one's Whorfian or anti-Whorfian heels in this respect, since, fortunately, the two traditions (or ideologies) have met over the issues at hand. Despite any remaining differences, this first meeting provides a basis for further common research.

Crosslinguistic comparisons of what are often called *polysemy* phenomena likewise speak against the original Whorf hypothesis. To quote just one from an ocean of possible examples, the English word *frame* has a rich polysemic spectrum ('picture frame', 'frame of a vehicle', 'door frame', 'frame of reference', 'template', 'rack', etc.) diverging widely from its lexical counterparts in other European languages, despite the basic cultural unity of the linguistic communities concerned.

A similar picture arises from the meaning of the English (or 'Saxon') genitive *'s*, as in *John's book*. The polysemy of this *'s*, and in general, of possession predicates worldwide, has been widely discussed in the literature for at least a century (for recent discussions, see Clark 1992: 311; Seuren 2009a: 24, 356; 2010: 222–8). The noun phrase *John's book* is interpretable in an unlimited variety of ways, depending on discourse and situation: it can mean 'the book owned by John', 'the book written by John', 'the

---

[23] Joe Blythe, of the Max Planck Institute for Psycholinguistics at Nijmegen (Netherlands), suggested to me that perhaps the ambiguity of Dutch *neef/nicht* or Italian *nipote*, as against the non-ambiguity of words for 'uncle' or 'aunt', could be due to the fact that in the latter case the members of the class denoted belong to one single generation, whereas in the former case they belong to different generations. We do not know if this is true, given the paucity of the available data and the primitive state of the theory. But whether or not this is the correct answer, the Whorf hypothesis is faced with the problem that, apparently, there are cognitive distinctions, at least in the field of kinship relations, that are not manifest in language, which makes it hard to keep maintaining that it is language that cuts up nature into cognitive categories.

book given by John', 'the book given to John', 'the book borrowed by John', 'the book bought by John', 'the book reviewed by John', 'the book in John's custody', etc. etc. The semantic description of the genitive will thus have to incorporate a parameter referring the listener to available shared knowledge, such as 'standing in some relation to possessor noun's referent, the relation being known to speaker and supposed to be known to hearer in virtue of situational, contextual or world knowledge' (Janssen 1976). Clearly, the *language*, in this case, *underdetermines* interpretation, because of a lack of specificity in the genitive morpheme, and appeals to a knowledge base presumed to be present in the hearer to achieve full interpretation.

This phenomenon, the *underdetermination of cognitive categorization and of interpretation by the linguistic material provided*, permeates the whole of language and language use. Utterances are, in fact, little more than rule-governed cues triggering a search for the most plausible way in which they can be integrated into the ongoing discourse as a cognitive process. This basic fact, whose ultimate consequences have not been sufficiently thought through even though it is in principle recognized worldwide by pragmaticists and semanticists studying textual coherence, speaks loudly against the Whorf hypothesis, in that it shows that the real work happens in the mind and that language is merely the mind's handmaiden.

2.4 Experimental testing

2.4.1 *Inconclusive experiments*

Let us consider first a few well-known experiments that do not seem to have achieved their purpose, which was either to weaken the Whorf hypothesis or, if not to strengthen it, at least to maintain the Whorfian tradition.

2.4.1.1 *Colour*   During the 1950s a few experiments were conducted with the purpose of testing the Whorf hypothesis. Prominent among these is the experiment on colour naming and colour perception conducted by Brown and Lenneberg, published in Brown and Lenneberg (1954) and commented upon in Lenneberg (1953).

These authors' argument was, in essence, as follows. In cases where one might expect linguistic and cognitive categories to be correlated, it should also be expected that naming and recognition of the lexically represented phenomena should be quicker and easier. Applied to colours—a category taken to be exemplary for a correlation between language and thought—this means that colour naming would have to be quicker and easier for colours that have monomorphemic vernacular names in the lexicon (e.g. black, white, red, blue, green) than for colours that are not or poorly represented lexically (e.g. magenta, turquoise, terracotta). This expectation was confirmed. It was also found, however, that speakers of a language where certain colours are not or are poorly represented in the lexicon had no difficulty recognizing and classifying those colours. The only difference was that the names of not or poorly represented colours took longer to retrieve or to process. The authors concluded that their experiments did not support the spirit of the Whorf hypothesis. From our modern vantage point we would say that what was tested was not the Whorf hypothesis, which is about world view and central thought, but rather the border area adaptation of thought processes to the specific language spoken.

What was not taken into account by Lenneberg and Brown is the fact that there are, possibly physiologically based, *universals* in both colour perception and colour naming. One should realize that the physiology of colour perception constitutes a research area that is still far from finally settled. Nor do we have complete certainty regarding the distribution of colour names across the languages of the world. All we can say is that there is, at present, a certain agreement with regard to a distinction between primary and secondary colours and the crosslinguistic distribution of their names.

The colours most readily identified and used by humans as primary points of reference appear to be—in addition to white and black—red, green (in some older theories yellow) and blue. The latter three are the *primary colours*. They are *additive*, in that their addition, in various proportions, in light-radiating sources produces all colours of the spectrum. The addition in light sources, in equal proportions, of red, green and blue produces white. For humans, there are also three *secondary colours*: yellow, cyan and magenta. These are *subtractive*, in that their combinations act as filters upon a spectrum of white light, which is what happens, for example, when one mixes paints. The secondary colours are somewhat less prominent or salient for identification or as points of reference (see also section 8.5.2). This system is species-specific: humans are *trichromats*, as opposed to other mammals, some of which are *monochromats, dichromats,* or *tetrachromats*.

As regards colour naming, there is Berlin and Kay (1969), a study widely considered classic. These authors posit a seven-stage classification, such that:[24]

Stage 1: every language L has at least two monomorphemic colour terms (MCT), these terms cover dark-cool (roughly *black*) and light-warm (roughly *white*);
Stage 2: if L has three MCT, *red* is added;
Stage 3: if L has four MCT, either *green* or *yellow* is added;
Stage 4: if L has five MCT, both *green* and *yellow* are added;
Stage 5: if L has six MCT, *blue* is added;
Stage 6: if L has seven MCT, *brown* is added;
Stage 7: if L has more than seven MCT, *purple, pink* and *orange* and/or *grey* are added.

---

[24] For the stages 1 to 4, the findings in Berlin and Kay (1969) are in agreement with Dixon (1977), which is restricted to *adjectival* colour terms and does not take into account cases where colours are expressed as verbs. (An alternation between adjective and verb for the same meaning is often found across the languages of the world, as shown in Wetzer 1996; cp. English *squint* and *be cross-eyed*, or *limp*, which is both an adjective and a verb, and, of course, a noun.)

It was also found that, within the gradual transitions of the colour spectrum, there was a high degree of agreement among speakers of all languages in identifying referential focal points for 'pure' colours, in particular the colours white, black, red, green, yellow and blue.

This classification, presented as valid for all languages, is criticized in Saunders (1998) and Saunders and Van Brakel (1997) on a number of counts. Saunders criticizes Berlin and Kay (1969) for its Americo-centrism, for technical deficiencies and even errors in the experiments, for 'a language sample that was not random, and a bilingual and colonial factor that was ignored', for the choice of informants, and, generally, for drawing foregone conclusions. The wide acclaim with which Berlin and Kay (1969) was received upon its publication is characterized as follows in Saunders (1998):

This suspension of critical faculties must be put down to such factors as weariness with the Relativist *Zeitgeist*, local factional politics, congruence with structuralist and Chomskian principles, the status of Berkeley Anthropology and a sychophantic [sic; PAMS] adulation of scientistic methodology.

This, perhaps a little too extreme, criticism was followed by the carefully researched Levinson (2001), which reports on the language isolate *Yélî Dnye*, spoken on Rossel Island (Papua New Guinea) by a community of just over 3500 speakers. This language lacks basic, monomorphemic colour terms, even for white and black. The colour terms it has are adjectival formations derived (by reduplication) from nouns for characteristic objects. 'Black' is a reduplication of the noun for 'night', 'white' reduplicates the noun for 'white cockatoo', 'red' reduplicates the noun for 'red parrot', and so on. These data speak against Berlin and Kay's graded classification. Yet Levinson also says (Levinson 2001: 9):

[. . .] ethnographic observation reveals little interest in color: there is no current artwork or handiwork in color, with the exception of baskets woven with patterns (usually natural versus black/blue). There is a keen interest in the multidenominational shell money, but color is an unreliable clue to the denominational values, and there is no special descriptive vocabulary.

This suggests that the colour terms used by Yélî Dnye speakers are relatively recent, introduced as a consequence of contact with the outside world. It is reasonable to assume that language contact is a powerful source of interference with otherwise valid universalist generalizations (cp. Levinson 2001: 40).

Also, significantly, in colour naming tasks, the subjects, even elderly ones with no scholastic education or outside experience at all, strictly followed the Berlin and Kay classification (Levinson 2001: 22):

All subjects used *kpaapîkpaapî* 'white', *kpêdêkpêdê* 'black' and *taataa* 'red' (despite the fact that the last term was said to belong to the neighboring dialect; all but one subject also used *mtyemtye*, the local dialect word). All subjects also used the phrase *yi kuu yââ* for some area of the green hues. Beyond that, the consensus rapidly breaks down. [...] Taken together, these facts suggest that only a handful of expressions are the conventional expressions for a perceptually salient hue: *kpaapîkpaapî* 'white', *kpêdêkpêdê* 'black', with *mtyemtye* and *taataa* vying for "reds" and the phrase *yi kuu yââ* predominantly chosen for "green."

There is, on the whole, a large amount of uncertainty regarding the (non-) universality of colour perception and colour terminology (see Saunders and Van Brakel 1997 for ample and informed comment). Even so, there seems to be no convincing evidence invalidating the generally accepted view (a) that there is a universal perceptual system, whether or not physiologically determined, of (most probably three) primary and (again probably three) secondary colours, besides black and white, and (b) that, as a rule, visually unimpaired members of all cultures are capable of recognizing fine distinctions in colour qualities. The Whorfian hypothesis that language affects thought is, in any case, not confirmed. Levinson's work in this regard is more relevant for the linguistic relativity thesis (see Chapter 3) than for the Whorf hypothesis. Levinson's final sentence 'it takes a culture of color to make a color terminology worthwhile' (Levinson 2001: 45) is uncontroversial, but obviously non-Whorfian.

What this means for the strict Whorf hypothesis is unclear. Whatever little Whorf says about colour (1956: 85, 147, 163, 209) appears to indicate that for him colour perception is a language-independent 'sensation', not corresponding to a conceptual interpretation, and hence universal: 'visual perception is basically the same for all normal persons past infancy' (Whorf 1956: 163). But how colour terms can have a meaning if there are no corresponding concepts, remains unclear. On p. 209, he speaks of 'words denoting [...] various sensations of blue' but no corresponding semantic theory is provided. (In general, the semantics of qualia remains unclear in the Whorfian perspective.)

The opposition between language-driven intellectual concepts on the one hand and less intellectual and more universal 'apprehension' or perception on the other, though stipulated by Whorf, remains vague and ambiguous. This stands out clearly when one considers his treatment of the question of whether the concepts of space, time and matter are universal. Having formulated this question on p. 138, he gives 'the right answer', first on p. 153: 'Newtonian space, time, and matter are no intuitions. They are recepts from culture and language.'[25] Then, on p. 158:

---

[25] The word *recept* stems from the Canadian-British Darwinist scholar George John Romanes (1888, Ch. ii: 36–7): 'In addition, then, to the terms Percept and Concept, I coin the word Recept. [...] Recepts, then, are spontaneous associations, formed unintentionally as what may be termed unperceived abstractions.' Romanes gives the following example (p. 50):

If I am crossing a street and hear behind me a sudden shout, I do not require to wait in order to predicate to myself that there is probably a hansom-cab just about to run me down: a cry of this kind, and in those circumstances, is so intimately associated in my mind with its purpose, that the idea which it arouses need not rise above the level of a recept; and the adaptive movements on my part which that idea immediately

To sum up the matter, our first question asked in the beginning (p. 138) is answered thus: Concepts of "time" and "matter" are not given in substantially the same form by experience to all men but depend upon the nature of the language or languages through the use of which they have been developed.

Further down on the same page 158, 'space' is given a somewhat different treatment from 'time' ('matter' being left out of the equation):

> But what about our concept of "space," which was also included in our first question? There is no such striking difference between Hopi and SAE [Standard Average European languages; PAMS] about space as about time, and probably the apprehension of space is given in substantially the same form by experience irrespective of language. The experiments of the Gestalt psychologists with visual perception appear to establish this as a fact. But the CONCEPT OF SPACE will vary somewhat with language, because, as an intellectual tool, it is so closely linked with the concomitant employment of other intellectual tools, of the order of "time" and "matter," which are linguistically conditioned.

His opposing of the *apprehension* of space to the intellectually conceived *concept* of space (earlier called a 'recept'; see note 25) is meant to save his thesis. The concept is then, without further argument, taken to be 'linguistically conditioned' (p. 159). That apprehension, in the sense of 'awareness of something in general terms', is not possible without corresponding general concepts (the alternative being behaviouristic conditioning) is not taken into consideration.

It is thus unclear whether the findings of Lenneberg and Brown described above confirm or disconfirm the Whorf hypothesis. One may try to save Whorf by saying that colour naming is exempt from his hypothesis, which is about central thought, not about universal experiences, apprehensions or percepts, which are based on the physiology and cerebral processing of visual stimuli. But this implies a semantic theory that accounts for the denoting of experiences, apprehensions and percepts without the intervention of (qualia) concepts, and no such theory seems in sight. Moreover, one has to explain why languages differ so markedly in their colour terminology and, in particular, how the effects measured by Brown and Lenneberg can come about.

2.4.1.2 *Levinson and absolute orientation*   Let us now consider Levinson's (2003) argument that the cognitive mindset of *absolute orientation* (horizontal spatial

---

prompts are performed without any intelligent reflection. Yet, on the other hand, they are neither reflex actions not instinctive actions; they are what may be termed receptual actions, or actions depending on recepts.

It seems to me that Whorf's recourse to the notion of 'recept', unaccompanied by any comment, is confused. For one thing, Whorf here equates recepts with concepts, whereas Romanes is anxious to distinguish them. But in general it seems clear that for Whorf the intellectual aspect of cognition is language-driven, while primary impressions are universal. His use of the term *thought* must then be understood as excluding primary impressions such as 'apprehensions' or percepts.

reference in terms of the cardinal directions north, south, east and west, or of dominant landmark features such as *uphill* or *downhill*) and our tendency to think rather in terms of *viewpoint-related orientation* for horizontal reference in cases where the compass points are not relevant, are determined by the language spoken in the communities in question.[26] According to Levinson (2003: 91–2), some cultures favour absolute frames of horizontal spatial reference at the expense of our familiar viewpoint-related orientation system, with words for 'left', 'right', 'in front of', 'behind', and the like. Such concepts lack corresponding words in languages with absolute orientation, which makes it 'impossible to give a general recipe for setting the table [...], with forks on the left and knives on the right' (Levinson 2003: 91).

Speakers of an absolute orientation language will have to be well trained in being able, all the time and at any place, to realize the position of the north–south and the east–west axes (or of the uphill and downhill directions): speakers of such languages 'clearly run a mental compass in the unconscious background as it were' (Levinson 2003: 152). Such phenomena are, of course, fascinating. Imagine yourself asking your friend where the teapot is and your friend answering that it is to the west of the milkbottle and analogously for every mundane horizontal place specification. Yet one has to be careful. As is explained in section 3.1, one must beware of what Keesing (1997) calls the *Frake syndrome*—that is, the tendency to write only about the 'exotic' and leave the unmarked or 'normal' undiscussed. In fact, Levinson's 'absolute' orientation systems are rare exceptions (and, as noted in Keesing 1997: 127, used only for special purposes) and the homely 'relative' orientation systems are the rule by a long shot.

Levinson describes a fair number of experiments with regard to absolute orientation, involving mainly speakers of the Australian Aboriginal language Guugu

---

[26] Actually, viewpoint-related orientation comes in two varieties (Miller and Johnson-Laird 1976: 394–405; Levelt 1996). We have (a) *deictic orientation*, which defines left–right or front–back relations as seen from the point of view of an external viewer (either ego or a discourse-defined 2nd or 3rd person replacement, a 'homunculus' moving about according to discourse and/or context) and (b) *intrinsic orientation*, which defines left–right or front–back relations from the point of view of the prepositional object referent itself (called *relatum* by Miller and Johnson-Laird and by Levelt). Deictic orientation involves three arguments, (a) the *viewer*, (b) the *subject* (the tree in *the tree is to the left of the fountain*, called the *referent* in Miller and Johnson-Laird and in Levelt), and (c) the *object* (the fountain). Intrinsic orientation has two arguments, (a) the *subject* (the tree) and (b) the *object* (the man). Intrinsic orientation is in principle limited to cases where the object has itself a front and a back and a left- and right-hand side. *To the left of the tree*, for example, can be interpreted only deictically, because a tree has itself no front, back, left- or right-hand side, but *to Mr. Cooper's left* is ambiguous, as it can also be interpreted intrinsically, since Mr. Cooper will have a front and a back and a left- and right-hand side of himself. This ambiguity is often manifest in captions of photographs, where, from the viewpoint of an external viewer, the qualifications 'right' and 'left' are in need of further comment. (English prefers the preposition *on*, as in *on Mr. Cooper's left*, for the intrinsic reading; see Levelt 1996: 89.) Intrinsic orientation is also possible for faceless objects when there is a known last path covered (which gives the object a face, as things are taken to move face forward), as in *After the ball had rolled to the tree, the house was on its left* (Levelt 1996: 105).

Yimithirr and the Mayan language Tzeltal, spoken in Tenejapa, Mexico. In one experiment, Guugu Yimithirr speakers were compared with speakers of Dutch (a language whose speakers normally use viewpoint-related orientation). Both groups of speakers were presented with an array of objects on a table in a room and were asked to memorize the array. They were then led into a different room, with the door, window and table in the same relative (left–right) arrangement as in the first room, but where everything was positioned at 180 degrees from the first room. The objects were also present on the table, but in a haphazard array. The subjects were then asked to place the objects in the same array they were in on the table in the first room. The Dutch subjects consistently placed the objects according to left–right and front–back parameters (they were, so to speak, 'setting the table'), whereas the Guugu Yimithirr subjects showed a significant preference for the arrangement in terms of the points of the compass (the less than 100 per cent preference being explained by the fact that the Guugu Yimithirr subjects were also fluent speakers of English).

This result does not show that it is the language that determines the choice of pattern. All it shows is that there is a correlation between the orientation style current in the language on the one hand and nonlinguistic—that is, cognitive—processes on the other. Levinson fully recognizes this. He makes it clear (Levinson 2003: 170–1) that the purpose of all experiments reported on in his (2003) is to show, first, the reality of the correlation and, secondly, that it is the linguistic factor that induces the correlation. In a final section 'Correlation and causation: chicken or egg', Levinson (2003: 210–3) explicitly addresses the latter question. There he attempts to show that it is the language that induces the cognitive structures (a conclusion that has been anticipated all along). Levinson posits first 'that language categories (LC) correlate with distinctive cognitive codings (CC)' (Levinson 2003: 211). Then, making it clear that '[t]he hypothesis I am entertaining is that LC is determinative of CC' (p. 211), and thus taking the 'strong version' of the hypothesis, he poses the question (Levinson 2003: 212):

How then would all members of a community come to share the locally predominant CC? There are a few distinct possibilities:
  1. there is human genetic diversity in this domain;
  2. some third factor—say, climate or ecology—induces a distinctive CC in the local population;
  3. the local population converges through communication.

Having rejected the answers (1) and (2), Levinson then settles on (3) (Levinson 2003: 213):

Thus we are thrown back on explanation (3)—that populations converge on a particular non-verbal coding strategy largely because they have learnt to do so by communicating with each other.

Apart from the fact that Levinson now recedes to the 'weak' version of the Whorf hypothesis—witness his use of the word *largely*—we see that he makes the buck stop at language. The mechanism by which 'communication'—that is, the use of language—can be seen to have this effect is squarely placed in the border area between language and thought, involving peripheral, not central, thinking, as is clearly argued on pages 302 and 303 of Levinson (2003), where explicit reference is made to Slobin's concept of 'thinking-for-speaking'. The actual argument runs as follows (2003: 301):

The argument is an architectural one. Language is an output system. The output must meet the local semantic requirements. Consequently, the input to language production must code for the right distinctions. As a consequence of that, scenes must be remembered complete with the relevant features. In order to code for those features, subsidiary processes must run—for example, to code for fixed bearings, a mental 'compass' must compute directions.

No problem so far. In fact, this concurs entirely with what I have said above regarding the 'packaging' and 'unpacking' of linguistic messages in the border area of language and thought. But then the 'architectural' aspect of the argument gives way to a certain amount of speculation, as Levinson continues thus (2003: 301):

An indirect consequence of coding for particular features is that inference will be done over those features. And other output systems like gesture will reflect the same coding of features in memory. So, given the architecture of the system, once one puts serious semantic constraints on the output, the rest of the system will be forced to support, code and operate on those features. And so the imprint of language-specific categories will run deep in cognitive processes.

Not quite. It does not follow, not even indirectly, that 'inference will be done over those features'. One cannot simply take it for granted that central thought, the seat of inference, is affected by peripheral demands. Nor does it follow that 'other output systems like gesture will reflect the same coding of features', even if that may be deemed probable. And although, given the architecture sketched, it follows by analytical necessity that 'the rest of the system will be forced to support [and] code' the features at issue, it does not follow that it will also 'operate on' them, since we do not know how 'deep', how vast and how language-independent the rest of the system is. Hence, the conclusion that 'the imprint of language-specific categories will run deep in cognitive processes' is circular. I do not say that this conclusion is false, but it is unwarranted. Levinson's reasoning here is a particularly sophisticated version of the fallacy of the failure to distinguish between the HOW and the WHAT. There still is absolutely no evidence that the type-level system of HOW speakers say things, whether lexically or grammatically, has an influence on the type-level cognitive mechanism of concept formation, the way we categorize and 'cut up' the world around us, while there is plenty of evidence that there is a considerable influence the other way (*pace* settling phenomena).

We see here the effects of a Whorfian past. While admitting that 'the kind of theory emerging from [his] book [...] is not Whorfian in any strict sense' (Levinson 2003: 301), Levinson still speaks of 'Whorfian effects', subsumed under the label of *Neo-Whorfianism*. And there is a tendency to generalize from the peripheral language-border to the 'system' as a whole, even though nothing supports that tendency.

It seems to me that Levinson's analysis is incomplete, as it focuses on too small a number of possibilities. As we have seen, he posits three distinct possible answers to the question of how a community may have come to share its dominant cognitive categorizations (Levinson 2003: 212): genetic diversity, climate or ecology, and 'communication'. Having rejected the first two, he plumps for the third, appealing to border-area effects of language on peripheral thought and raking in more than just border-area effects in the process. But surely, dominant cognitive categorizations in a community can come about in other ways as well, or, alternatively, Levinson's concept 'communication' must be taken to cover a great deal more than just border-area effects. West-African animistic voodoo beliefs, for example, clearly do not spring from the language spoken, as the beliefs are shared by speakers of wildly diverging and highly splintered language groups. Do they nevertheless spring from 'communication'? Only if one confuses the HOW and the WHAT. They do seem to spring from magic, that is, a lack of adequate knowledge of natural causes and a wish to influence natural courses of events by an appeal to thought-up forces and effects— a long process in which language is bound to play an instrumental role, in its quality of WHAT, not of HOW.

So let us suppose that absolute spatial orientation, as an instance of socially shared cognitive categorization, has come about one way or another, as a result of outdoor living or as a manifestation of tribally shared and cultivated prowess, or whatever. The cognitive categories of absolute orientation will then be part of the central thought system, just as they are part of the central thought systems of speakers of viewpoint-oriented languages, but their activation will be vastly more frequent in absolute orienters because they will be considered relevant in vastly more numerous situations than is the case for speakers of viewpoint-oriented languages. In fact, they are needed so often that, as Levinson says, the members of the community in question have been trained to carry a 'mental compass' around with them all the time.

In this perspective it is relevant to call attention to a specific feature of the lexical semantics of all languages which, though well known among practising lexicographers, is not often brought to the fore by theoretical lexicologists and hardly known to linguists in general. This is the dependency of the meanings of certain lexical items or grammatical forms (such as the genitive *'s* discussed above) on available encyclopedic or situational knowledge. An obvious example, in all languages, is provided by the *possessive complex*, which embraces all expressions denoting a relation usually described as 'possessive', such as verbs for 'have' or prepositions meaning 'with' or 'possessive' pronouns or 'possessive' nominal cases such as the genitive or dative

(Janssen 1976; Seuren 2009a: 24, 122, 356; 2010: 222–8). Although grammarians usually speak of 'possessive' in all such cases, the relation actually expressed is one of 'known appurtenance', with an appeal to available knowledge, taken to be shared by speaker and hearer. Other such relations are expressed by or implicit in *gradable adjectives* (which make an appeal to an agreed standard of comparison), *viewpoint-related orientation* (which appeals to contextually defined knowledge), or individual predicates such as *fond of* (*John is fond of cherries* versus *John is fond of dogs*). All such cases are instances of the more general fact that *language underdetermines cognition*, just as *speech underdetermines full interpretation*: language is but a handmaiden to the mind.

The point here is that the semantic complex of 'sameness' falls likewise into this category. To interpret an expression involving the notion of 'sameness', one needs an appeal to cognition in that it needs to be clear in what respects the 'sameness' (or lack of it) is said to hold. 'Sameness' involves an identification of tokens into types, which is a process driven by selective cognitive factors, contextual relevance being the most prominent. Thus, to decide whether John has *the same car* as Harry one needs criteria of 'sameness', and these may vary from situation to situation, depending on what is taken to be relevant. Normally, the expression will not imply that John and Harry are co-owners of the same vehicle. Rather, it will be interpreted as applying to two distinct vehicles which are 'the same' in certain respects. The make and type will have to be the same, but sameness of the year of manufacture, the engine or the colour may not be relevant and will then not fall under the concept of sameness.

The link between this fact and Levinson's analysis of absolute orientation is the following. All Levinson's experiments are predicated on the use of expressions involving the notion of *sameness* in the instructions given, as appears from Levinson (2003: 155)—a passage that is about the methodology applied in all the experiments reported on:

Clearly it is crucial that the instructions for the experiments, or the wording used in training sessions, do not suggest one or another of the frames of reference: instructions were of the kind 'Point to the pattern *you saw before*', 'Remake the array *just as it was*', 'Remember *just how it is*', i.e. devoid of spatial information as much as possible, and as closely matched in content as could be achieved across languages. [italics mine; PAMS]

Given the insight that the linguistic meanings of predicates expressing 'sameness' involve an open parameter referring speaker and hearer to available shared knowledge and activating contextually relevant cognitive features, the well-nigh ubiquitous use of absolute orientation expressions by speakers of languages such as Guugu Yimithirr or Tzeltal is explained by *the assumption that the cognitive categories involved in absolute orientation are considered relevant in the vast majority of the speech situations occurring in their daily lives* (but not, for example, in situations involving traffic rules, where absolute orientation is irrelevant and would quickly lead to disaster). The open parameter in the expression *the same array* is then given the value 'same according to the compass points'. No appeal to habit-based cognitive coding 'grooves', whether only in the language–thought border area or more deeply into central thought, is then required and the entire phenomenon of absolute orientation would be irrelevant to any Whorfian or non-Whorfian influence of language upon thought processes. This is not to say that there is no 'grooving' effect of the language on peripheral thought processes as regards absolute orientation. I personally expect there to be some such effect. But it has not been shown to be there and when it is, I expect it to be marginal.

To test the role of the relevance factor in spatial orientation, one may present speakers of a viewpoint-oriented language with an image where the north is indicated by an arrow pointing upward (or away from the subject) and a town is shown on the left (west) side and a hill on the right (east) side. Then present a different image where the north is indicated by an arrow pointing down (or towards the subject) and ask the same subjects to replicate the positions of the town and the hill. Chances are that a large proportion of the subjects will not do so according to the right–left parameter but according to the east–west axis, as that will be taken to be the relevant parameter. Analogously, one may present speakers of an absolute orientation language with an image of a car keeping left on a road and then, in a different room placed at 180 degrees with respect to the first room, present them with the image of only the road and ask them to place the car in the same position on the road as before. Again, chances are that these subjects, who will presumably be traffic-competent, will predominantly follow the left–right axis and forget about absolute orientation. Or present a number of absolute orienters with a photograph of objects on a table and ask them to replicate the arrangement seen on the photograph using real objects on a real table. My guess is that the subjects will, again, follow the left–right axis, as there is no absolute orientation model to follow. I have not carried out these or similar experiments, as I have neither the skill nor the wherewithal for doing so, but I invite any reader who has both to see if my prediction comes true. In any case, as long as such counterexperiments have not been carried out, Levinson's claim must be considered at least premature and probably false.

The same criticism and the same conclusion would seem to apply to an experiment reported in Lucy (1996: 50), where English and Yucatec speakers were asked to decide whether a small carton box was *more like* a similar box but made of plastic, or a small piece of carton. The English speakers all opted for the plastic box, whereas the Yucatec speakers all opted for the piece of carton. This is said to correspond with the fact that English speakers tend to attend more to the shape of objects, whereas for Yucatec speakers the material that objects are made of is a more dominant criterion. This may well be true, but since 'likeness' is a cognitively, not a linguistically defined criterion, subject to degrees of contextual relevance, this result is likely to be produced mainly by general attitudes of relevance and not, or less, by the fact that speakers are brought up in the terms of a specific linguistic system.

The conclusion I have reached with regard to Levinson's spatial orientation experiments is in broad accord with what was found in Levelt (1996), which tested ellipsis of direction terms in path descriptions through various 'stations' represented as circles, as in Figure 2.2. Levelt poses the question whether ellipsis in subsequent path descriptions requires *sameness of the word* after lexical selection (surface ellipsis) or *sameness (continuity) of direction in the mental layout* before lexical selection (deep ellipsis). He tested for deictic and intrinsic, not for absolute, orientation (see note 26). In the test set-up subjects saw a number of layouts of stations and connecting lines, Figure 2.2 being one example, and were asked to describe each layout. The experimenter looked for cases of ellipsis. Only those subjects' reports were taken into account that were consistently deictic or intrinsic. Reports with midway perspective changes were ignored. (Note that an expression like *straight (on)* requires an intrinsic perspective.)

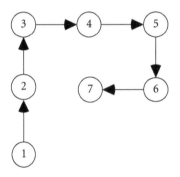

Figure 2.2 Example of layout of stations and paths in Levelt (1996)

To decide whether ellipsis is 'deep' or 'surface', Levelt looked at all cases of ellipsis in the reports and checked whether they reflected omissions of the second identical lexical item (in which case there is surface ellipsis) or of mention of identical spatial relations in the mental spatial image (in which case there is prelexical or deep ellipsis). Thus, if ellipsis in human language is of the surface type, one expects descriptions of Figure 2.2 like (2.13a) for deictic ellipsis and (2.13b) for intrinsic ellipsis:

(2.13) a. From 2 go up to 3. Then go right to 4 and *right* to 5.   (deictic)
        b. From 4 go straight to 5. Then go right to 6 and *right* to 7.   (intrinsic)

However, ellipsis of the type in (2.13b) was consistently absent in the material, which made Levelt conclude that ellipsis is 'deep': it is possible only when there is sameness (continuity) of direction in the mental layout of the stations.[27] The fact that the same

---

[27] It must be noted here that *ellipsis* must be taken in a strict sense, excluding quasi-anaphoric use of the word *again*. A formulation like *Then go right to 6 and again to 7* in (2.13b) seems perfectly adequate to describe the path from 5 to 6 to 7 in intrinsic terms.

lexical item may be called for in intrinsic descriptions is of no importance: the conditions for ellipsis are set once the orientation mode is chosen but before lexical selection. Unfortunately, the crucial results can only come from cases where the intrinsic mode has been chosen, because only for intrinsic descriptions can there be a discrepancy between lexical selection and mental layout. Deictic descriptions do not allow for discrimination on this parameter, as one can easily check. Yet since it is unlikely that ellipsis works differently for different orientation modes, Levelt felt justified to generalize from the orientation mode that allows for discriminatory results to the one that does not.

On the basis of these findings, Levelt concluded that (1996: 101):

When we describe [...] spatial patterns [...], we must decide on some order of description because speech is a linear medium of expression. The principles governing these linearization strategies [...] are nonlinguistic (and in fact nonsemantic) in character; they relate exclusively to the image itself.

As noted by Levelt, this conclusion is at odds with Levinson's position which implies that it is the language that makes absolute or relative orienters decide on parameters of sameness. Mentioning a discussion he had with Levinson on the matter, Levelt maintains his conclusion that sameness criteria for spatial orientation do not depend on the language but on relational pattern agreement in the mental layout after the selection of the orientation mode, but adds that mode selection may vary according to circumstances and relevance criteria. The criteria in question are thus to be located in the earliest stages of Slobin's 'thinking-for-speaking', in what Levinson calls 'experiencing-for-speaking' (Levinson 2003: 303), but not in the speaking.

2.4.2 *Getting closer*

There has recently been an increase of experiments, mostly but not exclusively to do with place or time, and mostly aiming to show that, one way or another, there is some truth in the Whorf hypothesis, at least in the weak version of it. Let us review some of them.

2.4.2.1 *Bowerman and Choi (2003)*   In the engaging study Bowerman and Choi (2003), the authors deal with the question of whether conceptual categorizations in first language acquisition are language-dependent and if so at how early a stage language begins to exert an influence. The paper opens with the following words, which show its Whorfian perspective (Bowerman and Choi 2003: 387):

Does language influence nonlinguistic cognition, and do different languages influence it in different ways? Testing these classical Whorfian questions presupposes speakers who are old enough to have mastered the relevant aspects of their language. For toddlers in the very early stages of linking meanings to language forms, we need to ask another question: do the concepts initially associated with language arise solely through nonlinguistic cognitive development, or are they formulated, at least in part, under linguistic guidance? Establishing where children's early meanings come from—the relative contributions of nonlinguistic cognition and exposure to language—is important to the debate about the Whorfian hypothesis because it provides clues to how flexible—hence how potentially malleable—children's cognitive structuring of their physical and social world is.

The authors then point out (p. 388) that 'recent comparisons of children learning different languages show that children adopt language-specific principles of categorization by as early as the one-word stage'. This, the authors hasten to add (p. 388), 'does not, of course, show that the linguistic categories, once acquired, exert an influence on nonlinguistic cognition, but it does set the stage for this possibility'.

After this, the authors focus on spatial cognition and language, and in particular on spatial relations and frames of reference. In this area, they found that 'both nonlinguistic cognition and language seem to influence early spatial semantic development, often in interaction', but always on the basis of a pre-existing 'grasp of many aspects of space, including when objects will fall, what objects can contain other objects, and the path objects can follow in moving from one place to another' (Bowerman and Choi 2003: 389). The authors present evidence 'that learning a language can affect nonlinguistic spatial cognition by selectively maintaining or discouraging sensitivity to spatial distinctions that are, or are not, relevant to that language' (p. 390).

The main focus in Bowerman and Choi (2003) is on a small set of locative prepositions or verbs in English, Korean and, to some extent, Dutch, in particular prepositions or verbs expressing relations of *containment*, *support* and *tight fit*. For example, the Korean verb *kkita* expresses a tight-fit relation as of a ring on a finger or a drawer in a chest or a Lego block on another, while the verb *nehta* expresses loose containment in a larger object, such as obtains for an apple in a bowl or a book in a bag. Korean uses *nohta* for putting something on top of a horizontal surface, *pwuchita* for putting something on a vertical surface, and *ssuta* for putting clothing on the head (pp. 393–4). By contrast, English *on* expresses a relation of attachment to a flat or round surface, but not necessarily of support, as when one speaks of a vase *on* a table or a fly *on* a ceiling or a picture *on* a wall or a ring *on* a finger. The preposition *in* is used for containment, whether tight or loose.

In an experiment eliciting descriptions of a wide range of actions, for both English and Korean speakers, each group consisting of 10 adults and 10 children from 2 to 31/2 years, Bowerman and Choi found that all English children, like the adults, distinguished systematically between events of containment, all described by means of the preposition *in*, and events of contact/support/surface attachment, all described by means of *on*. By contrast, all Korean children (Bowerman and Choi 2003: 397):

subdivided events of containment depending on whether they were loose [...] or tight [...], and they grouped tight containment events with tight surface attachment or encirclement events [...] (all *kkita*). They also used different verbs, as is appropriate, for putting clothing on the head, trunk and feet.

Thus, 'by at least 2 to 2½ years of age, children learning different languages classify space in strikingly different ways for purposes of talking about it' (p. 397).

This leaves the question of *how early* children learn these distinctions. In a cross-linguistic preferential looking experiment involving children aged from 18 to 23 months, the authors found that 'children understand these categories language-specifically at least by 18 to 23 months' (Bowerman and Choi 2003: 398)—that is, before they start to produce the target words. Similar results were found for the vertical *up–down* parameter and for correct and incorrect uses of words for *open* as used by English, Dutch and Korean children (pp. 398–406).

The authors then raise the question of the nonlinguistic starting position native language learners are in, which, they say (p. 410), 'is one of the most challenging and controversial questions facing developmentalists today'. This question is indeed extremely hard to answer, not only because the means for testing the 'subjects' are very limited but also because their brains are still developing, along with the skills they acquire. One thus has to tread very carefully and the authors do indeed leave ample room for doubt as they present their conclusions.

Reporting on an experiment by Casasola and Cohen (2002) regarding early infant categorization of containment, support and tight-fit relations, Bowerman and Choi agree that there is evidence that prelinguistic infants from the age of 10 months growing up in an English-speaking environment are sensitive to the category of 'containment' but not to those of 'support' or 'tight fit', which 'leaves open the possibility that these two categories are constructed in the course of learning the meaning of English *on* or Korean *kkita*' (Bowerman and Choi 2003: 411). A further preferential-looking experiment, by McDonough, Choi and Mandler (2003) on 9- to 14-month-old English and Korean infants compared with adults fluent in English or Korean, showed that both English and Korean babies in that age group can be made to categorize for tight versus loose containment by familiarizing them with scenes where these relations hold, which suggests conceptual readiness for that distinction, but that only Korean speakers keep the distinction alive in later life. Adult English speakers proved insensitive to it under default conditions, though the distinction can be reactivated if necessary. Korean speakers have the distinction 'ready to hand', so to speak, whereas English speakers have to dig it up from their reserves when they want to reactivate it.

The crucial question is, of course, what to make of these results. As regards the conceptual domain of space, Bowerman and Choi conclude that before language acquisition starts 'infants notice many different properties of specific spatial situations' (Bowerman and Choi 2003: 416), whereby guided or unguided comparisons of situations may be a crucial factor. In this process, 'an important stimulant to comparison can be hearing the same word' (p. 417). As the language acquisition process gets under way, the child will thus develop specific sensitivities for the recognition and use of specific spatial expressions. The authors continue (p. 417):

These linguistically relevant sensitivities achieve and maintain a high degree of standing readiness [...]. Sensitivities that are not needed for the local language may diminish over time [...]. Loss of sensitivity seems especially likely in the case of distinctions that are not only irrelevant to the lexical and grammatical distinctions of the local language, but also crosscut the distinctions that *are* relevant, since attending to linguistically irrelevant distinctions might interfere with developing the automaticity that is needed for the linguistically relevant ones.

After a parallel with the well-known early loss of sensitivity to phonetic distinctions that are irrelevant for the target language, the authors' final sentence is (p. 418):

One thing, however, is becoming clear: just as infants are geared from the beginning to discover underlying phonological regularities in the speech stream, so too are they born to zero in on language-specific patterns in the organization of meaning.

To this I may add that cognitive activation effects are likely to diminish as meaning distinctions are less truth-conditional and more of a *settling* nature—a third axis mentioned in relation with, but not incorporated into, Figure 2.1, shown at the outset of the present chapter. The reason for this assumption is that settled language has greater cognitive arbitrariness and thus requires fewer demands on cognitive correlations, but more on linguistic memory. Moreover, it is perhaps useful to mention, in this context, that language is quite possibly not the only peripheral border area with central thought: routine skills other than language (driving, operating a machine, bricklaying, etc. etc.) may require similar peripheral interface areas, with similar or comparable consequences. People become *alert* to a cognitive parameter or association or class of phenomena when that is necessary and this alertness becomes ingrained as a result of frequent activation.

2.4.2.2 *Which way does time fly?*   Some experiments have made it clear that there is some effect of culturally fixed cognitive time-line directionality (left-to-right or right-to-left) on left- or right-hand side responses for 'earlier' or 'later' (see, for example, Tversky et al. 1991; Torralbo et al. 2006; Fuhrman and Boroditsky 2007; Weger and Pratt 2008). While it seems to be the case in *all* speech communities that in event-relating reports earlier events are vocalized first and later events later (an iconic effect found universally: the difference between *She married and went to Spain* and *She went to Spain and married*), in *literate* speech communities spatial cognitive models for time-line directionality begin to make their appearance. These models appear to correlate with the writing directionality of the language spoken. (No information is provided on whether or how time-line directionality is cognitively modelled in non-literate cultures.) Thus, speakers of languages written from left to right, such as all European languages, are quicker to respond by pressing a left-hand side button when presented with a question to which the answer is 'earlier' (and analogously for the right-hand side and 'later') than speakers of languages written from right to left, such as Arabic, who show the opposite effect.

The acquisition of the skill of writing, which normally takes place around the age of six, thus influences cognitive models for the spatial representation of time: for left-to-right writers, time flies from left to right, and conversely for right-to-left writers. But this says nothing about the *languages* involved, nor about the cognitive categorizations in the minds of their speakers. In the *languages* involved, no correlation has been found between expressions for 'earlier' and the left- or right-hand side, or for 'later' and the right- or left-hand side, as the case may be. All that is found in the *languages* of the world is a mix of spatial metaphors for past and future, but no association with left or right. What is found is either (1) a model where *ego* moves through time from the past into the future, with either ego's face towards the future (1-a) or ego's face towards the past (1-b), or (2) a model where *ego* is stationary and time passes by, with no direction specified.[28]

Thus, in English, model (1-a) is manifest when it is said that we have the future *before* us or *look ahead* into the future, or leave the past *behind* us or *look back* into the past. Yet, at the same time, model (2) is manifest when it is said that *time flies* or, if event A precedes event B, that A takes place *before* B; and if B follows A, that B takes place *after* A (note that the original meaning of *after* is 'behind': B is 'at the back of' A).[29] Here the words *before* and *after* ('behind') are used for 'earlier' and 'later', respectively. Apparently, whereas English speakers see *themselves* as moving forward towards the future, they visualize *events* as moving face forward from the future into the past. When I say that I was born *before* the war, the war event, so to speak, is mentally presented as having the event of my birth 'before' it. And likewise in other European languages. French has *avant la guerre* ('before the war'), with the preposition *avant*, from Latin *ab-ante* ('in front of'). Italian has *dopo la guerra* ('after the war'), with the preposition *dopo*, from Latin *de-post* ('at the back of'). All this is somewhat confusing, since we say that we leave *behind* us the things that happened *before* us, without implying that we turn around. The confusion shows up in expressions like *move the meeting forward*, which is frequently misunderstood as 'postponing the meeting'.[30]

---

[28] The modulations and cognitive viewpoints of the 'movements' involved are expressed, if at all, through what is known as *aspect*.

[29] In Sranan, the English-based Creole language of Surinam, on the north coast of South America, the word for 'afternoon' is *bakanná*, from *bakadina* ('back-(of)-dinner').

[30] It is often said, no doubt correctly, that temporal expressions in the languages of the world are usually based on spatial metaphors (there are exceptions, such as English *brief*, French *bref*, Italian *breve*, which can be used only in a temporal sense). Yet it is not often observed that the expressions for temporal reference are always of the deictic or intrinsic and never of the absolute orientation kind: there is no record of any linguistic community where, for example, the ego-related notion 'yesterday' cannot be expressed and requires an expression in absolute terms, in terms of day, month and year, so to speak. The question thus arises how absolute spatial orienters express temporal references and relations. This question is not discussed in Levinson (2003), but it is, though very succinctly, in Boroditsky and Gaby (2010). There it is said that 'Pompuraawans [the Aboriginal people studied; PAMS] have a rich vocabulary dedicated to describing time, but there is no overlap between absolute spatial reference frames and time in the lexicon; absolute direction terms like 'north', 'south', 'east', and 'west' are not used to describe temporal relationships'.

In some cultures, speakers see themselves as moving backward into the future (model 1-b). The rationale behind this view is obvious: the future is uncertain and can only be projected from what is known about the present and the past (and is, as we have seen, expressed by means of an epistemic modal predicate), whereas the present and the past are clearly there, recorded by perception and knowledge (memory). It appears that Homeric Greek followed model (1-b): the word *opíssō* ('backwards, towards what is behind') is found used for 'in the future'.[31] The same has been observed in the Andean language Aymara (Núñez and Sweetser 2006). But although we literates imagine time as flying from left to right (or, if we have grown up as right-to-left writers, from right to left), *the left–right axis never seems to play a role in the way temporal notions are expressed.* In no language, as far as I am aware, is the past in any way codified as being on the left, or on the right, nor is the future ever linguistically codified as being on the right, or on the left as the case may be—even though involuntary gesturing during speech sometimes does follow the right–left axis (I will be happy to be told of any counterexamples to this claim). We have to move with the times, as is always said. For us, this means that we have to move forward, but whether for the Greeks in Homer's day or the speakers of Aymara it would mean that they have to move backward, is something we do not know.

Be that as it may, the studies referred to above show that the left–right axis is cognitively real (and manifest, for example, in gesturing). Of course this confirms our earlier conclusion that there are elements in cognition that are not traceable in, and even less to, language: language is seen to *underdetermine* cognition, which speaks against the Whorf hypothesis. More relevant at this stage of our enquiry is that the crossmodal transfer from writing to gesturing suggests that we are dealing with activation effects outside the area of language, which would entail that the writing skill is separate from the language module as such.[32]

2.4.2.3 *Handedness*   Some experiments have shown that the universal, linguistically fixed, association of 'right' with 'good' and of 'left' with 'bad' does not affect cognition. Across the globe, the right–hand side is conventionally—that is, culturally and linguistically—associated with 'good' and the left–hand side with 'bad' (Van Cleve and Frederick 1991; Casasanto 2009; Casasanto and Jasmin 2010). This correlation is expressed linguistically, for example, in the semantic spectrum of the English words *right*, which means both 'right-hand side' and 'correct', and *left* (derived from

---

[31] Cp., for example, Homer, *Odyssey* 20, 199, which says literally: 'May you prosper towards what is behind', meaning 'May you prosper in the future.'

[32] If that is so, an account must be given of cases of so-called 'spelling pronunciation', as when *Anthony* is pronounced not as the correct /ˈænt'ni/ but as /ˈænθ'ni/, with a spurious voiceless interdental caused by the spelling *th*, or when the word *southern* is pronounced ['saʷθern], etc. The most likely answer is that readers who take in the spelling behave as if they were still learning the language and accordingly correct, or add to, their existing competence. This would be possible only with relatively infrequent words or with subtle phonetic distinctions not immediately manifest to all hearers.

Old English *lyft* 'lame, weak, foolish'), which is also used in negative qualifications ('two left feet'; 'out in left field'). It is also apparent in the etymologies of the words in various languages for 'right' and 'left': 'right' is often, as in the case of English *right*, derived from a root meaning 'straight', while 'left' is often associated with 'crooked'. Latin *sinister*, originally meaning 'left' but widely associated with 'evil', is possibly (the etymology of *sinister* is uncertain) cognate with Latin *sinus* ('bend, concave space'), as in *sinuous*. Greek *aristerós* ('left') literally means 'better' (cp. the word *aristocracy*) but is explained by all authorities as an apotropaic euphemism employed to mislead magical evil forces. Outside language, one uses the right hand to accept things or to shake hands or to eat, while the left hand is reserved, in some cultures, for the performance of unclean bodily duties. And many such examples can be adduced.

Yet it was found in Casasanto (2009) that left-handers predominantly associate 'good' with the left-hand side and 'bad' with the right-hand side, and conversely for right-handers.[33] In the interesting but anecdotal study Casasanto and Jasmin (2010) this result was tested on a detailed analysis of video-recordings of two final American presidential debates, one between Kerry and Bush, both right-handers, in 2004 and one between Obama and McCain, both left-handers, in 2008. The analysis showed unambiguously that Kerry and Bush associated good with right and bad with left, whereas Obama and McCain did the opposite. It would be useful if this result could be replicated for larger numbers of speakers.

It is easy to see that the conventionally fixed cultural and linguistic correlation between 'good' and right-hand side on the one hand and between 'bad' and the left-hand side on the other is a matter of the overwhelming statistical preponderance of righthandedness (about 90 per cent) in populations across the world. The determining factor of the correlation is thus neither language-determined nor culturally determined 'thought' of whatever kind but the mere statistical preponderance in all populations of being right-handed rather than left-handed.

---

[33] Casasanto (2009) established, furthermore, that the association of *up* with 'good' and 'happy', and of *down* with 'bad' and 'unhappy' is independent of the handedness parameter and is, moreover, of a different, more directly cognitive, kind. In the case of the *up-good* and *down-bad* association, one is free to vary the linguistic expressions (*in the skies, over the moon, elated, skyrocketing*, etc. for 'good' versus *plummet, plunge, sink* for 'bad'), as long as the notions of 'up' and 'down' are somehow expressed. But in the case of the *right-good* versus *left-bad* association, the linguistic expressions cannot, or only by way of punning, be varied. Expressions like *dextrous, dexterity, maladroit* have no counterparts for the left-hand side (*gauche* is not the opposite of *dextrous* and not a synonym of *maladroit*) and *That's right* cannot be replaced with something like *That's how I eat my soup*—unless the latter becomes a jocular idiom. *Right-hand man*, meaning 'helpful associate', can be matched with *left-hand man* ('feckless associate') only jocularly. Casasanto's interpretation of this difference is that the *up-good* and *down-bad* association has retained its metaphorical character and is thus easily brought to awareness, whereas the *right-good* and *left-bad* association has become part of the language, without any remaining cognitively live, metaphorical value—at least in communities without any strong taboos on the use of the left hand for propitious purposes. In my interpretation, I say that the *right-good* and *left-bad* association is a result of a completed *settling* process in the languages in question, whereas the *up-good* versus *down-bad* association has only partially been integrated into the language as such.

Again, the fact that the left-handers Obama and McCain associated 'good' with the left hand and 'bad' with the right hand and thus remained uninfluenced by the language disconfirms the old Whorf hypothesis. What we have here is an instance of linguistically predominant cognitive categorization on the basis of genetic factors, not of language or 'communication' (cp. Levinson 2003: 212, quoted above). This cognitive categorization, moreover, has apparently not affected more central areas of cognition, as it has not been transferred to gesturing, despite, one may guess, a relatively high frequency of occurrence. This raises a few empirical questions. For example, how resistant are genetically determined nonlinguistic associations to linguistic activation effects? Is there a threshold value on a strength parameter for such transfer?

2.4.2.4 *Length versus quantity in time measurement expressions*   It has proved difficult to devise an experimental set-up enabling the experimenter to isolate the parameter of causal directionality. Correlations between linguistic and cognitive (thought) phenomena are relatively easy to establish, but the problem of what causes what has turned out to be elusive. What seems to be needed is, first, a set-up where two or more languages are selected that differ systematically in their expressions for a given semantic field. Then, native speakers of the languages involved should be asked to perform a strictly nonlinguistic task that isolates the cognitive parameter that triggered the originally semantic but now autonomous (socio-)linguistically calibrated phenomena. If it then appears that the results of the nonlinguistic task correspond significantly with the language spoken by the subjects, there is noncircular evidence for an influence of language upon the cognitive machinery of the subjects involved. As we have seen, such evidence has emerged and it appears that it is reducible to activation effects most strongly manifest where the activation is most frequent and most peripheral (closest to Slobin's 'thinking-for-speaking'). Since, as was suggested in section 2.1, settling is likely to reduce activation effects, the evidence will be stronger and more convincing to the extent that the linguistic phenomena used in the experiment are more clearly settled and thus less strongly associated with cognitive features or associations. In such cases, it is really *language*, as a modular system, that is seen to exert an influence upon nonlinguistic cognitive structures or processes.

In the experiments described in Bowerman and Choi (2003), discussed above in section 2.4.2.1, the degree of settling of the linguistic material involved was not crystal clear, since the linguistic and cognitive correlations were easily brought to consciousness and thus relatively obvious and salient. In the experiment reported on in Casasanto (2008), however, the phenomena tested are more integrated into autonomous language and thus much harder to notice and bring to consciousness. The results should, therefore, be more significant in the perspective of cognitive activation effects.

Casasanto, who is in overall sympathy with the Whorfian point of view, established first (by means of frequency counts in large corpora of English and Greek, respectively) that English and Modern Greek differ systematically in the ways they express duration. In English, one speaks of *long* and *short* durations (meetings, holidays, etc.), whereas in Modern Greek one cannot use the direct translation equivalents of these English adjectives, *makrós* and *kontós*, respectively, but one has to use quantity expressions. Greeks speak of 'a meeting that lasted *much*' (*sinántisi pou diárkese/krátise polí*, where *polí* means 'much') and when they wish to say that the fine weather will last longer, they say the equivalent of 'the fine weather will last *more*', (*Tha diarkísi/kratísi perissótero o kalós kerós*, where *perissótero* means 'more'). Casasanto comments (2008: 71):

These preliminary studies by no means captured all of the complexities of how duration is metaphorized in terms of space within or between languages, but findings corroborated native English and Greek speakers' intuitions and provided quantitative linguistic measures on which to base predictions about behavior in nonlinguistic tasks.

Casasanto does not consider the issue of whether the linguistic categories that are used to express duration are a result of settling. He simply wishes to test (a) whether there is a correlation between linguistic expressions and cognitive models or 'thinking', and (b) whether it is the language that causes the thinking or the other way round. The actual experiment and the results are described as follows (Casasanto 2008: 71–2):

[W]e asked English and Greek speakers to estimate the duration of brief events that contained either distracting information about linear distance (distance interference) or distracting information about amount (amount interference). In the distance interference condition, participants viewed a series of lines 'growing' across the screen, for various distances and durations. After each line disappeared, they were asked to reproduce its duration by clicking the mouse twice (in the same spot) to indicate the time that elapsed from the instant that the line appeared to the instant that it reached its maximum length. The distance that the line grew was irrelevant to the task and was varied orthogonally to the line's duration. As such, distance served as distractor: a piece of information that was irrelevant to the task but could potentially interfere with task performance. In the amount interference condition, subjects viewed a schematic drawing of a container filling gradually with liquid and were asked to reproduce the duration of the "filling" event. Analogously to the distance interference condition, the amount of fill varied orthogonally with the duration of the event and, as such, served as a distractor for the subjects' task of estimating duration. [. . .] English speakers should show more interference from distance than amount on their time estimates. Greek speakers should show the opposite pattern, being more distracted by amount than by distance interference. Results supported these predictions: [. . .] English speakers were strongly affected by the distance that a line traveled but only weakly affected by the fullness of a container, whereas Greek speakers showed the opposite pattern of cross-dimensional interference. The structure of people's low-level, nonlinguistic time representations is not universal: These simple psychophysical tasks indicate that at a basic level, the way we mentally represent time covaries with the way we talk about it in our native languages. However, does experience using different metaphors *cause* speakers of different languages to think differently?

To answer this question of causal directionality, Casasanto conducted the following training experiment (2008: 74–5):

A pair of training tasks […] was conducted to provide an in-principle demonstration that language can influence even the kinds of low-level mental representations that people construct while performing psychophysical tasks and to test the proposal that language shapes time representations, both in the laboratory and in natural settings, by adjusting the strengths of cross-domain mappings. Native English speakers were randomly assigned to perform either a "distance training" or "amount training" task. Participants completed 192 fill-in-the-blank sentences using the words *longer* or *shorter* for distance training and the words *more* or *less* for the amount training task. Half of the sentences compared the length or capacity of physical objects (e.g. An alley is *longer/shorter* than a clothesline; A teaspoon is *more/less* than an ocean) and the other half compared the duration of events (e.g. A sneeze is *longer/shorter* than a vacation; A sneeze is *more/less* than a vacation). By using distance terms to compare event durations, English speakers in the control condition were reinforcing the already preferred mapping between distance and time. By using amount terms, participants in the critical condition were describing event durations similarly to speakers of an amount-biased language like Greek, activating the nonlinguistic amount-time mapping that is normally dispreferred for English speakers. After this linguistic training phase, all participants performed the nonlinguistic filling container task. […] [N]ative English speakers' performance on the filling container task was statistically indistinguishable from the performance of the native Greek speakers. By encouraging the *habitual activation* [italics mine; PAMS] of either distance-time or amount-time conceptual mappings, our experience with natural language may influence our everyday thinking about time in much the same way as this laboratory training task.

In summary, people who talk differently about time also think about it differently, in ways that correspond to the preferred metaphors in their native languages. Language not only reflects the structure of our temporal representations, but it can also shape those representations.

What Casasanto describes in the training experiment is the successful temporary setting up of an *ad hoc* and short-lived routine that runs counter to long-term routines established earlier. The training experiment shows how repeated activation of a cognitive feature quickly leads to a routine—that is, to high frequency ratings and thus to high peripherality ratings in the sense of Figure 2.1 in section 2.1. (I equate Casasanto's *'low-level* thinking' with Slobin's 'thinking-for-speaking' border area of language and thought.) In no way do Casasanto's experiments show an involvement of central thought. There is, therefore, reason to narrow his indiscriminate use of the term 'thinking' down to 'peripheral thinking' and even to 'routine processing'. Casasanto himself concludes (p. 75):

The results summarized here suggest that conceptual mappings from space to time may be given in essentially the same form via correlation in physical experience to everyone and then *also* be conditioned by the languages we speak. [italics in the original; PAMS]

However, since the only (and marginal) causal effect of language on cognition that has been established is limited to, indeed low-level, processing mechanisms, Casasanto's extrapolation to presumably central conceptual mappings from space to time seems unwarranted. What Casasanto's results show is, rather, that, even at a level of thorough settling, a language, as a settled system on and for itself, may exert activation effects in the cognitive border area of 'thinking-for-speaking'.

2.5 Conclusion

The Whorfian tradition, from its origins in the intellectually confused but emotionally powerful German *Sturm und Drang* ('Storm and Urge') cultural movement of the late eighteenth century till the present day, has always been in need of clarity and rational argument. There has been plenty of rhetoric, where single cases were rhetorically exploited for or against the hypothesis, but of real arguments there have been precious few. Real arguments supporting the Whorf hypothesis will consist in showing that, in a general sense, linguistic variation and linguistic change correlate closely with culturally and socially shared conceptual variation and change without there being any other possible source of the correlation than the language of the community. This, however, has proved too tall an order: nothing of the kind has been shown.

What has been shown, especially in recent experiments, is that frequency of use patterns in the language that speakers grow up with and acquire command of establish automated routine lines for the activation and association of cognitive features—what I have called *activation effects*. These are most intensive in the peripheral border area of 'thinking-for-speaking' (Slobin 1987) or 'microplanning' (Levelt 1989, 1996), where conceptual thinking gels into propositions ready for linguistic expression. In this sense, language is seen to 'seep' into a border area of cognition, but without affecting central conceptual thinking.

A tentative, non-Whorfian but more functionality-centred, perspective has been developed in which, on the one hand, socially and culturally driven linguistic settling phenomena make for a proliferation of lexical distinctions and grammatical fineries, as social groups call for distinctive features setting them off from other social groups and giving them their specific identity, while, on the other hand, the corresponding routine-forming activation effects compensate for the resulting extra demands on cognition by facilitating the lexical and grammatical planning of utterances, as they allow speakers and hearers to bypass time- and energy-consuming appeals to central conceptual thinking for all nonessential semantic elements in the message. This perspective is to some extent supported by experimental findings discussed in the text (and, I hope, not contradicted by evidence not discussed). Yet it is underdetermined by these findings in that lines have been drawn that do not strictly follow from the available evidence but are hopefully useful in that they may contribute to a more complete total picture. Clearly, this non-Whorfian interpretation of experimental results obtained in what is presented as a neo-Whorfian framework is open to further debate and clarification, if only because it relies crucially on the as yet hypothetical framework of cognitively peripheral routine formation resulting from activation frequency, as cursorily and provisionally introduced in section 2.1 and illustrated in Figure 2.1.

The motto of this chapter, *Lingua ancilla mentis* ('Language is the mind's hand-maiden'), allegorizes this perspective: the mind is primary and reigns supreme. Language, being its maid, has little influence over her mistress, but the mistress will grant her maid a certain degree of autonomy and will facilitate the maid's work as far as possible and within the limits of the general constraints imposed on the mistress-maid relationship, while at the same time a good maid will help her mistress to deploy more activities and do so more efficiently than would have been possible without the maid's presence.

3

Relativism or a universal theory?

Ἁρμονίη ἀφανὴς φανερῆς κρείττων
Invisible harmony is stronger than visible harmony

(Heraclitus c. 500 BCE)

3.1 Some necessary preliminaries

3.1.1 A terminological observation

The term *relativism*, or *linguistic relativism*, is used here to denote the doctrine that human languages can vary without limit, or, to put it negatively, that there are no universal constraints on what can qualify as a human language. It was already pointed out in section 2.1 that this notion of linguistic relativism has been amalgamated with the notion that language determines or influences thought to form a theoretical complex known as Whorfianism. Whorfians now generally equate these two notions, as if they were inseparable or even identical. All Google entries I have found identify Whorfianism with linguistic relativism—though, as we saw in section 2.1, Lyons (1977: 245) defines linguistic relativism (or relativity) as follows:

[T]he actualization of particular phonological, grammatical and semantic distinctions in different language-systems is completely arbitrary. This can be referred to as the doctrine of linguistic relativity.

Yet Whorfianism as standardly conceived of by Whorfians consists of two logically independent theses: (a) the thesis that language influences or determines thought, and (b) the thesis that languages can vary without limits. These are two independent theses or claims. One can be a 'pure' Whorfian without being a relativist: all it takes is a Whorfian mindset combined with a tough view on the variability of languages. And conversely, one can be a relativist without being a 'pure' Whorfian, as when one holds, against Whorf, that thought determines or influences language and not vice versa, and that this influence may manifest itself in unrestricted ways—roughly the position taken in cultural anthropology. And one can be neither, as when one holds that language does not influence thought and that linguistic diversity is more apparent than real—the point of view taken by universalists. That the two positions syncretized into one thought complex is due to historical accident: both share the Romanticist fascination with the diverse manifestations of human languages and cultures, coupled with a now obsolete neopositivist philosophy of science banning 'abstract' underlying structures or machinery postulated for reasons of causal explanation (see Elffers 2012: 21–4 for an illuminating historical and conceptual discussion). This being so, an orderly discussion requires that the two theses be kept apart and are given distinct names. Following Lyons, I call thesis (b) *relativism*. Thesis (a) is embodied in what may be called *'pure' Whorfianism*. I have dealt with 'pure' Whorfianism in Chapter 2, while the present chapter deals with relativism.

In using the term *relativism* this way I not only follow Lyons, but I also conform to the use of the term *relativism* in the human sciences generally. In the human sciences, the term is used to denote the doctrine that human manifestations, such as culture in all its forms, judgements of what is true and false, good and bad, beautiful and ugly, same and different, desirable and undesirable, and so on, are relative to—that is, determined by—individuals' (socially shared) world construals and that these world construals may vary arbitrarily. In all these cases, the *causal relation* goes from the mental process of world construal to the manifestations. For relativists, all human manifestations that are in any way linked up with cognition are 'theory-laden'. I can see no reason why, in the case of language, the term 'relativism' should imply that the causal relation goes the other way, from the language to the world construal, so that the world construal should be 'language-laden'. Any doctrine assuming the latter would not be 'relativistic' in the accepted sense. To call 'pure' Whorfianism a relativist doctrine is thus not only notionally confused, it also goes against the accepted use of the term 'relativism'.

In the philosophical theory of truth, relativism says that there are no universal (or absolute) standards for truth and falsity, but that truth consists in what people take to be true—the Sophists' notion of truth, despised and attacked by Plato and Aristotle. In ethics, relativism stands for the doctrine that there are no universal (or, in the eyes of some, absolute) standards for good and bad and that good and bad are what any culture or society considers to be good or bad (which would make the *Universal Declaration of Human Rights* illegitimate). In cultural anthropology, relativism holds that cultures may vary indiscriminately, without any universal constraints and depending on the members of each culture's world construal. In general, relativism is opposed to universalism. It holds that human groups develop languages, ethical norms, truths, cultures, etc. relative to their own free decisions, without any specific limits imposed by the human species as such. Relativism weakens the definition of what defines the human species. Universalism tightens it up, presuming on the evolutionary development of the species.

In modern times, the various forms of relativism became widespread in philosophy and in the human sciences in the eighteenth century, again as a result of the discovery of exotic cultures. The seed of this generalized relativism lay in the relativization of the notion of truth, taking as its starting point the weakness of the notion of truth-as-correspondence with regard to value judgements in the realm of beauty or pleasure—let us say *value judgements of taste*—such as the Sophists' *There is a pleasant breeze today*. Such statements, or judgements, do not fit well into the classic notion of truth as correspondence with the facts. Until, roughly, the eighteenth century, the paradigm of truth as an absolute, metaphysical, semantically defined measure prevailed all over, as it still prevails in logic, most of Anglo-Saxon philosophy and the physical sciences. Then, however, increased familiarity with exotic cultures appeared to some philosophers and scholars in the humanities to justify an uncritical, in fact Romanticist, extension from value judgements of taste to all assertions, including pure statements of fact. This introduced a general relativist, anti-universalist attitude, which may well be called an ideology, with regard not only to the general notion of truth, but also to standards of morality and to humanist objects of study generally.

Nowadays, this relativist ideology is widespread in the human sciences and their applications, where the excuse for relativism is often sought in the fact that *context* codetermines perception and interpretation. While the recognition of this fact is in itself important and even essential for a proper understanding of these mental processes, as is witnessed, for example, by the impact of Gestalt psychology, to say that context *determines* perception and interpretation—and a heap of other things as well—is over the top and in fact incoherent. (If this were so, what would determine the perception and interpretation of the context?) Yet this is precisely the mistake made by many influential figures in the human sciences from the 1920s onward, leading to an intellectual climate in which relativism flourished. In the light of this historical perspective, it is easily understood why and how the relativist ideology has taken hold of large sections of anthropology and related subjects. To see how widespread relativism is, nowadays, in the human sciences, one only has to look at studies of public relations and communication, in particular mass communication, as they are practised and applied all over the modern Western world—philosophically and methodologically untenable and deeply pernicious in their consequences.

Be that as it may, I feel fully entitled to use the term *relativism* the way I do. In principle, of course, one is free to choose one's terminology, but in practice one tends to conform to existing terminology, and for good reasons. This is exactly what I do here, conforming to the use of the term 'relativism' in the broader field of the human sciences. The fact that the restricted group of Whorfians have taken to misusing the term is no reason for me to follow them. Whorfians will have to bear with me. They may even see my point.

3.1.2 *Some observations regarding scientific methodology*

Quite apart from 'pure' Whorfianism, a deep gulf exists in linguistics between universalists and relativists. It is not my purpose, in this chapter, to bridge that gulf. What I try to achieve in the present chapter is first of all of a methodological nature. I hope to convince my readers that relativism is methodologically counter-productive, whereas universalism represents a more constructive methodological attitude, seeking maximal unity in the diversity of human languages. I am thus clearly on the universalists' side, but my universalism is mainly methodological, which means that I am on the look-out for general properties and tendencies of human languages, with a view to developing a general theory of language. The question if and to what extent different languages converge into one overall system is, in the end, of an empirical nature and the answer will not be known until we have a solid and well-established general theory of the phonologies, grammars and lexicons of human languages—an ideal still unrealized. Meanwhile, however, one must observe the methodological principle that valid generalizations are to be welcomed and maximized, and not looked upon with suspicion from the start, as is done in relativist circles. Even if it were to turn out in the end that human languages are much more diverse than universalists had taken them to be, the methodological principle remains valid. I expect it to be the case, however, that human language is highly unified. It is up to us and future generations to show to what extent it actually is.

One often hears it said that universalism and relativism are two sides of the same coin. While it makes sense to ask why the languages of the world are so similar, it makes equal sense to ask why they are so different, or so it is said. I am inclined to maintain that the two questions are not on a par. The diversity of languages is an observable, and widely observed, fact. By contrast, the insight that languages show great similarity is the result of scientific analysis and description. The diversity of languages forms part of the domain of facts to be explained by a unifying theory, just as the diversity of physical matter is to be explained by reduction to unifying general hypotheses that are to be tested for empirical adequacy—the very principle of physics since the first beginnings of natural philosophy in pre-Socratic days.

For physicists, the question of why matter is as diverse as it is is to be answered by the general theory of matter—that is, theoretical physics. Matter is as diverse as it is because the general principles of theoretical physics allow for varieties to come about. General physical theory even predicts that specific varieties of matter will come about given specific circumstances. Linguistic theory, though much less advanced as regards theoretical power, is not all that different. The main difference lies in its predictive power as regards variability. While physical theory is (close to) fully deterministic in that it has (almost) full control of the parameters regulating the coming about of the various forms of matter, linguistic theory is unlikely ever to reach that state of precision, since the parameters controlling linguistic variability are as yet beyond the reach of any precise theory and may remain so forever. Settling phenomena, as described in Chapter 1, have so far proved too whimsical for any unifying theory. And the embedding of language in general cognition makes for further obstacles to a fully deterministic theory. That is why theoretical linguists speak of *constraints* on the variability of languages, refraining from any deterministic predictions on the precise forms languages will take under specified external circumstances. Other than that, however, the answer given by theoretical physics can be taken over literally: languages vary because the general principles of an adequate general theory of language allow for varieties to come about.

The problem is, however, that, despite centuries of professional linguistic theorizing, there is no generally accepted adequate theory of language that will specify both the necessary unity and the possible diversity of languages. Chomskyan theory has proposed that languages vary according to the values they (or rather their speakers) select on certain universally given parameters—an overall perspective that may well turn out to be fruitful and clearly deserves to be taken seriously. A further perspective was tentatively presented in section 1.4 above, in the context of the heteromorphy problem, involving both the notion of arbitrary settling and certain functional necessities of language. But, just as theoretical physics answers the question of the diversity of matter, the final answer to the question of why languages differ the way they do must come from theoretical linguistics. At present, however, that discipline is in a bad state.

One first requirement for a general theory of language is that the variability facts are well known. Until recently this was not the case: we only had a limited knowledge of the extent to which languages can vary. Meanwhile, however, the explosion of descriptive work on ever larger numbers of exotic languages has brought a radical improvement, which is a great blessing for our discipline. Never before have we, linguists, had such a rich supply of material from languages distributed all over the world, some of which are rapidly disappearing while others are consolidating their status. This has given an enormous boost, not only to general theorizing on grammar and lexicon, but also to our perspective on the relations between societal and cultural parameters on the one hand and the corresponding languages on the other, which in turn has greatly enriched our views on language change.

As a corollary of this development, however, we see that a split has arisen between those who love linguistic diversity for its own sake and those who rightly seek a maximally unified, general theory of language. (No such split seems ever to have occurred in physics, which is less open to emotions regarding the object of enquiry.) There exists a considerable amount of friction between the tribes of often anthropologically oriented fieldworking linguists, who tend to be relativists, and the universalist theorists. On the whole, this friction is generated by the diversity-loving fieldworkers, who cherish their newly found diversity so much that they want it to be the paramount factor in linguistic theory. Yet for a theorist, even the most colourful display of exotica becomes boring when none of the exhibits has any specific or crucial theoretical significance.

In a way, this is a continuation of a long-standing conflict (see section 3.2). The exploration of exotic languages began in a serious manner during the eighteenth century (Seuren 1998: 61–3). At the time, the newly reported findings from exotic languages were taken as confirmation of the basic unity of human languages across the world, linguistic diversity being but superficial appearance. This attitude is understandable, as, at the time, the Western world was suffering, much more than nowadays, from cultural and anthropological arrogance to the point of considering non-Western individuals inferior or even not fully human. While this lulled the conscience of colonial traders and of Western governments into a state of money-induced moral stupor, the intellectuals and the clergy reacted by stressing the fully human, and unspoilt, nature of 'savages', resulting in the philosophy of the 'Noble Savage'. In this context, it was important to stress language universals, which bring all humans under one linguistic umbrella, and to de-emphasize cross-linguistic differences. But when, during the nineteenth century, the fundamental equality of all humans was no longer an issue and anthropology began to develop into an autonomous academic discipline, a basically Romanticist fascination with exotic phenomena gained the ascendency. From then on, anthropological linguistics has been mainly diversity-oriented, while theoretical linguistics, continuing the old rationalist tradition and following the precepts of scientific method, has continued to look for what unifies human language despite the observed diversity.

The rationalist (universalist) attitude can be characterized as an effort to see to what extent existing universalist generalizations hold their own, can be extended or have to be modified amidst the barrage of new data. The relativist, diversity-oriented attitude can be seen as driven by the desire to get to know, and to preserve, the fascinating gamut of different ways in which humanity manifests itself. Taken this way, there is no intellectual conflict between the two attitudes: the former strives for insight and explanation, the latter for collection and exhibition. Problems arise when either party, or both parties, begin to claim exclusive territorial rights, which is what is happening today. The relativists are trying to push the rationalist universalists out of the arena, disregarding the right, nay the duty, of every theoretical discipline to pursue relentlessly any useful generalization.

A similar estrangement exists between lexicographers, who are experts in the down-to-earth details of words and their semantic versatility and settle for practical, workable general notions and categories, and lexicologists, who want a fully fledged, universal, explanatory theory of the lexicon as a main element in any language, without any practical compromises. In this case, however, it is the lexicographers who go about their invaluable business in silence, whereas the lexicologists are sometimes caught out telling the lexicographers how to do so.

Another parallel is found in ethology versus cultural anthropology. Ethology is the study of animal (including human) behaviour in interaction with the physical environment and with conspecifics (see, for example, Eibl-Eibesfeldt 1989). In ethology the notion 'innate' plays the role of what we call 'universal', and 'innate' is defined as covering all behaviour that is not learned but springs up spontaneously, as part of an inbuilt drive, often despite counteracting environmental factors or even despite physical handicaps or restraints. Obvious examples, among a vast multitude, are the squirrel's burying his food before the winter or the immediate and automatic suckling of newborn mammals or the fur-licking of cats. The challenge for ethologists is, first, to separate innate factors from factors originating in the physical environment or in the interaction with conspecifics, and, secondly, to try and pinpoint the origin of such innate traits in terms of phylogenetic evolutionary adaptation.

In (cultural) anthropology, which studies cultural systems and culturally defined forms of behaviour, the question of what is innate (universal) and what is acquired (relative) is more complex, as cultures, being specifically human, are much more open to free and conscious intervention than the largely compulsory forms of ethologically defined behaviour. Cultural behaviour is in principle rule-governed and to some extent constrained by an underlying *system* at a variety of levels. The link between what is universal in human cultures and what is innate in human individuals is also much weaker and less direct than in behaviour qualified as ethological. Consequently, (cultural) anthropology is less directly connected with biology than ethology is.

While the ethologists tend to favour innatism, the prevailing attitude in (cultural) anthropology is relativist, in that anthropologists, in the wake of the Noble Savage philosophy, tend to go out of their way to emphasize not only the differences between cultures but also the alleged moral and even the artistic superiority of those cultures that have not or hardly been affected by the now globally dominating culture and power of the Western world.

Not every anthropologist shares this attitude, however. For example, the great anthropologist James George Frazer (1854–1941) takes a straightforwardly universalist position as regards the religious and magical manifestations of culture in his monumental *The Golden Bough*, published in its full, twelve-volume, glory between 1906 and 1915 and reprinted many times, often in more or less abridged form. In modern times, Sandall (2001) gives a caustic critique of the relativist attitude in anthropology and pleads for an uncluttered application of universal standards and concepts to all cultures alike, but he belongs to a small minority.

Another notable member of this minority was the late Roger Keesing (1935–1993),[1] who wrote (Keesing 1997: 127):

---

[1] I owe this reference (as also the reference to Frazer) to my good friend Gunter Senft of the Max Planck Institute for Psycholinguistics at Nijmegen, Netherlands.

A few years ago Charles Frake, a pioneer in linguistically sophisticated ethnography, told me about a paper that never got finished. Frake had been invited to contribute an essay to a Festschrift for Claude Lévi-Strauss. He intended to write a structural analysis of spatial orientation among the Subanun of Mindanao. Having begun the analysis, Frake realized that the Subanun orientational system was basically the same as those of European languages—so he never finished the paper.

Now a close, cognitively based examination of spatial orientation in non-Western languages is belatedly being undertaken, there seems to me a serious danger that what I will call the Frake syndrome may contaminate our conclusions. We may write only about those languages that construct spatial relationships in ways that seem sufficiently exotic and unlike those familiar in European languages to challenge our takens-for-granted, and leave dozens of other papers unwritten, and languages thereby unexamined. This search for the exotic could cumulatively build up a spurious picture of the extent of diversity. Worse, it could serve to hide important constraints and perhaps even universals—what may be minimally marked and maximally 'natural' modes of spatial orientation experimentally laid down in humans' modes of perception and bodily engagement with the world. The evidence so far available on the systems of linguistically constructed spatial orientation being proposed as radically different from our own suggests that they coexist, as alternative schemata, with orientational systems much more closely akin to those of Western languages.

Then again (Keesing 1997: 139–40):

The Austronesian-speaking zone could, I think, serve as something of a laboratory for the comparative study of spatial conceptualization. However, it would be important in this project not simply to seek exotic and complex modes of encoding spatial relationships in the mountains of Halmahera or Flores or Sunda or New Britain, or spatial metaphors in High Javanese, but to examine as well the *less* elaborated and exotic systems. [...] In the Kwayo case, the ways space is used to conceptualize time, the way the body and bodily experience serve as points of conceptual reference and metaphoric elaboration, the ways in which envisioned space and its partitioning shape deictics, may guide us in thinking about possible universals underlying—and often hidden by—more exotic modes of representing space. They may help us to guard against Frake's Syndrome.

What Keesing is arguing for, correctly in my view, is that language is more than a curiosity shop of exotic phenomena and that criteria of naturalness or its opposite, markedness, should be given more weight in the study of the universal properties of human language. This wise admonition, coming from an anthropologist *nourri dans le sérail*, should figure prominently in any discussion about language universals.

In linguistics, the question is even more complex than in anthropology. Although the use of language is clearly a form of innately driven behaviour and thus falls under the ethologists' notion of innateness,[2] it differs from ethological forms of innate

---

[2] In this respect I concur with Jackendoff, who writes: 'Therefore, on general biological grounds, it should not be objectionable to posit unlearned special-purpose aspects of the human language-learning capacity.' (Jackendoff 2011: 588)

behaviour not only in that it, like cultural behaviour, is specifically human, it is also regulated by a highly intricate, coherent rule system valid for each specific language but with a large dose of common features, the nature of which is the topic of the present chapter. Linguistic rule systems are vastly more deterministic, more formal in the mathematical sense, and more detailed than what is found in cultures. The use of language differs, moreover, from cultural behaviour in that, in addition to being endowed with ethologically and culturally determined properties, it is also a highly deterministic *semiotic* system located in the brain, closely linked up with human cognition in ways that other forms of innate behaviour are not, and arbitrary in many respects, most obviously in the selection of lexical phonological form. It is this difference with general ethology and with (cultural) anthropology that makes it extremely hard to draw a well-motivated distinction between universal and arbitrary features of human language in general and of specific languages in particular.

In linguistic behaviour, the link between what is universal and what is innate is even weaker than in cultural behaviour, since there are many universal features of human language, more than of human culture, that are not due to innate, genetically fixed properties of the human brain specifically causing highly specialized forms of behaviour but rather to pre-existing factors such as the physical conditions of sound transmission, to the physiology of sound perception, to cognitive processing patterns and quite a few more such general ecological factors not specifically geared to the use of language. In general, when applied to language, the concept of innateness is much more fluid than when applied to the forms of innately determined compulsive behaviour studied by ethologists or even when applied to cultural behaviour as studied by anthropologists. The link with evolutionary biology is, accordingly, much more tenuous and indirect. The result has been a staggering amount of speculative literature, too often grounded in deficient expertise in one or more of the disciplines involved. In this respect, the drive for interdisciplinarity that has been felt for the past four or five decades has led to an excess of speculation—much like what happened during the mid-nineteenth century, when, in 1866, the *Société de linguistique de Paris* issued a statute (article 2) saying that no communication on either the origin of language or the creation of an artificial universal language would henceforth be admitted.

But let us not deviate too much from our present topic, which is the opposition between relativism and universalism from the viewpoint of the methodology of science. Neither relativism nor universalism is a scientific theory in the accepted sense of the term. Both are programmatic paradigms, providing perspectives for research questions and, importantly, defining hoped-for results. The universalists maintain that natural languages are subject to a universal charter of as yet unknown (probably largely evolutionary) origin, restricting the class of possible human languages and guiding the language acquisition process by young children, while the relativists posit that languages vary without any restrictions and even that 'linguistic diversity becomes the crucial datum for cognitive science: we are the only species with a communication system that is fundamentally variable at all levels' (Evans and Levinson 2009: 429).[3] This last statement seems a little over the top, since the 'crucial datum for cognitive science' will be delivered by the best theory. If human language is shown to be basically unified and diverse only in its surface manifestations, then that is the 'crucial datum'. But if it is shown to be basically diverse at all levels, then that is what cognitive science will have to reckon with. The answer depends on the extent to which theoretical linguists are able to come up with a machinery that will fit all languages into one unified scheme.

A minimal concession, from a relativist point of view, is that there must be some unity at least within socio-cultural communities and their internal subdivisions, or else no one would understand anyone else. The universalist, by contrast, must concede that, at least on the face of it, languages differ widely from each other and, moreover, display great internal geographical, sociological and interactional variation: variability is an essential part of language. The universalist's task is more hazardous in that he must show how unified human language is despite the obvious surface differences. To show the unity, he must go beyond the surface, a region that is accessible only by forming unifying hypotheses involving unobservables. The relativist who wants to stick to his guns is likely to be wary of such 'abstract' theorizing. However, an *a priori* attitude rejecting 'abstract' theorizing runs counter to the very principles of realist science, no matter whether it deals with physical matter or with the human mind in all its aspects. These principles tell us that 'abstract' theories are a prime tool for the explanation of observed data, provided they are interpretable in causal terms and do not proliferate assumptions beyond necessity. The Greek philosopher Heraclitus, who died around 480 BCE—a decade before Socrates was born—already saw this when he wrote, with regard to the dazzling variability of physical matter, 'Invisible harmony is stronger than visible harmony'.

Establishing universal properties of human language will show to what extent language is unified, but it does not by itself provide a causal answer to that unity. To the extent that universals have been established, they pose new causal problems, whose solutions will contribute to a better understanding of the ecological environment, including human cognition, in which language functions (see, for example, Hawkins 1988, 2004).

---

[3] The 2009 *BBS* article by Evans and Levinson is a frequent butt of criticism in the present chapter, for several reasons. Although *linguistic diversity* is the term used there for what I call *relativism*, it represents the relativist position in succinct, generally defining terms—something rarely found in the literature. It is extreme in its relativism, as it proclaims unlimited linguistic diversity and denies any universals; and it is highly outspoken, even provocative, unafraid of hurting feelings. It thus serves as an excellent reference point for a critique of linguistic relativism, whereby its provocative tone provides a licence for a vigorous and straightforward reaction.

Relativism is built on the *a priori* that all human languages are free to vary at all levels without any restrictions other than those imposed by general psychological, physiological, physical and social factors. This lighthearted thought is, however, dangerous and pre-emptive. It is dangerous because not enough is known about such factors and about language to avoid the charge of irresponsibility. It is pre-emptive because it precludes any possible further explanatory factors and because it precludes valid generalizations beyond those that follow from the factors mentioned. In fact, a relativist position risks blocking any discussion about the nature of language: languages differ indefinitely and fundamentally at all levels; discussion closed.

What is needed is a theory that maximizes explanation on the basis of a minimal set of generalizing assumptions, taking all relevant data into account. Such a theory requires a keen and open eye for troublesome data that might disturb the minimalist peace. There is always the risk of overconfidence in regard of one's own theory, which may lead to ignoring troublesome data and to underestimating the complexity of the object of enquiry. Behaviourism, as is now generally acknowledged, is a classic example of this kind of overconfidence. The strategy of keeping generalizations down to a minimum while covering a maximal area of data will work only if, besides being anxious to find such generalizations, one is also distrustful of them—just as an engineer trying to cut costs will have to be extremely distrustful of any minimalist construction, which he will have to subject to the most severe tests possible in order to avoid disaster. Unfortunately, this is not what the parties concerned do. The relativists are not looking for cost-saving generalizations. The universalists, at least the Chomsky-inspired theorists among them, are not distrustful enough.

It is claimed in Evans and Levinson (2009: 429) that linguistic relativism is, or should be, a source of inspiration for cognitive science:

Linguistic diversity [...] becomes the crucial datum for cognitive science: we are the only species with a communication system that is variable at all levels. Recognizing the true extent of structural diversity in human language opens up exciting new research directions for cognitive scientists, offering thousands of different natural experiments given by different languages, with new opportunities for dialogue with biological paradigms concerned with change and diversity, and confronting us with the extraordinary plasticity of the highest human skills.

This, however, is mere advertising copy. To begin with, it is unclear how a principled rejection of generalizations could ever be helpful in any science at all. For the rest, no universalist will deny that languages differ and that these differences 'open up exciting new research directions for cognitive scientists, offering thousands of differ-ent natural experiments given by different languages' etc. But the excitement lies not in a mere listing of differences but in the intelligent unearthing of a system, which will then be open to integration into the systems built by biologists and geneticists, who are likewise system builders and not collectors of curiosities.

A methodologically more constructive and more respectable strategy makes the researcher alert to possible universals, even if they look as if they might be arbitrary, while attempting to reduce them to conceptual or ecological necessity, thus actively contributing to the development of a proper theory of language. This way, the search for language universals will contribute directly to an adequate conceptual definition of human language as well as to the formulation of adequate conditions for conceptual or ecological necessity.[4] Any residual universals that look as if they may be quirks of nature will then constitute an empirical challenge. Thus, as our knowledge of the ecologically necessary conditions for human language increases, it will gradually become clearer which putative universals will be seen to be reducible to some form of necessity or inbuilt pressure and which continue to resist such a reduction, thus forming a residual empirical problem. This seems to me to be the right strategy in the search for possible language universals and generally in the construction of a proper theory of language.

3.2 Some history

The debate between the universalists and the relativists goes back to the late eighteenth century. Before that time, it had been, more or less implicitly, assumed that human language differs from other actual or thinkable communication systems in that it follows certain universal, or anyway nature-given, patterns not only of thought but also of modes of linguistic expression. The Greeks and Romans were decidedly vague on the issue, as they did not really feel that languages spoken by other peoples or races were worth considering. The best one can say is that they were naïve universalists. Medieval philosophers of language reflected on Latin, as they knew no Greek and weren't sure that the newly arising European vernaculars were indeed proper languages worth studying. They too were naïve universalists. In fact, it wasn't until the eighteenth century, in the wake of the great post-1500 European expansion into the Far West and the Far East and under the gradually increasing influence of various enlightened European religious and philosophical movements claiming human rights for non-European natives (the 'Noble Savage' philosophy), that European philosophers and budding linguists began to be serious about the question of the boundaries of human language.

---

[4] Jackendoff correctly points out that the notion of universal grammar is not to be confused with that of language universals (Jackendoff 2011: 587): 'For instance, UG might provide a set of options from which languages choose (such as parameters), or it might be a set of attractors toward which languages tend statistically without necessarily adhering to them rigidly.' This leaves open the possibility—unlikely though it may be—of a well-founded general theory of language, with many valid generalizations over the languages of the world but without any absolute language universals.

At first, the dominant attitude was conservative, in the tradition of Rationalism. As more and more reports on 'exotic' languages from all over the world reached the cultural centres of Europe, the general reaction was 'Look how similar all human languages really are!'. A typical representative of this attitude is the French grammarian *Nicolas Beauzée* (1717–1789; see Seuren 1998: 72), who distinguished, in his *Grammaire générale* of 1767, universal from language-specific principles (Beauzée 1767, I: ix–x) (translation mine):

Grammar, which takes as its object the expression of thought by means of spoken or written speech, thus allows for two sorts of principles. The ones are of an immutable and universal validity. Being connected with the very nature of thought they follow its analysis and thus result from it. The others [...] depend on fortuitous, arbitrary, and variable conventions, which have given rise to the different languages. The former constitute universal grammar, the latter are the object of the grammars of specific languages.

Beauzée also insisted on the Ockhamist razor principle and found that anyone who looks at exotic languages hits upon the same regular principles turning up again and again. He thus proved himself to be a true universalist (Beauzée 1767, I: xvi–xviii):

I believe that one must treat the principles of Language (French: *Langage*; PAMS) as one treats those of physics or geometry or any other science. For there is in effect just one logic, and the human mind, if I may venture this expression, is of necessity subjected to the same mechanism, no matter with what it occupies itself. I have thus, to the best of my ability, been sparing of principles. In order not to multiply them without necessity I have tried, wherever possible, to generalize over usages that appeared to be analogous. [...]

Constantly following this method I found everywhere the same views, the same general principles, the same universality in the laws common to Language. I saw that the differences of specific languages, the idioms, are nothing but different aspects of general principles or different applications of common fundamental laws, that these differences are limited, based on reason, reducible to fixed points, that therefore all the peoples of the earth, despite the differences of their tongues, speak, in a sense, the same Language, without anomalies or exceptions, and that, finally, one can reduce to a relatively small number *the necessary elements of Language*, and the teaching of all languages to a simple, brief, uniform and easy method.

I say 'necessary elements of Language' because they are, in fact, indispensably necessary in all languages to make the analytical and metaphysical deployment of thought perceptible. But I do not mean to speak of individual necessity which would not leave any language the liberty to leave one or more of them unused. What I am speaking of is a necessity of kind, which sets limits to the choice one can make of them.

Very few, if any, authors of the period defended the opposite, relativist, view. This is understandable if one takes into account the general mood among eighteenth-century philosophers, (mostly protestant) clergymen and other exponents of intellectual life, who mostly endorsed the 'Noble Savage' philosophy, insisting that 'exotic' natives are first and foremost humans and thus entitled to universal human rights—a prelude to the abolition of slavery in the nineteenth century (Bitterli 1989: 167). In academic circles and also among the rich bourgeoisie (but definitely not among the colonial traders, whose interests were of a more materialist nature), it was, if you like, 'politically incorrect' to emphasize the differences between the peoples, cultures and languages of the world. The eighteenth-century Rationalist intellectuals were thus predisposed towards what we now call universalism, though their universalism was already much less naïve than that of their medieval and ancient forebears.

It did not take long, however, for travellers, investigators and the wealthy European bourgeoisie to become fascinated with the exoticisms found in overseas, mostly tropical, lands and islands. Governments and learned societies began to finance large expeditions to explore the still numerous and vast white spots on the world map (Bitterli 1989: 155) and enterprising individuals began to undertake hazardous travels to head-hunting tribes in the dark recesses of Africa, Asia, Oceania and the Americas, either on the strength of their own wealth or commissioned by some official body.[5] All this was part of the great wave of Romanticism—the universal movement in Western civilization that made people wish to have direct personal experience of both the remote past (one thinks of the birth of professional archaeology in the 1770s) and the remote parts of the world, still making itself felt in present-day Western culture. In this period, anthropology, and anthropological-descriptive linguistics with it, became a recognized intellectual occupation in Europe (see Chapter 8 in Bitterli 1989).

The fascination quickly spread to the newly founded American Republic, where the interest was narrowed down mainly to the native North American Indians. A typical feature of the American development was the almost immediate professionalization under the aegis of the American government, which was, in principle at least though not always in practice, keen to establish morally justified relations with the native population, based on adequate knowledge and understanding. It was here that, during the nineteenth century, *anthropology* became an autonomous, state-subsidized, academic discipline studying the cultural and linguistic idiosyncrasies of the various American Indian populations. That indigenous natives all over the world are fully human was no longer an issue. The issue was now not the *unity* of mankind, which was taken for granted, but the *diversity* of its various physical, social, cultural and linguistic manifestations. From a professional point of view, idiosyncratic

---

[5] One thinks in particular of the travels undertaken by Captain James Cook (1728–1779) at the behest of the British Royal Society, or by the French mathematician-explorer Louis Antoine de Bougainville (1729–1811), name-giver of the Oceanic island Bougainville and of the originally Brazilian plant Bougainvillea, who was commissioned by the French king to circumnavigate the world; and, of course, one thinks of the famous *Beagle* expedition (1831–1836) under Captain Robert Fitzroy, with Charles Darwin as the most prominent passenger. Bougainville and Cook were the first to have scientific specialists as passengers on board, which shows that that kind of expedition sprang from a genuine desire to know the earth and its vegetal and animal inhabitants.

curiosities were now valued more than similarities. This predisposed the new anthropologists to a frame of mind that we now identify as relativism.

Philosophically, the new Romanticist relativists found their inspiration to a large extent in the writings of the seventeenth-century English empiricist philosopher *John Locke* (1632–1704), especially his *An Essay Concerning Human Understanding* of 1689. His minimalist theory of human cognition made him deny the reality of species-specific innate truths while remaining vague and noncommittal with regard to any innate species-specific principles of cognitive processing of sensory input. He made sensory input determine all cognitive content without taking into account specifically human ways of processing that input—a point of view massively disproved by modern cognitive science.[6] The net result was a drastic cutting down on universal properties of the human species. This epistemological relativism strongly appealed to the Neapolitan philosopher *Giambattista Vico* (1668–1744) and even more to the French philosopher *Étienne Bonnot de Condillac* (1714–1780), who in turn influenced the German savant-cum-linguist-cum-diplomat *Wilhelm von Humboldt* (1767–1835) and thus much of the nineteenth-century complex of ideas about the nature of human language (see Seuren 1998: 49–56, 108–19).

The new anthropology, especially its more linguistically oriented department, then struck up an alliance with neopositivism, the excessively data-oriented philosophy of science that developed and became fashionable during the late nineteenth and early twentieth century both in Europe and in America in the wake of Lockean empiricism. *Neopositivism was a scientific methodology that reduced all knowledge to sensory input and all reality to matter.* It held that theories postulating 'abstract' underlying, not directly observable, structures with a view to a *causal* explanation of the phenomena observed were unscientific and should, therefore, be exorcised from the realm of science. In fact, the entire notion of causality was placed under a cloud of metaphysical suspicion: in the neopositivist book, all there is is observable matter and regular

---

[6] It is not generally recognized, yet true, that not only modern cognitive science but also the physical sciences as a whole are at odds with the entire Lockean view of cognition, his 'human understanding', and in strict agreement with the rationalist view of cognition developed, notably, by Kant, who did not take the appearance of things for granted but postulated heavy cognitive processing machinery. Locke's non-answer to the great Cartesian and Kantian question of the unprovability and the unknowability in principle of the world as it is 'in and of itself', regardless of how it appears through the senses, amounted to a mere banausic 'Don't be a nuisance; you know the world is real and you know the way it is for your sense organs tell you, so don't fuss'. (There is a great deal of discussion and confusion among philosophers about what Locke actually meant to say, but on a recent rereading of the *Essay*, this is what I found his answer to amount to.) This naïve realism has had disastrous consequences not only for semantics (see Chapter 9), but also, in a wider sense, for the human sciences as a whole, as we see demonstrated here. Physics has, fortunately, not bothered about Locke but went its own way, though perennially hampered by the question of any possible *realist* interpretation of its mathematical equations. Modern cognitive science has made it clear that the mind is not simply a *tabula rasa*, a passive receptacle of sensory impressions, but a powerful active force in shaping the cognitive results of sensory input, which accords with the Kantian view that our picture of the world is the product of an active, species-specific process of world construal. See Seuren (2009a: 80–4) for a more detailed discussion of the Kantian 'paradox of knowledge'.

correspondences claimed to be universal, no causal 'invisible harmony' explaining the observable phenomena.

For those who were affected by this frame of mind, this meant that all that counts in the study of language is surface phenomena and, for many, phenomena of actual use in particular. The postulation of 'abstract' underlying rule systems forming the grammars of the languages being studied was, and still is, considered anathema or at least undesirable. The very word *abstract* has thus become an icon of rejection in relativist circles. Curiously, no sustained philosophical or methodological defence of this neopositivist attitude is found in the literature emanating from the quarters concerned. As a result, relativists tend to look only at surface phenomena that fall under agreed criteria of direct observability, considering any possible universals in the 'abstract' rule systems postulated by more theoretically oriented linguists illegitimate or irrelevant or in any case not worthy of serious attention. And worse, in limiting themselves to the observation of observables, anthropological linguists, following the Polish-British anthropologist Bronislaw Malinowski (1884–1942), have had a predilection for conventionalized or ritualized forms of speech, such as greeting formulas, where linguistic meaning plays a subordinate role and the main function is social bonding, claiming or suggesting that such marginal forms of language use form the core of natural human language.

This is, in fact, a typical feature of anthropological linguists and their close colleagues, the pragmaticists. They claim to study language when what they do is study the use that language is put to, whereby they focus on uses that may be socially or anthropologically relevant but are marginal from a linguistic point of view. If it wasn't for the inaccessibility of the mental machinery of language to scientific observation, the situation would be like that of studying the Hell's Angels, who, as I take it the reader will be aware, use their motorcycles not, as normal people do, as a means of transport but to show off, intimidate or worse. It is perfectly legitimate, and even useful, to study the Hell's Angels' untypical use of motorcycles and the place of this behaviour in the psychology and sociology of human group formation, but that study is not the study of motorcycles. Studying motorcycles is a technical business, whereby the primary or normal function of those machines as a means of rapid locomotion can be taken into account. In the study of their users' behaviour, the mechanics of motorcycles is taken for granted. Similarly in the study of language. Studying language is a technical business, whereby the primary or normal function of language may play an explanatory role. In the study of the *use* of language, the mechanics of language is taken for granted. The source of this confusion, widespread among anthropological linguists and pragmaticists, is the misguided neopositivist tenet that the scientific understanding of reality must not go beyond observables and that any assumption of underlying causal factors or structures is illegitimate. Motorcycles are tangible objects but language systems (grammars and lexicons) are not: they are software stored in the brain, which is a 'machine' that is very hard to gain physical access to.

The neopositivist attitude that has pervaded anthropological linguistics has also had a negative effect on modern linguistic typology. Typologists are by definition not relativists. It is the specific task of linguistic typology to detect universals in human languages, and the results that have been attained over the past three or four decades have indeed been impressive (see section 3.8.1). Unfortunately, however, the main focus of attention in typological research is on surface phenomena, with little or no interest in more 'abstract' parameters developed, or to be developed, and meant to create a perspective in which human languages are seen as manifestations of a unified underlying system.[7] This is to some extent excusable, given the not very flourishing state of theoretical linguistics, especially in its more formal manifestations, which are, or used to be, dominated by the Chomskyan school of Autonomous Generative Grammar. In fact, one often sees and hears typologists complain that no sufficiently reliable beneath-the-surface grammatical analyses exist for them to fall back on. Yet one hardly ever sees typologists themselves engage in the kind of grammatical theorizing they decry the uncertainty of. Perhaps it is felt that one cannot do everything at the same time. Yet a greater integration of the two branches of research would be most welcome, especially because never before have we had at our disposal such a massive amount of descriptive work on such a large number of languages spread all over the world. The profession should jump at this chance.

3.3 Attitudes

Relativists prefer it to be the case that observable, Greenberg-type, universal properties of language as proposed in the typological literature, turn out not to be universal after all, so that no 'abstract' theory is required to explain them. They are, on the whole, wary of any theory that posits non-observable, so-called 'abstract', systems that would capture the observable data in terms of general or universal principles. This, as has been said, gives their methodology a distinctly neopositivist flavour, in that neopositivism lives by observed data alone and rejects any notion of a causal theory positing explanatory systems or mechanisms underlying the observable data.

---

[7] There exists, for example, hardly any typological work on how languages deal with complementation (clauses as arguments to predicates) in their grammars. Yet one suspects that in those languages that do not leave their argument clauses intact or nominalize them, but reduce full clause embedding by raising either the subject term (Subject Raising or SR) or the verb (Predicate Raising or PR, leading to verb-clusters) from the lower argument clause into the higher matrix clause, the SR-solution appears to have a default status, probably because it requires less processing effort (Hawkins 2004). The more 'marked' (see Greenberg 1966) PR-solution (widespread in, for example, German and Dutch and clearly present in French and Italian, where it is primarily associated with higher causative predicates) is subject to heavy restrictions on recursion (as recursive processing quickly runs into trouble) and is typically given up in favour of the SR-solution when problems arise (Seuren 1986b, 1990). A typology of complementation solutions would be most welcome, but it is not available. See Seuren (1972a, 1985, 1996), Seuren and Hamans (2010).

When a relativism-prone linguist is confronted with a nontrivial close grammatical parallel in two or more unrelated languages in different parts of the world, the reaction is, as a rule, not the 'How interesting!' that will come from the universalism-prone linguist, but a rather disappointing refusal to take the parallel seriously. Likewise, relativism-prone linguists who hit upon a linguistic phenomenon that will strike the average, possibly Eurocentric, theoretical linguist as curious or outlandish, will emphasize the difference and the apparently idiosyncratic nature of the phenomenon in question, whereas the more universalist-minded linguist will try to develop an empathy with the phenomenon, so that it can be understood 'from within', so to speak.

Consider, for example, the so-called 'mother-in-law' lexicon discussed in Dixon (1972: 32–4, 292–6) in relation to the Australian language Dyirbal. The phenomenon, widespread among some Australian Aboriginal language groups until about 1930 but now virtually extinct, consists in the fact that, in the presence of taboo relatives (in-law parents of the opposite sex and father's sister's or mother's brother's child, but one normally speaks just of 'mother-in-law'), only words from a special so-called 'nuclear' lexicon (called 'Dyalnuy') may be used, whereas those 'nuclear' Dyalnuy words are not used in normal everyday use (called 'Guwal') when no taboo relatives are present. The Dyalnuy 'mother-in-law' lexicon contains only neutral and general words of a highly restricted sociolinguistic register, comparable with English words like *consume* (for 'eat'), *amble* (for 'walk'), *cast* (for 'throw'), or *abode* (for 'house'). It contains no specialized or graphic non-nuclear words like possible equivalents for *trundle*, *swagger*, *trip*, *rush* as hyponyms of the Dyalnuy word for *amble*.

This is, of course, a remarkable phenomenon. But there are different ways of looking at it. One can regard it as a highly idiosyncratic phenomenon, totally alien to anything Westerners can fathom, something, so to speak, from a different planet. But one can also try to empathize, describing it as a, perhaps excessive, outgrowth of phenomena regularly found in many other speech communities. It is commonly found, for example, that words of an elevated register are preferred in official texts, or in public speeches by highly placed persons, or when speakers in a lower social position address persons in a higher position. In an official context, or in the presence of persons commanding respect, one will (or, rather, one would, in the good old days), for example, rather not speak of a *car* but, more respectfully, of a *vehicle*. This will, in principle, account for the elevated character of the Dyalnuy lexicon. Moreover, one can easily imagine that one who addresses a highly placed person, or speaks in the presence of such, is expected to keep a low profile and not to indulge in language that is too graphic or too profuse, that kind of artistry or showmanship being reserved for talk among equals. This would, in principle, account for the nuclear character of the Dyalnuy lexicon. All it takes to arrive at a situation as sketched by Dixon for Dyirbal is a high degree of institutionalization of phenomena found all over the world in less extremely institutionalized forms.[8]

It seems to me that the empathizing attitude is more constructive and more conducive to a better understanding of human language and of mankind in general. It makes one see the general pattern and thus contributes to a unified theory of language and mankind. In this respect, our old friend Nicolas Beauzée, quoted in section 3.2, was entirely right. For him, a good methodology requires that one should be 'sparing of principles' and that one should not 'multiply them without necessity' but try 'wherever possible, to generalize over usages that appear to be analogous' (Beauzée 1767, I: xvi).

It is true, of course, that linguists have to work with imperfect analytical tools. There is, for example, as yet no generally valid definition of the concept 'word'. And of course we do not have universally applicable empirical definitions for the main word classes of verb, noun, adjective and so on. Yet it is an undeniable fact that, on the whole, linguists know what they are doing when they set up classes of verbs, nouns or adjectives for the languages they describe or when they say, for example, that a language has no adjectives.[9] Does this lack of universal definitions make linguistics an academically worthless exercise? No one has ever seriously maintained that it does. And rightly so, for a number of reasons. First, like any science, linguistics lives by bootstrapping. Imperfections are taken for granted as long as it is felt that progress is made. Intuitively plausible notions are often given precise definitions in hindsight, with much experience and plenty of material in the bag. Disciplined hypothesizing is part of that process. But secondly, and more importantly, if it had not been for the largely intuitive word class assignments linguists have become accustomed to using, all the intriguing cross-linguistic generalizations linguists have developed and use with remarkable success would have been impossible. In other words, as so often in science, the results justify the hypothesis. Anyone coming

---

[8] Gunter Senft called my attention to Irvine (1992), where the author describes the existence of a specific 'respect' vocabulary in Zulu, to be used *inter alia* by male speakers to refer to or address mother-in-law, and by female speakers to refer to or address father-in-law, and originating from the social necessity of avoiding affinal promiscuity.

[9] Sometimes, the lack of adequate, testable definitions plays up. It used to be generally accepted, for example, that Sranan, the English-based Creole of Surinam, lacks adjectives in predicative use, all adjectival predicates being expressed as stative verbs. In Seuren (1986a), however, I could demonstrate that most such adjectival 'verbs' behave differently from other, normal verbs. For example, adjectives, but not verbs, can be turned into zero-marked causative verbs, as in *Alen e tranga yu*, 'rain makes-strong you', with the preverbal particle *e* for non-durative verbs in the present tense. Degree adverbs, such as *moro* ('more') or *so* ('so') always follow verbs but may precede adjectives, depending on their syntactic position, as in a sentence like *A liba so/moro bradi* ('the river <is> so/more broad'). Adjectives are optionally copied in sentences like *O bradi a liba bradi?* ('how broad the river <is> broad?'), but verbs cannot be. When no copying takes place, the copula *de* appears: *O bradi a liba de?* ('how broad the river is?'), which is impossible for verbs. Such differences, though not definitional for the notion of adjective in general, seem to justify the conclusion that Sranan has adjectives after all.

up with better generalizations using other word classes is welcome, but no one seems to have raised their hand so far.

It is counterproductive to reject notions, insights or perspectives simply because they are not satisfactorily defined. To condemn universalist efforts on such grounds (as is done, for example, in Evans and Levinson 2009: 439–40) is not defensible: as long as one is in the process of theory construction, a licence is needed for incompletely defined but intuitively convincing categories. No work would get off the ground without such a licence. We would never have come to know what we do know about language if our linguistic ancestors had all been relativists.

One possible answer to the problem of the cross-linguistic definition of word classes might lie in a yet to be developed theory of concepts. Suppose it proved possible to establish that concepts fall into two main categories, the *primarily nominal* and the higher-order *primarily predicative* concepts (the latter being subdivided again into a number of subcategories, including *primarily adjectival* and *primarily verbal* concepts). Then it would be possible to say that every language will have SOME means to make a formal distinction between nouns and verbs. It would then be up to the linguists to find out WHAT means are used in each language and what types of nominal and verbal marking there would be in the languages of the world (see note 9 above about adjectives in Sranan).

It is likewise not very helpful to insist imperiously that universalists should come up with clearly defined absolute language universals, seen to be present in all languages. Such strict universals, like any universal statement over an unmanageably large range of entities, are never fully verifiable, if only because we necessarily lack evidence both from lost and from future languages. It is more productive to focus on phenomena that recur with great frequency in all sorts of unrelated languages all over the world. Such phenomena require an explanation for the simple reason that they are not random, and the explanation naturally starts with the assumption of an underlying universal system designed in such a way that it will automatically produce the recurrent patterns unless counteracted by some other, pre-emptive factor, such as language contact or the gradual transition from one language type to another (for example, from verb-final to verb-first). Such a system is likely to be functionality-driven, just as evolution favours the fittest. But, for all we know, antifunctional or functionally neutral factors also play a role (Seuren and Hamans 2010).

Viewed this way, universalism is not so much a search for a list of specific, concrete, absolutely universal properties of individual languages as an effort to formulate a maximally restricted general theory of human language that will make us see how languages come about and why recurrent patterns are found so frequently. And for such a theory to have maximal empirical clout it should be as restricted as possible— that is, it should maximize universal features. Reduction of varieties of facts to general principles has been the hallmark of science ever since the pre-Socratic philosophers of nature (such as Heraclitus, whose motto heads the present chapter).

3.4 Further notional clarity

We must be clearer on what relativism and universalism actually amount to. Summarily speaking, linguistic relativism is the doctrine that human languages can differ arbitrarily. If unqualified, however, this would soon lead to absurdity. It would mean that there could be a natural human language, used as a means of communication in a community, which is entirely like English but where every second occurrence of the phoneme /u/ is replaced with a giggle, or, less absurdly but still absurd, where the negation of a sentence would consist in its repetition, or would invert the word order of the non-negative sentence (which would be highly iconic!).

We note, meanwhile, that relativists have so far failed to present any qualification of their general thesis that languages can vary indiscriminately that would rule out giggle-English or sentence repetition or inversion for negation. On the contrary, they vaunt any unusual feature of Australian or other exotic languages as confirmation of their relativistic stance, which means that they would have to admit, say, giggle-English as a possible human language. More sensible linguists, however, feel that it is not. These linguists thus need some rationale for ruling it out. In fact, all serious phonological theories do present or contain such a rationale, though in general terms, not just for giggle-English. But this means that no serious phonological theory is relativist in the outspoken sense of Evans and Levinson (2009). Nor, for that matter, is any other serious general theory about any other domain of natural language.

What is needed, therefore, is, to begin with, a reasonably precise conceptual, or 'essential', definition of what a natural language amounts to, and in addition a specification of the ecological environment in which human languages function.

Such an 'essential' definition (still lacking a phonological component) might perhaps run as follows:

(3.1)   A human language is by definition a socially sanctioned symbolic system for converting an unlimited array of intents (speech acts over propositions) into structurally analysable perceptible form and vice versa—whereby a proposition is taken to be the mental act of assigning a property to one or more mentally defined entities in the real or a virtual world.

The remaining, non-essential conditions will then be, at least in part, of an ecological nature and will follow from the general physical make-up of the world, the species-specific physiological and anatomical make-up of the human body, the species-specific make-up of the human mind and the species-specific processes and structures occurring when humans form communities or societies. Properties of human languages that follow from the conceptual and ecological conditions of language either as necessary consequences for each individual language or as statistically predominant tendencies over (types of) languages must be taken into account by anyone who seriously looks at the question of possible universal properties of human language. Let us call such conceptual or ecological conditions *intrinsic universals* (which may be universal in an absolute sense or be reflected in statistical preponderances). Both relativists and universalists have to accept in principle that there are intrinsic universals. The empirical debate between the two parties will, therefore, be (a) about what intrinsic universals there are, since it is far from clear what the consequences are that follow either from the ecological conditions in which human language is used or from a conceptual definition of language, as proposed in (3.1) or any other reasonable 'essential' definition, and (b) whether there are any *extrinsic universals*, not fitting into any available theory of intrinsic universals. But such a debate, being of a strictly empirical nature, then becomes neutral as regards universalism versus relativism.

This is indeed the direction the debate is moving. What serious relativists mean when they say that languages may vary arbitrarily is that the arbitrariness is restricted by the intrinsic conditions imposed by ecological or conceptual necessity.[10] Beyond those, they say, there is total freedom, the implication being that *there is nothing in language that is not also found in general cognition: language is a mere derivate of general cognition*. This, however, can only be a programmatic statement as long as our knowledge of the intrinsic conditions on human languages and of the workings of human cognition is as deficient as it is. The research programme set up in these terms is motivated by the *desire* to establish that languages differ arbitrarily within the limits imposed by intrinsic conditions. There is thus a *parti pris*, which is why relativists are averse to the notion of extrinsic universals which look as if they resist an explanation in terms of conceptual necessity or ecological functionality and may have to be explained as unpredictable choices made by nature regarding general principles governing the composition of sentences, or as cases of not optimally functional evolutionary exaptation.[11] This is what makes linguistic relativism an ideology.

At the other extreme, Chomsky's (1995) 'Minimalist Program', to the extent that it is comprehensible, appears to be a (totally unsubstantiated; see Seuren 2004a) claim

---

[10]   According to Evans and Levinson (2009: 429), 'significant recurrent patterns in organization [...] are better explained [that is, better than in universalist terms; PAMS] as stable engineering solutions satisfying multiple design constraints, reflecting both cultural historical facts and the constraints of human cognition'. There is, however, no opposition between universalism and an explanation in terms of ecological (including cognitive) functionality. If the 'recurrent patterns in organization', which pervade languages all over the world, can indeed be reduced to factors of functionality, so much the better, since that would enhance insight into language and its physical, social and cognitive ecology. Nothing in the universalist doctrine speaks against that.

[11]   *Exaptation* (Gould and Vrba 1982) is the term for the use of an evolutionary trait, such as an organ, in a later evolutionary stage for a different purpose from what it served in the first place. Such a trait is sometimes called a *spandrel* (Gould and Lewontin 1979). A well-known example is bird feathers, which originally evolved for temperature regulation but subsequently served for flying.

to the effect that natural language is the best possible engineering solution to the problem of designing a symbolic system that fulfills the requirements to be met by any institution that can call itself 'natural language'. One consequence of this, so far vacuous, *a priori* is that there are no extrinsic universals, which would make Chomsky's stance in principle indistinguishable from the stance taken in, for example, Evans and Levinson (2009). Even the terminology used is seen to merge, as both Chomsky and Evans and Levinson speak of 'engineering solutions' (see note 10). In fact, however, the Chomskyan Minimalist and the relativist camps could not be more opposed. How is that possible? It seems to me that the reason why they can be so opposed, while their *a priori* premises are so similar, is ideological: both parties—and all others taking part in the by now widely raging debates—are lost in speculations about very different but equally eerie virtual realities, one based on the desire to deny, the other on the desire to affirm, unity in human language, while neither party has any serious empirical grip on the matter at hand. In this welter of shadow boxing, the present chapter argues that the participants in this debate should realize that we are only at the very beginning of a serious universal theory of human language—a stage where grandiose visions and claims about the eventual outcome are not only premature but also futile and damaging to the advancement of knowledge.

Old-fashioned universalists (of the kind I belong to) work towards a unified theory of human language, as part of the more general enterprise of formulating a unified theory of mankind. They feel that the more of language can be captured by the fewer general principles and tendencies, the more constrained and unified a general theory of human language—and thus of human nature—will be and thus the more empirical clout such a theory will have, all in accord with the Ockhamist principle that a scientific theory must maximize its generalizations, avoiding unnecessary distinctions. Universalists subscribe to the opening sentences of Greenberg (1966: 9):

> The problem of universals in the study of human language as in that of human culture in general concerns the possibility of generalizations which have as their scope all languages or all cultures. The question is whether underlying the diversities which are observable with relative ease there exist valid general principles. Such invariants would serve to specify in a precise manner the notion of 'human nature' whether in language or in other aspects of human behavior.

Universalism says that there is a universal, specifically linguistic, charter of regularities, principles and restrictions putting a brake on how human languages can develop, possibly beyond the intrinsic restrictions imposed by the necessity or functionality of nature and reason. The intrinsic restrictions are, naturally, accepted. In this respect, there is full agreement with the extreme relativistic Evans and Levinson (2009: 444):

> [T]here is a growing body of work that shows exactly where the language sciences are headed, which is to tame the diversity with theories and methods that stem ultimately from the

biological sciences. Evolutionary approaches, in the broadest sense, are transforming the theoretical terrain.

The programme of 'taming the diversity with theories and methods that stem ultimately from the biological sciences' is a central element in universalism, where the main concern, apart from serious data collecting and theorizing, is to show the unity—that is, the 'tameness'—of human language. But universalism is prepared to go further than relativism and envisage also the possibility of extrinsic universals, implicitly accepting that an explanation will eventually have to be sought for them, possibly in terms of contingent evolutionary development or of exaptation or some other not optimally functional or functionally indifferent evolutionary process or social universal.

For example, it has been shown (Greenberg 1963, 1966; Hawkins 1983, 2004; Hawkins and Cutler 1988; Dryer 1992, 2005a, 2005b, 2009) that the position of a language on the Verb-Object (VO) versus Object-Verb (OV) parameter is a powerful determinant for that language having (a) prenominal or postnominal adjectives, (b) prepositions or postpositions and (c) postnominal or prenominal relative clauses. A VO language is very strongly predisposed towards prepositions and postnominal relative clauses, while OV languages predominantly take postpositions and prenominal relative clauses. This correlation is naturally captured in terms of *branching directionality* (Dryer 1992, 2009; Seuren 1996): VO languages have a right-branching syntax and thus favour prepositions and postnominal relative clauses, while OV languages favour a left-branching syntax, which means that they will have postpositions and prenominal relative clauses. A mixture of types is also found, though those cases seem to be statistically marginal.[12]

But why do languages have the left-right-branching parameter at all in their syntax? For all we know, human language is quite thinkable without that parameter—which, by the way, is expressible only in terms of hierarchically branching constituent diagrams (see section 3.8.2), not in terms of dependency diagrams à la Tesnière (1959). Computer languages, for example, lack this parameter altogether (and mostly operate with Tesnière-type dependency diagrams). Hawkins, in many publications, explores

---

[12] Hawkins and Cutler (1988) point out that this correlation is skewed in that OV languages show a significantly lower proportion of prenominal relative clauses than predicted. These authors attribute the skewing to the fact that prenominal relative clauses are likely to produce garden-path processing obstacles, as in the (SOV) Japanese sentence (i) (p. 283):

(i)   Zoo-ga   RelCl[kirin-o   taoshi-ta]   shika-o   nade-ta
      elephant-subj   giraffe-obj   knocked-down   deer-obj   patted
      'The elephant patted the deer that knocked down the giraffe.'

Hearers would first understand 'the elephant knocked down the giraffe', only to realize, as the following words come in, that this was a garden path and that the correct interpretation is as given in (i). Cases like this support Hawkins's general thesis that processing demands constrain or influence grammatical structure.

to what extent utterance processing factors can be held responsible for universals or universal tendencies in language. This makes a great deal of sense, yet such processing factors have not so far been shown to be powerful enough to explain the far-reaching role of the branching directionality parameter in human languages and no alternative avenue of explanation has so far proved successful. Is this parameter a quirk of nature or is there a more organic explanation that has so far escaped us? Relativists are uncomfortable with such facts and such questions, whereas universalists are eager to collect relevant data in this regard and to formulate relevant hypotheses, while not demanding an immediate explanation.

3.5 What are 'universals of language'?

The answer to the question of what are universals of language looks, but is not, simple. Of course, one can say: 'Any property adhering to all human languages is a language universal.' But this simplicity masks the real state of affairs. It is also conducive to imperiousness on the part of anti-universalists: show us absolute universals or you can go! But this is not the way it is. As has just been argued, for now and the near future, universalism is a perspective, a well-founded scientific research programme that will, if successful, yield nontrivial, counterevidence-proof language universals of an absolute or a gradual or an implicational kind, either because it predicts them or because it hits on them during fact-finding missions. It is no false modesty to say that we are not even yet in a position to define the main parameters of a universal theory of language variation that would, eventually, define the limits within which any specific language is free to vary.

To demand of universalists that they come up right away with putative absolute universals with the sole purpose of demolishing them amounts to an effort to demean serious science. It is like denying the effects of medication because in some cases the medicine does not work. What we want to find out is to what extent putative universals are indeed universal, just as pharmacologists want to find out to what extent their medicines work and why they don't work when they don't. There may, after all, be inhibiting or disturbing factors.[13]

Moreover, when we speak of a 'universal theory of natural language', we have in mind a theory that defines what is *natural* in human language, as opposed to what is non-natural or artificial. Non-natural forms of language are found in (sub)languages

---

[13] Obviously, complete induction from all the actually existing languages in the world, now, in the past and in the future, is impossible. But what is not impossible is psychological experimenting. One could, for example, teach one group of subjects a rule system (using a small artificial vocabulary) that follows a putative grammatical universal u and another group of subjects a different syntactic rule system (using the same vocabulary) that violates u. If it were to be found that, after an equal amount of training, the first group achieved significantly better than the second, then that would count as evidence for the view that u is indeed somehow part of an innate system of universals, whether intrinsic or extrinsic.

cultivated in specific academic disciplines and/or cultural circles. Technical jargons are 'non-natural' in this sense, and may thus transgress the boundaries of what is to be considered 'natural'. Yet they do occur and their 'non-natural' features may thus, incorrectly, be held up as (false) counterexamples to what is otherwise a sound universal theory of natural language.

Even so, however, good reason demands acceptance of the fact that there are universal properties common to all natural human languages, whether spoken or signed. Such properties come in different kinds. Some are essential, or in more up-to-date parlance, *conceptually necessary*. They are defined by the very notion of human language, made explicit in some hopefully adequate general definition such as given in (3.1) above. They thus constitute the necessary and sufficient conditions for anything to count as a natural human language. Anything satisfying such an 'essential' definition would qualify as a potential natural human language and failure to satisfy it would mean that the object in question is not a natural human language. This sounds trite but it is nevertheless important, because there is as yet no unanimity as regards the defining characteristics of human language. The search for conceptually necessary universal conditions on human languages may thus well contribute to our knowledge in this respect.

But there are other kinds of necessity than conceptual necessity, further delimiting the notion of a potential natural language. There is, as has been said, *physical necessity*, defined by the laws of physics, or *physiological necessity*, defined by the physiological make-up of the human body, or *psychological necessity*, defined by the make-up of the human mind, and also *social necessity*, defined by interactive processes universally taking place when humans are placed together in communities. Since, trivially, all human languages are used by humans with their physiological and psychological make-up, in a world subject to universal physical laws and in communities subject to universal social laws and principles, there are universal consequences of the ecological environment common to all human languages. These, too, will count as universals of language, but not of a conceptual or 'essential' order. For if a language were to be found spoken by humans but escaping some or other of the physical, psychological or social laws governing all existing human languages, this language would still count as a human language as long as it satisfies some agreed set of conceptually necessary conditions such as presented in (3.1). For example, if a human race were to be discovered with respiratory organs differing from those of the rest of humanity, a deviant oral or glottal physiology and an accordingly deviant auditory system (with a different optimal discrimination range), so that this race would produce and perceive speech sounds that differ from those found in the spoken languages we have so far encountered, this would not make its language or languages non-human—though it would make for a separate subclass.

This leaves room for so-called *implicational universals* (Greenberg 1963), which say that if a language has the property X it also always or most of the time has the property Y. To take a concrete proposal, Universal 34 in Greenberg (1963: 94), not contradicted so far,[14] says: 'No language has a trial number unless it also has a dual. No language has a dual unless it also has a plural.' An implicational universal such as this is likely to be of an extrinsic nature, given the state of our present knowledge, and thus unlikely to be due to physical, physiological, psychological or social necessity, nor is it likely to be of a conceptual nature, though it may be a consequence of 'markedness' as a feature of human cognition (Greenberg 1966)—a topic yet to be studied in greater depth in cognitive science.[15]

Room is likewise left for phenomena that may or may not be, strictly speaking, universal but can be shown to be, if not *necessary*, at any rate *functional* in that they enhance or facilitate the functioning of the language machine in its ecological environment—a perspective explored in particular detail in the works of John Hawkins. In cases where such functionality-driven phenomena are not universal in the strict sense but are widely found among the languages of the world, one may justifiably speak of *universal tendencies* or *recurrent patterns*. They are often reflected in the diachronical development of language or dialect groups. One also often finds that a particular phenomenon or development is functional from one point of view but antifunctional from another. It may, for example, be functional when applied with moderation but antifunctional when applied profusely, as is clearly the case with acronyms, usually written in capital letters. Or it may be functional from a production and/or comprehension processing point of view but antifunctional from a sociolinguistic point of view, or vice versa (Francis and Michaelis 2003, Gaeta 2010,

---

[14] In Evans and Levinson (2009: 439) it is maintained, without reference, that this universal is counter-evidenced by Nen, a language in South-West Papua New Guinea. The claim is that 'Basic verb stems in Nen are dual, with non-duals indicated by a suffix meaning "either singular or three-or-more", the singular and the plural sharing an inflection!'. No further comment is provided. A Google search yielded one short unpublished seminar paper on Nen, written by one of the two authors (Evans 2011). The evidence provided in this paper shows that most verbs in Nen take three formally distinct affixes, for singular, dual and plural ('more than two'). But adjectives and verbs of location and position do not take a number suffix (number being expressed by a pronominal prefix) but an affix marking stativity. This stativity affix appears to be the same for singular and plural (more than two), dual use requiring a separate (marked) form. The pronominal prefixes have no dual and merely distinguish between singular and nonsingular (dual or plural). (We know anyway that duals are usually a residual and restricted category, as is also stressed by Greenberg himself.) No trace of 'basic dual verb stems' could be found. There seems to be no reason, therefore, to consider Nen a counterexample to Greenberg's Universal 34. All there is, is a marked stativity suffix for adjectives and verbs of location and position with a dual subject. Such is the relativist desire to do away with language universals. See also the enlightening comment by Daniel Harbour (Harbour 2009) on Evans and Levinson (2009).

[15] From a cognitive point of view, Greenberg's Universal 34 is remarkable, as one would expect the implicational order *singular < dual < trial < plural*, since this is the order found in the typology of counting systems: in tribal languages spoken in less culturally developed communities it is often found that the counting system is: *one – two – three – many*. In language, however, one finds the order *singular < plural < dual < trial*.

Seuren and Hamans 2010). It is mainly because of such functional conflicts that the languages of the world do not all develop unidirectionally towards some asymptotic ideal of maximal functionality.

There are, finally, many phenomena that are empirically found to be very widespread among totally unrelated languages and perhaps even universal, but do not seem to be reducible to either conceptual or ecological necessity and serve no obvious functional purpose. An outstanding example is the special cross-linguistic status of *causative* verbs or affixes. All over the world, one finds that what are, semantically speaking, predicates expressing causation are structurally united with the predicates in their embedded propositions standing for what is caused to be the case or to happen. This 'unification' results in either a verb cluster or a morphologically complex verb with a causative affix (sometimes a zero affix). Syntactic causative verb clustering is found in, for example, French (the *faire*-construction), Italian, German, Dutch.[16] Morphological causativization is much more frequent. It is found in Japanese, Turkish, Uto-Aztecan, Tagalog and thousands of other languages, including English, which mostly has a zero causative morpheme for verbs (e.g. *drop*) and overt alternation only idiosyncratically, as in *rise* vs *raise* or *fall* versus *fell*. (For nominal-to-verb derivation, English has a variety of affixes, such as the suffix *-en* as in *blacken* or the prefix *en-* as in *enlarge* or *endear*.) When one sees, in any of the now numerous descriptions of exotic languages, a section about 'valency increasing' or whatever it is called, one is bound to find causative affixation as the first and foremost instance, often flanked by similar procedures for predicates of 'letting' or 'allowing'. Is this a universal? Not in so far as there are languages that do not have it, such as Latin, Ancient Greek or Portuguese. But then, why should this phenomenon be so frequent across languages?

Such apparently contingent, yet widespread and in some cases even universal, phenomena pose an empirical problem in that one will wish to know the causal origin of their being so widespread and so typical for human languages. In some cases, the origin is unclear. It may lie, for example, in evolutionary processes of exaptation of certain parts of the brain, or in general, as yet unknown, features of cerebral or cognitive processing, or, indeed, in the make-up of a postulated innate module for the processing of certain aspects of utterances. In the case mentioned above of semantically causative predicates being united with their lower verbs, one might say, in the innatist spirit, that this phenomenon is an inherent feature of the innate language faculty, which is built in such a way that causatives, not unlike negation, tenses and modalities, are prone to clustering with the verb commanded by

---

[16] In English, syntactic causative verb clustering is found only in very few fully lexicalized instances such as *let go* or *make do*. In German and Dutch, the clustering procedure has been generalized to become the standard syntactic embedding procedure for most complement-embedding verbs (Seuren 1972a, 2003; Evers 1975).

them, either syntactically, as still separate verbs, or as adverbial particles or morphological elements. In this perspective, the clustering tendency is, so to speak, waiting in the wings, ready to be given the seal of approval by 'the people' and thus to emerge overtly under certain conditions yet to be specified, just as potatoes will sprout and form roots when put back in the soil. One may perhaps speak of a universal *pressure* rather than a *tendency*. A proper theory of universals should give such phenomena their proper place.

A no doubt functionally motivated example is *haplology*, the tendency, or pressure to do something about immediate successions of short functional words. Dutch has a sentence like (3.2a), where the first *er* corresponds to English existential *there* and the second *er* is a partitive pronominal:

(3.2)   a. Er   waren er   twee.
          there were   thereof two
          'There were two of them.'

      b. ...dat er   (*er)   twee waren.
         ...that there (*thereof) two were
         '...that there were two (of them).'

Since in Dutch (as in German), the verb of non-main clauses or infinitivals is moved to final position, (3.2b) should have two successive occurrences of *er*. Yet one occurrence must be deleted, on pain of ungrammaticality (intuition says that the one deleted is the second, partitive *er*). In Italian, immediate successions of clitics get modified. In (3.3a), the succession *ci si* should 'really' be *si si*, as in the ungrammatical (3.3b), the first *si* being the form for the impersonal 'one', the second being the reflexive *si* required with the reflexive verb *svegliarsi* ('wake up'):

(3.3)   a. Ci si   sveglia   presto in montagna.
          one oneself wake-up early in the mountains
          'One wakes up early in the mountains.'

      b. *Si si sveglia presto in montagna.

Similarly, still in Italian, for two successive occurrences of the clitic pronoun *le*, as in (3.4b), where the first *le* is changed into the masculine *gli* ('to him'), making *gliele* ambiguous between 'them to him' and 'them to her', and amalgamated with the following *le* (as happens with *gli* generally):

(3.4)   a. Non   gliele   voleva   dare.
          not to her/him-them(fem.) wanted(3sg.) give
          '(S)he did not want to give them (fem.) to her/him.'

      b. *Non le le voleva dare

In general, languages tend to avoid a succession of small functional words and many of them do something about it, though what they do about it, if anything, differs from language to language. Here again, we see a widespread, but not universal tendency, this time clearly motivated by functionality factors. Such phenomena are part of a universal theory of language, even if they are not absolute universals occurring in all languages.

Generic noun phrases are another case in point. It is often assumed in the literature that the same, semantically defined, principle applies to all languages, but even a superficial inspection of the facts shows that this is not so. Generic noun phrases are problematic not only from a semantic and logical point of view (Aristotle devoted a fairly long passage to them in his *On Interpretation*, trying to capture them in quantificational terms, but he failed to reach a conclusion), but also as regards their grammatical treatment in the languages of the world. There seem to be two competing principles at work: the use of so-called 'bare plurals' (plural noun forms without any determiner), as in English *Elephants have a good memory*, versus the use of the definite article, as in the French equivalent *Les éléphants ont une bonne mémoire*. Likewise in Portuguese *João ama café* (John likes coffee), without the definite article, versus Italian *Gianni ama il caffè*, with the definite article. The use of the definite article in such a sentence in Portuguese, or leaving it out in the corresponding Italian sentences, makes these sentences ungrammatical in their respective languages.[17] The correct method would seem to be a maximizing of any general principle within each language and across languages, and thus a minimizing of the influence of the social settling factor. This way, any possible universal factor will stand the best chance of coming to the surface.

3.6 What to do with counterevidence?

As always in science, the question arises of what to do with real or apparent counter-evidence. Surely, we will not automatically let a single counterexample, or even a handful of them, destroy a theory or theoretical complex that has so far satisfactorily and organically accounted for a large number of instances. Such a theory is too good to be thrown out lightly. Yet the counterevidence, if serious and not the result of sloppy observation, has to be accounted for, which means that the theory in question is not complete, or perhaps faulty in some detail. And this is, of course, the situation we are in in linguistics: linguistic theories are all obviously imperfect and incomplete.

First of all, it must be noted that a universal theory of language aims at establishing what is *natural* in language, as has been said above. Yet humans and human societies have an inbuilt urge to create cultures and thus to enhance sophisticated acting and

---

[17] One should note that the rules or principles for the grammatically correct use of the definite article in English have so far escaped explicit formulation.

thinking, which will soon rise above the level of primitive naturalness. It is not excluded in principle that non-natural features of language will appear at more developed levels of cultural sophistication. Such features are not to be taken to constitute counterexamples to a universal theory of natural language. Yet we have no well-established method to separate basic-natural from more sophisticated, and thus potentially non-natural, features of languages. This forms one obstacle to a universal theory of natural human language. In the circumstances, all we can do is be aware of this danger and act accordingly.

Apart from this, there is the fact that languages change continually and may change from one linguistic type to another, for example, from SOV to SVO, for whatever reason. During the change, a language may exhibit features of both types, perhaps distributed over different age groups, thereby disturbing the picture. Again, one may hold up such cases as counterexamples, but a closer look may show the opposite. Let us consider one such potential counterexample. Greenberg's Universal 3 (Greenberg 1963: 78) says: 'Languages with dominant VSO order are always prepositional.' This universal is not without exceptions. One such exception seems to be the language Katukina-Kanamari (KK for short), spoken by a small community of Amazonian Indians in Brazil (Dos Anjos 2011). KK is verb-first but does seem to have only postpositions. The question is thus whether there are reasonable grounds that may explain how and why this anomaly can have occurred.

These are the details. KK is, in principle, verb-first and ergative, though SVO also seems to occur, as appears from (3.8) below and also from an SVO sentence like (3.5a), whose regular form should be (3.5b), where the ergative is marked by the suffix *-na* (Dos Anjos 2011: 268):

(3.5)   a. Aiobi hak   tucunaré.
           Aiobi pierce tucunaré (strong river fish)
           'Aiobi pierced the tucunaré.'

        b. Aiobi-na   hak   tucunaré.
           Aiobi- ergat pierce tucunaré
           'Aiobi pierced the tucunaré.'

But cases like (3.5a) appear to be rare. The ergative character of KK may be grounds for saying that KK is not VSO but only verb-first, because ergative languages have no direct object, or else EVS (Ergative-Verb-Subject). Perhaps this objection is valid: it may be the case that Greenberg's Universal 3 holds for VSO but not for ergative verb-first (or EVS) languages. But it may also be the case that verb-first, possibly preceded by Ergative, is the crucial condition.

Then, KK has two classes of postpositions. The first requires that the suffix -*na* is added to the preceding nominal object. The suffix -*na* is a jack-of-all trades, but its central function seems to be to signal a possessive or genitive relation. It is also obligatory with the ergative argument (not unlike the obsolete English *of* as a passive preposition, as in *instituted of God*). Postpositions that require -*na* are, for example, *katu* ('with' for animate objects), *iton* ('without'), *ama* ('for'), *toi* ('deep inside'). One thus has postpositional phrases as in (3.6) (Dos Anjos 2011: 324):

(3.6) No:k   ha-owamok-**na**   iton.
       be good   3sg.poss-wife-**of**   without
       'He behaved well in his wife's absence.'

This reminds one of the Latin postposition, but really ablative noun, *gratia* ('for the sake of'), which is preceded by a genitive, as in *exempli gratia* ('for (the sake of an) example', usually shortened to *e.g.*). One would thus expect these postpositions to be based on original nouns, in a zero locative case, meaning 'company' (for 'with'), 'absence' (for 'without'), 'advantage' (for 'for'), 'inside' (for 'deep inside'), but no evidence for or against this hypothesis is available.

The second class of postpositions just takes a preceding object noun without -*na*. This class includes *to* ('at, near'), *han* ('with' for inanimate objects), *iki* ('inside') and the obviously compound forms *tona* ('at the foot of'), *todik* ('below'), *patudik* (centripetal 'towards'), *patuna* (centrifugal 'towards'), *ton* ('on top of'). Thus, one has (Dos Anjos 2011: 318):

(3.7) Hi:ran   adu   hi:tyan   patuna.
       go away   I   wild hog   towards (centrifugal; deictic)
       'I went away towards the wild hog.'

(3.8) Rosa   daan   hi:tyan   patudik.
       Rosa   come   wild hog   towards (centripetal; intrinsic)
       'Rosa came closer to the wild hog.'

A universalist will now try to reconcile these data with existing generalizations, such as Greenberg's Universal 3. Suppose there is a tendency in KK to drop the affix-*na* under certain conditions. We have already seen that -*na* is missing in (3.5a) for the ergative case. Conceivably, (3.5a) is a sign or symptom of reanalysis, whereby the order ERGATIVE–VERB–SUBJECT is reinterpreted as SUBJECT–VERB–OBJECT, with a semantic change from a passive to an active meaning of the now transitive verb. A similar dropping of -*na* would then account for the postpositions not requiring -*na* attached to their object noun. Optional or conditional dropping of the genitive suffix is not unknown in other languages. In Turkish, for example, the normal genitive construction is formed by two elements, the suffix -*in*[4] attached to the genitive possessor noun plus the possessive suffix -*(s)i*[4] attached to the possessed object noun, as in *Ahmed-in araba-sı*, literally 'Ahmet-of car-his'.[18] Yet when the connection between the possessor and the posessed object noun has become conventional-ized, the genitive suffix *-in⁴* is dropped, as in *benzin istasyon-u*, literally 'petrol station-its'. In a similar way, one might hypothesize that the genitive suffix *-na* in KK is beginning to be allowed to be left out.

A hypothesis along these lines, if supported by further data from KK and other languages, would not only provide an 'excuse' for KK apparently not following Greenberg's Universal 3, but would also reveal a pattern of development in KK from verb-first ergative to SVO, with postpositions, whereby it is noted that Greenberg's theory of universals does not take into account any transitional phenomena occurring when a language changes from one word order type to another. I am not saying that the hypothesis just put forward is the correct answer. Perhaps it is, but it may also be wildly off the mark. My point is that the effort to save a tentative generalization stimulates further research, as long as the researcher is not carried away by excessive enthusiasm for his or her hypothesis. Such an effort is thus likely to lead to more and improved generalizations providing a better insight into what is going on.

3.7 Modularity, innateness, and the 'no negative evidence' problem

3.7.1 *Modularity and innateness*

Universalism comes in different varieties. One main division is between the typologists and the theoretical linguists. Typologists, on the whole, restrict their search for universals to observable surface phenomena, remaining sceptical as regards explanatory theories that may involve the postulation of non-observable, 'abstract' principles, rules or mechanisms. Theoretical linguists, by contrast, are prone to posit what some call 'abstract' universal properties definable in terms of non-observable mental machineries postulated to explain speakers' competence in their language. They reject the neopositivist method, and follow a more classical methodology which incites scientists to construct explanatory theories involving non-observable principles, rules or mechanisms that provide a causal explanation of the observable data. Theirs is the Heraclitean motto: 'Invisible harmony is stronger than visible harmony.'

The theoretical linguists, furthermore, fall into two more or less distinct classes. There are those who hold that language consists in non-specialized use of the general functions of the mind/brain. They are mostly found among the *cognitivists*, for whom any theory positing linguistic specialization in the brain is anathema: for them, language is fully explainable in terms of general functions of cognition and the

---

[18] The superscript '4' attached to the suffixes *-in⁴* and *-(s)i⁴* indicates that these suffixes belong to the class of suffixes that take four different vowels according to the last preceding vowel. The *s* in *-(s)i⁴* is inserted when the preceding syllable ends in a vowel.

brain. Given this *a priori*, they tend to have greater sympathy for relativism than for universalism.

There are also those, however, who hold that each language reflects a specific instantiation of a general human *language module* (Fodor 1983), innately present in the brain, probably not in a single brain area but rather as a set of brain functions specialized for the acquisition and use of specifically human languages. They see the innate module as still unspecific (and probably also still not full-grown) at birth and in need of linguistic input to create full socially integrated competence in a specific language. The process whereby the 'blank' and possibly not yet full-grown linguistic module grows into mature linguistic competence is called *language acquisition*.

Most universalist theorists of language are also modularists and hence innatists, positing what is called an innate *Universal Grammar* which provides an implicitly given, automatic 'manual', so to speak, for the construction of any language-specific grammar internalized by a language learner. Quite apart from the merits of theories implying such a 'universal grammar', it would seem that the term *Universal Grammar* is at least misleading, in that it suggests one single universal grammar for the whole of mankind. This may sound like Chomsky's view, but even Chomsky does not take that literally. What is called 'universal grammar' is in fact (a theory of) the *universal principles* underlying all language-specific grammars. For that reason I shall henceforth speak not of 'universal grammar', no matter how time-honoured the term, but of the *universal principles of grammar* or UPG.

Innatism can be seen as an attempt at incorporating extrinsic universals into a theory of intrinsic universals, in that, with an innate language module, the species-specific mental make-up of humans will be such that it has all universal linguistic properties as necessary consequences. According to opponents, this reasoning is circular, as it offers the very same problematic facts as their explanation. Defenders say that this may be so for the moment—in fact, all hypotheses are circular without additional confirming evidence—but that future empirical evidence coupled with good theorizing may break the circle and show them right or wrong.

To say of universals that they are innate implies that they no longer merely follow from conceptual necessity or from ecological factors, but that, in addition, these consequences (and possible other, extrinsic, features as well) are *prewired*, or *hard-wired*, into a specifically linguistic part or aspect of human genetic structure, in the form of one or more modular learning and/or processing programmes, thereby predisposing language learners to the easy and natural acquisition of languages that stay within the limits posed by these prewired universals and pre-empting the natural acquisition of languages that transgress them. It has often been observed, not without reason, that the speed, ease, regularity and universal inevitability of infant language acquisition during the critical learning period, in the face of fragmentary and contaminated linguistic input, strongly suggests such a programmatic prewiring.

And indeed, it takes a very severe cerebral, articulatory or sensory handicap in early life for the natural language learning process not to take place.

The innateness of a language faculty is perhaps what relativists are most eager to deny, as it gainsays the Lockean *tabula rasa* principle (see note 6) and threatens the entire neopositivist frame of mind, thereby profoundly affecting one's overall view of human nature. Yet infant language acquisition strikes one as highly programmatic, just as learning to walk upright, the development of perceptual faculties, of memory, and, in more general terms, the ubiquitous manifestations of animal instinctive behaviour. This makes one see native language acquisition as a very robust natural process of growth, requiring external sensory input for it to be triggered. Yet as long as so little is known about the physiological implementation of such programmed learning processes, the innate argument, for all its plausibility, must remain restricted to non-hardware hypotheses. And this is what theorists have started doing: formulate non-hardware hypotheses about certain aspects of UPG, entirely in the spirit of formulating non-hardware specifications of grammar systems for specific languages. The following section gives some examples of non-hardware UPG hypotheses showing in formal, but not physiological, detail how possible UPG principles and procedures can be seen to facilitate the process of language acquisition.

3.7.2. *The 'no negative evidence' problem*

A much debated issue in this context is the *'no negative evidence' problem*: how do children learn that certain ways of expressing thoughts are ungrammatical or certain interpretations illegitimate, given the absence of explicit marking for illicitness in the linguistic material offered and given the fact that, despite their being illicit, illicit expressions and interpretations do occur? How do learning children draw the line between what is correct and what is incorrect in the language they are acquiring? How do they know where to stop applying a general rule? UPG is standardly offered by universalists as the most obvious answer. This is, however, called into question by some authors. Hawkins, for example says (Hawkins 2004: 11): '[T]he whole relevance of UG to learnability must be considered moot.'

I do not wish to argue that there is no 'no negative evidence' problem: there certainly is, and I cannot claim to have an answer to all cases where it rears its head. But I do argue that at least in some cases where the problem has been diagnosed, the diagnosis can be withdrawn because a proper version of UPG does seem to provide an answer. Some such cases are discussed in the present section.

3.7.2.1 *Internal anaphora resolution of definite terms*   The problem of internal anaphora resolution of definite pronouns with regard to definite antecedents within the same sentence has been known for a long time. Quantified antecedents are a different matter, as they bind their bound-variable pronouns. Moreover, reflexivity

plays a much more important role than it is usually given credit for.[19] Apart from these complicating factors, however, the internal anaphora resolution problem requires finding an answer to the question why *he* (the *pronoun*) in (3.9a–d) is interpretable as coreferential with *John* (the *antecedent*) in (3.9a,b,c), but not in (3.9d), where *John* is not a possible antecedent:

(3.9)   a. While John stood on the balcony, he watched the crowd.
        b. While he stood on the balcony, John watched the crowd.
        c. John watched the crowd, while he stood on the balcony.
        d. He watched the crowd, while John stood on the balcony.

From the point of view of first-language acquisition, the question is: how does the child learn that coreferentiality of *John* and *he* is possible, even preferred, in (3.9a,b,c) but not in (3.9d)? This is a 'no negative evidence' question because the child must be kept from generalizing coreference relations to include (3.9d).

The standard answer is that there is a UPG principle ensuring the correct restriction:

Internal Definite Anaphora Principle (IDAP):
For a pronoun p to be coreferential with its antecedent A, A must precede p or, if A follows p, p must occur in a high-peripheral subordinate clause or at least in a high-peripheral prepositional phrase (for the notion of high-peripherality, see the sections 3.7.2.2, 5.2.1 and 5.2.2.2).

The antecedent must thus be somehow 'superior' to the pronoun, in that it either precedes the pronoun or has a higher status in the hierarchy of the corresponding constituent tree analysis. In this respect, there is a similarity with the case of internal versus external datives discussed in the following section.

The question is, of course, is IDAP universal? As far as we know, the answer is 'yes'—as simple as that. Does this mean that IDAP follows from the general make-up of the mind or brain or from processing procedures? The answer is uncertain, since we know too little about those things. If so, IDAP does not by itself require a language module; if not, the possibility that IDAP is innate as part of a language module is distinctly open. Most researchers feel that it is unlikely that IDAP follows from general cognitive or processing principles, which makes them favour the innate or modular hypothesis.

In this context, let me relate an anecdote. A few years ago I was on holiday in Bali but I had my laptop with me so that I could do some work. A friend of mine's son, whose native language is Balinese and who studied English at the local university, saw me working and asked if he could have a look. On my screen were four sentences like those in (3.9) and I explained the coreference relation to him. As he came to the last of the four sentences, he jumped up in surprise, realizing that there was no possible

---

[19] See Seuren (1985: 346–86) for an extensive discussion of the entire anaphora problem, inclusive of quantified and reflexive anaphora. For reflexivity, see section 5.2.2.1 and Chapter 7 in the present volume.

coreference. I had not told him about the fourth sentence, nor had he ever been taught the working of IDAP. Yet he immediately saw the difference. The reason can only be that IDAP does not have to be taught because it comes with human nature, one way or another. Learning by exposure is ruled out, or at least highly unlikely, precisely because of the lack of evidence that would have made the young man correctly exclude a reading for (3.9d) that is available for (3.9a,b,c)—a clear instance of the 'no negative evidence' problem.

3.7.2.2 *Internal versus external datives*   A similar phenomenon is the asymmetry of internal and external datives. In this case, however, the UPG principle accounting for the asymmetry is of a more technical nature, requiring a formally more elaborate analysis and description. To follow the argument, therefore, you will have to raise your level of concentration a little and switch off your TV.

Bowerman (1988) discusses this problem in detail, arguing that the problematic lack of negative evidence in this case is of a language-specific nature, so that UPG cannot be of help in ruling out ungrammatical occurrences. Her argument pertains to cases in English where the internal dative is ungrammatical despite the rule, allegedly valid for English, that datives may alternate between an internal dative, as in *John gave Mary a book*, and an external dative, as in *John gave a book to Mary*.[20] Thus, with the verb *donate*, the internal dative is barred:

(3.10)   a. She donated her fortune to the Church.
         b. *She donated the Church her fortune.

Many other verbs behave in a similar way. We have, for example, *say, demonstrate, reveal, assign, explain, whisper, relate, propose, advise, devote, dedicate, dispatch, transfer, let* (to a tenant), and many more. Assuming a meaning-preserving transformation rule of *Dative Movement* in the syntax of English, whereby external datives are transformed into internal datives, Bowerman wonders (1988: 75): 'how does [the child] learn that *say, demonstrate*, etc. are exceptions to the rule?'

The answer to the question is not simple. In the following few pages I will show that, on the assumption of an innate universal machinery, all the child has to do to exclude sentences like (3.10b) from the grammar is decide that *donate* and the other members of that class are two-place predicates and not three-place predicates such as *give, offer, write, lend, hand, sell, read, refuse, telegraph*, and many others. This (non-conscious) decision has many consequences, some of which are discussed below and all or most of which have never been noted in the literature. The learning task is thus seen to be enormously facilitated, but only on the assumption of a fairly complex

---

[20] Bowerman does not discuss cases where the opposite holds: only internal and no external datives, as with the verb *ask*, as in *I asked the man a question* versus **I asked a question to the man*, or with expressions like *give a kiss*, as in *John gave Mary a kiss* versus **John gave a kiss to Mary*. See Green (1974) for extensive discussion.

innate machinery, whose details cannot be described without a certain amount of technicality.

I argue, first, that the assumption of a meaning-preserving Dative Movement rule for English and similar languages had better be given up. The facts seem to be accounted for more adequately by the assumption that in English and related languages there are two classes of verbs of 'giving', a class of *two-place verbs*, such as *donate*, which take an obligatory subject and direct object, but no indirect object, and a class of *three-place verbs*, such as *give*, which take an obligatory subject and direct object, and an optional indirect object. The external dative with verbs of the *give*-class is analysed as a two-argument use of the verbs in question plus a prepositional phrase (PP) representing a semantic operator over a nuclear Matrix structure. Internal—that is, argument—datives are, if I am not mistaken, always optional in English and in almost all cases the 'beneficiary' role they express can be expressed differently, mostly by means of a peripheral PP under the preposition *to*. An exception is the verb *ask* (see note 20) which does not allow for rephrasing in terms of a peripheral PP under *to*. This exception is peculiar to English; Dutch, for example, does allow for an external dative with *vragen* ('ask').[21]

The terms of this description are applicable to other languages, which, however, differ considerably in the details. German has no external dative for the three-argument verbs of the *give*-class, only for the two-argument verbs of the *donate*-class (though this restriction is being relaxed in modern spoken German). In French, Italian and Modern Greek, the verbs of 'giving' form one single class allowing for a three-argument structure only when the (internal) dative is pronominal and not flanked by a first- or second-person or third-person reflexive direct-object pronoun. In all other cases these verbs take a two-argument structure, non-pronominal datives being obligatorily expressed by means of an external prepositional phrase. The pronominal internal datives are then cliticized (for a detailed analysis see Seuren 2009b). (These facts would again raise the 'no negative evidence' problem unless seen to follow from a presumed—probably extrinsic—feature of UPG.) Some, in particular Creole, languages, have no internal datives at all, expressing the beneficiary role by means of a serial verb construction (Seuren 1991) under a serial verb of 'giving' which then normally develops into a preposition meaning 'to': 'John sold a book *give* Mary'. Such facts suggest that in UPG indirect-object argument terms have a weak status, in

---

[21] The reason may be that in English the dative under *ask* is not interpreted as expressing a 'beneficiary' role but, as in French and other Romance languages, as expressing the opposite, a role in which the argument NP (here the indirect object) is the giver while the subject is the beneficiary. In the Romance languages, the dative is also used for that 'non-beneficiary' role, as appears from the fact that the dative is regular for verbs of 'taking', such as (French) *prendre* ('take') or *voler* ('steal'): *Il m'a pris dix dollars* ('he took ten dollars from me'; *Il a pris dix dollars à ma tante* ('he took ten dollars from my aunt'). How English children get to 'know' that the indirect object with *ask* is to be interpreted that way, is indeed a difficult question, an instance of the 'no negative evidence' problem.

the sense that a language can do without them, expressing the 'beneficiary' role in other ways that do not imply argument status.

The assumption of a semantic operator status of the external dative is motivated by the fact that close observation reveals subtle semantic differences between internal and external datives. Consider the following sentence pairs, with the verbs *leave*, *offer* and *pay a visit*, which allow for both kinds of dative:

(3.11)   a. She left her fortune to the Church.
        b. She left the Church her fortune.

(3.12)   a. She left two hundred pounds to me.
        b. She left me two hundred pounds.

(3.13)   a. He offered his services to the king.
        b. He offered the king his services.

(3.14)   a. She paid a visit to her native village.
        b. She paid her native village a visit.

The (a)-sentences all present the acts described as something honourable or ceremonial. The (b)-sentences, by contrast, are more neutral in this respect, allowing for a less honourable interpretation of the acts described. Note that (3.11b) sounds perfectly normal when changed into *She left me her books*, and (3.14b) when changed into *She paid her son a visit*. (3.12a) could be said by a person who is proud to have inherited such a large sum, whereas (3.12b) may be said by a speaker who finds two hundred pounds a pittance. (3.13a), again, describes an honourable act, but (3.13b) is easily open to a somewhat more suspect, or perhaps even louche, interpretation. (3.14a), describes an act of piety or of a somewhat ceremonial nature, whereas (3.14b) is clearly inappropriate for such an act. This accords with the general fact that peripheral prepositional phrases (PPPs) tend to bestow greater dignity on the prepositional object referent than regular arguments to their referents. Thus, *I shook hands with the President* is more appropriate for me to say than *The President shook hands with me*, and *Hubert loves God* is more appropriate than *God is loved by Hubert* (McCawley 1970: 292), even though the members of each pair are logically equivalent.

The explanation I favour is that PPPs represent semantic operators over the lexical Matrix clause which contains the main predicate and its arguments (see Seuren 1969, where the Matrix clause is called 'Nucleus'). Impressionistically speaking, one might say that the operator status of PPPs makes them take a certain distance from the predicate-argument Matrix structure of the sentence, which might be taken to explain why they bestow a certain dignity on the prepositional object referent. More formally, it is observed that external datives behave like all other PPPs in that they are scope-sensitive, though they are so in a specific way, different from other scope-sensitive sentence constituents. In general, sentence-final peripheral PPs make for scope-ambiguity, whereas sentence-initial PPPs do not, under non-contrastive intonation. Consider the following examples:[22]

(3.15) a. I gave two books to nobody.
        b. To nobody did I give two books.
        c. I gave nobody two books.

(3.16) a. I read two poems every morning.
        b. Every morning I read two poems.

(3.17) a. I didn't go home because of the rain.
        b. Because of the rain I didn't go home.

The three (a)-sentences are scope-ambiguous, whereas the (b)-sentences and (3.15c) are not (under non-contrastive intonation). (3.15a) means either 'there are two books that I gave to nobody' or 'there is nobody I gave two books to'. (3.15b) and (3.15c) can only mean the latter. Analogously, (3.16a) can mean either 'there are two specific poems that I read every morning' or 'every morning there are two poems (not necessarily the same ones) that I read'. (3.16b) can only mean the latter. And, again, (3.17a) can mean either 'it is not the case that it was because of the rain that I went home' or 'it was because of the rain that I did not go home'. (3.17b) can only mean the latter. (To illustrate the force of logico-semantic scope in surface structure, one may consider the somewhat artificial sentence *Not because of the rain did I go home*, which is again unambiguous and means 'it is not the case that it was because of the rain that I went home'.) These facts are not generally taken into account in language acquisition research (or indeed in linguistics generally), but if they were, they would again raise the 'no negative evidence' problem in that there is nothing in the data offered to the language-learning child to support such an interpretative distinction.

Why should this be so? In my analysis, which originates in Seuren (1969), the reason lies in the fact that *not*, *two books* and *somebody* in (3.15), *two poems* and *every morning* in (3.16), and *because of* and *not* in (3.17) represent *scope-sensitive logico-semantic operators*, standing over a lexical *Matrix clause* in a scope hierarchy in the semantic analyses (SAs) of their sentences. Logicians have taught us to write the

---

[22] These scope differences are denied in model-theoretic formal semantics, for the simple reason that the formal apparatus used is unable to account for them. To support their view, formal semanticists make liberal use of allegedly pragmatic contrastive intonation patterns, which are in fact accounted for, like quite a few other phenomena, by different underlying topic-comment structures and are demonstrably not pragmatic but semantic (see Seuren 2010: 378–408). The scope differences in question are, however, linguistically real, as appears, for example, from a sentence like *Some books were not sold*, which is in no way interpretable as 'it is not the case that any books were sold'—that is, as equivalent to *No books were sold*. Another example is (3.15b), which is not open to the interpretation 'there are two books that I gave to nobody', no matter what contrastive intonation one tries to force on it. The interpretation 'there are two books that I gave to nobody', for an English sentence where *nobody* precedes *two books*, is possible only without aux-inversion, as in the heavily marked *To nobody I gave two books*.

operator with the highest scope in leftmost position, followed by the operator with one-but-highest scope, etc. If we apply this natural convention to the cases at hand, the last element will be the Matrix clause, which contains the main predicate plus its arguments (whereby the predicate (verb) stands in initial, middle or final position, depending on the language type). The grammar of a language is taken to contain a machinery that incorporates the operators into the Matrix clause in a cyclic way: the lowest operator is incorporated, or lowered, first, then the one-but-lowest, and so on, till the highest operator has been lowered. At the end, if no obstacles are met (see below), the Matrix clause has incorporated all higher operators. In Seuren (2004a: 195–6), this universal tendency in the grammars of all languages is called *Matrix Greed* (see (3.32) in section 3.8.1 below; see also section 4.4 for a discussion of the basic machinery of operator lowering).

Most operators, in particular the negation and the quantifiers, are *strongly scope-sensitive*. Others, such as prepositional operators, are only *weakly scope-sensitive*. The lowering of strongly scope-sensitive operators is subject to the universal *Scope-Ordering Constraint* (SOC), which says that, in principle, *higher-scope operators precede lower-scope operators in the syntax (not the morphology) of surface structure* (Seuren 1985: 143; 1996: 304–9). (SOC is probably motivated by Hawkins-type processing factors, since scope is semantically essential and needs to be marked in surface structure. And what is more natural than having the highest operator come first in the flow of speech?) A strongly scope-sensitive operator, once lowered, is thus 'flagged' in the Matrix clause in a way that can be formally written as a numerical (superscript) index. In principle, any lower index has to stay to the left of its higher-indexed predecessor, as shown in the analyses given below. At the same time, however, quantifying operators, which bind a variable in the Matrix clause, are obliged to 'land' in the position of the variable bound by them. And this position is defined by the syntax of the Matrix clause.

This may lead to conflicts. In English, for example, when an existentially quantified direct object has scope over the negation, the derivation aborts, because the negation has to stay with the finite verb, which has to precede the direct object. An SA of the form 'there is a candidate x such that it is not the case that I know x' cannot be processed by the normal English operator-lowering system and a periphrastic solution must be found, such as *There is a candidate I don't know*. Not so in Dutch or German, where the negation normally follows the direct object. There we have sentences like (Dutch) *Ik ken een kandidaat niet* or (German) *Ich kenne einen Kandidaten nicht*, which are processed in the normal way by the lowering machinery.

Some operators are prepositional (postpositional, according to the language concerned). They turn up as a prepositional (postpositional) phrase in surface structure, where they tend to occupy a left-peripheral or right-peripheral position, becoming a PPP. *To nobody* in (3.15a,b), *every morning* in (3.16a,b) and *because of the rain* in (3.17a,b) are PPPs (*every morning* is taken to contain a tacit preposition indicating position in time). The crucial point is that PPPs by themselves—that is, when they contain no strongly scope-sensitive operators and thus only definite noun phrases or variables in prepositional object position—are *weakly scope-sensitive*, which means that they have the privilege to override SOC in certain ways in surface structure (but, it seems, with certain prosodic consequences). To account for this complication, we introduce the following *PPP-statute*, which is more complex than it need be, owing to the fact that the lowering statute for variable-binding operators (quantifiers) has not been specified earlier. ('OP_w' stands for 'weakly scope-sensitive operator'; 'OP_s' for 'strongly scope-sensitive operator'.)

PPP-statute:

An OP_w may freely cross any operators lowered earlier and then attract any higher variable-binding OP_s that has to land inside it owing to variable binding. But an OP_s to be lowered later may not cross an OP_w lowered earlier, unless the higher OP_s binds a variable whose position it has to reach. The PPP-statute is cancelled and SOC applies again in full force as soon as the PPP resulting from an OP_w has attracted a flagged OP_s.

This means that:

(a) An OP_w is allowed to ignore the flagging of any OP_s lowered earlier but may not be ignored by any OP_s to be lowered later, unless OP_s has to land in the position of the variable bound by it. Having been lowered, an OP_w may freely attract a higher variable-binding OP_s that is obliged to land inside the OP_w owing to variable binding.

(b) A higher variable-binding OP_s that is obliged to land across a PPP owing to variable binding is allowed to ignore the flagging of that PPP but not of any OP_s that has landed inside it.

(Possibly, the high-peripheral status of PPPs in surface structure lies at the bottom of the licence to violate SOC: PPPs are only peripherally attached high up in their surface structure main clause and thus have greater freedom to 'swivel around' than flagged elements somewhere down the middle of the tree structure.)

PPPs are thus not flagged by means of a numerical superscript in the normal way. Instead, I give them the superscript flagging 'PPP' which indicates that they fall under the PPP-statute.

SOC is restricted to the syntax. It appears not to apply in respect of morphological elements, although further detailed study in this regard is called for. Thus, when English *not* is morphologically united with the existential quantifier *somebody*, giving *nobody*, as, for example, in (3.19d) below, SOC may be overridden.[23]

---

[23] In Seuren (2010: 114–21) I argue that, in natural language, the negative quantifiers *no, nothing, nobody* etc. are non-complex, primitive negative quantifiers. If that position is taken, the derivational processes sketched below are simplified.

Under these conditions, sentence (3.15a) must be seen to be derivable from either (3.18a) or (3.18b), but (3.15b) from (3.18a) only, whereas (3.15c) must be derivable from (3.18c) only, not from (3.18d). I use 'for some' and 'for two' to express the existential quantifier, also often expressed as 'there is/are.' The subscript M stands for 'Matrix clause':

(3.18)   a. $_{OP_1}$[not $_{OP_2}$[for some person x $_{OP_3}$[for two books y $_{OP_4}$[to x $_M$[give (I, y)]]]]]
        b. $_{OP_1}$[for two books y $_{OP_2}$[not $_{OP_3}$[for some person x $_{OP_4}$ [to x $_M$[give (I, y)]]]]]
        c. $_{OP_1}$[not $_{OP_2}$[for some person x $_{OP_3}$[for two books y $_M$[give(I, x, y)]]]]
        d. $_{OP_1}$[for two books y $_{OP_2}$[not $_{OP_3}$[for some person x $_M$[give(I, x, y)]]]]

The structures in (3.18) are actually right-branching constituent tree structures. Figure 3.1 shows the tree structures corresponding to (3.18a) and (3.19a), thus illustrating the lowering process of OP_4 of (3.18a) into the Matrix clause. Whoever should wish to rewrite all structures and operations on them involved in the analysis given here in terms of tree structures is encouraged to do so. In the present context, however, we will do without that luxury. One notes that all structures are right-branching. I assume provisionally that this is universal, also for verb-final languages, whose verb-final nature is expressed in the verb-final position of V in the Matrix clause. It is possible also, however, to map the whole machinery onto a left-branching 'mirror' system. Which of the two is preferable is a question I leave open here.

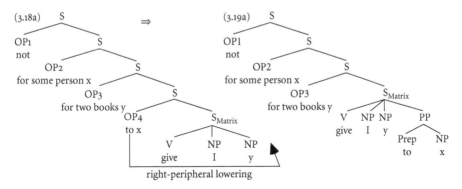

FIGURE 3.1 Constituent tree structures corresponding to (3.18a) and (3.19a), illustrating the lowering of OP_4 into the Matrix clause

One notes that the verb *give* in (3.18a) and (3.18b) has two arguments, the subject *I* and the direct object *y*, whereas in (3.18c) it has three arguments, the subject *I*, the indirect object *x* and the direct object *y*. This implies that *give* is listed in the mental lexicon as occurring with either two or three arguments, the optional argument being the indirect object. There is thus no Dative Movement rule. The so-called external dative represents a prepositional operator under the preposition *to*, which is lowered into the Matrix clause.

Let us first derive (3.15a) from (3.18a) (ignoring tense). The lowering process is cyclic, which means that the operator closest to the Matrix clause is incorporated first, and so on. Prepositional operators are incorporated into either a left-peripheral or a right-peripheral position in the Matrix clause. To get (3.15a) we let OP_4 be lowered to the right-peripheral position, as in (3.19a). The resulting peripheral prepositional phrase is flagged by the superscript PPP. Then OP_3 is lowered, giving (3.19b). No problem here: *two books$_3$* stays before *to x^{PPP}*. Now we lower OP_2, giving (3.19c). This apparent violation of SOC is permitted because the PP *to x^{PPP}* represents a prepositional operator, which, on account of the PPP-statute, allows higher operators that must be incorporated into it owing to variable binding to ignore the flagging of operators lowered earlier. (3.19d) is legitimate because it results from the morphological unification of *not* with the existential quantifier *some person*:

(3.19)   a. $_{OP1}$[not $_{OP2}$[for some person x $_{OP3}$[for two books y $_M$[give(I, y to x^{PPP})]]]]
         b. $_{OP1}$[not $_{OP2}$[for some person x $_M$[give(I, two books^3 to x^{PPP})]]]
         c. $_{OP1}$[not $_M$[give(I, two books^3 [to a person^2]^{PPP})]]
         d. $_M$[give(I, two books^3 [to not^1-a-person^2]^{PPP})]

The rest of the grammar then gives (3.15a). Note that the grammar also allows for (3.20), where the negation has not been morphologized but has gone with the finite verb, as usual:

(3.20)   I did not^1 give two books^2 to anybody^3.

Here, however, the meaning represented by (3.18b) is excluded for the same reason that aborted 'there is a candidate *x* such that it is not the case that I know *x*' from becoming a non-periphrastic English sentence. SOC requires that the negation of (3.18b) comes after *two books*, which is possible only if the negation is morphologically united with 'a person'. Without such morphological unification, English grammar requires the negation to go with the finite verb, which comes before *two books*.

   Now derive (3.15a) from the input structure (3.18b). First, OP_4 is lowered, giving (3.21a). Then, lowering of OP_3 gives (3.21b). Lowering of OP_2 (the negation *not*) to a morphologizing position gives (3.21c). (Non-morphologized, the result is (3.21c'), which, however, has no future because OP_1 cannot be lowered, owing to SOC.) The lowering of OP_1 gives (3.21d), which is again further processed to end up as (3.15a).

(3.21)   a. $_{OP1}$[for two books y $_{OP2}$[not $_{OP3}$[for some person x $_M$[give(I, y to x^{PPP})]]]]
         b. $_{OP1}$[for two books y $_{OP2}$[not $_M$[give(I, y [to a person^3]^{PPP})]]]
         c. $_{OP1}$[for two books y $_M$[give(I, y [to not^2-a-person^3]^{PPP})]]
         (c' $_{OP1}$[for two books y $_M$[not^2 give(I, y [to a person^3]^{PPP})]])
         d. $_M$[give(I, two books^1 [to not^1-a-person^2]^{PPP})]

This accounts for the ambiguity of (3.15a). A similar analysis accounts for the ambiguity of (3.16a). (3.17a) with high scope for *because of the rain* is accounted for by the PPP-statute. Note that the PPP *because of the rain* in (3.17a,b) contains no strongly scope-sensitive operator and is thus only weakly scope-sensitive.

We now pass on to (3.15b) and show why (3.15b) can only be derived from (3.18a) and not from (3.18b). To get (3.15b) from (3.18a), we repeat the process shown in (3.19a–d), but now with the PP *to x* lowered left-peripherally, as in (3.22a). (3.22b) is permitted on account of the PPP-statute because *to x* is a PPP not containing a flagged operator and OP_3 has to reach the y-position in the Matrix clause. Lowering of OP_2 gives (3.22c), which is further processed into (3.15b):

(3.22)   a. $_{OP_1}$[not $_{OP_2}$[for some person x $_{OP_3}$[for two books y $_M$[to x^{PPP} give (I, y)]]]]
          b. $_{OP_1}$[not $_{OP_2}$[for some person x $_M$[to x^{PPP} give(I, two books^3)]]]
          c. $_{OP_1}$[not $_M$[[to a person^2]^{PPP} give(I, two books^3)]]
          d. $_M$[[to not^1-a-person^2]^{PPP} give(I, two books^3)]

The derivation of (3.15b) from (3.18b) is blocked, as is shown as follows. The lowering of the operators 4, 3 and 2 takes place without any problem, giving (3.23a), (3.23b) and (3.23c) respectively. Then, however, OP_1 has no choice but to be lowered into the position of the variable bound by it, which violates SOC. Hence, (3.23d) is blocked and the derivation is aborted:

(3.23)   a. $_{OP_1}$[for two books y $_{OP_2}$[not $_{OP_3}$[for some person x $_M$[to x^{PPP} give (I, y)]]]]
          b. $_{OP_1}$[for two books y $_{OP_2}$[not $_M$[[to a person^3]^{PPP} give(I, y)]]]
          c. $_{OP_1}$[for two books y $_M$[[to not^2-a-person^3]^{PPP} give(I, y)]]
          d.   ***$_M$[[to not^2-a-person^3]^{PPP} give(I, two books^1)]

(3.15b) is thus not scope-ambiguous, as (3.15a) is, but can only mean 'there is nobody that I gave two books to'. (3.16b) is likewise unambiguous, meaning 'every morning there are two poems (not necessarily the same ones) that I read'. Likewise for (3.17b), which can only mean 'because of the rain it was not the case that I went home'.

The derivation of (3.15c) is as follows. We will see that (3.15c) can only be derived from (3.18c), not from (3.18b). The input structure for (3.15c) we will try out first is (3.18c). The first operator to be lowered is OP_3. The lowering results in (3.24a). Now OP_2 is to be lowered, giving (3.24b), which corresponds with (3.15c) or (3.24d) corresponding with *I didn't give anybody two books*. No problems here: SOC has been fully observed:

(3.24)   a. $_{OP_1}$[not $_{OP_2}$[for some person x $_M$[give(I, x, two books^3)]]]
          b. $_{OP_1}$[not $_M$[give(I, a person^2, two books^3)]]
          c. $_M$[give(I, not^1-a-person^2, two books^3)]
          d. $_M$[not^1 give(I, a person^2, two books^3)]

As is easily seen, an attempt at deriving (3.15c) from (3.18d) is doomed owing to an SOC violation in the lowering of OP_1 'for two books y', which would have to land across the two operators lowered earlier.

Further confirmation for the analysis presented above comes from cases like (3.25a,b) or (3.26a,b):

(3.25) a. The sheriff of Nottingham jailed Robin Hood for two years.
        b. For two years the sheriff of Nottingham jailed Robin Hood.

(3.26) a. I lent him my bicycle for six weeks.
        b. For six weeks I lent him my bicycle.

Again, the (a)-sentences are scope-ambiguous in a way the (b)-sentences are not. (3.25a) can mean either (3.27a) or (3.27b), but (3.25b) can only mean the latter:

(3.27) a. [the sheriff of Nottingham caused [for two years [Robin Hood be in jail]]]
        b. [for two years [the sheriff of Nottingham caused [Robin Hood be in jail]]]

Likewise, (3.26a) can mean either (3.28a) or (3.28b), but (3.26b) can only mean the latter:

(3.28) a. [I allowed [for six weeks [he use my bicycle]]]
        b. [for six weeks [I allowed [he use my bicycle]]]

The same explanation applies here as was given for (3.15) and (3.16) above, except that here we must assume an internal lexical analysis for the verbs *jail* and *lend*, which are taken to contain the internal lexical elements 'cause-to-be-in-jail' and 'allow-to-use', respectively. I will not go into the precise details here, but the general idea is that the 'abstract' predicates *cause* and *allow* function as strongly scope-sensitive operators and the prepositional operators giving *for two years* and *for six weeks* are taken to occur either inside or outside the scope of *cause* and *allow*, respectively.

What, then, is the upshot of this long, technical story? The upshot is that the absence of an internal dative with verbs of the *donate*-class is not part of the 'no negative evidence' problem. We are not dealing with exceptions to a rule but with manifestations of two different argument structures. All the language-learning child has to do—well below awareness, of course—to be able to mark sentences like *She dispatched her cousin a letter* as ungrammatical and sentences like *She sent her cousin a letter* as grammatical is to classify verbs like *dispatch* as two-place predicates but verbs like *send* as three-place predicates. All the rest is done automatically by the inbuilt machinery the child is equipped with *in nucleo* at birth. External datives are not part of the argument structure of the verbs concerned but are peripheral prepositional phrases (PPPs) representing higher operators to be lowered cyclically into the Matrix clause, in virtue of universal Matrix Greed, according to the Scope-Ordering Constraint (SOC). The evidence for this analysis consists in the fact that the lowering of operators underlying PPPs, including external datives, is subject to a special asymmetrical *PPP-statute*. External datives thus fit into a general analysis of PPPs with all the consequences thereof. The task of assigning the correct argument structure to verbs does not seem too hazardous, especially because the machinery itself will require the child to fill in the blanks, so to speak.

Here we have a case where it can be shown in a detailed and formally precise way how a hidden machinery interfaces with the infant user in a maximally functional and user-friendly way, merely asking the child to fill in a few blanks. The machinery thus not only accounts for a collection of apparently unrelated data, which by themselves would have raised the 'no negative evidence' problem if they had been observed, it is also seen to be extremely user-friendly, since the learning child does not have to bother at all about what goes on 'below the bonnet'.

The solution offered is thus of a 'lexicalist' nature. Bowerman (1988) criticizes earlier 'lexicalist' proposals for not being able to account for children's well-known overgeneralization of provisionally postulated rules of grammar. While this criticism may apply to the earlier proposals she refers to—I won't go into that here—it does not seem to hold for the analysis presented above, for the simple reason that as long as the child has not settled on the proper argument-structure assignment to the verbs involved, illicit internal datives will occur.

Is it preposterous to postulate such a complex machinery to explain the natural, apparently preprogrammed process of first-language acquisition? Only if the complexity of language or the programmatic nature of first-language acquisition are underestimated, as they often are in relativist circles. Otherwise, such a postulation is as preposterous as it is to postulate a complex machinery underlying, say, perspectival vision, or as it would have been in times past to postulate the complex machinery of the middle and inner ear in order to explain acoustic sound discrimination. One may, if one wishes, compare the situation to that of a person who knows well how to operate a computer but has no idea of what goes on behind the screen. How preposterous would it be for such a person to postulate a complex machinery needed to link his keyboard and mouse actions with the computer's performance?

Given the extreme complexity of the language machinery as a whole, the 'hidden-machine' view must have a certain appeal and it is, therefore, unclear to me why there should be so much resistance to it. If carried out with the care and caution required in all academic work, the research programme delineated by this approach should be pursued with spirited enthusiasm.

3.7.2.3 English zero-causatives and un-*verbs: a universal theory of the lexicon?*   Two further classes of cases where Bowerman (1988) spots the 'no negative evidence' problem are English zero-causatives and English *un*-verbs. Zero-causatives are verbs occurring not only intransitively but also transitively in a causative meaning without any morphological change. *Un*-verbs are verbs (not adjectives or adjectival past participles) with the prefix *un*-. The two classes have in common that they are productive under certain semantic criteria (which are, however, hard to define) but with odd-looking exceptions—as is typical for settling phenomena. The problem is: how do children manage to identify the exceptions if their learning takes place in terms of (semantic) rules or regularities based on evidence presented?

To see the problem with greater clarity, we must have a somewhat closer look at the facts, which look rather messy, despite some overall regularities. First, there is the presumably universal *Monomorphemic Alternative Priority Principle* (MAPP), which says that when there is a monomorphemic alternative, such as *kill* for 'cause-to-die' or *raise* for 'cause-to-rise', zero-causativization does not take place. This may be taken to be unproblematic for the language-learning child, even though instances of *die* for *kill* do occur, up to a certain age, in child language corpora (Bowerman 1988: 80).

Then, causatives often cover different, usually more restricted, semantic ground from their non-causative counterparts. Thus, intransitive *grow* has a wider range of possible uses than causative *grow*: you don't grow children or horses, but you do grow plants or cattle. Similarly for *trot*, whose causative uses are restricted to idioms (*He trotted out an excuse*) or to horses as object referents. *Gallop* and *jump* can be used causatively only with regard to horses (**That jumped me*). Causative *fly* is restricted to transport by air and in a restricted causative meaning (*He flew me to Boston*, but **That flew the bird*). Causative *hang* has different forms for the past tense and the past participle, according to whether it means 'execute by hanging' (*The executioner hanged the murderer*) or 'cause to hang for decorative purposes' (*I hung the picture over the mantle piece*). But one also says *hang a gallery* (with paintings). Causative *dare* (*He dared me to contradict him*) is not quite the same as 'cause-to-dare'. In fact, it comes closer to 'cause-not-to-dare'.

Conversely, intransitives may be more restricted in their use than causatives. The verb *build*, for example, has a rather restricted range of intransitive uses (*Pressure is building on the Prime Minister*), which the more normal causative *build* does not share (**Parliament is building pressure on the Prime Minister*).

Third, causatives often incorporate an inchoative intransitive 'come about', as in the case of *write, draw, build* or *put together*.[24] *John is drawing a circle* is then interpreted as 'John is causing a circle to come about by drawing'. This is generally so for verbs of production, often referred to by the German term *effizierend* (the object comes about as a result of the action described in the verb). A special case is the verb *mount*, which, as a causative, means 'cause-to-come-about-by-mounting'. Yet it also has a non-causative transitive use, as in *He mounted the platform*, which is thus ambiguous between 'he climbed up to the platform' and 'he caused the platform to come about by mounting'. Here, causative *mount* is not the causative of non-

---

[24] There is also a 'bicausative' use of *build* meaning 'cause to cause to come about by building, as in *The City Council is building a community centre over there*, meaning 'the Council is causing (a builder) to cause a community centre to come about by building'.

causative *mount*. Another special case is the verb *grow* as when you say of a man that he is *growing a beard*. In a way, this *grow* is *effizierend* but the incorporated higher predicate is not *cause* but, rather, *allow*. And when you say of an adolescent male that he is *growing hair on his upper lip*, even *allow* won't do, as it is simply happening to him, whether he likes it or not.

Then, some intransitives simply lack a causative version. Thus, the intransitive *look good* has no causative: **That will look you good*. Likewise for the verbs *go*, *laugh*, *vomit*, *limp*, *squint* and others. Other idiosyncrasies, and thus pitfalls for language-learning children, are easily found. Problems galore.

That lexicons differ from grammars in that they are less rule-governed and contain more idiosyncratic exceptions has been known for a long time. Bloomfield went so far as to say (1933: 274): 'The lexicon is really an appendix of the grammar, a list of basic irregularities.' Since Bloomfield we have learned that the lexicon also contains many regularities, but it remains true that such regularities do not allow for reliable *predictions*; they can only be established *retrodictively*, which will make it hard for the young child to detect exactly where in the lexicon formal and semantic regularities stop. The child may be helped by an innate 'knowledge' of the categories that are operative in the lexicon, but it will have a hard job determining where lines have to be drawn. It is thus not surprising that full lexical competence comes late in the language acquisition process.

Bowerman is right, therefore, in recognizing the 'no negative evidence' problem all over the lexicon. She attempts to detect semantic regularities for zero-causative formation, but has to admit that in many cases English simply goes its own way. Her tentative criteria include (Bowerman 1988: 85):

... 'cause of a change of physical state' (*open, melt, shatter* ...), 'cause of motion in a particular manner' (*float, roll, bounce* ...), 'coerced or encouraged locomotion in a particular manner' (*walk, gallop, run, jump* [your horse] ...) and 'enabling and accompanying of willful transportation in some manner' (*fly, boat, motor* [someone to New York] ...). [Causativization] does *not* apply to verbs specifying 'motion in a direction' (cf. **I went my son to school*; **I rose the flag*) and verbs of 'internally caused acts' (**Bill vomited Jill, *Fred laughed the baby, *John died Harry*), although there may be suppletive forms with the same meaning (*I took my son to school, I raised the flag, John killed Harry*), and some verbs are 'positive exceptions', in that they causativize even though they belong to a class whose members in general do not (*Mom burped the baby*, 'internally caused act'; *Mary dropped the ball*, 'motion in a direction').

Further exceptions are not too hard to find. *The wind drifted the ship to the shore* or *The wind headed us south* violate the 'motion in a direction' criterion—unless they fall under 'coerced locomotion', in which case they stand for 'cause-to-go in a particular manner'. *Wake up, fatten, bleed, swell* seem to violate the 'internally caused acts' criterion. And so on. Yet Bowerman is right in seeking semantic generalizations, since productivity of zero-causativization is clearly channelled through and restricted by intuitive semantic criteria. Certain causatives 'feel right' whereas others have a totally unnatural 'feel' about them.

An analogous story can be told about *un*-verbs. According to Whorf (1956: 71), *un*-verbs share 'a covering, enclosing, and surface-attaching meaning [...]. Hence we say "uncover, uncoil, undress, unfasten, unfold, unlock, unroll, untangle, untie, unwind", but not "unbreak, undry, unhang, unheat, unlift, unmelt, unopen, unpress, unspill".' Again, we find a combination of semantic regularity and irregularity. *Unbalance, unbend, unsettle, unhang* (which, *pace* Whorf, does occur, as in *unhang a door*), *unhook* appear to contradict Whorf's criterion, just as Shakespeare's *un-provoke* (in the famous drunken porter scene in *Macbeth* II, iii, 29–31: 'Lechery, sir, it provokes, and unprovokes. It provokes the desire, but it takes away the perform-ance.'). By contrast, one would expect verbs like **unjoin, *unfit, *unroof,* which do not exist. **Unfill, *unclose, *unshut, *unsqueeze* (Bowerman 1988: 84) can perhaps be explained by an appeal to MAPP, since English has *empty, open* and *loosen,* respect-ively, as monomorphemic alternatives.

The case of zero-causatives and that of *un*-verbs are not too dissimilar from that of locative prepositions in different languages (see section 2.4.2.1), or of Dutch locative verbs (see section 1.2.5). In all such cases we are dealing with, on the one hand, certain discernible semantic patterns that seem to be definable in terms of bundles of (universal) cognitive features and, on the other, with idiosyncrasies cutting through the semantic patterns. It seems to me that such a state of affairs, which is typical for the lexicons of all languages, is adequately described as the result of *settling*, as discussed in Chapter 1. The lexicon is the primary repository of settling phenomena.

How the child manages to acquire full competence of the language in this respect is a good question. I think the child gradually settles on the correct bundles of cognitive-semantic features at play but at the same time learns to accept incidental positive and negative infractions of the conditions defined by such bundles. The mastery of all the subtleties involved will then be the joint product of both the cognitive-semantic criteria and the incidental liberties taken with them and individu-ally recorded in the mental lexicon. But this is not good enough. That it is not good enough for the implementation of a computer learning program may be forgivable for the time being, but it is not good enough as an explanation in general.

For such cases as have been discussed, a theory of UPG will be of little use. One might, however, well think of a theory of the *universal principles of the lexicon,* or UPL. Given the serious embarrassment caused by the 'no negative evidence' problem, some theory of universal principles of the lexicon would seem to be potentially of great help. Equipped with an adequate UPL, the child will at least be able to expect what (s)he will be faced with. The child will then willingly accept what would otherwise be weird combinations of cognitive-semantic motivations behind lexical uses and regularities on the one hand and settling phenomena on the other. (S)he will then 'know' that lexical generalizations are less forceful than grammatical generalizations and that retrodiction is a more fruitful method in building up a lexicon than prediction. If Bowerman (1988) is to be criticized at all, it is because it considers only the possible role of a UPG, not that of a UPL yet to be developed.

There is already a large body of doctrine and general theory about the lexicon, but less than the much larger body of expertise built up by lexicographers. It would be a good thing if the lexicographers' expertise were made better use of in theoretical lexicology, which may then develop a respectable UPL that may be of help in solving the 'no negative evidence' problem.

3.8 Towards a general theory of human language

To ask 'Are there universals of language?' is asking the wrong question. The right question, as is argued in Jackendoff (2011: 587; see note 4 above), is: 'Can we develop a general theory of human language?' The proper implementation of such a theory will then tell us to what extent human language is unified and to what extent it is diverse—which is the real question. In developing such a theory a certain courage is not unwelcome: science is helped by daring, but responsible, generalizing proposals, which will then have to stand up to possible falsification. Let us see if we can mention a few new proposals, in addition to the many published in the literature.

3.8.1 *A few proposals for universal properties of languages and grammars*

It is not very likely that a universal theory of language will emerge without any rigid universals of language. In fact, it is almost impossible to talk about language without implying or positing universals. Even Evans and Levinson (2009) do so. For example, one absolutely valid universal property of human language, part of its conceptually necessary definition, is presented in Evans and Levinson (2009: 444): '[I]t is always possible in any language to express complex propositions.' This universal is proposed in the context of these authors' (correct) argument that the universal property of human language expressed by it does not entail that the *syntax* must have unrestricted recursion: recursion is not 'the criterial feature of the human language capacity' (p. 442). On the contrary, 'the generative power would seem to lie in the semantics/pragmatics or the conceptual structure in all languages, but only in some is it also a property of the syntax' (p. 443). Apart from the fact that it can hardly be the *pragmatics* of language or language use that has the power to generate complex propositions, this is one sensible contribution to the general theory of language—in full agreement with, for example, Levelt (1989) or Seuren (1985, 1996, 2009a), and of course, with the conceptually necessary universal (3.1) proposed in the present chapter (see also the end of section 6.3.2.1).

Another universal of great generality will be yielded by an answer to the question regarding the formal mathematical type natural language grammars belong to (see

Chapter 6). Are they finite state grammars or context-free phrase structure grammars or context-sensitive phrase structure grammars, or are they transformational—that is, not constrained by mathematical restrictions (though highly constrained by non-mathematical restrictions)? Readers familiar with my work will know that I take the view that natural language grammars are transformational by conceptual necessity but constrained by non-mathematical, empirical restrictions such as have been proposed by typologists and theoretical linguists. Many, however, still cling to the idea that they belong to one of the three remaining types.

A further, very well-known, contribution, of a more detailed and technical nature (not discussed in Evans and Levinson 2009), is the *Keenan-Comrie Relative Accessibility Hierarchy* (RAH), proposed in Keenan and Comrie (1977) and Comrie and Keenan (1979). This proposed universal, which has not so far met with counter-evidence, says that non-resumptive relative clauses—that is, relative clauses with full relative pronouns, not a relative particle plus a resumptive pronoun, as, for example, in Demotic Arabic—show a hierarchical ranking in that some languages allow only for subject relativization, as in (3.29a), others also for direct-object relativization, as in (3.29b), others again also for indirect-object and prepositional-object relativization, as in (3.29c), and finally others also for genitive-relativization, as in (3.29d):[25]

(3.29)   a. the man who sold the woman the house
          b. the house which the man sold (to) the woman
          c. the woman (to) whom the man sold the house
          d. the man whose father sold the woman the house

The Relative Accessibility Hierarchy states that if a language L has genitive-relativization, it also has internal or external indirect-object relativization; if L has indirect-object and/or prepositional-object relativization, it also has direct-object relativization; if L has direct-object-relativization, it also has subject-relativization. Or:

(3.30)   **The Keenan-Comrie Relative Accessibility Hierarchy (RAH):**
          SU ⊃ DO ⊃ IO ⊃ GEN ⊃ . . . . . .

RAH amounts to saying that genitive-relativization is more marked (in the sense of Greenberg 1966) than indirect-object and/or prepositional-object relativization, which is more marked than direct-object relativization, which is more marked than subject-relativization.

If we are lucky, RAH will be a specific instance of a more general putative universal property of language, which I would call the *Predicate-Argument Hierarchy* or PAH, saying that all languages have subject arguments, some also have direct-object

---

[25] Non-resumptive relative clauses are relative clauses with relative pronouns linking up a nominal clause constituent with an antecedent, in contrast with relative clauses that start with a 'such-that' particle and replace the relativized nominal clause constituent with a resumptive pronoun.

arguments, some of these also have internal (dative) indirect objects, some of these also have morphological genitives—after which come further morphological cases as found in, for example, Latin or Finnish.

(3.31) **The Predicate-Argument Hierarchy (PAH):**[26]
SU ⊃ DO ⊃ IO ⊃ GEN ⊃ . . . . . .

Ergative languages only have subject terms. What are object terms in non-ergative languages are subject terms of intransitive-passive verbs in ergative languages. What are subject terms in transitive sentences of non-ergative languages are the equivalent of agent-phrases in ergative languages. The prediction is that ergative languages will have no case system beyond subject and ergative case. Ergative languages may de-ergativize and 'grow' direct object terms, as, possibly, in example (3.5) above of the Amazonian language Katukina-Kanamari discussed in section 3.6. Creole languages (see section 3.7.2.2 above), which have only subject and direct-object terms, tend to 'grow' first external indirect objects (via verb serialization) and then, in some cases, internal datives, starting with pronominal datives—though the dominant lexifier language may interfere with this development. Languages with case-marked datives, such as Latin or German, tend to drop external indirect objects. Modern Greek, which no longer has a case-marked dative (except for pronouns) but still has a case system, makes do with external indirect objects only (unless they are pronominal, in which case they are cliticized). There may thus be an implicational-developmental subsystem for indirect objects/datives, whereby case marking and/or pronominal status play a role.

The much-discussed typological proposals in Greenberg (1963) are to be taken very seriously, even if they are based on a relatively small sample of languages, mainly because they have proved to be extremely robust. Later writers, such as Comrie (1981), Stassen (1985, 1997, 2009), Dryer (1992, 2005a, 2005b, 2009) and many, many others have likewise put forward intriguing and sometimes highly refined typological universals, most of which have withstood falsification attempts till the present day. I cannot, in the present context, discuss this vast body of literature, built up by competent professionals, in any detail, but I can at least mention its existence.

Some universals, such as *Matrix Greed* and the related *Scope-Ordering Constraint*, are proposed in the present chapter:

(3.32) **Matrix Greed:**
In all languages, operators in the logico-semantic representations of sentences (quantifiers, negation, tenses, modalities, prepositional operators, adverbial clause operators, and possibly others) are lowered into the Matrix

---

[26] One notes the analogy with Greenberg (1966: 38), who proposed a markedness hierarchy in terms of frequency of occurrence for case-marked predicate arguments: NOM/ACC > DAT > . . . .

Clause containing the main lexical predicate and its argument terms. Each category of operators has its own lowering charter (quantifiers lower onto the variables bound by them, negation and tenses mostly lower on verbs, prepositional and adverbial clause operators mostly lower peripherally, etc.). When the grammar blocks lowering (for example, because of SOC), a logico-semantic periphrastic phrasing is required.

(3.33)   **Scope-Ordering Constraint (SOC):**
Higher-scope strongly scope-sensitive operators precede lower-scope strongly scope-sensitive operators in the syntax (not the morphology) of surface structure.

Some have wondered why there should be such a structural gap between surface structure and semantic analysis (SA) in natural language (Chomsky 1995: 317; 1998: 24; Seuren 2004a: 138–43, 162–4, 173–4; see also section 1.4 above on the heteromorphy problem). Why should conceptually motivated sentence structure manifest itself in the wildly diverging surface structures of the languages of the world? Why do we, as the human species, not speak in the language of predicate logic, with universal lexical items (differing only phonologically, the choice of phonological form being arbitrary, just as the choice of symbols is arbitrary in logic) for its lexical variables, given that predicate logic is 'the best instrument available so far for the systematic expression of both mathematical and truth-conditional content, as well as for the calculus of logical entailments', if I may quote myself (Seuren 2004a: 133)? This problem, which I have dubbed the *heteromorphy problem* (section 1.4), has not received a satisfactory answer so far, other than only partially convincing suggestions to the effect that such a universal logical language might make for non-optimal processing procedures ('facilitation of parsing on certain assumptions, the separation of theme-rheme structures from base-determined semantic (θ) relations, and so on'; Chomsky 1995: 317).

Part of the answer, it seems to me, may perhaps be found in a universal tendency to maximize the structural properties of the Matrix structure, consisting of the main lexical predicate and its argument terms, as opposed to the operators that stand over it in the underlying logical SA-structure. This tendency automatically leads to the lowering of the operators into the Matrix structure, which thus turns up in surface structure under a heavy load of operator material. This tendency of *Matrix Greed* is probably motivated mainly by factors of processing facility, though precise knowledge in this respect is still to be gained.

A collateral advantage is the fact that the lowering of operators opens up the possibility of more word or constituent classes than just 'S', 'NP', 'predicate', 'determiner' and 'variable'—the only categories needed for SA-structures—and thus allows them greater freedom to vary. As was said in Chapter 1, language not only serves the purpose of communication of intents (speech acts over propositions), but is also a primary means of social self-manifestation. This answer only needs to be partially correct for Matrix Greed to be a demonstration of the fact that settling processes are themselves subject to universal constraints: speakers do not 'settle' their languages arbitrarily but stay within certain pre-established constraints defined by UPG. Both Matrix Greed and SOC vividly demonstrate this.

In section 3.7.2.2 the *PPP-statute* is proposed as a universal principle (in the wake of SOC), mainly because it does not have to be taught and is thus not part of a grammatical description of any specific language but is operative in all languages, as far as is known. Is the PPP-statute an intrinsic or an extrinsic universal? I believe it is extrinsic, because even if it follows from, or fits into, a general UPG principle in virtue of which there is a trade-off between temporal precedence and high constituent status, it is not clear that such a principle, no matter how impressionistically plausible, is operative in general cognition.

In section 3.7.2.1, I propose the *Internal Definite Anaphora Principle* or IDAP, following the standard literature on anaphora resolution. This is another example of a putative universal whose universal status is suggested by the fact that it does not have to be taught, since learners apply it spontaneously, as was vividly demonstrated by the Balinese student's surprise reaction described in section 3.7.2.1. Why is this a sensible proposal? Because if it is a valid principle for all speakers of European languages and a Balinese speaker has it too, what reason could there be for denying it to speakers of any other language? Like the PPP-statute, IDAP seems to be an extrinsic universal, forming part of the same trade-off between temporal precedence and high constituent status as mentioned in the preceding paragraph.

The *Monomorphemic Alternative Priority Principle* or MAPP, discussed in section 3.7.2.3, is likewise a worthy candidate, but of a different nature from the two preceding proposals. MAPP is not part of the processing machinery and is thus not reflected in immediately available semantic intuitions, but is constitutive in the formation of a lexicon. It cannot, therefore, be validated by an appeal to intuitive judgements but requires punctilious checking through masses of languages. For that reason, it cannot be proposed with the same confidence as IDAP or the PPP-statute. Yet it is worth trying.

Before I start being too long-winded, I will mention two final putatively universal properties of language:

(3.34) When a language turns modal predicates into bound morphemes (affixes), it is always the futurity modal that goes first.

(3.35) When a language allows for the process whereby a higher lexical predicate Phigh and a lower lexical predicate Plow at the level of Semantic Analysis are incorporated into a verbal cluster or a morphological unit, the first Phigh to undergo such a process is always a predicate of causation, followed by a predicate of permission.

Here again, intuitive judgments cannot be relied on because neither (3.34) nor (3.35) are operative in the processing of utterances. They have to be validated inductively, which means that they always risk falsification. According to what has been said at the end of section 3.5, these are potential instances of universal pressure, in that they suggest a natural process of growth rather than a static formal system.

One could easily go on for a long time proposing and testing putative universals. Every general theory of grammar is an attempt at formulating a part of UPG and although most such theories will no doubt prove to be inadequate, the very fact that linguists keep undertaking efforts of this nature shows that general linguistics, as an academic subject, crucially depends on an implicit or explicit search for universals.

3.8.2 *How about constituent structure?*

A widely accepted universal is that *sentences are built up in terms of hierarchically ordered constituents*—a view first proposed in the medieval *Grammatica Speculativa*, rediscovered in Wundt (1880) and elaborated in Bloomfield (1933) and the ensuing development of structuralist linguistics and then generative grammar (Seuren 1998: 35–6, 219–27). In fact, the introduction of the notion of hierarchical constituent structure has been a main factor in the formation of modern linguistic theory. As with all other universalist proposals, Evans and Levinson (2009: 440–2) try to shoot this one down as well. They re-interpret this universal as saying that surface structures of sentences are built up in terms of *continuous* hierarchically ordered constituents, so that surface constituent structure can be exhaustively rendered in terms of labelled bracketing (see section 6.3.1). This presumed universal is then rejected on the (trivial) grounds that in many languages one finds discontinuous constituents, whose members belong together semantically but are separated by intervening syntactic material. According to these authors (p. 441), 'syntactic theories developed in the English-speaking world have primarily focused on constituency, no doubt because English fits this bill' (which, by the way, it does not, as we shall see in a moment). To support their rejection, they adduce examples of wildly discontinuous constituents from Latin poetry (Virgil) and from two Australian languages, Jiwarli and Thalanyje.

There appears, however, to be a notional confusion here between constituency as defined by *semantic dependency relations* (including scope) on the one hand and *syntactic constituency assignments in surface structure* on the other. That the two do not run parallel is well-known. This is why a distinction is made between surface and semantic representations for sentences, the grammar of the language in question being the bridge between the two. English, for example, has cases like *She told the man off* or *How does this work?*, where *told … off* and *does … work* each form one semantic constituent but are separated in surface structure. In fact, I don't know of any language that does not have discontinuous constituents, in the semantic dependency sense, one way or another, whether in its syntax or its morphology. They are found all over the place, as in Latin *magna in urbe* 'in the big city', or German *Er hat sie geliebt* 'he has loved her' (where *hat...geliebt* 'has loved' is discontinuous), or French *Il ne travaille pas* 'he does not work' (where the negation *ne...pas* is discontinuous), or Italian *Lo voglio fare* 'I want to do it', with *lo* ('it') as the direct object of *fare* ('do'). Wundt, the originator of modern constituent structure analysis, gave the example of the perfectly normal, nonliterary Latin sentence *Socrates venenum laetus hausit* ('Socrates happily drank the poison') (Wundt 1880: 57), which has the discontinuous constituents *Socrates...laetus* ('happy Socrates') and *venenum... hausit* ('drank the poison'), implying that the analysis into these two discontinuous constituents reflects semantic structure (see Seuren 1998: 220). Bloomfield, who, in his younger years, was a great admirer of Wundt and introduced constituent analysis into linguistics, wrote, in his abstruse terminology: 'In languages which use highly complex taxemes of selection, order is largely non-distinctive and connotative' (Bloomfield 1933: 197), giving examples from Latin, German and French. *The problem is precisely how to relate the, often discontinuous, surface structure constituents to a system of (continuous) semantic constituents.*

The question of whether semantic relations that are discontinuous in surface structure should be represented by crossing lines or whether there is an independent constraint prohibiting crossing dependencies in surface structure constituency assignments is intriguing but undecided. In some cases it is clear that discontinuous constituents are not to be united by crossing lines in surface structure constituent analysis. In the French sentence *Il ne me l'a pas donné* ('he hasn't given it to me'), for example, grammatical analysis shows that *ne* is part of the clitic cluster *ne-me-le* within the auxiliary (AUX) constituent *ne-me-le-a*, whereas *pas* is an adverbial particle between AUX and the past participle *donné* (see Seuren 1996: 169–84 for extensive discussion). In this case, therefore, it would be wrong to connect *ne* and *pas* by a crossing line in the surface structure. By contrast, the Latin cases cited in Wundt (1880: 57) and in Evans and Levinson (2009: 441) look as if they might well require crossing lines in their surface structure constituent analysis.

It is as yet unknown if there is a general (universal) principle in this regard, and if so what it should be. In most current varieties of linguistic theory the question of surface structure constituency is underexposed, probably because that is where syntax ends and morphology begins, and linguistic theory is more focused on syntax than on morphology. In Seuren (1996: 60), a universal end-of-syntax rule or principle called MINCE, mincing tree structures into consecutive subtrees, is proposed to fashion constituency structures resulting from the transformational mappings into an acceptable format suitable to be fed into the morphology. But it must be admitted that, on the whole, the question of surface constituency has not been given the attention it deserves.

In Evans and Levinson (2009) it is proposed or suggested that some languages are best analysed in terms of dependency relations, introduced in Tesnière (1959) and used in some linguistic theories and, widely, in computational linguistics, while tree-structure analyses are more suitable for other languages, such as English, which the authors (wrongly, as we have seen) reckon not to have discontinuous constituents. It is even suggested that some languages may use both methods, combining them in some mysterious way. This proposal shows great levity of mind. Tesnière-type dependency relations are meant to hold at the level of semantic structure and say nothing about surface grammar. Tesnière-type structures are thus at best a method of semantic representation for sentences, but they say nothing about surface structures or about the relation between the two levels of representation—that is, about grammar. Moreover, they are not suitable as a system for semantic representations since they cannot, other than in highly artificial ways, render scope relations and, in particular, quantificational structure. (The computer scientists' enthusiasm for them should be seen in the light of the general neglect of semantic scope relations in that area of studies, where predicate-argument structure is the focus of attention.) In serious semantics, hierarchical constituency is of the essence, since, as has been universally accepted since the 1960s, semantic representations require the regularity of *logical structure*, which crucially depends on the format of hierarchical tree structures (bracketed strings).

The proposal to treat some languages in terms of Tesnière-type dependency relations and others in terms of tree structures thus amounts to a category mistake. Once it is accepted that semantic structures are organized as hierarchical constituent trees expressing scope relations, the passage to Tesnière-type structures is by definition a passed station. And even when Tesnière-type structures are taken to represent meanings, the problem of mapping these onto discontinuous surface constituents still exists. Furthermore, rejecting constituent trees amounts to rejecting a vast body of work in the theory of grammar that has been more successful than any other brand of work in the same field. For example, the universal importance of the *branching directionality* parameter in hierarchical constituent structures is, by definition, expressible only in terms of constituent trees. Tesnière-type dependency diagrams are useless in this respect.

To give just one quick example, the German version of the English clause *that I wanted to see her dance* is *daß ich sie tanzen sehen wollte*, with the verbal cluster *tanzen sehen wollte* ('dance see wanted'). The Dutch version, by contrast, is *dat ik haar wilde zien dansen*, with the verbal cluster *wilde zien dansen* ('wanted see dance'). The Dutch cluster is thus the mirror image of the German cluster. As is well-known among serious grammarians, this difference is due to the fact that German is (mainly) left-branching while Dutch is (mainly) right-branching in verbal clusters. To uphold this explanation, which has no viable alternative in grammatical theory, it is necessary to assign constituent tree structure to the word groups in question. Denying tree structure to certain languages, such as Latin or Evans and Levinson's Australian languages Jiwarli and Thalanyje, would stand a better chance if the authors had actually *shown* in what sort of alternative structural terms these languages, or Latin, could, according to them, be described and to what extent such a description would have explanatory value with regard to the languages in question and to other languages. Yet no indication is provided in that regard. All we have is the authors' statement that this can, or should, be done, which rather weakens their position, since detailed descriptions of the German and Dutch constructions in question have actually been provided, with close parallels in other, often totally unrelated, languages (e.g. Evers 1975, Seuren 1972a, 1996, 2003).

Moreover, the question arises of a possible alternative to hierarchical tree structures as an analytic or descriptive device for the *surface structure* of sentences. One option is to assign no structure at all, but this can be ruled out straight away since order is never totally arbitrary. Every language has to distinguish, for example, 'not one person was injured' from 'one person was not injured', and all languages use ordering as at least one means of doing so. Another option would be to assign sentences a purely linear order, as was done in what used to be called, during the 1950s, 'information science' or 'information technology' (see section 6.1). The notion 'grammaticality' would then be reduced to 'nth-order statistical approximation', given n-1 preceding 'symbols' (see section 6.3.2). And natural languages would then, in the terminology of the Chomsky-hierarchy of grammar types (see Chapter 6), belong to the class of the highly restricted type-3 monotone right- or monotone left-branching finite state languages. This would make it impossible to formulate a systematic relation between surface and semantic structure. It would, moreover, be a reversal to a view that has been so thoroughly discredited that resurrecting it would require a very solid underpinning indeed—something not provided in Evans and Levinson (2009). (For one thing, it would be impossible to distinguish between the two possible constituent structures of expressions like *ancient manuscript collection*, which is either an ancient collection of manuscripts or a collection of ancient manuscripts, as was already noted in Bloomfield (1933).) All further alternatives beyond type-3 finite state grammars, whether semantically viable or not, likewise require continuous or discontinuous hierarchically layered tree structure analyses.

What responsible theoretical linguists, following Wundt, are inclined to posit as a universal in this respect is the following:

(3.36)   At some, non-surface, level of representation, semantic constituency is continuous (and thus expressible in terms of bracketing).

This universal makes a great deal of sense and has not so far met with any resistance either from the facts or from serious theorizing. Actually, universal (3.36) can be strengthened to (3.37), which is in conformity with the fact that the formal languages of logic and mathematics lack discontinuous constituents and are thus fully expressible in terms of labelled bracketing—a fact that is of great significance in theories of semantic processing:

(3.37)   At the level of Semantic Analysis, semantic constituency is continuous (and thus expressible in terms of bracketing).

This constraint on the structure of semantic representations is relaxed in surface structure, as we have seen. Yet it is still recognizably there, enough for psychologists and linguists to have spotted it. In this perspective it becomes an interesting question *to what extent* universal (3.37) can be violated in surface structure—a further quarry for possible universals. Obviously, when any kind of non-surface representation of sentences is rejected in principle, there can be no universal such as (3.36) or (3.37), but the question is how serious such theories can be taken to be.

3.9 Conclusion

The main upshot of the present chapter is methodological. Theorists of language need to be driven by a basic urge to seek unity. In this search for unity, they must, first of all, take due account of all known facts and welcome any new facts and potentially fruitful analyses and perspectives, even if these threaten existing generalizations or may force a change in the perspective taken so far. Then, it is imperative to develop a unified perspective, or even a theory, in terms of which all the known facts can be given a proper place. Lastly, a causal explanation must be sought of all that is known about the object of enquiry.

To elevate linguistic relativism to the status of an overarching *a priori* principle, at the expense of any possible outcome of a general theory of language to the effect that human language is basically unified, is unconstructive, methodologically unsound and above all pre-emptive. For the first time ever, we now have detailed descriptions of thousands of different languages distributed all over the world and thus forming, or coming close to, what we may consider to be a representative corpus. Now is the time for proper theorizing, in close collaboration with the typologists.

When we look at the state of our present knowledge, we see that a relativist position is no longer defensible. Everything points to an underlying universal systematicity in language, which is not obviously reducible either to any sensible conceptually necessary definition of human language or to its ecological embedding, and thus suggests at least the possibility of extrinsic universal properties of language. The hypothesis of an *innate language module*, in the sense of a bundle of specialized functions in cognition and/or the brain, thus presents itself as a realistic possibility. Such an innate language module will be much like a system of, probably hierarchically ordered, parameters, in need of values to be provided by any specific language— which for the young child will be the language it grows up in.

At the same time, however, it looks very much as if such an innate language module is not a formally fixed system, fully present at birth in the way of a ready-made, complete 'blueprint' for action. On the contrary, it rather looks like an organic system present at birth *in nucleo* and developing itself along largely predisposed lines as material input fills the blanks. In this way, a language can 'grow' new features, as the underlying module develops into new but universally constrained directions. One must in any case reckon with a cognitive machinery of great complexity and, as some say, 'abstractness'. The physical, or physiological, implementation of such a machinery has only recently begun to come within the horizon. In sorting out the cerebral details of language and its use, it is important not to underestimate the complexity of the object whose workings one seeks to capture in physiological terms.

4

What does language have to do with logic and mathematics?

4.1 Introduction

The present chapter is meant as a prelude to the chapters that follow, initiating the reader into areas of research and ways of thinking many linguists and psycholinguists are less accustomed to. The question 'What is the relevance of logic and mathematics for the study of language?' plays a central and all-important role in the theory of language. (The obverse question of the relevance of language for logic and mathematics is not discussed here.) Unfortunately, however, the question we do discuss here is also one that has become unpopular among linguists and psycholinguists, even though it is an obvious question, one that is often present in the minds of interested non-professionals and of beginning students of language. However, as the students progress or the outsiders look a little further, they soon learn to avoid this issue and to take for granted what is taught in courses and in current textbooks, where the question of the relation between language, logic and mathematics is simply not raised. The impression is thus created that this question should not be asked and that whoever does so is out of line, or just stupid. Yet it is a perfectly legitimate and normal question, which should not only be asked but also be answered.

In this chapter, I try to bring some clarity in this central issue. My answer is, in principle, twofold. First, I argue that natural language has an inherent *natural logic*, probably the same for all languages, in that linguistic words or morphemes stand proxy for logical operators whose meanings jointly define a logical system. Secondly, since by definition logical operators have scope and since logical structure is determined by scope relations, semantic comprehension of sentences likewise crucially depends on scope relations, which means that there must be a regular mapping procedure relating surface structures of sentences to logical structures in which scope relations are expressed in explicit structural terms. In simple language, this means that the grammar of a language is in principle a mapping relation mediating between lexically filled logical structures on the one hand and linguistic surface structures on the other. This answer is, obviously, in need of a great deal of further elaboration and elucidation, some of which is given in the remainder of the present chapter and in some of the later chapters in the present book (section 3.7.2.2 took an advance loan), but, in principle, this is what it amounts to: (a) surface sentential structure can only be properly understood if it is considered to be the product of a grammatical mapping relation from logically structured semantic analyses (SAs) onto the surface structures of any specific language, and (b) the linguistically defined interpretation of surface structures proceeds via the underlying logically structured SAs in the semantic terms of the logical system inherent in human cognition. The process leading to this insight has been long-winded and in many ways painful, but there it is.

The question making up the title of the present chapter and the answer given may not please those who consider themselves representatives of what they claim to be the 'standard' body of opinion and thus feel that they are entitled to full command of the market. Yet, in the human sciences more so than anywhere else, command of the market is no guarantee for quality—though academic administrators often misguidedly think it is. So I ask: what does language have to do with logic and mathematics?

One part of this question, the part about the relation between linguistic and logical structure, has a long history going back to Aristotle (384–322 BCE), the ancient Stoa school of philosophy and the Alexandrian linguists active during the last few centuries BCE. It concerned mostly the relation between the structure and meaning of sentences on the one hand and of propositions in traditional predicate logic on the other. In fact, the traditional grammatical notions of *subject* and *predicate*, at the time often also called *noun* and *verb*, originate in Greek philosophy, in particular in Aristotelian predicate logic.

Only lately, in the course of the twentieth century, has logic begun to play new and different roles in the study of language. We have witnessed an application of the modern notion of *formal derivation*, one of the first products of the formalization of logic during the nineteenth and twentieth centuries, to linguistic structure, as a result of which grammars came to be seen as *generative algorithms*—a development discussed briefly in section 4.2.3 and less briefly in Chapter 6. During the late 1960s and the early 1970s a more semantically oriented relation between the structures of language and those of logic was explored in the school of what used to be called *Generative Semantics* (renamed *Semantic Syntax* by the present author). In this school it is hypothesized that every sentence S has an underlying structure, its *Semantic Analysis* (SA), which not only specifies the meaning of S in the analytical terms of a variety of the modern language of predicate logic but also serves as the input to an algorithmic transformational machinery (the grammar) mapping the SA onto a well-formed surface structure in the language concerned (McCawley 1973; Seuren 1969, 1996). This approach is, in fact, a formal elaboration in modern terms of the ancient view that saw sentence structure as based on the subject-predicate structure of logical sentences.

At the same time, during the 1960s, the American logician Richard Montague (1930–1971) presented his likewise logic-derived theory of model-theoretic semantic interpretation of natural-language sentences (Montague 1974). This formally highly complex theory is a spin-off of logical proof theory by means of an ontology of possible worlds, based in turn on Tarski's theory of *meaning-as-truth-conditions* (Tarski 1944; Tarski and Vaught 1956). Against Tarski's explicit advice, Montague applied Tarski's model-theoretic semantics, which was meant for mathematical purposes, to natural language, deluded by the false notion, developed in the context of modern logic and mathematics, that natural language is just a variety of the class of 'formal' languages. The untenability of this approach is discussed in Chapter 9.

In the general excitement of the application of logico-mathematical methods to the study of natural language many essential questions and obstacles were overlooked. First, one lost sight of the essential facts (a) that natural languages are part of social reality and thus subject to settling (Chapter 1) cutting in on any regular form-meaning correspondence and (b) that, contrary to formal or artificial languages, the interpretation of natural language sentences requires appeals, at a well-organized variety of distinct levels, to available general, contextual and situational knowledge. In addition, it was also totally forgotten that logical systems are defined by the meanings of their operators (the binary sentential connectives *and* and *or*, quantifiers, negation, and more) and that these operators have representatives in natural languages, usually as words but sometimes also as bound morphemes or morpheme variations, which makes it worthwhile to see if natural language has a logic of its own, based on the lexical meanings of the operators, and, if so, to compare this logic with the established logical system or systems. This question is briefly discussed in section 4.2.6 and treated more fully in Chapter 8. Chapter 7, on reflexivity in language, shows one particular logico-semantic aspect that is unique to natural language and not found at all in any of the formal languages devised by logicians or computer scientists.

That mathematics has meanwhile made a conspicuous entrance into linguistics will be clear from the above. In fact, most practitioners of the model-theoretic approach are not linguists but mathematicians by trade—with the inevitable consequence that they tend to underestimate the complexity of natural language emphasized in Chapter 5. But apart from that, the elaboration of a natural logic as an emergent property of the linguistic meanings of the logical operators makes it necessary to go into mathematical set theory as the proper instrument for the semantic definition of the operators in natural language. In this sense, it is clear that logic, and in particular predicate logic, is directly based on set theory, since the linguistic meanings of the predicate-logic operators are straightforwardly definable in terms of set-theoretical relations. In fact, just as language has its own logic, humans have their own 'naïve' set theory, and it is therefore to be expected that the linguistic meanings of the logical operators in natural language are to be defined in terms of what one may suppose 'natural' set theory to amount to.

It is a deplorable fact that this point of view is anathema in circles of model-theoretic semanticists, owing to an unwillingness to discuss the foundations of logic and mathematics in terms of naturally given human cognition instead of the terms set by a cognitionless, strictly extensional ontology. For this reason, the Amsterdam-based programme of reducing the cognitive aspects of natural language to, or combining them with, model-theoretic semantics is unlikely to succeed. To the extent that this school of thought produces formal analyses in terms of 'objective' logic or mathematics, it will miss the connection with cognitive reality.

4.2 Language and logic

4.2.1 *What is (a) logic?*

Logic was discovered by Aristotle while he was a student in Plato's Academy in Athens around the year 360 BCE. Aristotle found that there are a few words in language—in his case Ancient Greek—which, when placed in certain positions in sentences, allow one to draw immediate conclusions based on the meanings and positions of those words alone, without taking into account the meanings of other words in the same sentence. Thus, when I say *All Romans are mortal*, I am entitled to conclude that *Some Romans are mortal*, merely on the grounds of what the words *all* and *some* mean and their position in the sentences involved. He also found that, together with the negation word *not*, a system of relations comes into view that allows one to draw conclusions from premises in a systematic, and thus formalizable, way. The words that have this magical property, he found, are few in number. He identified *all, some, not, possible* and *necessary* as members of this class. Not long after his death, the Stoic philosophers added *and, or* and *if* to this small inventory. Together they form what we now call *logical operators*. Since antiquity, only few operators have been added to this small but explosively powerful class, and those that were added (such as the comparative morpheme *more* or *-er*) do not seem to be part of any interesting logical system. On the basis of the operators *all, some* and *not* Aristotle formulated the first predicate-logic in history, now (with an important modification)[1] known as the *Square of Opposition*.

---

[1] As is made clear in Chapter 8, the form in which this Square dominated predicate logic for fifteen centuries until c. 1900 is not the one devised by Aristotle. What is now known as the *'classic' Square of Opposition* is an adaptation made by later commentators, mainly Apuleius (c. 125–180 CE), Ammonius (c. 440–520 CE) and especially Boethius (c. 480–524 CE), who 'streamlined' Aristotle's original system and in doing so introduced the logical error of *Undue Existential Import* (explained below in section 4.3). The French medieval philosopher Peter Abelard (1079–1142) was the first to detect this error and restore Aristotle's logic to its pristine, logically correct, form (see Seuren 2010: 147–80 for detailed discussion and references).

It is called *predicate* logic because with the quantifiers *all* and *some* and the negation *not* as constants—the only terms with their own meaning—the *predicates* (*Roman* and *mortal* in the example given) are represented by linguistic variables.[2] Analogously, *propositional logic*, developed by the Stoic philosophers, is so called because while the constants normally used are the logical operators *and*, *or* and *not* (and *if*, if you like), the linguistic variables represent the actual *propositions* dealt with in this system. Predicate logic thus deals with predicates, while propositional logic deals with propositions. There is, furthermore, *syllogistic logic*, or simply *syllogistic*, which takes a combination of logical sentences and allows for the deduction of one or more conclusions following from the combined input sentences on the basis of their formal structure. Syllogistic logic, often caught under the rubric of *reasoning*, is less directly related to the semantics and grammar of natural language and is not discussed in the present book.

Taking a *proposition* to be a *mental act of truly or falsely assigning a property to one or more entities*, we can define *a logic* as follows:

A *logic* **LOG** is expressed in a symbolic language whose lexicon consists of constants (operators) with mathematically defined meanings and of variables ranging over linguistic elements, and whose formulae represent schemata of primitive or complex propositions. **LOG** forms a logic because the language it is expressed in enables a human person or a machine to derive new formulae from given formulae *salva veritate* (under maintenance of truth) and without inconsistency, merely on the basis of the meanings of the operators in **LOG**.

A logic is by definition *formal* in that a 'machine' can do the logical work: no appeal is needed to the individual meanings of the linguistic elements that can stand in for the variables since all the work is done by the operators, whose mathematically defined meanings determine what derivations are legitimate.[3]

We say that when a logical formula F_1 expressing a proposition allows for the formal or automatic derivation of a logical formula F_2 *salva veritate*, F_1 **logically entails** F_2. Entailment is the backbone of any logical system and is defined as follows:

To say that a formula F_1 *entails* a formula F_2 is to say that whenever F_1 is true F_2 is necessarily also true in virtue of the meanings of F_1 and F_2.

---

[2] I distinguish between *linguistic* and *objectual* variables. The former, already used by Aristotle, represent, or range over, linguistic entities such as predicates or propositional structures. The latter, usually written as *x*, *y* or *z*, range over (sets of) elements in the ontology posited; they were introduced during the late nineteenth century and are part of a machinery computing the truth value of a predicate-logical formula in a given model.

[3] The actual practice of logic in daily life requires a great deal of scholastic education. Unschooled individuals are usually unable to conduct even simple logical arguments, abstracting from concrete *hic et nunc* circumstances (well-schooled individuals are often no more than a little better in this respect). See Hallpike (1979: 117–20) for telling examples. The inability to conceive or formulate a general principle—a necessary condition for logical reasoning—is often reflected in proverbs, which take individual cases and use them as exemplars for a general principle.

The entailment relation in logic is, therefore, a *semantic* or, in Kantian terms, an *analytic* relation, which holds in virtue of the *meanings* of the formulae involved, not in virtue of, say, physical necessity or inductive regularity. A sentence like *John has been buried* does not entail the sentence *John is dead*, even though, normally, when one has been buried, one is dead. Likewise, a sentence like *John has been decapitated* does not entail, in the semantically analytic sense intended here, that John is dead, even though one can be pretty certain that death will follow when a person has been decapitated. By contrast, a sentence like *John has been murdered* does have the semantic entailment *John is dead*, because it is in the meanings of the predicate *have been murdered* that whoever has been murdered is necessarily dead.

How is this difference to be tested more precisely and more reliably than by mere intuition? This question is raised in, notably, Cruse (1986: 14). The answer given by Cruse (and many other authors dealing with the question) is based on the *conceivability* of any situation where the entailing sentence is true but the entailed sentence is false. One may protest that this is not good enough, since there are considerable differences in individual persons' imaginative powers. Cruse attempts to counter this criticism by proposing a few tests, centered around the concept of possibility and the logical properties of material implication, in particular contraposition. He thus proposes, if one wants to test whether (4.1) indeed expresses a semantically valid analytic entailment relation, to ask subjects whether they agree with (4.2a–c) and disagree with (4.3a–c):

(4.1)   This is a dog   <entails?>   This is an animal

(4.2)   a. This can't possibly be a dog and not an animal.
        b. This is a dog, therefore it is an animal.
        c. If this is not an animal, it follows that it is not a dog.

(4.3)   a. This is a dog, so it must be a cat.
        b. This is not an animal, but it is just possible that it is a dog.
        c. This is a dog, so this might be an animal.

The problem with these tests is that the concepts underlying the words 'possible', 'therefore', 'follow', encompass both physical and conceptual (analytical) necessity. Yet Cruse's tests can be refined in such a way that an interpretation in terms of physical necessity is eliminated, or at least pushed into the background, and conceptual necessity is singled out. The crucial notion to be tested, to make the notion of entailment operational, is *consistency*. In Seuren (2010: 331–2), in a discussion of possible operational criteria for the entailment relation, it is argued that there is one crucial operational criterion that does seem to single out analytical necessity, separating it from physical necessity. This criterion consists in eliciting consistency judgements for sentences like:

(4.4)   a. This may not be an animal, yet it is a dog.
      b. John may not be dead, yet he has been murdered.
      c. John may not be dead, yet he has been buried.
      d. John may not be dead, yet he has been decapitated.

The criterion is based on the argument that *may not p*, or 'it is possible that not-p' for any proposition *p*, contains the epistemic operator *possible that not* and expresses a speaker's commitment to the effect that the speaker's knowledge base **K** is reliable enough to be considered correct and that it follows from **K** that *not-p* cannot be excluded (see Seuren 2010: 203–6 for further discussion). Now, if a speaker assumes a commitment as to the truth of the entailing sentence (the second clauses in (4.4)) and at the same time, without becoming inconsistent, can leave open the possibility of the entailed sentence (the first clauses in (4.4) without the *may-not* operator) being false, then there is no entailment relation. By contrast, if it is felt that inconsistency arises, one can be certain that there is an entailment relation in the analytic, semantic sense of entailment.

According to this criterion, (4.4a) and (4.4b) will come out as incoherent, so that there is a semantic entailment from being a dog to being an animal, and from having been murdered to being dead. Yet (4.4c) and (4.4d) allow for a coherent interpretation. All that is needed is a story where buried persons can stay alive or where decapitation of a living person does not necessarily lead to death, for example because it can be followed by a re-attachment of the severed head to the body without the interruption of life, no matter how unattainable such an achievement is in the actual world. Moreover, eggs can be buried and already dead bodies, as well as statues, can be decapitated, but not murdered. For lexicographers, this has the practical consequence that the meanings of words like *bury* or *decapitate* should not be specified as implying the notion of death but merely as 'put underground' for *bury* and 'sever the head (from a body)' for *decapitate*. Death is merely a practical condition or consequence in prototypical cases.[4]

Thus, to say of an individual *N* that *N* barks does not entail that *N* is a dog, since (4.5) is open to an interpretation in which it is consistent. All that is needed is a story in which Captain Walrus is a barking human:

(4.5)   Captain Walrus may not be a dog, yet he barks.

---

[4] With one exception, all English dictionaries I have consulted indeed leave out any mention of killing or death in their meaning descriptions of the words *bury* or *decapitate*. The one exception is the *Collins Cobuild English Language Dictionary* (1987), based on corpus frequency counts in the Birmingham University International Language Database and written in 'ordinary, everyday English'. The word *behead* would seem to differ from *decapitate* in that it conveys an official or ceremonial status to the decapitation event, which would strengthen the implication of ensuing death. To what extent this is actually so is a question that needs further lexicographical research. The existing dictionaries make no mention of this possible semantic difference.

In a way, this amounts to an exploration of the limits of fiction: when one has the feeling that a certain fictional story transgresses the limits of consistency and begins to be incoherent, the text has touched an analytical, and thus a semantic, nerve.

We distinguish *semantic* from *logical entailments* by stipulating that when a semantic entailment follows from a logical system with logical constants and linguistic variables, we call it a *logical entailment*. A logical system is thus a formal calculus of entailments.

It also follows that a logic needs a logical language: there can be no logic without a well-defined logical language. It has been known since Aristotle that natural language sentences are not suitable for logical purposes: they need to be reduced to, or 'regimented' into, formulae of a logical language to do their logical work. In section 4.2.4, I argue that every sentence of a natural language L has an underlying representation in terms of a *natural logical language* (with values for the linguistic variables); the grammar of L turns these logical expressions into well-formed surface sentences of L.

Logical systems may thus differ according to (a) the metalogical axioms regarding the notions of truth and falsity, (b) the choice of constants (operators), (c) the meanings of the operators chosen, and (d) the ontology adopted and the ranges of the linguistic variables. Of particular interest in the present context is (c), the possible semantic variation of formally similar operators. The quantifying operator *all* has different meaning descriptions in Aristotelian and, say, modern Russellian logic, which is why Aristotelian and Russellian logic are two different logical systems. It is, therefore, nonsense to say that there is only one possible logical system: variations in the meaning descriptions of logical operators may lead to distinct but perfectly valid logical systems. It is argued in Chapter 8 that the natural logic of human language is one such (non-standard) variety.

The totality of meaning descriptions of the operators involved will give rise to a logical system when the various meaning descriptions are *consistent*, so that no contrary conclusions can be derived. It is important to realize, however, that when we speak of a *natural logical system*, there is no implication that this system is present as such in the human mind. What is (non-consciously) present in the human mind is the meanings of the lexical elements that jointly form the logical system (if any). The logical system itself is *epiphenomenal*, or *emergent*, in the sense that it follows from the existing machinery and can be constructed through scholarly analysis on the basis of the existing lexical meanings of the operators and the structure of the logically expressed propositions involved.

This account of what makes a logic is unusual. Current definitions of logic, to the extent that they can be found, carry a heavy imprint of neopositivist (or logical-empiricist) philosophy and modern mathematics, whereas the linguistic and cognitive elements remain unmentioned. In fact, modern logic has done all it could do to dissociate itself from language and cognition, making sure that it applies faultlessly to the physical world we live in. But what is needed, when it is our purpose to understand *language*, is a mathematics and logic that can be considered to be somehow implemented in or result from the human mind as part of the cognitive machinery. This, incidentally, makes one wonder why and how the same modern logic has been so actively seeking for applications to natural language—pre-eminently a cognitive phenomenon. Yet, despite the basic differences between the standard empiricist and the ecological approach advocated in the present study, the definition given here of what makes for a logical system is perfectly compatible with the more mathematically oriented concept of logic current today. This common ground should make it possible to have a fruitful exchange of views and perspectives, thus restoring the balance somewhat in favour of the cognitive and natural-linguistic aspects of logic, so abhorred by Russell and his followers and treated with such distrust by modern formal semanticists and philosophers of language.

4.2.2 *The tradition*

In what is called 'the tradition'—the period from Aristotle till, roughly speaking, the beginning of the twentieth century—there was never any clarity regarding the relation between language and logic. The earliest grammatical analyses were produced around 300 BCE in Alexandria, then the capital of Egypt, whose king, Ptolemy the First, a half-brother of the Macedonian conqueror Alexander the Great (356–323 BCE), had taken Egypt after Alexander's death and had made the preparations for the first university in the Western world, the *Mouseion*, Latinized to *Museum*. Linguistics was an important subject in this university, since Egyptian youngsters needed adequate knowledge of Greek for a career in the army, the civil service or in commerce. The Alexandrian 'philologists' had no other analysis of sentence structure available than Aristotle's logical analysis in terms of subject and predicate, which they were keen to borrow for the purpose of teaching Greek to Egyptians, the more so because Aristotle was a Macedonian, just like Ptolemy and Alexander, who had been taught by Aristotle as a boy, (see Seuren 1998: 18–23). But little thought was given to the question of *why* a logical analysis should be relevant to grammar.

This situation did not change much in the twenty-two centuries that followed, despite all kinds of metaphysical speculations about the threefold mutual conformity of language, the mind and the structure of the world. The common view was that surface sentences somehow reflect a logico-semantic thought structure much like the analyses provided in Aristotelian predicate logic, which again reflects the ontologial structure of the world, but few attempts were made to make this threefold relation more explicit. One of the few who made a detailed attempt at greater explicitness regarding the relation between the postulated thought structures on the one hand and linguistic surface structures on the other was the Spaniard *Franciscus Sanctius* or *Sánchez* (1523–1600), professor of rhetoric, Latin and Greek at the University of

Salamanca (Breva-Claramonte 1983; Seuren 1998: 41–6). In his principal work *Minerva, seu de Causis Linguae Latinae* ('Minerva, or on the causes of the Latin Language'), published in 1587, Sanctius presented a detailed account of the reasons why and the manner in which language and thought must be taken to be related. Yet there is—understandably in the light of the almost total absence of formal descriptive and analytical tools—still relatively little on the precise relation between language and logico-semantic structure. Sanctius provides little in the way of explicit rules mapping SAs onto surface structures or vice versa, but he does provide surprisingly precise observations and well-formulated problems. He observes, for example, that the subject of a clause always takes nominative case when constructed with a finite verb but accusative case in construction with infinitives—still an important question in the theory of grammar (see section 5.3.2).

Other than that, however, what one sees happening is a gradual process of linguists taking greater distance from logic. At the beginning of our Common Era, word classes other than noun and verb, nominal cases and verbal conjugations had been distinguished, for both Greek and Latin, without any help from logic, but the link with logic was not severed until the middle of the nineteenth century, when it was discovered that the *linguistic* notions of subject and predicate do not correspond very well with the *Aristotelian* notions of the same name. In other words, the Alexandrian philologists had, apparently, been rash in taking over Aristotle's logical distinction between subject and predicate for the purpose of grammar.

The German linguist-philosopher Heymann Steinthal observed, for example, (Steinthal 1855: 199), that in a sentence like *The patient slept well*, the grammatical subject is *the patient* and the grammatical predicate is *slept well*, but when one asks what property is assigned to what entity, the answer is that the property *good* is assigned to the entity *the patient's sleep*, the sentence being understood as 'The patient's sleep was good'. (The correctness of this observation is confirmed by the fact that the negation of this sentence, *The patient did not sleep well*, does not deny that the patient slept but only that the patient's sleep was not good.) This observation stands proxy for a widely discussed but unanswered question in the philosophy of language of the period: what is the relation between the grammatical and the cognitive-semantic structure of sentences? Thus arose the great *subject-predicate debate*, which dominated linguistic thinking until the 1930s but failed to lead to any clear solution, mainly because of the unclarity of the notions to do with logic and human cognition (see Seuren 1998: 120–33 for extensive discussion).

The debate was, moreover, overtaken and made redundant by the new wave of neopositivism, later called logical empiricism, which swept through both the natural and the human sciences, convincing the academic world that the study of meaning in relation to cognition was unscientific and thus anathema. This led to a state of mind where it was considered mandatory to study language without cognitive meaning, and logic without cognition. In the early years of the twentieth century, logic became forbidden ground for linguists, language being considered autonomous and independent of logic, and cognition became forbidden ground for logicians, logic being considered autonomous and independent of the human mind.

We are still coping with the consequences of this bizarre episode in the history of science. While it is undeniably true that the great developments in logic and mathematics over the past 150 years have provided us with a treasure of indispensable new insights and analytical tools, it is also true that there is still a profound unclarity regarding the relation between language and logic. This unclarity was not removed by the Montagovian hubris of imposing a neopositivist logico-mathematical 'semantics' on natural language. This formal, model-theoretic semantics has failed to take into account that language could not function or even exist without the fabric of cognition from which it arose and that languages could not become the historically stable systems they are without the fabric of society. It is time to realize that, if one wishes to gain entrance to the secrets of language, one has no choice but to do away with neopositivism or logical empiricism as a philosophy of the human sciences. Cognitive science, social psychology and related approaches are helping us on the way, but a philosophical analysis of the central role of cognitive processing in all human dealings with the 'world', including human linguistic dealings, is still lacking. In this respect, the human sciences are badly in need of a philosophical overhaul.

4.2.3 *Syntax: the notion of a grammatical algorithm*

Around 1950, the intellectual climate was thus strongly influenced by neopositivism (or logical empiricism), for which the human mind was not a suitable object of enquiry. To the extent that mental functions were studied, it was in terms of the natural sciences—psychology had become totally behaviouristic—and, at least in circles of empiricist philosophers and mathematicians, natural languages were increasingly seen as (somewhat peculiar) varieties of the kind of formal logical language busily explored by the mathematicians and logicians of the day. In succinct terms, a natural language (mostly English, of course) was considered to be a formal mathematical language with interesting handicaps. Montague's seminal 1970 paper 'English as a formal language' (reprinted in Montague 1974) bears witness to this fact.

It was in this general intellectual climate that the American linguist Zellig S. Harris (1909–1992), followed by his student Noam Chomsky (b. 1928), developed the idea of a natural language L as a set of well-formed sentences produced by a *generative algorithm* in the sense of an abstract or concrete device generating all and only the well-formed sentences of L from (a) an initial symbol ('S'), (b) a given lexicon (list of word forms grouped in classes) and (c) a set of rules or rewrite instructions taking 'S' as input and delivering the sentences of L as output.

The notion of *algorithm* stems from arithmetic. During the ninth century, the mathematician-astronomer *Muḥammad Ibn Mūsa Al-Ḥuārizmi*, born in Uzbekistan, then called Chorasmia or Ḥuārezm, and later working at the newly founded 'House of Wisdom' (in fact a university) in Baghdad, formulated the four classic algorithms of addition, subtraction, multiplication and division, using the newly introduced zero as position indicator. He counts as the father of algebra and his added name *Al-Ḥuārizmi* ('the man from Ḥuārezm') became eponymous of the term *algorithm*. It was not until the 1930s that this classic notion of algorithm was generalized, mainly by the Polish-American mathematician Emil Post (1897–1954) (see Post 1944), to what the word means nowadays: an automatic, formal procedure for the generation of a well-defined set of strings of symbols. During the 1950s, Harris and Chomsky applied this modern notion to language, presenting a language as a set of strings of symbols and a grammar as an algorithm generating the set. This view of grammar has become known as *autonomous syntax*—that is, syntax as a random sentence generator without taking into account any semantic, cognitive or contextual factors. Chomsky's famous *hierarchy of algorithmic systems*, which was developed during the late 1950s and early 1960s, is a direct product of this development. Chapter 6 is a critical discussion of the validity of this concept of grammar. It argues that the Chomsky hierarchy is ultimately irrelevant for the study of language.

4.2.4 *Semantic syntax: propositions in logic, sentences in language*

So far, we haven't found much in the way of a valid link between language and logic, other than, perhaps, the traditional view of sentence structure as a somewhat garbled reflection of the structure of a formula in a proper logical language. By 1960, however, this view had not been sufficiently supported by analysis and empirical results. This changed when, in or around 1965, some young linguists and philosophers began to realize that the recently introduced Chomskyan notion of a grammar as an explicit theory of a native speaker's *linguistic competence* did not tally very well with the then current view of grammar as a random sentence generator. After all, a person able to produce well-formed sentences at random, without any knowledge of what they might mean or how they could fit the situation and the context at hand, can hardly be called a competent speaker. So something had to be done with regard to meaning.

The first sign of this new insight was the 1963 article in *Language* by the philosophers Jerrold Katz and Jerry Fodor (Katz and Fodor 1963). In this article, the authors proposed to add a 'semantic component' to the Chomskyan generative grammar, taking its input not only from the postulated 'deep structure' but also from the surface structure of sentences. However, what the output of this 'component' should be taken to look like and what sort of operations would be needed to get from deep or surface structures to an output specifying meanings remained totally opaque. A year later a book appeared, written by Jerrold Katz and the linguist Paul Postal (Katz and Postal 1964), in which detailed syntactic arguments were proposed to the effect that a Chomskyan autonomous grammar would be considerably simplified if it were assumed that the postulated semantic component took its input only from deep structure and no longer from surface structure.

This book made quite an impression because it worked with *syntactic arguments*— a form of arguing that was familiar to and fully accepted by the linguistic community. Not much later it was concluded by some young linguists, notably James McCawley, George Lakoff, Haj Ross and, if I may say so, myself (I was working independently in the UK at Cambridge University at the time), that if deep structure was the only input to the semantic component and if the form of the output of that component, a *semantic representation* or *semantic analysis* (SA), was unclear, it made sense to explore the hypothesis that the deep structure, postulated on syntactic grounds, is itself the semantic analysis sought after. This idea marked the beginning of the movement known as *Generative Semantics (Semantic Syntax)*. Soon, McCawley proposed that the deep-structure-cum-SA should be taken to be cast in some variety of the language of modern predicate calculus—an idea strongly supported by the fact that there is a notable degree of isomorphy between the scope of logical operators on the one hand and the left-to-right order of their representatives in surface structure on the other (see Seuren 1969 and section 3.7.2.2 in the present book).

At first, Chomsky, whose knowledge of and ideas about semantics have always been badly underdeveloped, went along with this idea, as is apparent from his book *Aspects of the Theory of Syntax* of 1965. Soon, however, he turned against it, bewilderingly calling his *Aspects* theory the *standard theory* and replacing it with what he called the *revised standard theory* (Chomsky 1972), which, however, was less a revision than a total reversal of the Generative Semantics theory developed by McCawley, Ross and others a few years earlier and adopted by himself in his (1965). Here, Chomsky reverted to the idea presented in Katz and Fodor (1963) to the effect that a semantic analysis should take its input from both deep and surface structure, not from deep structure alone. At times, in subsequent years, he also proposed that a semantic analysis should take its input from surface structure alone, but never from deep structure alone. At present, he seems to hold that SAs result from a structure somewhere in the middle between deep and surface structure. In any case, since the late 1960s he has systematically rejected the identification of deep structure with SA, though he concurred with McCawley's view that SAs ('logical form') should be taken to have the structure of the language of modern predicate logic. The *value* of his views, however, has always been determined more by the prestige he has managed to acquire in the field than by the force of his analyses or his arguments.

Chomsky thus rejected the idea of a grammar as a transformational mediator between cognitively produced SAs and surface structures, insisting, against all reason, that a grammar is a random sentence generator whose products are subject to semantic interpretation on the one hand, just as they are subject to phonetic interpretation on the other. This theory is known as the theory of *autonomous syntax*. It is argued in Seuren (2004a) that autonomous syntax is untenable not only on empirical grounds but also, in a general sense, because as a *realist* theory of grammar, reflecting what goes on in the mind, it is absurd, while as an *instrumentalist* theory of grammar, meant merely to capture the data in terms of maximal generalizations, it is unnecessarily twisted—that is, 'perverse' in a technical sense.

In fact—but this was not generally recognized during the 1970s and 1980s—Chomsky clung, and still clings, to an essentially behaviourist and neopositivist view of language, whereas the angry young generative semanticists were breaking away from the neopositivist enclosure, wishing to explore the wider possibilities of less doctrinal but, of course, still solidly scientific means of studying the nature of cognitive reality. Chomsky's unwillingness, or inability, to adapt to this new scientific paradigm was, in all likelihood, the main cause, besides his obvious lack of expertise in semantic matters, of his unrelenting resistance to the frame of mind expressing itself in Generative Semantics.

Be that as it may, the Generative Semantics (or Semantic Syntax) approach clearly is an effort to make explicit, and find empirical support for, the traditional idea of a (partial) commonality between linguistic and logical structure. Like Sanctius, mentioned in section 4.2.2, it places this commonality in the perspective of a relation between two levels of representation, the semantic-analysis (SA) level and the surface level, linked by transformational mapping rules—whereby , as shown in section 5.2.2, discourse-conditioned topic-comment modulation gets interwoven with discourse-independent syntactic structure.

The much improved analytical tools that are available today—owing largely to the great developments in logic and mathematics over the past 150 years—enable the development of precise and empirically testable theories that make this relation explicit. We are thus free to lift the ban on logic imposed upon linguistic theory during the early years of the twentieth century and to revert to an older past shaped by the work of ancient, medieval and renaissance scholars, with Sanctius as a shining example.

4.2.5 *Semantics: model-theoretic semantic interpretation*

Meanwhile, logic and linguistics came into contact at a totally different plane. The prominent and, at the time, promising American mathematical logician Richard Montague (1930–1971) gave a new meaning to the phrase that natural languages are formal languages of the type developed in logic and computer science. Whereas for Chomskyans and related schools of linguistic thought it meant that languages are sets of meaningless symbols arranged according to an algorithmic production procedure, Montague, playing on 'semantic' proof methods in logic, developed a system whereby (a) phrases in (English) sentences are 'translated' into, or reduced to, elements of expressions in the language of standard modern 'Russellian' predicate logic (so-called 'Montague grammar') and (b) the resulting logical expressions are tested for truth in any given possible world. The set of possible worlds in which a given sentence S is true will then be the meaning of S. This system, which showed great formal prowess, was based on Tarski's dictum that 'meaning is truth conditions'. This was semantics-cum-grammar in a neopositivist, non-cognitive garb.

One of Montague's main points was that the possible worlds approach, with the notion of 'truth in a model', would solve the still unsolved problem posed by the fact that natural language allows speakers to utter true sentences about non-existing, or 'intensional', entities, such as (4.6a) or (4.6b):

(4.6)   a. Apollo was worshipped in Delphi.
        b. The UFO John claimed to have seen was the talk of the town.

This should be impossible according to the neopositivist book, which wants talk about non-existing entities, such as the Greek god Apollo or 'unidentified flying objects' (UFOs), to be false or without a truth value or, at best, meaningless. Yet these sentences have no problem being true. In fact, (4.6a) IS true. For Montague, they are true in some possible worlds but not in others. And since meaning is truth conditions and truth conditions are realized as sets of possible worlds, truth for such sentences is reserved for certain sets of possible worlds, which may or may not include the actual world. This 'programme of extensionalization of intensions' was Montague's neopositivist answer to the problem of intensional entities.

The same 'programme of extensionalization of intensions' was thought to solve the old Fregean problem of the nonsubstitutability of co-extensive terms in so-called 'intensional contexts'. In simple terms, this is the problem that the denoting phrases *the morning star* and *the evening star*, normally substitutable *salva veritate* because they refer to the same object, the planet Venus, are not substitutable *salva veritate* in sentences like (4.7a). If the phrase *the morning star* is replaced with *the evening star*, it is no longer guaranteed that if (4.7a) is true, (4.7b) is necessarily also true:

(4.7)   a. John believes that the morning star is inhabited.
        b. John believes that the evening star is inhabited.

Gottlob Frege (1848–1925) had noticed this in his epochal (1892) and had posed the question of how semantic theory could account for this apparent discrepancy. His answer was that verbs like *believe* are 'intensional' in that their object clauses do not denote a truth value but a thought, and the thought that the morning star is inhabited is not the same as the thought that the evening star is inhabited (see section 9.4.1 for a full discussion). Montague, whose neopositivism did not allow for such eerie things as 'thoughts', disagreed. Feeling more comfortable with possible worlds, which he apparently considered less eerie than thoughts, he translated Frege's solution into a possible-world framework, saying that the object clauses of intensional verbs such as *believe* do not denote truth values but sets of possible worlds. Equality of such sets of possible worlds is equality of propositional meaning. Since the set of possible worlds in which the morning star is inhabited is not the same as the set of possible worlds in which the evening star is inhabited, it follows that the object clauses of (4.7a) and (4.7b) cannot be interchanged *salva veritate*.

Soon after Montague's untimely death, however, it was observed by a number of his followers that this 'programme of extensionalization of intensions' leads to a serious predicament when the object clause of a verb like *believe* represents a necessarily false or a necessarily true proposition. If propositions, like propositional meanings, are taken to be sets of possible worlds, then a necessarily false proposition is by definition the null set of possible worlds, and a necessarily true proposition is by definition the full set of possible worlds. This means that it should always be possible to substitute one necessary falsity, or one necessary truth, for another *salva veritate*. This, however, is clearly not so. It may well be the case that John believes (4.8a) but not (4.8b), even though the object clauses in these sentences are both necessarily false, and John may well believe (4.9a) but not (4.9b), even though the object clauses in both sentences are necessarily true:

(4.8)   a. John believes that all bachelors are married.
        b. John believes that the square root of 4000 is 200.

(4.9)   a. John believes that all dogs are animals.
        b. John believes that the square root of 40,000 is 200.

This problem has become known as the *problem of propositional attitudes*. Despite frantic efforts, in particular Cresswell (1985) (see note 5 in Chapter 9), it has remained unsolved till the present day. This fact forms one of the planks of the basic critique of Montagovian possible world semantics put forward in Chapter 9, which claims that the prophecy voiced in Dowty et al. (1981: 175) has come true:

> We must acknowledge that the problem of propositional attitude sentences is a fundamental one for possible world semantics, and for all we know, could eventually turn out to be a reason for rejecting or drastically modifying the whole possible worlds framework.

In the wider perspective adopted here, we observe that Montague's programme of extensionalization of intensions shows how and why the neopositivist philosophy of science, when applied to the human sciences, ultimately runs aground on the cliffs of the human mind and thus of natural language. Chapter 9 is a detailed demonstration of this thesis. Natural language does not admit treatment as a 'formal language with interesting handicaps'. Not only is there the problem of propositional attitude sentences, anyone looking at language with an eye for its cognitive bindings will find similar problems all over. The flexibility of its lexical meanings, manifest in phenomena such as polysemy or the dependence on values for open, cognition-dependent parameters,[5] sociolinguistic settling phenomena in the widest sense (Chapter 1), and many other properties of natural language vividly demonstrate the *a priori* fruitlessness of any attempt to dissociate language from cognition.

We must, therefore, conclude that the possible world approach to natural language grammar and semantics throws no light at all on natural language, let alone on the relation between language and logic. The alternative, presented in Chapter 9 of the present volume and in many of my previous publications, is to accept the reality, though not the existence, of thought-up *intensional entities*, which can be referred to and quantified over just like actually existing *extensional entities*, together with a mental machinery of *discourse domains* modelling previous discourse in terms of *cognitive content*, with open access to the whole of cognition. Only thus can we make progress on the long road to an understanding of human language and cognition.

Given the failure of modern mathematical logic to serve as a model for either an autonomous algorithmic sentence generator or a truth-value-assigning machine in a universe of possible worlds, all we are left with in the way of a relation between language and logic is the object-language structural and semantic link envisaged by Aristotle and applied by later generations of Alexandrian philologists and Stoic philosophers. In modern terms this means a recognition of the fact that the logical faculty of mankind originates in the lexical meanings of what we have learned to identify as logical operators plus the (re)discovery, on more detailed and more solid empirical grounds than were available to the ancients, of the structural mapping relations between semantic analyses as logically analytic expressions of propositions on the one hand and linguistic surface structures on the other. That is, we are back with Aristotle and 'the tradition', but now with a vastly improved toolbox and within vastly expanded horizons.

Yet, despite our fundamental and, I am sure, justified critique of the application of neopositivist or logical-empiricist methods to the human sciences, it must be admitted that our improved toolbox would not have become available and our expanded horizons would not have opened themselves to us had it not been for the great explosion of formalization in mathematics, logic and the sciences taking place over the past 150 years. The fault lies not with these recent developments, which have been uniquely beneficial in many ways, but with the failure to recognize that the study of

---

[5] Notably for the group of possession predicates, such as *have*, which has different conditions for truth in sentences like (i) and (ii):

(i) This hotel room has a bathroom.
(ii) This student has a supervisor.

Sentence (i) is false when the room in question has to share a bathroom with other rooms, but (ii) is still true when the student in question has to share the supervisor with other students. This is not a question of competence in English but of world knowledge: no English proficiency course will teach this difference; one has to know the way things are in the worlds of hotels and faculties. It follows that the semantic specification of the predicate *have* must be taken to contain an open parameter for a 'relation of appurtenance', whose value is provided by speaker-hearer's *world knowledge*. Similar open parameters are part of the meanings of gradable adjectives ('clever for a human/monkey', etc.), as well as for other lexical categories.

mankind, and in particular of human cognition, requires a methodology that is more adapted to its object of enquiry.

4.3 Natural logic and natural set theory

What goes for logic goes for its underlying mathematics, in particular set theory, which forms the basis of any logical system in that it creates an ontological model for logical languages and a mathematics to deal with it. Here again, the set theory underlying natural logic cannot be the standard mathematical set theory that is applicable to physical reality. It must be a *natural set theory* taken to be innately and implicitly built into human thinking. Given the fact that standard mathematical set theory (SMST) strikes the naïve observer as in many ways unnatural, natural set theory (NST) is likely to differ from SMST in a number of ways.

First, NST is sensibly taken not to contain a notion of *null set*. What is known as the null set (∅) in modern mathematics is for ordinary humans the absence of an extension for a concept. If anything shows the unnaturalness of the concept of null set, no matter how indispensable in mathematical set theory, it is the fact, known to all teachers of SMST, that beginning students invariably have great difficulty under-standing it and tend to continue making mistakes for a considerable time. Let us assume, therefore, that NST will have to do without the null set, which alone makes for massive differences between NST and SMST. The concept of the *totality of all entities* (**Ent**) seems likewise cognitively unrealistic, though to a lesser extent than the null set. Universally quantified statements are usually made with regard to restricted, contextually delimited totalities, as already observed in De Morgan (1847: 37–8).

Then, it makes sense to surmise that naïve cognition considers the operation of *union* or *addition* only for sets that are completely distinct and thus have no common intersection, with the result that when two or more sets are placed under the union operator—that is, added—the total number of elements (the cardinality) of the resulting set equals the arithmetical addition of the cardinality of the sets that have been added up. Analogously for the set-theoretic operation of *intersection*, which very much looks as if it is naturally understood as mutual partial intersection, whereby the sets involved always share a part (not the whole) with all other sets involved and whereby the resulting set does not equal **Ent**. Both the operations of union and of intersection are thus, in the terms of this hypothesis, restricted to certain set configurations and are, therefore, not applicable to any arbitrary pair (number) of sets, as in SMST. This is, of course, fatally wrong in mathematical set theory, but it looks very much as if it is cognitive reality.

More such restrictions are likely to hold with regard to SMST (for a fuller discussion see Chapter 3 in Seuren 2010). Empirical investigations will have to confirm or disconfirm the claims made here regarding NST. But the point is that any such restrictions have a direct bearing on the logic or logics constructed on the basis of mankind's natural way of looking at and operating with sets of entities.

This is most easily shown for predicate logic. To avoid the wrath of professional logicians, let us consider first how this works for standard modern predicate logic (SMPL). The two classic operators for predicate logic, the universal and existential quantifiers, are insightfully described, in the spirit of *generalized quantification analysis* (Mostowski 1957), as higher-order predicates expressing binary relations over sets of entities. Thus, the universal quantifier, usually symbolized as ∀, is describable as saying that one set is (classically) included in the other. A sentence like (4.10a) is then analysed, or rewritten logically, as (4.10b):

(4.10)   a. All Romans are mortal.
         b. $\forall_x$(Romans(x), Mortal(x))

where 'Romans(x)' denotes the set of all Romans, or [[Roman]], and 'Mortal(x)' denotes the set of all mortals, or [[Mortal]]. The sentence says that [[Roman]] is included in [[Mortal]], or [[Roman]] ⊆ [[Mortal]]. Similarly for the existential quantifier, standardly symbolized as ∃. A sentence like (4.11a), rendered as (4.11b), says that the two sets [[Roman]] and [[Famous]] have a non-null intersection:[6]

(4.11)   a. Some Romans are famous.
         b. $\exists_x$(Romans(x), Famous(x))

These two quantifiers are thus defined in set-theoretical terms. More formally, we can say that the universal quantifier ∀ and the existential quantifier ∃, both higher order predicates (that is, predicates over sets rather than individuals), are semantically defined as in (4.12), where the square-brackets notation is used to denote the extension of the predicates in question and where the variables X and Y range over (*n*th-order) sets:

(4.12)   a. [[∀]] = { <X,Y> | X ⊆ Y }
             (the extension of the predicate ∀ is precisely the set of all pairs of sets X and Y such that X is included in Y)

         b. [[∃]] = { <X,Y> | X ∩ Y ≠ ∅ }
             (the extension of the predicate ∃ is precisely the set of all pairs of sets X and Y such that X and Y have a non-null intersection)

This is the semantic definition of these two quantifiers in standard modern (Russellian) predicate logic or SMPL. In Aristotle's original logic (Aristotelian-Abelardian logic or AAPL; see section 8.4.1), the definition of the universal quantifier

---

[6] Objectual variables (see note 2 for the term *objectual*), such as *x* and *y*, are needed only to differentiate which term is bound by which quantifier. Thus, in a formula like $\forall_x$(Child(x), $\exists_y$(Footballer(y), Admire(x, y))), corresponding to *All children admire some footballer*, it is essential to have *x* and *y* in the proper order in 'Admire(x,y)'. The inverse order, as in 'Admire(y,x)', would result in a sentence like *For all children there is a football player who admires them*, or *All children are admired by some football player*. (Note that this is another clear case where the Scope-Ordering Constraint or SOC, discussed in section 3.7.2.2 and in many of my earlier publications going back to 1969, is seen to be at work.)

is slightly different. There, $\forall$ is defined as in (4.13) (the definition of $\exists$ remains unchanged):

(4.13) $[[\forall]] = \{ <X,Y> \mid X \subseteq Y \text{ and } X \neq \varnothing \}$
(the extension of the predicate $\forall$ is precisely the set of all pairs of sets X and Y such that X is included in Y and X is non-null)

As is shown in detail in Chapter 8, the added condition that $X \neq \varnothing$ leads to a very different logic, richer than SMPL and providing a better fit with natural logical intuitions. In this logic, sentences of the form *All R is M* (for example, *All Romans are mortal*) entail sentences of the form *Some R is M*, or *Some Romans are mortal* (the so-called *subaltern entailment schema*). In SMPL, as is well-known, the subaltern entailment schema does not hold. By contrast, the *Conversions*—that is, the equivalence of *Some R is M* with *Not all R is not M* and of *All R is M* with *No R is not M*—do hold in SMPL but not in AAPL. (For proofs, see section 8.4.1). Here we have a clear demonstration of the fact that different semantic definitions of the quantifiers will lead to different logical systems. It is thus easily understood that what I call the *natural logic* of mankind is unlikely to be the standardly accepted modern predicate logic, developed by such towering figures as Frege and Russell, but is defined by the *natural* meanings of the words that represent the logical operators. The question is: what do these meanings look like?

It was implicitly thought for many centuries that the traditional *Square of Opposition*—usually but mistakenly thought to be Aristotle's own logic whereas it is in fact an adulteration of his system brought about by later commentators—is the natural logic we are looking for. This may well be so, even though it suffers from the fatal logical defect of *undue existential import* or UEI, about which more in a moment. First let us introduce a simple nomenclature for logical sentence types, inspired by, but different from, the nomenclature traditionally used in treatments of the Square of Opposition. We use the sentence-types as specified in (4.14a–h), with the English (or Angloid) versions in the first column, the nomenclature (type names) in the second column and the translation into logical quantifier language in the third column. One will note that, in the middle column, $\neg$ signifies the *external* or *sentence negation* ('it is not the case that...') and * the *internal* or *matrix predicate negation*:

(4.14)
a.	All R is M	A	$\forall_x(Rx, Mx)$
b.	Some R is M	I	$\exists_x(Rx, Mx)$
c.	Not all R is M	$\neg$A	$\neg\forall_x(Rx, Mx)$
d.	Not some (=No) R is M	$\neg$I	$\neg\exists_x(Rx, Mx)$
e.	All R is not M	A*	$\forall_x(Rx, \neg Mx)$
f.	Some R is not M	I*	$\exists_x(Rx, \neg Mx)$
g.	Not all R is not M	$\neg$A*	$\neg\forall_x(Rx, \neg Mx)$
h.	Not some (=No) R is not M	$\neg$I*	$\neg\exists_x(Rx, \neg Mx)$

Given this, what is undue existential import or UEI? The defect of UEI consists in the fact that the Square fails as a logical system in all cases where the predicate of the subject term has a null extension, or, in all cases where [[R]] = ∅. And why does the Square suffer from UEI? Because the quantifiers cannot be defined consistently in set-theoretical terms in such a way that they give rise to the Square as a logical system.

This is quickly shown. The Square has both the subaltern entailment schema (from A to I and thus also from A* to I*) and the Conversions (the equivalence of A and ¬I* and of I and ¬A*). But this means that, in the Square of Opposition, the universal quantifier ∀ is defined both with and without the extra condition that X ≠ ∅, which makes that logic unsound. The unsoundness shows up when one asks whether A-type sentences (All R is M) are true or false, according to the Square, in cases where [[R]] = ∅. If true, it follows by the subaltern entailment schema that the corresponding I-type sentence (Some R is M) is also true, but that is impossible because an I-type sentence requires for truth that [[R]] and [[M]] have a non-null intersection—a condition that is incompatible with [[R]] being equal to ∅. Therefore, when [[R]] = ∅, an A-type sentence cannot be true. Since the logic is governed by the *principle of strict bivalence*, which says (a) that there are only two truth values, true and false, and (b) that every formula in the logical language must have a truth value, it follows that, when [[R]] = ∅, an A-type sentence must be false, since it cannot be true. This makes ¬A true. But this again runs foul of the Conversions, since the Conversions say that ¬A (Not all R is M) is equivalent with I* (Some R is not M), which requires for truth that there be a non-null intersection of [[R]] and [[M̄]] (the complement of [[M]]) , which again requires the non-nullness of [[R]]. Therefore, when [[R]] = ∅, an A-type sentence can be neither true nor false, which violates the strict bivalence principle. The subaltern entailment schema and the Conversions cannot be combined into one consistent system, as is done in the Square. In the end, we will save the Square by incorporating it into a larger system of three-valued presuppositional logic (see Seuren 2010, Ch. 10), but this is not at issue here. What is at issue here, is the fact that the operators of any logical language are best defined exclusively in terms of set theory, whether standard or natural, and that the price to be paid for any fudging with that condition is logical disaster.

All this goes to show that the quantifiers are best described as binary predicates over pairs of sets (in the simplest cases, second-order predicates over pairs of sets of first-order entities), defined exclusively in set-theoretic terms. As regards the main operators of *propositional logic, not* (¬), *and* (∧) and *or* (∨), a similar analysis is applicable. In propositional logic, it is not sets of entities that are input to the calculus but sets of situations (for the theory behind this analysis in terms of sets of possible situations, see Chapter 8). If a proposition *P* is true in the set of possible situations /P/ in the universe **Uni** of possible situations, then *not-P* (¬P), with the standard bivalent negation ¬, is true in the complement of /P/ in **Uni**. Analogously, if the propositions

P and *Q* are true in the sets of possible situations /P/ and /Q/, respectively, then the composite proposition *P* ∧ *Q* (*P and Q*) is true in the set /P/∩/Q/ of possible situations, so that /P ∧ Q/ equals /P/∩/Q/. And the composite proposition *P* ∨ *Q* (*P or Q*) is true in the set /P/∪/Q/ of possible situations, so that /P ∨ Q/ equals /P/∪/Q/.

4.4 The importance of scope relations

So far, we have been through some logic but it may well be felt that the importance of logic for an adequate understanding of natural language has not been convincingly demonstrated. This is now going to change with the introduction of the notion of logical scope. The notion of logical scope stems from logic but it has a much wider application than in logic alone. In structural terms, the notion of scope is defined as the Matrix-S functioning as the subject term under a logical or non-logical operator. Consider, for example, the sentences (4.15a) and (4.16a), logically represented as (4.15b) and (4.16b), respectively. These latter two expressions, however, are linear (bracketed) representations of tree structures that consist of hierarchically ordered constituents, as in (4.15c) and (4.16c), respectively. Tense is disregarded, so as to keep the exposé within limits of immediate comprehensibility. Note that constituent order is taken to be Verb-Subject-Object (VSO) throughout. The grammatical treatment of tense makes for a surface SVO-order (see Seuren 1996):

(4.15) a. John is not an Englishman.

  b. ¬ [Englishman(John)]

  c.

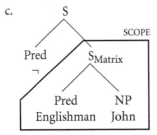

(4.16) a. All flags are green.

  b. ∀ₓ(Green(x), Flag(x))

  c.

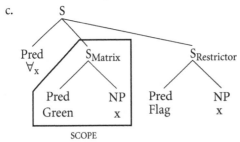

In both cases, the scope consists of the Matrix-S, whose predicate will be the main predicate of the surface sentence. In general, the scope of an operator OP is the Matrix-S it is lowered into. OP can be a logical operator, as in (4.15c) and (4.16c), but it can also be a non-logical, semantic operator, as in the case of the prepositional operators discussed in section 3.7.2.2.

One should note that in (4.16b,c), against the general convention of placing the restrictor term ('Flag(x)') in first and the matrix term ('Green(x)') in second position, I have surreptitiously inverted the order. Logically speaking, there is no difference, as one can adapt the semantic definitions of the operators involved. But the advantage is that the scope of all operators in all cases can now be defined as the *subject-* or *Matrix-S* of the operator in question. Grammatically speaking, moreover, this 'inverted' order has the advantage that the transformational conversion process leading from structures like (4.16c) to the corresponding surface structures like (4.16a) is channelled through more familiar routes. The first step in this process is the unification of the quantifier predicate with the restrictor term, to be followed by the lowering of the new complex predicate into the position of the objectual variable in the matrix term. If the restrictor term is placed in second position—that is, treated as an object term—the unification of the quantifier predicate with the restrictor term is a form of OBJECT INCORPORATION, a well-known process in the syntax of languages. By contrast, SUBJECT INCORPORATION is extremely rare and mostly limited to impersonal weather verbs ('rain is falling' → 'it is raining'). (Note that, for reasons of ease of exposition, OBJECT INCORPORATION has already been applied in the structure (3.18a) of Figure 3.1 in section 3.7.2.2.)

What is called the Matrix-S is, to begin with, the bare S-structure containing the main predicate of the surface sentence plus its argument terms (which may be bound variables). This is how the Matrix-S appears at SA-level, where the SA-structure is input to the grammar, as also in (4.15c) and (4.16c). However, since all kinds of operators may occur between some operator high up in the SA-structure and the original Matrix-S, and since, in virtue of the universal property of grammars called *Matrix Greed* (see (3.32) in section 3.8.1), these intermediate operators all have to be cyclically incorporated (lowered) into the S-structure commanded by them, starting from the lowest operator and gradually moving up until the highest operator has been lowered, the original bare Matrix-S is gradually enriched with operators cyclically incorporated into it. To maintain the generalization that the scope of an operator is its Matrix-S, we keep calling the enriched Matrix structure the Matrix-S. To have an idea of what is meant and how the machinery works, consider the following example:

(4.17)   a. All children admire some footballer.

   b. $\forall_x(\exists_y(Admire(x,y), Footballer(y)), Child(x))$

(4.17b) is represented as a constituent tree structure in (4.18a), which is the SA of (4.17a), and thus input to the grammar of English. The first cyclic operation to be performed on (4.18a) is OBJECT INCORPORATION (OI) on the quantifier ∃ just above the Matrix-S. The result is (4.18b). Then OPERATOR LOWERING (LOW) applies to the complex predicate ∃$_y$:Footballer(y), which lands in the position of the variable bound by it in the Matrix-S. The result is (4.18c). Now the machinery moves one cycle up, to the quantifier ∀$_x$. Again, OI applies first, giving (4.18d), followed by LOW, giving (4.18e). The Matrix-S has now swallowed all higher operators except the tense operators, which will result in the surface structure (4.17a). This shows why, in structural terms, we can say that the scope of any operator OP is the Matrix-S as it is the moment OP is about to be processed. At SA-level, the scope of any OP is its subject-S—that is, the first S-structure after OP.

(4.18)

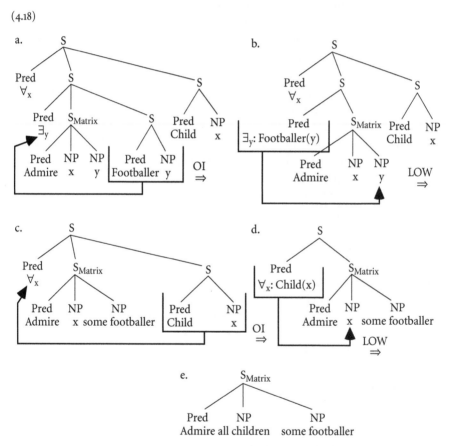

Semantically speaking, the relation of an operator to its scope is no different from the relation of a predicate to its argument terms: the predicate assigns a property to whatever is denoted by each argument term. In the proposition underlying the sentence *John is an Englishman*, the property of being an Englishman is assigned to the person John, resulting in a virtual fact which is also an actual fact when the sentence is true but remains a virtual fact when the sentence is false. Likewise, the predicate *not* ($\neg$) assigns to this virtual fact the property of not being an actual fact. In the proposition underlying the sentence *All flags are green*, the predicate *all* ($\forall$) assigns to the denotation of its subject- or Matrix-S (the set of all green things) the property of including the set of flags.

For what seem to be mostly practical reasons, we speak of scope only in relation to 'abstract' predicates that are lowered into a Matrix-S during the grammatical processing, not in relation to Matrix predicates or to nominal terms (note that all operators, whether logical or non-logical, are treated as predicates at SA-level). The reason why we do not speak of the *scope* of ordinary lexical predicates with regard to their nominal argument terms lies mainly in the fact that in sentences with two or more scope-bearing logical or semantic operators these operators can be interchanged with regard to each other, which will, in most cases, lead to a different meaning, whereas 'ordinary' nominal argument terms cannot swap places with their own predicates and thus take scope over them. Thus, one can say both *It is possible that not p* and *It is not possible that p* (where *p* stands for an embedded subject-S). But while one can say *John is an Englishman*, one cannot turn *John* into a predicate over *be an Englishman*.[7] Scope differences thus typically arise according to what position is assigned to what operator above any Matrix-S.

The important general fact is that natural language sentences are full of both logical and non-logical scope-bearing operators, whose hierarchy must be established for a proper interpretation. Since surface sentences are often ambiguous in this respect, a proper interpretation requires a semantic representation where the hierarchical relations of the operators in question are expressed unambiguously and explicitly. This is the basis of the hypothesis that surface sentences require underlying semantic analyses (SAs) where scope relations are expressed explicitly—that is, in a semantically explicit language that incorporates logical structure.

4.5 Conclusion

It is thus clear that the relation between natural language and logic lies mainly in the fact that language contains expressions for what have been identified as logical or non-logical operators. The meanings of the logical operators determine the logic of

[7] A punctilious reader might observe that a nominal argument term may well become a predicate over the remainder of the Matrix-structure in which it occurs. This happens, in particular, in cleft sentences of the form *It is John who is an Englishman*, analysable as 'the one who is an Englishman is John', where *John* is the predicate and *the one who is an Englishman* is the subject term. (This operation is known in logic as *λ-abstraction*.) Although this objection is probably justified, it does not seem to have had any impact on the practical use of the term *scope* in logic and semantics.

language and the positions of both kinds of operator with respect to each other in the logico-semantic analyses of sentences determine their scope relations and thus co-determine sentence meanings. The logical operators are represented by words or morphemes in natural languages. These words or morphemes have lexical meanings which, when defined in set-theoretical terms, yield a (natural) logic. This is what, in my analysis, the relation between language, logic and mathematics amounts to. It follows that the interpretation of sentences requires a structural sentence representation in terms of logical structure, owing to the fact that logical and non-logical operators are predicates over subject clauses, which may again contain operators over subject clauses, etc. Since the hierarchical scope relations of operators with respect to each other are crucial for the proper interpretation of sentences, and since it is only in logical representations that scope relations are systematically expressed, it follows that semantic representations of sentences require logical structure. This is a central tenet in the theory of language.

5

A test bed for grammatical theories

'Test beds allow for rigorous, transparent and replicable testing of scientific theories, computational tools and new technologies'

(Wikipedia*)

5.1 Introduction

Language is difficult and treacherous. Good observers have known that for a long time, but especially over the past half century this insight has been rubbed in with some force by theoretical linguists, who, however, did not always find a willing ear among those who prefer claims to insight. Studying language is not an easy option. When I was still teaching, I used to tell my students that language is always more complex than you think, recursively. It is necessary to be aware of that, when you study language, because students and even professional linguists, let alone those who come from other disciplines and deal with language as an incidental sideline, regularly underestimate the complexity of language: we all use it effortlessly all the time, so it must be easy. Well, it isn't, not as an object of enquiry, one reason being that language is intricately interwoven, at all levels, with the cognitive and emotional mind, whether individually or socially, and another that the grammars and semantics of languages incorporate formally complex systems that can only be unearthed by meticulous and systematic observation and consequent so-called 'abstract' hypothesis formation in terms of a general theory of human language aiming at the strongest possible generalizations over all human languages—that is, a maximally compact universal theory of human language.

For the past one hundred years or so, linguistics has tried hard to become 'scientific' and to leave behind the stage where its theories were based on visceral feelings. But when one applies the criteria of modern science to the study of language, it soon becomes clear that language, like all mental phenomena, is more refractory than non-mental physical nature. Those who think that language can be understood without the help of sometimes complex descriptive and analytical 'abstract' formalisms are seriously mistaken. Language gives the impression of being easily understood, as easily as we understand a language when we use it. Ease of use is confounded with

---

* //en.wikipedia.org/wiki/Testbed [last accessed 06/08/13].

simplicity of the system behind it, whereas one reason for that system to be as complex as it is, is precisely the drive to make it user-friendly. An example of this has been given in section 3.7.2.2. The appearance of simplicity is due to the fact that most of the language machinery is hidden from view. As with computers, almost everything goes on behind the screen. We use our computers every day with the greatest ease, yet if we were called upon to understand how they work merely on the basis of visible evidence, without any knowledge of the hidden software or the technology of the hardware, we would be at a loss. And the brain, with language as an element in it, is more difficult than computers.

This fact is of basic importance to non-linguists who engage in interdisciplinary research involving natural language as an object of study, in particular, but not exclusively, neuroscientists unravelling the neurophysiological basis of active and passive linguistic processing. The subtlety and complexity of natural language(s) is often lost on such 'outsiders', though, fortunately, there are notable exceptions. Linguists, vying for their favour, often do not find it in their interest to pull out batteries of problematic linguistic data that show the full complex depth of language. To the extent that this becomes accepted policy, it gives rise to a climate of opinion where the complexity of language is severely underestimated and experimental results are given interpretations that go way beyond what is warranted on grounds of serious linguistic analysis and theory—much to the detriment of real progress in science.

Within the precincts of linguistics proper, one result of underestimating the difficulty of language has been a proliferation of theories of, or approaches to, language and, in their wake, of theories of grammar or ideas of what a grammar of a language should be taken to be or not to be. Most of these would-be theories can be discarded simply because they fall foul of the facts. Unfortunately, however, they continue to be cultivated, often in restricted circles where language is looked at only from one particular angle yet claims are made that pertain to language as a whole. This has not been good for the discipline of linguistics, which now offers to the outside world a picture of fragmentation and deep-running internal oppositions, without it being known to the outside world that a large portion of the existing theories and approaches, though advertised as general theories of language, only cover certain, often quite superficial or marginal, aspects of it, and that often in badly inadequate ways.

Of course, no theory is perfect and every theory has to cope with disturbing facts, usually in the form of counterexamples. But ordinary counterexamples are not primarily the facts I have in mind. What I mean is cases where a given theory or group of theories is *in principle* unable to adopt an obvious solution on account of the fact that the solution envisaged requires machinery of a kind that is *in principle* excluded by the theory or theories in question, which claim proprietary rights to the whole of language.

This applies in particular to the many theories, or rather approaches, on the market today which reject, as a matter of principle, any 'abstract' theorizing. (Prominent among these approaches are those that go under the banner of 'cognitivism'.) What is meant by 'abstract' is not always clear, but, on the whole, what authors rejecting anything 'abstract' in the theory of language mean is that phonologically null elements are not admitted, that sentences have only one representation, the surface structure, without any null elements, retrievable deletions or whatever (except, surprisingly, in morphology, where null elements are considered admissible), that there are no movement, deletion or copying rules: all there is is what is visible at the surface (except in morphology). Generalizations are allowed only in terms of statistical trends. This extreme and naïve neopositivism is strangely combined with an appeal to introspection as regards non-observable structures and regularities. Usually, such theories claim not only an account of syntax but also of semantics and the relation between these two, which is noble but not very helpful as long as no comprehensible account of meaning is provided. And it never is, in these surface oriented, non-'abstract', quasi-scientific and essentially visceral theories.

A further typical feature of 'cognitivism' in linguistics is the tenet that natural first-language acquisition is based exclusively on statistical frequency measures in the linguistic material offered to the learning infant. Any thought of an innate faculty specifically guiding the natural process of language acquisition, and thus any thought of language universals, is explicitly and *a priori* rejected with a fervour that comes close to religious fanaticism. Many of the observations adduced below are meant to show that such an exclusively statistics-based theory of language acquisition is hopelessly inadequate and stands no chance of accounting for the facts observed. Unfortunately, however, ideology too often seems to have the upper hand.

An obvious example is the following. Every English speaker immediately understands a sentence like *The first Americans landed on the moon in 1969*. Yet when one asks 'Who are or were the first Americans?', the answer must be that the noun phrase *the first Americans* does not refer to any 'first Americans', whoever they may be or have been, but to 'the first Americans who landed on the moon'. The sentence is thus to be paraphrased as something like 'the first Americans *to do so* landed on the moon in 1969', whereby a VP-anaphor of the form *to do so*, standing for the main predicate 'to land on the moon', is added to the phrase *the first Americans*. This would also explain why negation is problematic in such sentences. A negative sentence like *The first guests were not arriving* may be syntactically well-formed but it is semantically repugnant and highly abnormal. The reason would seem to be that such a sentence suffers from internal contradiction, as it would say that the first guests to arrive were not arriving—hardly a coherent message.

How a theory can account for such phenomena without assuming deletions, movements and other 'abstract' elements, or how an infant can learn the proper meaning of such sentences merely on the basis of statistics, remains a mystery. It is the purpose of the present chapter to give many more such examples and invite others to make their own contributions, and thus to spread the insight that any attempt, in grammatical theorizing, to steer clear of 'abstract' elements or rule formalisms, or of an innate learning programme, is doomed to failure on merely empirical grounds.

Sometimes, none of the existing theories has an answer and one simply has no idea of what a proper solution might look like. Such cases are useful to keep in mind as they provide a good reason for all linguists to tune down any claim to full adequacy and generality of their theories. But the argument value of such 'insolubles' is limited, given the state of the art. More directly valuable are facts or observations for which the solution is clear enough, at least in principle but where the solution cannot be fitted into some given theoretical framework. When faced with such cases, that theory is in trouble. Yet the discipline of linguistics is so divided and so fragmented that schools faced with such cases are able to carry on and acquire funding regardless.

The present chapter thus gives the reader an idea of how hard a nut to crack language is and, in a more practical vein, presents some crucial facts with a direct bearing on existing grammatical theories and approaches, so that one can say with confidence that this or that theory or approach is in principle still in the race or has to be given up on account of basic inadequacy. The facts presented—mostly taken from English, though other languages are not eschewed—pose basic problems for all or some of the current theories or approaches to language.

Some of these facts—let us call them *class A facts*—are typically not the result of language learning and thus do not reflect settling phenomena of the kind discussed in Chapter 1. That they are not learned and memorized, appears from the fact that their occurrence is too rare to serve as a basis for implicit language acquisition by spontaneous learners, whether infants or adults. Moreover, they are unknown to language teachers and thus never form the object of explicit language teaching. Yet speakers assent immediately to these observations, which shows that there is more to language than what is learned during language acquisition. One should note that any given class A facts do not necessarily occur in all languages: they are not themselves language universals but are reasonably taken to follow from language universals in that when they occur, they are immediately interpreted the proper way, without special teaching or habituation. But they may be inhibited by language-specific restrictions or regulations, as in the case of accented comment lowering in French (see the examples (5.11) and (5.12) and note 10 below).

The existence of class A facts means that it makes sense to entertain the possibility of a species-specific, universal, innate set of grammatical and semantic principles restricting the shape of natural language grammars and guiding the language-acquisition process. The observation of class A facts thus places heavy demands on general theories of language.

Other facts, the *class B facts*, represent language-specific acquisition results, in that one has to have a high degree of language-specific competence to judge their correctness. The argument value of these facts is that if the machinery required to account for them in a maximally generalized way—that is, the machinery capturing the widest and most significant generalizations—is not admitted in some specific general theory or model, that theory or model is in trouble, unless it can provide an alternative, *non-ad-hoc*, analysis that accounts at least equally well for the facts in question in a different framework. And if no existing type of analysis can take the observed fact or facts into its stride, then that very fact should remind all linguists of the fact that we are still some way removed from a full understanding of human language.

In general, for both categories of facts, a full and detailed account of how the observed phenomena fit into a fully formalized analysis is not aimed at in the present study. Only occasionally do I provide a succinct statement of the rule system that appears adequately to account for the facts. More often, I try to formulate an underlying explanatory or leading principle or a rough formal analysis that seems to have to guide any fuller analysis and explanation of the facts in question. And occasionally, I have to leave the observation unexplained, as no one seems to have an inkling of how to tackle it in a *non-ad-hoc* way. The practical point is that theories which, as a matter of principle, do not allow for the analysis or for the explanatory leading principle given will then either have to find an (unlikely) alternative avenue of explanation or have to give way to theories that provide a natural and convincing explanation of the facts in question.[1]

The observations presented in the present chapter are in some ways similar to what are known in the linguistic literature as *squibs*—that is, observations that pose as yet unsolved problems in terms of any given theory or set of theories.[2] Squibs tend to expose some problematic gap in current grammatical, lexical, phonological or semantic knowledge and thus constitute a challenge and an admonition to do more

---

[1] The first option, that of an alternative course, is often pursued in anthropologically oriented linguistics and also in cognitivist circles. The course taken there consists in a wholesale denial of grammatical systematicity, embedded in a feeling that 'real' language is primarily found in everyday interactional and conversational data (a confusion of the language *system* and the *use* of that system). The focus is on paralinguistic phenomena, such as gesturing, pauses, non-integrated exclamations or facial expressions. The result, in many such studies, is then a claim to the effect that the whole of the language system is reducible to such essentially paralinguistic—that is, non-linguistic—phenomena. While the validity and usefulness of the study of paralinguistic phenomena is beyond dispute, when this study leads to a denial of the specific systematicity of human language it is mandatory to raise the alarm and point to facts that make such a denial untenable.

[2] The term *squib* was introduced in this sense during the late 1960s by the linguist John R. (Haj) Ross, himself the most productive source of squibs known in the field (on the internet one can find a collection of several thousand handwritten squibs he came up with over the years). Since its inception in 1970, the periodical *Linguistic Inquiry* has featured a regular column 'Squibs and Discussion', containing problematic observations of all kinds offered by a large variety of linguists.

work. On the whole, however, they are not aimed at testing entire theoretical frameworks. The observations presented here are. They are, so to speak, squibs with an edge.

Theoretically crucial observations of the kind presented here form a *test bed*, meant to eliminate not only grammatical theories but also theories of language in a wider sense. A test bed is of great value when a theory is required to be reliable, robust and as error-free as possible, and in particular when different theories or approaches are to be evaluated with regard to each other. No generally acknowledged test bed for grammatical theories has so far come into being in the discipline. Yet it would be useful to have such an institution. A linguistic test bed is by its very nature open-ended, in that everyone is free to contribute their crucial observations and, of course, the nature of the observations will change as new theories arise. What I present here is a highly selective and still small collection of crucial, discriminatory observations in the sense intended. More are likely to be found among the squibs already published in *Linguistic Inquiry* or in the so far unpublished Ross collection mentioned in note 2. The Ross squibs are not used here, as they have not been published. Occasionally, as the reader will notice, I fall back on a squib taken from *Linguistic Inquiry*.

5.2 Some class A facts

Class A facts are typically linguistic facts that do not have to be taught or learned individually and do not follow from any language-specific rule or rule system, yet are immediately recognized by anyone with a normal command of the language in question and even by adult beginning learners. Such facts strongly suggest that they follow from as yet only partially known universal principles. Let us start with some facts to do with anaphora.

5.2.1 *The epithet pronoun test*

To show what the epithet pronoun test amounts to, we must first have a quick overall look at pronouns and anaphora in general. Anaphora is notoriously complex. As a rough, overall definition, I say that *anaphora is reference by proxy*, whereby the proxy authorizer is called the *antecedent*. To create some order, it is necessary to distinguish various kinds of anaphora.[3]

Two main and partially crossing distinctions are to be made first. On the one hand, a distinction is to be made between *referential* and *bound* anaphora. On the other, we need to distinguish *external* from *internal* anaphora, according to whether the

---

[3] See Seuren (1985: 346–86) for an extensive discussion of the anaphora problem, including quantified and reflexive anaphora. For reflexivity, see section 5.2.2.1 and Chapter 7 in the present volume.

antecedent is found outside or inside the sentence in which the anaphoric expression occurs. External anaphora is always referential (as binding does not occur outside the sentence); internal anaphora is sometimes of the referential and sometimes of the bound variety. The epithet test, about which more below, separates referential from bound anaphora.

In cases of external anaphora, the antecedent can often be linked to immediately preceding linguistic context, as in (5.1a) or, more rarely, in subsequent discourse, as in (5.1b).[4] Often also, the antecedent cannot be linked to explicit preceding (or following) verbal context but must be retrieved from world knowledge regarding typical situations, as in (5.1c)—a process falling under what is called 'bridging' in the psycholinguistic literature. Sometimes, as in (5.1d), an externally anaphoric pronoun picks up the value of a parameter (in this case the parameter 'Pope'), which means that cognition must be taken to allow for variable entity representations. This phenomenon is known as 'sloppy identity' anaphora. Sometimes also, the antecedent of an external pronoun is provided by an existentially quantified noun phrase, as in (5.1e). In such cases, cataphora (see note 4) appears to be much less natural, as appears from (5.1f). Generalizing, we can say that in all cases of external anaphora the antecedent, licensing the proxy reference made by the anaphoric expression, is not a linguistic expression but the *cognitive representation* of a really existing or imaginary entity.[5] This explains (5.1g), where the anaphor takes as its antecedent a cognitive representation that has just been said not to have a counterpart in the actual world— which shows that anaphora is basically distinct from presupposition (see Seuren 2010: 372–7).

Whether the generalization that the antecedent is in all cases a cognitive representation and not a linguistic expression can be upheld for internal anaphora as well, is a question that needs further discussion. Precise analysis will possibly reveal that, for internal anaphora, one will have to fall back on the notion that what is called the antecedent is a linguistic expression. But we can leave this question aside here.

---

[4] In traditional grammar, (5.1b) is considered to be a case of *cataphora*, not of *anaphora*. In ancient Greek, *katá* meant, among other things, 'downstream' and *aná* 'upstream'. Note that in (5.1b) there is a cataphoric relation not only between *he* and *Harry* but also between *it* and the clause *Harry is in for a big surprise*.

[5] There is a question, much discussed in the pragmatically oriented literature on discourse anaphora, regarding the difference between *anaphora* and *deixis*. The view taken here is that deixis differs from anaphora mainly in that deixis is not reference by proxy but reference by pointing. In deixis there is no antecedent. Deictic expressions are themselves directly referring expressions, more directly even than definite descriptions or proper names. In this respect, deixis is the opposite of anaphora. The difficulty is that in many languages the pronouns used for anaphora and those used for deixis show considerable overlap. I will not here go any further into the bulky literature on how anaphora differs from deixis, as this question is not germane to the discussion at hand.

Typical examples of external anaphora are the following:

(5.1) a. *Harry* left without a word. *He* went straight home.[6]
       b. *He* doesn't know it yet, but *Harry* is in for a big surprise.
       c. He is not the sort of man to go steady. But *they* are always extremely attractive.
       d. In 1650, *the Pope* wore a beard, but in 1950 *he* was clean-shaven.
       e. A *woman* entered the room. *She* attracted admiring gazes from everyone.
       f. ?*She* doesn't know it yet, but a *woman* is in for a big surprise.
       g. John has no *children*. So *they* can't have misbehaved.

The specific form of anaphora demonstrated in (5.1e) deserves a special name as it has a precisely defined function in the semantics of discourse. I have called it *primary anaphora* (Seuren 2010: 293–310). Its specific function in discourse semantics is as follows. Indefinite noun phrases are usually, correctly, taken to introduce a new entity representation ('address') into the discourse domain D by means of an existential statement. A sentence like *A woman entered the room* establishes a new *woman*-address in the current D. It does so by means of the corresponding underlying existential proposition 'there was a woman x such that x entered the room'. This, being a proposition, is either true or false. The new *woman*-address is thus a propositional addition to D, which means that it does not have referential status and does not stand for a possible individual in the situation given. It cannot, therefore, without special provisions, function as a nominal antecedent for a subsequent anaphoric pronoun, since nominal antecedents must be entity addresses, not propositional increments, and thus have referential value. It is the function of primary anaphora to make that possible. Primary anaphora turns a newly introduced 'open' (that is, still propositional) address into a 'closed' referential address standing for an entity. Referential addresses do not have a truth value (are not true or false) but are the mental representation of entities in the real or a thought-up world. This transition from an 'open' to a 'closed' address is called *address closure* in Seuren (1985: 318–9; 2010: 230–3). Address closure as a result of primary anaphora accounts for the difference between, for example, (5.2a) and (5.2b) (cp. Seuren 2010: 248):

(5.2) a. Nob has few customers who are dissatisfied.
       b. Nob has few customers, and they are dissatisfied.

(5.2a) simply makes a new propositional addition to D, thereby setting up a new open address, which can be true or false. The occurrence of the pronoun *they* in (5.2b), immediately following the introduction of the open *customers*-address, causes the

---

[6] In the example sentences to do with anaphora, italics stand for possible co-reference. An asterisk signals impossible and a question mark doubtful co-reference. Small capitals or bold print, as in (5.11) ff., indicate prosodic prominence.

closure of this address, so that this pronoun can now take the new *customers*-address as sentence-external antecedent. That this has semantic, in fact truth-conditional, consequences will be obvious, for example, from the difference between (5.2a) and (5.2b).

In Montagovian possible-world semantics (PWS), primary anaphora has led to the much advertised problem of *donkey anaphora*, consisting in the fact that primary anaphora pronouns, such as *they* in (5.2b), cannot be given a place in standard Russellian logic, which serves as the logical vehicle for PWS.[7] Since this logic only admits of bound objectual variables (for the term *objectual*, see Chapter 4, note 2) as argument terms to predicates, and since primary anaphora pronouns such as *they* in (5.2b) cannot be treated as bound variables, it must be concluded that Russellian logic is inadequate not only for the purpose of PWS but for the purpose of natural language semantics in general. And this inadequacy is a direct consequence of the fact that standard Russellian logic is unable to deal with contextual or discourse factors.

One will note that this problem did not come about as a result of an empirical question arising from available data but is theory-generated, in that it shows up the inadequacy of Russellian logic for the purpose for which it is used. Those who have little faith in that logic (or in PWS)—and are unfamiliar with problems such as the one posed by (5.2)—will thus hardly be excited by the donkey anaphora problem and merely see their scepticism confirmed. Yet those who have put all their money on PWS, complete with Russellian logic, are in trouble, for the mere reason that the formal machinery adopted leads to a quandary. (The empirical obstacle posed by (5.2) above played no role in PWS, as the semantic difference between (5.2a) and (5.2b) was never observed in PWS quarters.)

The answer given in Kamp (1981) and Kamp and Reyle (1993), both firmly rooted in the PWS camp, is that the notion of a discourse domain **D** must be introduced into the theory—just as had been argued in Seuren (1972c; 1975) on entirely different, mainly presuppositional, grounds—and that Russellian logic must be adapted to incorporate elements functioning as what I call primary anaphora pronouns. This theory has become known as *Discourse Representation Theory* (DRT). In this perspective, the donkey anaphora problem merely shows the basic inadequacy of the Russellian (and Quinean) programme of reducing all definite referring argument

---

[7] Besides cases like *Nob owns a donkey and he feeds it*, donkey anaphora also covers cases like *If Nob owns a donkey, he feeds it*, *Either Nob owns no donkey or he feeds it* and *Every farmer who owns a donkey feeds it*. I do not discuss the latter three classes of cases here, because they can be shown, in terms of discourse incrementation, to incorporate *and*-conjunction (see Seuren 2010: 307–10). One notes, meanwhile, that in all three cases the pronoun is replaceable with an epithet: *If Nob owns a donkey, he feeds the wretched animal*; *Either Nob owns no donkey or he feeds the wretched animal*; *Every farmer who owns a donkey feeds the wretched animal*. This is a clear sign that 'donkey' pronouns do not represent bound variables but are of a referential nature.

terms to bound variables. The real problem, not mentioned in the PWS or DRT literature, is the empirical question posed by the semantic difference between (5.2a) and (5.2b). This problem is solved by a theory of primary anaphora and address closure. Primary anaphora is thus a special case of external anaphora.

External anaphora resolution is not, on the whole, subject to principles defined in terms of sentence structure and much more to principles in the sphere of situational or world knowledge, or to that perennially elusive thing called 'common sense'. Those who have occupied themselves with external anaphora are, on the whole, psycholinguists and pragmatically oriented text linguists, not theoretical linguists looking at the formal aspects of language and grammar.

Next to external anaphora, we have *internal anaphora*—that is, relations between anaphoric pronouns and antecedents within the sentence. Here, the principles at work are clearly much more of a structural nature, definable in terms of surface or deep sentence structure, depending on the kind of pronoun at issue. Different categories must be distinguished for internal anaphora, in particular *internal referential anaphora* on the one hand and, on the other, *reflexive* and *quantificational anaphora*, which involve some kind of binding, forming the category of *bound anaphora* mentioned above.

In section 3.7.2.1 the problem of internal referential anaphora resolution was discussed using as examples the four sentences in (3.9) repeated here for convenience as (5.3) (italics indicate anaphoric relations; asterisks say that there is no anaphoric relation):

(5.3)   a. While *John* stood on the balcony, *he* watched the crowd.
         b. While *he* stood on the balcony, *John* watched the crowd.
         c. *John* watched the crowd, while *he* stood on the balcony.
         d. **He* watched the crowd, while *John* stood on the balcony.

As one will remember, the problem is why in (5.3a–c) the pronoun *he* is naturally taken to be coreferential with *John*, while in (5.3d) such a relation of coreferentiality is excluded. The answer given in section 3.7.2.1 consists in an appeal to a universal principle, the *Internal Definite Anaphora Principle* or IDAP, which says that for a pronoun *p* to be coreferential with its antecedent *A*, *A* must precede *p* or, if *A* follows *p*, *p* must occur in a high-peripheral subordinate clause or at least in a high-peripheral prepositional phrase.

On the whole, IDAP works quite well, provided non-referring or bound pronouns, such as cases of covert reflexivity or of variable binding, are singled out and treated separately. Thus, an example like (5.4), taken from Akmajian and Jackendoff (1970: 125), an early squib in *Linguistic Inquiry*, does not contradict IDAP, because *his* in (5.4a), if interpreted as coreferential with *John*, is a *covertly reflexive possessive pronoun*, which, in Latin, would be the overtly reflexive *sua*, not the non-reflexive *eius*, and in Swedish would be the overtly reflexive *sin*, not the non-reflexive *hans* (cp. the discussion around example (7.13) in section 7.3):

(5.4) a. In *his* room, *John* smokes cigars.
       b. *In *John's* room, *he* smokes cigars.

In a relation of reflexivity, the *governor* is the term that makes the *governee* (the reflexive pronoun) reflexive. The governee can never occupy the position of the governor. Since reflexivity is, in principle,[8] governed by the subject term, *his* in (5.4a) is interpretable as reflexively coreferential with the governing subject term *John*, but in (5.4b) the subject is *he* and the possessive phrase is *John's*, which excludes a relation of reflexive co-reference, despite the fact that *John*, as a possible antecedent, precedes the pronoun *he*, which should, according to IDAP, make a definite internal anaphoric relation possible. Note that IDAP takes over when no reflexivity is involved, as in (5.5a,b). In (5.5a), (non-reflexive) coreference is possible, owing to the fact that *John* precedes *him*. In (5.5b) coreference is still possible because, although *him* precedes *John*, it is in a high-peripheral prepositional phrase. In (5.5c) coreference is blocked because the pronoun precedes the antecedent and is not in a high-peripheral clause or prepositional phrase:

(5.5) a. In *John's* room, I hit *him* on the nose.
       b. In *his* room, I hit *John* on the nose.
       c. *I hit *him* on the nose in *John's* room.

A weak form of reflexivity, perhaps best called *indirect reflexivity*, occurs when a pronoun is analysable as part of the complex predicate of the main subject term in a subject-predicate analysis, where all non-subject argument terms and all non-peripheral adverbial adjuncts (clauses) are considered part of the complex main predicate. An example of such a complex predicate is 'assert that one does not covet one's neighbour's wife', where the two occurrences of *one* are indirect reflexive variables taking any specific main subject term as value. The main subject is then the governing argument term and any following pronouns are of the indirect reflexive class. It is typical of adverbial phrases or clauses that belong to the predicate in this sense that they cannot be preposed other than under heavily marked contextual conditions of contrastivity. The sentences (5.6a,b) contain instances of indirect reflexivity:

(5.6) a. *John* wished *he* had said nothing about the garden party.
       b. *John* often watches TV because *he* is bored.

---

[8] I must say 'in principle' because there are cases where the reflexivity-commanding argument term is not the subject but the object, as in *His mother loved John*, or a dative, as in the Latin legal phrase *Suum cuique dare* ('to give everyone what they are entitled to', literally 'to give everyone their own thing').

One notes, of course, the surface-structural parallel of (5.6b) with (5.3c). This would suggest that sentence-final adverbial clauses may have a different structural status according to whether they modify the main clause and are thus high-peripheral, as in (5.3c), or belong to the predicate (are part of the Verb Phrase or VP), as in (5.6b). The difference is comparable to the ambiguous status of the prepositional phrase in a sentence pair like *John was waiting on the platform* versus *John was waiting on the Prime Minister*. In the former sentence, *on the platform* has high-peripheral status, which appears from the fact that the sentence cannot be passivized into *!The platform was waited on by John* (the sign *! is used to indicate ill-formedness on semantic grounds), and that the subordinate adverbial can be (non-contrastively) preposed, as in *On the platform, John was waiting*. In the latter sentence, *on the Prime Minister* is part of the Verb Phrase—that is, of the predicate. Here, passivization is normal: *The Prime Minister was waited on by John* and preposing of the adverbial is not possible: *!On the Prime Minister, John was waiting* (see Seuren 1996: 116–28 for ample discussion). In (5.3c), the subordinate clause *while he stood on the balcony* is naturally taken to be a high-peripheral sentence constituent. In (5.6b), the subordinate clause *because he is bored* invites an interpretation in which it has a lower status, as part of the complex predicate 'watch TV because one is bored'. This makes the clause *because he is bored* a VP-constituent and the pronoun *he* an indirect reflexive pronoun. The important point in the present context is that (non-contrastively) preposed adverbial clauses or phrases cannot be part of the complex predicate and can only have high-peripheral status.

Pronouns that represent bound variables, as in (5.7a,b), likewise appear to have their own statute. Consider (5.7a,b).

(5.7)   a. I advised *all students* to ask *their* lecturer to mark *their* papers before Easter.
   b. Roger had warned *some students* not to cheat in *their* exam.

It is clear that the three occurrences of *their* in (5.7a,b) represent variables bound by the superordinate quantifier (*all* or *some*). Whether the statute of bound-variable pronouns and that of indirect reflexive pronouns coincide or are different is a question I can leave open here.

In this context, we can present the *epithet pronoun test*. As is well-known, definite pronouns can, in many cases, be replaced with a so-called epithet pronoun consisting of a full lexical noun phrase whose noun has an emotional, evaluative, ironical or bleached general meaning, as in (5.8a–c). Externally anaphoric pronouns can always be replaced with an epithet pronoun; internally anaphoric pronouns only when they are referential. *The generalization is thus that referential pronouns are open to replacement with an epithet pronoun; bound pronouns never are.* In all cases, the epithet pronoun is unaccented (has low prosodic profile):

(5.8)   a. I was looking for *Trisha*, but I couldn't find *the little girl*.

      b. When *the professor* ascended the lectern, nobody paid any attention to *the fool*.

      c. When I saw *the man*, I realized that *your father* had been through hell.

The same goes for the sentences (5.3a–c): in all three cases, the pronoun *he* can be replaced with an epithet pronoun like *the fool* or *the great genius*. The only difference this makes is that the speaker adds the truth-conditionally irrelevant information that (s)he hereby qualifies the person referred to as a fool, or a great genius, or whatever. What interests us here is the conditions under which internally anaphoric pronouns can be replaced with an epithet pronoun.

Epithet replacement appears not to be possible for non-referential or bound pronouns, in particular for direct and indirect reflexives and for bound-variable pronouns, as can be seen from (5.9a) and (5.9c–f), in all of which co-reference is hard or impossible to get. Only (5.9b) seems to allow for co-reference, as *John* does not have subject status:

(5.9)   a. *In *the fool's* room, *John* smokes cigars.   (cp. (5.4a))

      b. In *the fool's* room, I hit *John* on the nose.   (cp. (5.5b))

      c. *John* wished *the fool* had said nothing about the garden party.   (cp. (5.6a))

      d. *Roger had warned *a student* not to cheat in *the fool's* exam.   (cp. (5.7b))

      e. *I promised *John* that I would never try to cheat *the fool*.

      f. *That *the fools* would never pass *all students* knew.

The judgements expressed in (5.8) and (5.9) are not based on explicit teaching or learning but follow from the mere fact that one has acquired command of English (or any other language). The difference between (5.6a) and (5.9c) shows in particular that there is a category of indirect reflexives—something that might not have come to light otherwise. The epithet pronoun test shows that any adequate theory of pronouns will have to make the distinctions indicated above, with all the consequences this must have for a theory of language. The ball is now in the park of those who, as a matter of principle, reject any 'abstract' machinery needed to explain the facts mentioned.

5.2.2 *Topic-comment structure*

The following cases show that the assignment of contrastive accent is not just a matter of taking a surface sentence and placing contrastive accent on any arbitrary element in it, but is constrained by, and thus requires the assumption of, an underlying topic-comment structure of the general form (5.10), where 'the x such that [... x ...]' denotes a specific parameter, usually called the *topic*, whose value, the *comment*, needs to be filled in:

(5.10)   the x such that [... x ...] be_{val} Y

Y is the comment predicate providing the value of the topic parameter, and be_{val} is the value-assigning copula *be*.[9] The value predicate *Y* receives strong predicate accent which is maintained in surface structure, where it is recognized as either *emphatic* or *contrastive accent*. In most cases, the accented *Y* predicate is lowered into the Matrix structure [. . . x . . .] onto the position occupied by the variable *x*, which thus receives emphatic or contrastive accent. Sometimes, however, the grammar of the language in question blocks lowering and demands a more direct rendering of (5.10) in surface structure terms. Thus, whereas English has both (5.11a) and (5.11b), their French equivalents are not equally acceptable in that language: French requires (5.12b) and rejects (5.12a):[10]

(5.11)   a.   JOAN wants to read the book, not JACK.

        b.   It's JOAN who wants to read the book, not JACK.

(5.12)   a.   *JEANNE veut lire le livre, pas JACQUES.

        b.   C'est JEANNE qui veut lire le livre, pas JACQUES.

5.2.2.1 *Topic-comment structure and reflexivity*   The examples (5.13) and (5.14), also discussed below in section 7.3, provide crucial evidence. Consider the following little

---

[9] There is a metalinguistic variant of (5.10) for cases where a linguistic correction is intended, as in, for example, *I didn't* RETAIN *the man, I* DETAINED *him.*

[10] The French ban on lowering of contrastively opposed elements only holds for nominal expressions (NPs) in non-metalinguistic use (Horn 1985), not for other grammatical categories or for metalinguistic correction. Thus, (i), (ii) and (iii) are good French (capitalization in the French sentences stands for prosodic prominence, not for stress):

(i) Dieu DISPOSE, il ne PROPOSE pas.
   (God DISPOSES, he does not PROPOSE)

(ii) Il ne l'a pas PRIS, il l'a VOLÉ.
    (He didn't TAKE it, he STOLE it)

(iii) LA REINE, mon petit, pas CETTE FEMME-LÀ!
    (THE QUEEN, my boy, not THAT WOMAN!)

(iii) is typically interpreted as a correction (uttered, say, by a mother to her little son) of the choice of words in a previous utterance made by the boy, such as *Cette femme-là vient de tousser* ('That woman has just coughed') (see Horn 1985). In (iii), only one person is referred to and the correction applies not to the reference made but to the expression used to make the reference. By contrast, (iv) does not allow for this metalinguistic interpretation. In (iv), the correction implies a *referential* correction, so that two different persons are involved, referred to by the phrases *la reine* and *cette femme-là*, respectively.

(iv) C'est LA REINE, mon petit, pas CETTE FEMME-LÀ, qui vient de tousser.
    (It is THE QUEEN, my boy, not THAT WOMAN, who has just coughed.)

Interestingly, the English translation of (iii) is ambiguous between the referential and the metalinguistic corrective reading, whereas the English translation of (iv), like its French original, can only have the referential reading. The underlying topic-comment structure of metalinguistic corrections does not involve expressions referring to world entities but names referring to expressions. (I must thank Olivier le Guen of the *Centro de Investigaciones y Estudios Superiores en Antropologia Social* in Mexico City, and native speaker of French, for validating the observations made.)

dialogue between a father and his young son, who is crying because he has just hurt himself:

(5.13)   a. Father: Well-educated boys don't cry.
            b. Son: Í didn't educate me!

Had the boy answered (5.14), with the (expected) reflexive pronoun *myself*, his reply would have had a different meaning and would have been inappropriate in the situation at hand:

(5.14)   Í didn't educate myself!

There seems to be no other way to explain this difference between (5.13b) and (5.14) than by means of an underlying structure that somehow brings out non-reflexivity in (5.13b) and reflexivity in (5.14). One obvious way of formulating such an analysis is shown in (5.15a,b), corresponding to (5.13b) and (5.14), respectively:

(5.15)   a. not [the x such that x educated me] be$_{val}$ I
            b. not [the x such that x educated x] be$_{val}$ I

There is no reflexivity in the Matrix structure *x educated me* of (5.15a), but there is in (5.15b), with the reflexive Matrix structure *x educated x*. Lowering of the value (comment) predicate *I* into the Matrix structure *x educated me* of (5.15a) leads to (5.13b); for the Matrix structure *x educated x* (or *x self-educated*; see section 7.2) of (5.15b), the final result is (5.14).

   Likewise for (5.16), which is due to the late medieval literature on *exclusives*, as a category of *exponibles* (see Seuren 2010: 314–15), and was taken up in Geach (1962: 132):

(5.16)   a. Only Satan pities himself.
            b. Only Satan pities Satan.

According to most current analyses, *only*-structures are likewise cases of topic-comment modulation: (5.16a) is taken to correspond to (5.17a); (5.16b) to (5.17b):

(5.17)   a. the x such that [x pities x] be$_{val}$ only SATAN
               (the one who self-pities is only Satan)

            b. the x such that [x pities Satan] be$_{val}$ only SATAN
               (the one who pities Satan is only Satan)

Here lies the key to the answer: in (5.17a) there is the reflexive predicate *x pities x* (or *x self-pities*), whereas in (5.17b) one finds the non-reflexive predicate *x pities Satan*. It would seem that any solution to this apparent riddle would have to fall back on something like the difference between (5.17a) and (5.17b). (Even so, it still has to be explained why (5.16b) does not allow for an internal anaphoric pronoun: as in *Only Satan pities him*, where Satan and him cannot be coreferential.) In any case, the above observations show that linguistic analysis cannot do without the assumption of 'abstract' analytical structures underlying the surface form of sentences.

5.2.2.2 *Topic-comment structure and anaphoric relations*   The same conclusion follows from the following facts, also due to Akmajian and Jackendoff (1970) (an exceptionally rich quarry for troublesome observations related to anaphora resolution under contrastive accent, of which I can only discuss a few). The authors observe that, in cases such as (5.18), without contrastive accent, the pronoun is used ambiguously in that it may have an internal or an external antecedent. However, the anaphoric ambiguity disappears when either the internal antecedent or the pronoun is contrastively accented, as in (5.19a) or (5.19b), where the contrastive accent is indicative of an underlying topic-comment structure. To illustrate their point, they present the examples (5.18) and (5.19a,b). In (5.18), we have *John* as a possible antecedent, besides any possible unmentioned external antecedent. In (5.19a) and (5.19b), however, *John* is no longer a possible antecedent: the pronoun *he* must refer to a sentence-external referent. (I have added (5.19c) and (5.19d) to show that the matter is even more complex than might appear on the basis of the observations made in Akmajian and Jackendoff (1970).)

(5.18)   After *he* woke up, *John* went to town.

(5.19)   a. *After HE woke up, *John* went to town.
       b. *After *he* woke up, JOHN went to town.
       c. *John* went to town after HE woke up.
       d. JOHN went to town after *he* woke up.

In (5.19c) and (5.19d), where the subordinate clause introduced by *after* has been placed after the main clause, the possibility of a co-reference relation between *John* and *he* is restored again. (5.19c) comes naturally in a context where someone has said that John went to town after, say, a person called Harold woke up. The speaker of (5.19c) corrects this by saying 'No, John went to town after HE (himself) woke up'. (5.19d) is naturally understood as a correction of someone else's 'Harold went to town after he (= Harold) woke up'. The speaker of (5.19d) now says 'No, JOHN went to town after he (= John) woke up'.

No explanation for these observations has been offered to date, which is an indication that the problem posed by them is unusually tricky and that its possible solution does not fit into any grammatical, semantic or pragmatic theory that has a stall in today's market place. In the following I will sketch the outline of what I see as a possible solution.

The topic-comment structure analyses of (5.19a–d), respectively, may be taken to be something like the following:

(5.20)   a. the x such that [after x woke up John went to town] be$_{val}$ HE
        b. the x such that [after he woke up x went to town] be$_{val}$ JOHN
        c. the x such that [John went to town after x woke up] be$_{val}$ HE
        d. the x such that [x went to town after x woke up] be$_{val}$ JOHN

In (5.20a) and (5.20b), the subordinate clause *after x/he woke up* has high-peripheral status, as appears from the fact that it stands in Matrix-initial position (see the discussion above around the examples (5.3)–(5.6)). In such sentences, any anaphoric relation obtaining between a pronoun and an antecedent will thus have to be of the kind controlled by IDAP. By contrast, the Matrix-final occurrence of the clause *after x woke up* makes it structurally ambiguous between a high-peripheral and a VP adverbial clause. In the former case, the clause represents a higher operator, in the latter it is part of the predicate 'go to town after waking up'.

The regularity emerging from these examples and analyses seems to be this:

(5.21)   Reservations being made for specific languages (French!), the topic predicate can always be lowered into the position of the first occurring variable, with retention of strong predicate accent. But a (nonreflexive) anaphoric relation between the lowered comment predicate, whether lexical or pronominal, and a corresponding pronoun or lexical constituent, respectively, can only come about when the lowered comment predicate, if lexical, has landed in the position of the governing argument term or, if pronominal, has landed in the complex predicate of the governing argument term.

In practical terms this means that no IDAP relation can exist between a pronoun and a full lexical constituent if either has the status of comment in a topic-comment structure (as in (5.20a,b)). A relation of (indirect) reflexivity or variable binding can exist, but only if the lowering process results in a structure where the full lexical constituent is a governing argument term and the pronoun is part of its (complex) predicate.

One notes, in particular, that epithet substitution is possible in (5.18), resulting in (5.22a), but not in (5.19c,d), which would give (5.22b,c), respectively:[11]

(5.22)   a. After *the fool* woke up, *John* went to town.
        b. *John went to town after THE FOOL woke up.
        c. *JOHN went to town after *the fool* woke up.

---

[11] One notes that in (5.22b) the status of THE FOOL as an epithet pronoun is made doubtful by the fact that what is intended to be an epithet pronoun, which has to be unaccented to be able to function as one, here occurs under contrastive accent.

This confirms the analysis presented in (5.21), since the anaphoric relation in (5.18) is of the IDAP type and thus allows for epithet substitution, whereas in (5.19c,d) the relation is one of binding and thus disallows for epithet substitution.

This principle makes intuitive sense in that IDAP pronouns are typically referential and reference is a function of argument terms, not of predicates, not even nominal predicates of the kind occurring as comments in topic-comment structures. By contrast, indirect reflexive and bound-variable pronouns are not referential but act as open places, in the Fregean sense, in, structurally speaking, subordinate or commanded definite argument positions whose fillers (values) are selected from restricted classes (ranges) for truth to be achieved. It will be clear, in any case, that mere usage-based or surface-based theories of grammars are too poorly equipped to come even near a solution for this category of data.

5.2.2.3 *Truth-conditional differences in topic-comment structures*   Let us now move on to another class of cases showing that contrastive accent goes way below the surface. Contrastive accent is not simply a matter of taking any arbitrary word or constituent from any given surface sentence and fitting it out with contrastive accent *salva veritate*—that is, without any change in truth conditions—as is maintained, for example, in Chomsky (1972: 99–100). That this is so is shown, for example, by the difference between (5.23a) and (5.23b) (the example, often quoted in the formal-semantics literature, seems to go back to Rooth 1985):

(5.23) a. In old St. Petersburg, OFFICERS always escorted ballerinas.
            (In old St. Petersburg, the one who escorted a ballerina was always an officer.)

        b. In old St. Petersburg, officers always escorted BALLERINAS.
            (In old St. Petersburg, the one who an officer escorted was always a ballerina.)

Clearly, (5.23a) and (5.23b) are true under different conditions, yet on the surface they differ only in the choice of the constituent under contrastive accent. The semantic difference is made visible when these sentences are analysed according to the pattern shown in (5.10) above, as in (5.24a) and (5.24b), respectively:

(5.24) a. In old St. Petersburg [always [the x such that [x escorted ballerinas] be$_{val}$ OFFICERS]]

        b. In old St. Petersburg [always [the x such that [officers escorted x] be$_{val}$ BALLERINAS]]

It follows that a proper interpretation of sentences like (5.23a) or (5.23b) requires a cognitive machinery relating these surface sentences to a form that allows for a well-regulated semantic processing procedure, such as (5.24a) and (5.24b), respectively.

Any theory excluding such a mapping relation must, therefore, be reckoned to be inadequate in principle, unless it presents a well-motivated different analysis that does not make use of 'abstract' levels of representation and rule systems.

The same conclusion follows from examples like (5.25a,b) (Seuren 2004a: 177; 2010: 406–8):

(5.25)   a. She was angry that JOHN had sold the car.
         b. She was angry that John had sold the CAR.

In general, in emotive or evaluative factive contexts, contrastive accent causes truth-conditional differences.[12] As is easily checked, (5.25a) may be true while (5.25b) is false and vice versa. Again, the difference is expressed clearly and systematically in an analysis that makes the topic-comment structure explicit:

(5.26)   a. She was angry that [the x such that [x had sold the car] be$_{val}$ JOHN]
         b. She was angry that [the x such that [John had sold x] be$_{val}$ the CAR]

It would seem that analyses formulated exclusively in terms of GIVEN and NEW, as are standardly found in the pragmatically oriented literature on 'information structure', lack the formal precision and specificity needed to account for cases like the above. To the extent that analyses as presented in (5.26a,b) are allowed in this literature, there seems to be little awareness that the theory must provide a machinery for relating such structures to the corresponding surface structures.

5.2.3 *Scope and negation*

No account of any language in the world can do without a theory of logico-semantic scope. This is particularly clear in the case of negation, whose scope properties are crucial to a proper understanding of sentences in any natural language. An obvious example is (5.27a,b), taken from Klima (1964), where a scope swap between *not* and *many*, expressed in a different left-to-right order of the operators concerned, makes for a crucial semantic difference:

(5.27)   a. Many smokers don't chew gum.
         b. Not many smokers chew gum.

Similarly for (5.28a,b):

(5.28)   a. Two soldiers did not march in step.
         b. No two soldiers marched in step.

---

[12] A *factive context* is any argument clause whose truth is presupposed by the sentence as a whole in virtue of the fact that the higher predicate—*angry* in (5.25a,b)—carries a presuppositional condition of truth for its argument clause. A factive context is emotive or evaluative when the higher factive predicate expresses an emotion or an evaluation.

This is generally so for scope-bearing operators, even though in some cases no truth-conditional differences arise, due to the semantics of the operator(s) in question, as in:

(5.29)   a. Some men love some women.
         b. Some women are loved by some men.

In some cases, an apparent scope swap occurs, making no truth-conditional difference, despite the different left-to-right order and despite the semantics of the operators involved. A well-known example is the swap between *not* and *all* in sentences like the following (Horn 1989: 226–7):

(5.30)   a. All that glitters is not gold.
         b. Not all that glitters is gold.

Why this should be so is not known. But the fact is that native speakers know perfectly well that the most obvious meaning of (5.30a) is what is expressed less ambiguously in (5.30b), despite the apparent scope swap in the former.

In some cases, a scope swap may even lead to ungrammaticality, as in (5.31a,b), taken from Seuren (2004a: 180, 188):

(5.31)   a. John is often not in the least interested.
         b. *John isn't often in the least interested.

The reason here is that *in the least* is a negative polarity item requiring a negation as the first operator commanding it in the underlying semantic analysis. This condition is satified in (5.31a), but not in (5.31b), where the operator *often* occurs between *in the least* and *not*.

The point of these facts in the present context is that any theory that wants to incorporate an account of the semantic and syntactic differences involved, which unsophisticated native speakers can easily be made aware of, requires a system of semantically regular scope representations plus an account of how these are related to the surface structures occurring in any language under analysis. The least one can conclude is that this cannot be done without the help of 'abstract' representations and rule systems. It reflects badly on the discipline that most schools of linguistic thought simply prefer to ignore such well-known facts.

5.2.3.1 *NEG-Raising*   NEG-Raising is the phenomenon that a negation which appears at the surface as the negation of the main verb is semantically interpreted as taking scope over a subordinate subject or object clause. Examples are given in (5.32). There is a fairly substantial literature on the phenomenon of NEG-Raising, observable in sentences of the type:

(5.32)   a. I don't think you are right.

b. I don't want to die.

c. She never thought he would lift a finger to help her.

d. It is not likely that he will be in the least interested.

It has been known for centuries that such sentences are normally interpreted as if the negation did not stand over the main verb (*think, want, likely*) but over the subordinate clause, so that these sentences are taken 'really' to express the following sentences:

(5.33)   a. I think you are not right.

b. I want not to die.

c. She thought he would never lift a finger to help her.

d. It is likely that he will not be in the least interested.

In fact, up till way into the twentieth century, normative school grammars in Britain and other countries told children that sentences like those in (5.32), or their equivalents in other languages, should not be used in polite company and that sentences like those in (5.33) should be considered the proper way of expressing the underlying thought.[13] However, when descriptive grammar replaced normative grammar, the schools no longer tried to impose unrealistic standards of 'correct usage' and linguists began to wonder what was going on in sentences like those in (5.32). Not long after, the term *NEG-Raising* (sometimes also *Negative Transportation*) became current.[14]

In (5.32c) and (5.32d) one notes in particular that the object clauses as they stand are ungrammatical, due to the negative polarity items *lift a finger* and *in the least*, which require a negation in the same clause: *He would lift a finger to help her* or *He will be in the least interested* are ungrammatical, but *He wouldn't lift a finger to help her* and *He will not be in the least interested* are good English. Facts such as these have been used to argue that NEG-Raising is a rule of syntax, since speakers know perfectly well that the surface form of sentences like (5.32a–d) misrepresents the true meaning of the sentences in question.

As regards the status of NEG-Raising (NR), I concur with Horn (1978: 215–16):[15]

---

[13] NEG-Raising is a universal in that it occurs in all languages unless there is some independent grammatical constraint blocking the raising of the negation from a subordinate clause (Horn 1978: 215).

[14] The basic texts for studies on negation are Jespersen (1917), followed first by the seminal study Klima (1964), representing early transformational grammar, and then by Horn (1989), which has become a classic and represents a synthesis of pragmatics, semantics and grammar, supported by a philosophical perspective. On the specific phenomenon of NEG-Raising, one may profitably consult R. Lakoff (1969), Horn (1971, 1978, 1989: 308–30), Seuren (1974).

[15] Though I do not share Horn's apparent disappointment at having to concede that NEG-Raising is, after all, a rule of syntax: 'Having perhaps been forced to concede the extension and even the significance of NR as a linguistic process, what can we conclude about its character?' (Horn 1978: 215). Linguistic settling tends to step in early on in the piece.

The view proposed here is [...] that NR originates as a functional device for signaling negative force as early in a negative sentence as possible. The determination of how soon possible is will be dependent upon the interaction of pragmatic, syntactic, semantic, and idiosyncratic factors; the result is that, faute de mieux, NR must be regarded as a rule in the synchronic grammar of English and other languages. NR would thus constitute an example of a pragmatic process which has become grammaticized or syntacticized [...].

The crucial point here is that NEG-Raising, whatever its origin and semantic or pragmatic nuances, is a rule of syntax. Besides the evidence based on negative polarity items, there is also the fact that (5.34a) and (5.34b), both good English sentences, differ in meaning (see Seuren 2004a: 188):

(5.34)   a. I don't think either Harry or John were late.
         b. I don't think either Harry or John was late.

Sentence (5.34a) is interpreted as (5.35a). This is first transformed, by a more 'abstract' form of NEG-Raising induced by the abstract predicate *and* (see Seuren 1974), to (5.35b)—a syntactic manifestation of one of De Morgan's logical equivalences—and subsequently, again by NEG-Raising but now induced by the predicate *think*, to (5.35c), which directly underlies (5.34a):

(5.35)   a. I think [not [Harry was late] and not [John was late]]
         b. I think [not [either Harry was late or John was late]]
         c. Not [I think [either Harry was late or John was late]]

The plural verb form *were* in (5.34a) can only be due to the fact that the object clause in (5.35a), which is the semantic input to the grammar, speaks of two persons who were thought not to be late, Harry and John. This semantic plurality is somehow preserved in the corresponding surface structure. Sentence (5.34b), by contrast, is much simpler, as it says merely that it is not the case that I think that either Harry or John was late. (For as yet unclear reasons, the *not* in (5.34b) carries a so-called *echo-effect*, in that it evokes a correction of a previous speaker's utterance saying or implying that this speaker thought that either Harry or John was late.)

One may well have a different opinion regarding the proper analysis of the observations made, but one thing is clear: any adequate analysis and description will have to involve a fairly complex mental machinery lurking behind the surface phenomena. All it takes to see this is a good eye for detail. Again we must conclude that a speaker's competence in his or her language cannot be described in mere terms of statistical frequency of linguistic input during the learning period. On the contrary, although linguistic input frequency factors undoubtedly play a crucial role in stimulating and guiding the acquisition process, it is hard to escape from the conclusion that what is actually happening in the learner's mind is inductive *rule formation*, whereby the inductive process is guided and constrained by an innate charter, evolutionarily crystallized in the form of specific prewired schemata waiting to be activated, in this case the attachment of the negation to a higher predicate. This charter is what is known as *universal grammar* or, preferably, the *universal principles of grammar*.

5.2.3.2 *AUX-Inversion, yes or no?*

In this section I discuss some curious cases in which, in English, so-called AUX-Inversion does not apply. As has been well-known since at least the beginning of the twentieth century, when the great grammars of Modern English, such as Poutsma (1904–1929), Jespersen (1909–1949) or Kruisinga (1911), were written, the Auxiliary constituent and the subject term are inverted, in English sentences, when the sentence starts with the negation or a negative or so-called semi-negative word or adjunct (such as *nor, only* or *hardly*). Examples are:[16]

(5.36) a. Hardly ever *did I visit* my ageing aunt. (**I visited*)
      b. Never before *had we* been so frightened. (**we had*)
      c. Not until last summer *did he make* headlines. (**he made*)
      d. No sooner *had she* shut the door than she started to cry. (**she had*)
      e. Only in the garden *would she* allow herself a cigarette. (**she would*)
      f. Nor *is it* my purpose to do so here. (**it is*)

These examples show that something like an AUX-constituent must be assumed as a structural unit in English sentences with an inflected main verb. The sentences (5.36a) and (5.36c), moreover, show that a well generalized description of AUX-Inversion will require the assumption of an underlying AUX-constituent (with a null *do*-support verb) even in ordinary inflected main verbs.

But apart from this, it must be observed that there are cases which look as if they satisfy the criteria for AUX-Inversion but do not necessarily have it, often showing a semantic difference with their counterparts that do exhibit AUX-Inversion. The following are examples of this phenomenon:

(5.37) a. Only last summer *he made* headlines (. . . and now he is dead).
      b. Not much later *it was* realized that a theory of competence requires an account of meaning. (**was it realized*)
      c. Not six years later *he became* chairman. (**did he become*)
      d. Not long after the summer *they married*. (**did they marry*)

One notes, in particular, that, other than (5.37b–d), (5.37a) has a grammatical counterpart, (5.38), with AUX-Inversion, but also with a different meaning. What exactly this semantic difference amounts to, is hard to specify in precise terms (nor is

---

[16] According to Kruisinga (1932: 325), '[T]he reason for this word order is that a negative word, put at the beginning of the sentence for the sake of emphasis, naturally attracts the predicative verb'—which shows that standards of explanation have been raised somewhat since Kruisinga's days.

it my purpose to try to do so here), but the reader will find it easy to evoke the difference by considering possible continuations such as those given in (5.37a) and (5.38). (The latter is closely synonymous with (5.36c):

(5.38)   Only last summer *did he* make headlines (. . . after many years of trying).

The phenomenon was observed, among others, by Kruisinga, who wrote (Kruisinga (1932: 327): 'When a negative adjunct is clearly understood as a word-modifier to the subject, it naturally precedes the subject without causing inversion.' This, however, is merely an (unsuccessful) attempt at stating the facts, not an explanation—unless the concept expressed in the word *naturally*, as also in note 16, is taken to suffice. According to our modern standards, we are led to look for a formal analysis and a formal rule system automatically yielding the correct surface structure. Such a formally precise solution has not been presented so far. All we have is the *intuition* that in cases like (5.37a–d) the negation does not take scope over a whole sentence or clause but merely over a part of a complex operator. Such an 'encapsulated' negation may thus be expected not to exert an influence upon the main structure of the Matrix clause. This, however, boils down to Kruisinga's intuitive 'explanation' rephrased in fancy modern terminology. We thus have a case here of a phenomenon not (yet) covered by modern formal theorizing.

Yet the preliminary intuitive analysis clearly shows that any formally precise solution will inevitably involve a great deal of formal—that is, 'abstract'—machinery, probably in terms of tree structures and command relations. A rejection in principle of such machinery, as is found in the cognitivist linguistic literature, means a reversal to pre-structuralist linguistics, where the concept 'naturally' was taken to constitute an explanation. By contrast, we do not take that concept to provide an explanation but to indicate the problem to be explained. The phenomena in question are indeed 'natural' in the sense that it requires remarkably little effort to acquire full command of them, which justifies the expectation that, in this small-scale acquisition process, the learning component will prove to be far less prominent than the innate component.

5.3 Some class B facts

As will be remembered, class B facts are linguistic facts where learning plays a dominant role and any assumed factor of an innate nature, though probably still indispensable, is operative much more in the background. Class B facts have a strong settling component and thus require a highly developed language-specific competence in the language in question. The class B facts we are interested in here are typically part of a rule system driven by lexical features, applicable to specific classes of syntactic structures and leading to structures that have a codified position in any theory of the universal principles of grammar.

5.3.1 *German and Dutch verb clustering*

A prominent collection of class B facts is provided by the German and Dutch system of verb clustering. A great deal has been written over the past forty years about this system, a synthesis of which is provided in Seuren and Kempen (2003). My own last contribution in this respect is Seuren (2003), which provides a detailed description and analysis of the facts together with a compact rule system in terms of *Semantic Syntax* (Seuren 1996), juxtaposed, in Seuren and Kempen (2003), to a handful of alternative explanatory rule systems in terms of other theories, in particular in the traditions of lexicalist grammar, transformational grammar, categorial grammar, performance grammar and tree adjunction grammar. In all these theories, the German-Dutch verb clustering system poses a formidable challenge, but no matter to what extent this challenge is met in the various theories, it is clear that vaguely formulated, surface-based approaches not allowing for any underlying 'abstract' theorizing, such as what is found in the existing varieties of so-called cognitivist linguistics, are in principle unequal to it.

Let us have a quick look at the main facts. Consider the German clauses in (5.39) and their Dutch equivalents in (5.40).[17] All four sentences have the same meaning, without any detectable truth-conditional or usage difference, rendered as '...that Hans wanted to try to get the dog to fetch the newspaper':

(5.39) a. ... daß Hans versuchen wollte, den Hund die Zeitung   holen zu lassen.
      ... that Hans try   wanted the dog   the newspaper fetch to get

    b. ... daß Hans den Hund die Zeitung   holen zu lassen versuchen wollte.
      ... that Hans the dog   the newspaper fetch to get   try   wanted

(5.40) a. ... dat Hans wilde   proberen de hond de krant   te laten halen.
      ... that Hans wanted try   the dog   the newspaper to get   fetch

    b. ... dat Hans de hond de krant   wilde   proberen te laten halen.
      ... that Hans the dog   the newspaper wanted try   to get   fetch

The derivational history of these sentences is no mystery. The semantic analysis (SA), which serves as input to the grammatical derivation is the same for German, Dutch and English, but for the obvious phonologically different lexical forms and, crucially, the rule features associated with them. Leaving out the Auxiliary component, which is not relevant to the present analysis, and assuming an underlying VSO-order

---

[17] In German and Dutch syntactic studies, it is customary to present example sentences in the garb of subordinate *that*-clauses. This is done in order to avoid the complicating but irrelevant fact that in German and Dutch there is a rule, called VERB-FINAL, which, in main clauses, moves the non-finite part of the verb cluster within a VERB PHRASE (VP) to the far right, stopping before any further embedded verb phrase. In subordinate clauses and infinitivals, the entire verb cluster is moved to the far right (but stopping before any embedded VP). If one wants to study the structure of the verb cluster, it is obviously more convenient to leave the verb cluster intact, which is what happens in subordinate clauses.

(McCawley 1970), the underlying SA-structure for the three languages alike is taken
to be as in (5.41):

(5.41)

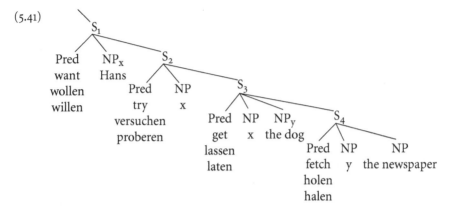

In English, the treatment of (5.41) is simple and straightforward. The verbs *get, try*
and *want* carry the rule feature *Subject Deletion* (SD; at one time *Equi-NP-Deletion*),
which deletes the subject-NP of the embedded object clause when that subject-NP is
an indirect reflexive (indicated by the bound variable x or y) and adds the particle *to*
to the verb of the embedded object clause. This happens cyclically, that is, starting
with the lowest embedded S-structure whose predicate induces SD, in this case S_3.
The result is first... *get x the dog to fetch the newspaper*. This process is repeated on
the S_2-cycle, giving... *try x to get the dog to fetch the newspaper*. Then again on the
S_1-cycle, giving... *want Hans to try to get the dog to fetch the newspaper*. Further
processing under the simple past tense operator leads to... *that Hans wanted to try to
get the dog to fetch the newspaper*.

German and Dutch are more complicated in this respect. Besides SD, they make
ample use of the rule of *Predicate Raising* (PR), sometimes called *Verb Raising* (VR)
(Seuren 1972a; Evers 1975), which takes the lower predicate constituent and unites it
with the higher predicate into a complex predicate (Verb) constituent, deleting the
dominating S and adding any further material to the higher S in the order given.
German has left-branching PR, which leads to the lower verb getting attached to the
left of the higher verb. Dutch has right-branching PR, leading to the lower verb
getting attached to the right of the higher verb. Some PR-inducing predicates require
the particle *zu* (German) or *te* (Dutch) to be added to the lower verb. PR is obligatory
(but without *zu/te*) for *lassen/laten* (let, get to), optional (with *zu/te*) for *versuchen/
proberen* (try) and obligatory (without *zu/te*) again for *wollen/willen* (want).

The derivations for German and Dutch are thus as follows, whereby labelled
bracketing is provided to the extent that it is relevant (for full tree structures, see
Seuren 1996 or 2003). The label 'Pred' is replaced with 'V' (verb) as soon as the S in
question has been through its cycle:

German:

S₃: $_V[_V[\text{holen}]_V[\text{lassen}]]$ x den Hund die Zeitung   (SD, PR)

S₂: versuchen x $_{VP}[_V[_V[\text{holen}]_V[\text{zu lassen}]]$ den Hund die Zeitung]   (SD)

or: $_V[_V[_V[\text{holen}]_V[\text{zu lassen}]]_V[\text{versuchen}]]$ x den Hund die Zeitung   (SD, PR)

S₁: $_V[_V[\text{versuchen}]_V[\text{wollen}]]$ Hans $_{VP}[_V[_V[\text{holen}]_V[\text{zu lassen}]]$ den   (SD)
Hund die Zeitung]

or: $_V[_V[_V[_V[\text{holen}]_V[\text{zu lassen}]]_V[\text{versuchen}]]_V[\text{wollen}]]$ Hans den   (SD, PR)
Hund die Zeitung

Dutch:

S₃: $_V[_V[\text{laten}]_V[\text{halen}]]$ x de hond de krant   (SD, PR)

S₂: proberen x $_{VP}[_V[_V[\text{te laten}]_V[\text{halen}]]$ de hond de krant]   (SD)

or: $_V[_V[\text{proberen}]_V[_V[\text{te laten}]_V[\text{halen}]]]$ x de hond de krant   (SD, PR)

S₁: $_V[_V[\text{willen}]_V[\text{proberen}]]$ Hans $_{VP}[_V[_V[\text{te laten}]_V[\text{halen}]]$ de hond de   (SD)
krant]

or: $_V[_V[\text{willen}]_V[_V[\text{proberen}]_V[_V[\text{te laten}]_V[\text{halen}]]]]$ Hans de hond de   (SD, PR)
krant

The routine treatment of tense and other auxiliary elements leads to the structures (5.42a,b) for German and (5.43a,b) for Dutch:

(5.42) a. Hans $_{VP}[_V[_V[\text{versuchen}]_V[\text{wollte}]]$ $_{VP}[_V[_V[\text{holen}]_V[\text{zu lassen}]]$ den Hund
die Zeitung]]

        b. Hans $_{VP}[_V[_V[_V[_V[\text{holen}]_V[\text{zu lassen}]]_V[\text{versuchen}]]_V[\text{wollte}]]$ den Hund
die Zeitung]

(5.43) a. Hans $_{VP}[_V[_V[\text{wilde}]_V[\text{proberen}]]$ $_{VP}[_V[_V[\text{te laten}]_V[\text{halen}]]$ de hond de
krant]]

        b. Hans $_{VP}[_V[_V[\text{wilde}]_V[_V[\text{proberen}]_V[_V[\text{te laten}]_V[\text{halen}]]]]$ de hond de
krant]

Postcyclic Verb-Final (see note 17) moves the verbal clusters to the end of their respective VPs but stopping short of entering or crossing an embedded VP:

(5.44) a. Hans $_{VP}[_V[_V[\text{versuchen}]_V[\text{wollte}]]$ $_{VP}[\text{den Hund die Zeitung} _V[_V[\text{holen}]$
$_V[\text{zu lassen}]]]]$

        b. Hans $_{VP}[\text{den Hund die Zeitung} _V[_V[_V[\text{holen}]_V[\text{zu lassen}]]_V[\text{versuchen}]]$
$_V[\text{wollte}]]]$

(5.45) a. Hans $_{VP}[_V[_V[\text{wilde}]_V[\text{proberen}]]$ $_{VP}[\text{de hond de krant} _V[_V[\text{te laten}]$
$_V[\text{halen}]]]]$

        b. Hans $_{VP}[\text{de hond de krant} _V[_V[\text{wilde}]_V[_V[\text{proberen}]_V[_V[\text{te laten}]$
$_V[\text{halen}]]]]]$

(5.44a) is now seen to be the surface structure corresponding to (5.39a), while (5.44b) is (5.39b). Likewise for Dutch: (5.45a) is (5.40a), while (5.45b) is (5.40b).

But there is more. German has the peculiar feature, known in German grammar as *Oberfeldumstellung* (see Seuren 1996; 2003). This phenomenon, which we may call *Right-Branching Switch* or RBS, consists in the fact that, for certain verbs (the **R-class**), PR becomes right-branching under the so-called **R-condition**. The **R-class** consists of the following verbs:

R-class:

sehen (see) (optional)	können (can, be able)	mögen (like, may)
hören (hear) (optional)	müssen (must)	dürfen (be allowed)
fühlen (feel) (optional)	sollen (must)	
lassen (let, get to)	wollen (want)	

Apart from a few refinements (see Seuren 2003: 281–4), which we will pass over here, the **R-condition** is as follows:

When an **R-verb** V_R is the highest matrix-V of a (left-branching) V-cluster below the perfect tense auxiliary verb *haben* ('have') or the future tense auxiliary *werden* ('will'), further additions to the V-cluster are right-branching—obligatorily for *haben* and optionally for *werden*. When the **R-condition** applies, the past participle expected under *haben* is replaced with an infinitive (known as *Ersatzinfinitiv*).

As a result of RBS, we have the following grammatical and ungrammatical sentences. The superscripts indicate the position in the SA-tree of the verb in question. Left-branching thus means a descending order, while right-branching means an ascending numerical order:[18]

(5.46) a. ...dass sie hat^1 ausgehen^3 wollen^2　　　　(+RBS)
　　　　　　'...that she has wanted to go out'
　　　b. *...dass sie ausgehen^3 gewollt^2 hat^1　　　　(−RBS)
　　　　　　'...that she has wanted to go out'
　　　c. ...dass sie mich hat^1 ausgehen^3 sehen^2　　　(+RBS)
　　　　　　'...that she has seen me go out'
　　　d. ...dass sie mich ausgehen^3 gesehen^2 hat^1　　(−RBS)
　　　　　　'...that she has seen me go out'
　　　e. *...dass sie mich hat^1 ausgehen^3 gesehen^2　(+RBS but no infinitive)
　　　　　　'...that she has seen me go out'
　　　f. ...dass ich sie habe^1 tanzen^4 gehen^3 lassen^2　(+RBS)
　　　　　　'...that I have let her go dancing'

---

[18] The grammaticality judgements have been tested on eleven native speakers of German from all over Germany, of both sexes and of all ages (Seuren 2003: 284–8).

g. ...dass sie wird[1] ausgehen[2]   (+RBS)
    '...that she will go out'
h. ...dass sie ausgehen[2] wird[1]   (−RBS)
    '...that she will go out'
i. ...dass sie das wird[1] haben[2] tun[4] können[3]   (+RBS on *haben* and
    '...that she will have been able to do that'   *werden*)
j. *...dass sie das haben[2] tun[4] können[3] wird[1]   (+RBS on *haben*, −RBS on
    '...that she will have been able to do that'   *werden*)

It will be clear that this system not only gets the facts crucially right—as well as any theory can hope for—but also does so in the general terms of a well-known (transformational) theoretical paradigm. Adherents of 'cognitivist' or 'usage-based' grammar, who claim that native language acquisition is exclusively a matter of statistical learning, of the kind that could be simulated in a general purpose computer, should realize that a crucial and well-tested difference in grammaticality status such as found between (5.46i) and (5.46j), to take just one example, cannot realistically be taken to be based on frequency statistics for the simple reason that such sentences are extremely rare in any corpus, if they occur at all. Yet native speakers readily offer their grammaticality judgements, which turn out to be remarkably uniform.

It may be argued that speakers could base their grammaticality judgements on extrapolation from simpler and more frequently occurring cases. Yet, given the specific nature of the cases at hand (the combination of the futuricity modal *werden* with the perfective auxiliary *haben* over R-class verbs), one wonders what such simpler and more frequently occurring cases might look like: (5.46i) and (5.46j) are themselves just about the simplest possible instantiations of the phenomenon at hand. Moreover, even if such simpler and more frequently occurring cases could be found or constructed, the argument still stands, since such extrapolation again requires the 'abstract' analyses in terms of which the construction is described.

The combination of rarity of occurrence combined with firm grammaticality judgements strongly argues against any form of radical 'usage-based' grammar.[19] Frequency of occurrence is no doubt one factor in the language acquisition process, as it is in the settling processes of language change, yet it cannot claim exclusive rights either in language acquisition or in language change.

An additional argument, strongly supporting the claim that 'abstract' structures and universal principles of grammar, or at least factors that transcend individual

---

[19] The parallel with physics is striking. Crucial data in physics are not obtained by observing ordinary events, such as children playing in a playground, but by means of, at times extremely costly, artificial laboratory set-ups. In physics, moreover, the news of any counterevidence to existing theories is sensational and spreads like wildfire. In linguistics, the tendency is still to cover up unwelcome facts.

specific languages, are at work is provided by the fact that *auxiliation processes* lead to the loss of non-finite verb forms, as shown in the defective paradigm of the English modals and of the German futuricity verb *werden* (see Seuren 1996 for a structural account of this loss of non-finite forms). Here, community-specific settling cannot be invoked as the sole explanatory factor, as there was hardly any social interaction between the communities concerned during the relevant period. What happened was that each community separately 'decided' to embark upon the auxiliation road made available by UPG. The details of this interplay between settling factors and universal (specific-language-transcending) constraints are as yet largely unknown.

It is a remarkable and somewhat alarming fact that in large sections of theoretical and descriptive linguistics the entire area of verb clustering and auxiliation in English, German and Dutch and the solutions proposed in various theoretical approaches (including the Semantic Syntax solution outlined above) are simply ignored, despite the fact that the crucial test value of this problem area, especially as regards verb clustering, has been widely publicized. The only academic reason I can think of for such bizarre behaviour is an *a priori* ideological aversion to 'abstract' rule systems and an equally irrational predilection for what is, oddly, taken to be 'real language' (see note 1 in Chapter 2).[20] One would guess that in more mature disciplines such wilful neglect of crucial facts would not pass without sanctions.

5.3.2 *The inflected infinitive in Portuguese*

At the risk of becoming tedious, I will give a final set of examples, this time taken from (Brazilian and European) Portuguese.[21] The phenomenon at issue is what is called the *inflected infinitive*. Let us first look at some data:

(5.47) a. Ele   lamenta   eu   ter   trabalhado   demais.
            he   regrets I_{nom} have$_{infin?}$ worked   too much
            'He regrets that I have worked too much.'

        b. Ele   entrou   em   casa   sem   eu   ver.
            he   entered   in   house   without I_{nom} see$_{infin?}$
            'He entered the house without me noticing.'

        c. Ele   lamenta   os   trabalhadores   ter*em*   trabalhado   demais.
            he   regrets   the   workers$_{nom}$ have$_{3plurinfin}$ worked   too much
            'He regrets that the workers have worked too much.'

---

[20] There is also the extraneous circumstance that in many universities maximization of student numbers is a top priority, and many heads of linguistic departments soon discovered that 'abstract' formalisms attract fewer students than a populist promise, under the banner of 'communication studies', to work with 'real' language used by real people in real-life situations. Whether this will bring forth great new insights into the nature of language is another matter.

[21] For a discussion of the same facts in the light of Chomsky's *Minimalist Program*, see Seuren (2004a: 195–8).

d. Ele entrou em casa sem os meninos ver*em*.
   he entered in house without the children$_{nom}$ see$_{3plur\text{-}infin}$
   'He entered the house without the children noticing.'

The forms *ter* ('have') and *ver* ('see') in (5.47a,b) are the bare infinitival forms for these two verbs in Portuguese. Yet, contrary to expectations, the form *eu* ('I') in both sentences is in the nominative case, where one would have expected the accusative *me*. By analogy, one may assign nominative case to *os trabalhadores* ('the workers') in (5.47c) and *os meninos* ('the children') in (5.47d). In these latter two cases, however, the alleged infinitives *ter* and *ver* are inflected in that they obligatorily take the plural suffix *-em*. The paradigm for such 'inflected infinitives' is rudimentary and simple, and unique to inflected infinitives, but it is a paradigm, assigning the suffix *-em* to all forms with a plural subject.

The problem posed by the Portuguese inflected infinitive (which occurs also in neighbouring Galego) is twofold. First, inflecting an infinitive and keeping the semantic subject in nominative case goes against all known generalizations regarding the formation of infinitival clauses in a vast number of languages studied, in that one has either accusative plus bare infinitive or a full subordinate clause. Here, however, we have something in between: a construction that looks both infinitival and clausal (but without complementizer). Secondly, it has proved impossible to date to identify a general condition, let alone a motivation, for the obligatory or optional occurrence of the inflected infinitive in Portuguese (see Raposo 1987 for a brave but unsuccessful attempt).[22] One should note that in (5.47a–d) the plural suffix attached to the infinitive is obligatory, but in a causative construction like (5.48) it appears to be optional, at least in Brazilian Portuguese (my two European Portuguese informants told me they had a strong preference for the *-em* suffix to be added):

(5.48) A nova lei fez os trabalhadores vender*(em)* a sua casa.
      The new law made the workers$_{acc}$ sell$_{(3plur\text{-}infin)}$ the their house
      'The new law made the workers sell their house.'

One should note that *os trabalhadores* in (5.48) cannot be a nominative, given the ungrammaticality of (5.49a), which requires the cliticized accusative form *me* ('me') instead of the nominative *eu* ('I'), as in (5.49b):

---

[22] Luca Ciucci, PhD student at the Scuola Normale Superiore of Pisa, Italy, informs me that the Portuguese (and adjacent Galego) inflected infinitive derives from the Latin Active Past Subjunctive, which is formed by placing the suffixes *-m*, *-s*, *-t* after the infinitive for singular 1st, 2nd and 3rd persons, and the suffixes *-mus*, *-tis* and *-nt* for the plural 1st, 2nd and 3rd persons, respectively. This provides a historical source for the nominative case of the semantic subject and the unified plural suffix *-em* of the inflected infinitive in Portuguese, but it does not solve the structural puzzle in synchronic terms. We probably have to do here with grammatical re-analysis of some sort, but the hybrid nature of the resulting inflected infinitive has so far not found a place in linguistic theory.

(5.49) a. *A   nova lei   fez   eu   vender a   minha casa.
            The   new   law   made I$_{nom}$ sell   the   my   house
            'The new law made me sell my house.'

        b. A   nova lei   me   fez   vender a   minha casa.
            the   new   law   me$_{acc}$ made   sell   the   my   house
            'The new law made me sell my house.'

The conclusion must be, therefore, that *os trabalhadores* in (5.48) is an accusative—the result of Subject Raising, which is the standard rule in Portuguese for infinitival complements—other than the subjects of other inflected infinitives, which are all in the nominative case, as we have seen. This may well have to do with the uncertainty regarding the inflectional ending of the infinitive *vender(em)* in (5.48).

The long and the short of it is that one will look in vain for the relevant generalizations in terms of language-specific surface structure alone. Whatever the solution will turn out to be, it will require a fairly 'abstract' machinery in terms of underlying structures and of a theory that transcends individual languages.

5.4 Conclusion

The main argument of this chapter has been to establish that it is not possible to reject on rational grounds, as a matter of principle, any attempt at constructing 'abstract' analytical and descriptive theories or any form of universalist, or universalizing, theory. The proponents or defenders of the many theories or approaches to natural language that do so implicitly or explicitly, are now forced into a position in which they must either reply to the objections raised in this chapter, or by anyone in the future, against such 'flat' theories or simply give up and turn to more sophisticated forms of theorizing. Such is the discipline of science. One understands, of course, that for most academics giving up one's pet theory is psychologically beyond their powers. Be that as it may, however, their conscience should now be rattled and those for whom false theories are not pet theories but just products on the market now know that they are missing out on the central works of language if they do not accept that human language can only be understood in terms of a complex set of interrelated machineries that are not open to direct observation but must be approximated by setting up hypothetical, assuredly 'abstract', explanatory causal theories. The old Heraclitean saying 'Invisible harmony is stronger than visible harmony', quoted as the motto for Chapter 3, has once again proved its mettle.

6

The Chomsky hierarchy
in perspective

6.1 Introduction*

The Chomsky hierarchy, developed by Chomsky and others during the late 1950s, is a formal classification of algorithmic production systems ('grammars') and the languages generated by them into four types, called types 3, 2, 1 and 0, such that each higher type is a proper subset of each lower type (see Chomsky 1963 for a full, technically elaborate survey). The question raised is to which type natural language grammars, seen as algorithmic production systems, belong. This question presupposes that grammars, as implemented in the human brain, are *productive* or *active*, and not *interpretative* or *passive*, so that full competence in a language is to be measured by the *speaker's* ability to produce utterances considered correct in a speech community. It also presupposes that active competence is fully formalizable by means of an algorithmic grammar. Both assumptions are taken for granted here—though under the strict proviso that the algorithmic grammar is not to be seen as a device producing strings of symbols from a start symbol but as a device converting a semantic input into a well-formed, language-specific output.

It is also taken for granted that utterance processing (semantic parsing) is unlikely to be fully formalizable, as it involves multiple appeals to cognition as a whole, which has so far escaped full formalization (for a full discussion see Seuren 2009a: Ch. 7). These premises have to be mentioned because it is widely, but wrongly, held nowadays that grammars are by definition hearer's decoding devices, whereas they are, in fact, speaker's encoding devices (this issue will come up repeatedly in the following text). In this respect, therefore, it is assumed that the Chomsky hierarchy, which is about the generation or production of strings of symbols, is on the right track.

In other respects, however, it seems to be on the wrong track. The Chomsky hierarchy is predicated on Chomksy's notion of *Autonomous Syntax*, in which

* I am grateful to Geoff Pullum of Edinburgh University and to Karl Magnus Petersson of the Max Planck Institute for Psycholinguistics at Nijmegen for helpful suggestions and critical comments.

sentences are taken to be algorithmically produced from an initial symbol, without any regard for what sentences mean. Grammars constructed along this pattern are said to reflect speakers' competence in their language, implying that knowledge of what sentences mean is not part of speakers' competence—as if a speaker who is able to separate grammatical from ungrammatical strings of symbols but has no inkling of what they mean can be called 'competent' (see Seuren 1972b). This notion of grammar is 'caught between absurdity and perversity' (Seuren 2004a: 70): from an empirical-realist point of view it is absurd and from a purely formal, instrumentalist point of view it is unnatural, unnecessary and apt to raise the wrong questions—that is, 'perverse'. Autonomous Syntax is thus ruled out *per se*.

In the present chapter, I argue that the Chomsky hierarchy is skewed in that it fails to distinguish between *primitive* and *non-primitive* production algorithms. Primitive production algorithms open with a single start signal, whereas non-primitive production algorithms are put into motion by any string of symbols taken from a well-defined set that may but need not itself be the product of a primitive algorithm and deliver transformed structures as output. The Chomskyan types 3, 2 and 1 belong to the class of primitive production algorithms, whereas type 0 should be defined as comprising the class of non-primitive or transformational production algorithms. What psychologists sometimes call a *module* (Fodor 1983) is typically a non-primitive algorithm converting signals of one kind to signals of another. Grammars for natural languages are modules in this sense, and thus belong to type 0, as they convert mind-generated propositional structures into an output that is realizable phonetically or in the form of writing or gestures. Natural-language grammars, though not subject to mathematically definable constraints (being of type 0), are clearly subject to universal or typologically restricted constraints of a non-mathematical, empirical nature (see section 3.8.1), but there is no unanimity on the precise form of such constraints (see Chapter 3).

My claim is that the Chomsky hierarchy, though valuable at the time, as it introduced a level of abstraction and generality into the study of grammar that had not been seen before, has lost much of its relevance for the study of natural language because it is now clearly seen and recognized that the idea that natural languages should be defined by means of a primitive algorithm is fundamentally at odds with any realist modelling. When the Chomsky hierarchy was developed, around 1960, this was not clear. At that time, the notion that a language could be seen as the product of a generative algorithm was brand new and exciting, especially in the context of the then developing theory of formal programming languages. In that context, Chomsky could write with some justification (Chomsky 1963: 325):

It appears that a deeper understanding of generative systems of this sort, and the languages that they are capable of describing, is a necessary prerequisite to any attempt to raise serious questions concerning the formal properties of the richer and much more complex systems that do offer some hope of empirical adequacy on a broad scale. For the present, this seems to be the area in which the study of mathematical models is most likely to provide significant insight into linguistic structure and the capacities of the language user.

He also wrote, however, without any justification (Chomsky 1963: 330):

...Saussure did propose a kind of account of the speaker as a device with a sequence of concepts as inputs and a physical event as output. But this doctrine cannot survive critical analysis. In the present state of our understanding, the problem of constructing an input-output model for the speaker cannot even be formulated coherently.

First, it is at least tendentious to suggest that De Saussure proposed or envisaged any kind of formal 'model' for the conversion of thought content into physical form. All he did was represent the then universally accepted view of utterances as expressions of thoughts—a view that has, fortunately, managed to survive the late twentieth-century onslaught. Other than that, however, the statement made in this last quote just shows ignorance of, and contempt for, the state of affairs prior to the birth of Generative Grammar in the school of Zellig Harris during the late 1940s. Not only did Chomsky despise American structuralism, in particular Leonard Bloomfield, but also European scholars like Heymann Steinthal (1823–1899), Theodor Lipps (1851–1914), Philipp Wegener (1848–1916), Wilhelm Wundt (1832–1920), George Stout (1860–1944), Karl Bühler (1879–1963) and many others, who had done massive amounts of solid preparatory work regarding 'an input-output model for the speaker' and were certainly able to formulate the problem coherently (if by 'coherent formulation' is meant the formulation of a research programme). Chomsky dismissed these authors and the tradition they stood in with a disdain that defies belief.

But even if it had been true that, in the year 1963, 'the problem of constructing an input-output model for the speaker [could] not even be formulated coherently', in the sense of a coherent research programme, this would, of course, have been no reason to claim that 'this doctrine cannot survive critical analysis'. When Aristarchus of Samos, during the third century BCE, proposed that the earth revolved around the sun—as we know from a brief mention in Archimedes' *The Sand Reckoner*—his proposal could probably not be 'formulated coherently', in the sense indicated, yet it has gloriously survived critical analysis. As so often, Chomsky's 'argument' here is without foundation and merely rhetorical. In fact, as is well-known, Chomsky has till the present day combated the theory of 'an input-output model for the speaker'—that is, a *Generative Semantics* type of grammar—as a correct model for natural language grammars. But, as is equally well-known, neither Chomsky nor anyone else has ever put forward a single valid argument to show that his Autonomous Syntax is in any way superior to the Semantic Syntax (Generative Semantics) model of a grammar mediating between thought and language (see Seuren 2004a: 169–90). Nor have any arguments to the effect that the Semantic Syntax model is superior on all counts ever been answered. Here we see that his arrogant *a priori* rejection of anything resembling a theory that sees utterances as expressions of thought goes back to at least 1963.

Meanwhile, the situation has changed dramatically and for the better. An input-output model for the speaker can now be formulated more coherently than ever. Psychologists have developed well-founded theories of the kind of 'thinking-for-speaking' (Slobin 1987) or 'microplanning' (Levelt 1989) needed to get to a proper input for precisely an input-output model for the speaker. Linguists (in particular the late Jim McCawley; see section 6.3.3 below) have developed solid theories of semantic representation in terms of a well-motivated variety of the language of modern predicate calculus, as well as a solid and empirically well-motivated theory of grammar, in which grammars convert semantic representations to surface structures (Seuren 1996).

There are, of course, still many open questions, such as the question of whether the language of Semantic Analyses is subject to the constraints that hold for any of the four grammar types defined in the Chomsky hierarchy, but that question does not have a high priority (the language of Semantic Analysis or SA probably conforms to the type of language generated by context-sensitive phrase structure grammars). Much higher on the agenda is the question of how the cognitive mind gets to the formulation of an SA that is ready to be fed into a transformational grammar so that it will result in a well-formed surface structure of the language concerned. Given what is known in this respect, the formal typology of grammars as set out in the Chomsky hierarchy has lost the relevance it once had. Even if it were technically possible to generate natural languages from a single initial symbol, this would be irrelevant for the theory of language—though it may still be relevant for programming languages, where such a theory may act as a filter for unwellformed strings of symbols, provided the formal language used is deterministically parsable.

Natural languages are defined not by primitive production algorithms but by non-primitive transformation systems, taking as input, for each sentence generated, an SA, itself delivered by cognition in ways that we are beginning to understand in ever more precise detail, and delivering surface structures plus instructions for phonetic or other kinds of perceptible form as output. The notion of Autonomous Syntax, in the sense of a grammar defining the well-formedness of uninterpreted strings of symbols, may make sense in the context of formal mathematical or programming languages—which was, in fact, part of the context in which this notion was born—but it has no relevance for natural language, and it most certainly does not reflect native speakers' linguistic competence. All Chomsky has to say on this subject is (Chomsky 1963: 328):

Our discussion departs from a strict Saussurian conception in two ways. First, we say nothing on the semantic side of *langue*. The few coherent remarks that might be made concerning this subject lie outside the scope of the present survey.

What we see here is a hangover from behaviourism, a brand of psychology Chomsky has been unable to detach himself from completely, despite his severe criticism of it.

Although the notion of Autonomous Syntax has played a dominant role in late twentieth-century linguistic thought, it is now widely accepted that languages are systems that mediate between semantic structures (SAs) on the one hand and linguistic surface structures on the other, exactly as tradition (including De Saussure) has always taken it to be. We now have robust theories of semantic form and robust formal systems for transforming them into surface structures. These elements were lacking in traditional grammar, with the result that the traditional view came into disrepute during the twentieth century, when the focus lay on formalized analyses and descriptions. Nowadays, thanks to a combined effort of cognitive scientists, philosophers and linguists, we are in a position to satisfy all justified formalization demands while avoiding the aberrations that arose from the inability to do so adequately.

Even so, however, it must be admitted that there were other dangers threatening a sound view of language during the period concerned—dangers that Chomsky rightly attempted to ward off. One of these was the alarming influence on linguistic theory, during the 1940s and 1950s, of what used to be called 'information science' or 'information technology', with its probability and entropy measures (see below). The Chomsky hierarchy was a welcome relief from these basically misguided notions regarding natural language. Yet the various models of autonomous generative grammar that replaced those based on information science have suffered the same fate in that they have turned out to be themselves basically misguided.

This is not without consequences for those recent studies in the evolution of human language that take their cue from the Chomskyan notion of Autonomous Syntax, such as Hauser et al. (2002), Fitch and Hauser (2004), Fitch (2010). Despite the many useful and stimulating insights expressed in these studies, they bark up the wrong tree when it comes to the evolution of syntax. First, the experiments in question are based on *comprehension* or *reception* (in whatever sense), not on *production*. Then, these studies are, like Chomskyan Autonomous Syntax, unable to come to terms with linguistic meaning, even though the drive to express meanings has undoubtedly been the main force motivating the evolution of language. Although the Chomsky hierarchy may have been relevant in the 1950s, when linguistic theory had to rid itself of the unrealistic notions developed in information technology, it has lost relevance for the study of natural language in the light of more up-to-date insights, especially insights into the nature and structure of meaning and into the relation between meaning and structured linguistic form.

6.2 What is an algorithm and why is this notion relevant for the study of language?

In the most general sense, an algorithm is a finite formal rule system that manipulates given input structures consisting of discrete symbols in well-defined structural positions and delivers structured output strings, likewise consisting of discrete symbols in well-defined structural positions. An algorithm thus consists of (a) a set of symbols, its *vocabulary* (which is finite for a primitive algorithm, but may be infinite if the algorithm is linked with a primitive algorithm generating an infinite vocabulary), (b) a set of initial input symbols or structured strings of initial input symbols, its *input*, and (c) a finite set of *instructions* or *rules* yielding the output.

The term *algorithm* derives from the birthplace of the ninth-century Baghdad astronomer and mathematician *Muḥammad Ibn Mūsa*, mostly known as *Al-Ḥuārizmi*, that is, from the province of Ḥuārizm (ancient Chorasmia, present-day Uzbekistan), where the man was born.[1] On the basis of available, mostly Indian, expertise (such as the zero as a position indicator) and helped by the Arabic number system, Al-Ḥuārizmi developed the four classic operations in arithmetic: addition, subtraction, multiplication and division, now called the *classic algorithms*. It was not until the thirteenth century that this system of arithmetic began to conquer Europe, spreading from Spain and Sicily, against the widespread and long-lasting interdiction in many commercial centres of the use of the zero in bookkeeping (as it would be conducive to fiddling the books). During the 1930s and 1940s, the notion of algorithm was generalized so as to comprise all formally defined symbolic systems generating outputs from given inputs (Post 1944; Rosenbloom 1950).

Algorithms come in many varieties. In the present context, which sees grammars of natural languages as algorithms, it seems useful to make a first primary distinction between *production* and *reception algorithms*. The former are subdivided into *primitive* and *non-primitive production algorithms*. The main difference consists in the fact that primitive production algorithms take as input a single initial symbol, say S. The initial symbol is expanded through so-called REWRITE RULES into strings of one or more symbols, all taken from a given vocabulary, which may include intermediate (nonterminal) symbols but must include terminal symbols, which occur in the final output strings. By contrast, non-primitive algorithms accept any symbolic input *I*, whether or not produced by a preceding algorithm, and transform or convert *I* into a well-defined structured output. The class of primitive production algorithms has

---

[1] The original Latin borrowed form was *algorismus* (sometimes also *algobarismus*), still recognized in the now obsolete Spanish word *algorismo* 'number'. The *s* was replaced with *th* in France during the seventeenth century by a false analogy with the then new term *logarithm*, which derives from the Greek words *lógos* (reason) and *arithmós* (number). By the end of the nineteenth century, the form *algorithm* had become generally accepted. Yet until the middle of the twentieth century, purists would still write (and say) *algorism*.

been studied much more intensively than the class of non-primitive production algorithms.

A specific kind of reception algorithm is a *decision algorithm*, where input structures are 'transformed' into, or mapped onto, one of two symbols: 'yes' or 'no'. When the output for a given input structure *I* is 'yes', *I* is a legitimate product of a given primitive or non-primitive production algorithm **A**. When the answer is 'no', *I* is not generated by **A**. Algorithms whose output is always this way decidable are called *decidable algorithms*. Infinite sets of finite symbol strings ('infinite languages') that allow for a decision algorithm, given a primitive or non-primitive algorithm of any kind generating the strings of the language, are called *decidable languages*. Infinite languages that are characterizable through an algorithm of any type, whether or not decidable, are standardly called *recursively enumerable* or *canonical languages*. An infinite language that is not recursively enumerable, is algorithmically undefinable (though it may be definable in other ways).[2]

In linguistics, the distinction between primitive and non-primitive production algorithms is of great importance in the light of the controversy between Chomskyan *Autonomous Syntax* and erstwhile *Generative Semantics*, more properly called *Semantic Syntax* (see section 6.1). Autonomous Syntax considers syntactic structures to have their own formally definable properties, regardless of any communicative or interactional needs. (In fact, Chomsky denies that language is made for 'communication' in any sense of the term: he holds the curious view that language is primarily used for the purpose of soliloquy.) Semantic Syntax, by contrast, sees grammar as a rule-governed system for the conversion of SAs into surface structures (SSs). Grammar is thus subservient to, and arising from, the speaker's need or wish to enter a social commitment, through a speech act operator, with regard to a proposition—that is, a mental act in which a property is assigned to one or more entities (see Seuren 2009a: 85–98). It is clear that Autonomous Syntax fits a framework that sees grammars as primitive production algorithms, whereas Semantic Syntax requires a non-primitive production algorithm that takes structured SAs—that is, crystallizations of propositional thoughts under a commitment operator—as input and delivers well-formed surface structures. The argument that the Chomsky hierarchy is irrelevant for the study of natural language must be seen in this light.

When a language **L** is decidable, its complement—that is, the set of strings not generated by the algorithm generating **L**—is also decidable, since all and only the strings in the given vocabulary that are rejected by the decision algorithm belong to the complement of **L**. A decidable language **L**, whether generated by a primitive or a non-primitive production algorithm, must have a matching non-primitive decision

---

[2] *Finite* languages are always enumerable since they can be enumerated as simple lists of strings of symbols. This also makes them decidable, as there is a finite procedure (checking the finite list) for deciding, for each string, whether or not it is on the list.

algorithm. When natural or computer languages are concerned, a decision algorithm is called a *parser*.

The term *parsing* is, however, also often used for *semantic parsing*—that is, the reduction of surface structures to their corresponding semantic representations or SAs. This use is less relevant in a discussion of the Chomsky hierarchy of generative systems, since this hierarchy leaves meaning out of account. What is relevant in a wider context is that there seems to be no practically viable algorithmic procedure for the reduction of phonologically analysed surface structures to their corresponding SAs (Seuren 2009a: 268–76). The topdown process, from SA to SS, is largely deterministic, allowance being made for a certain but manageable degree of SS variability, stylistic or other, given an input SA. The bottom-up mapping, however, from SS to SA, is of a different nature. Here, as is well-known among computational linguists, the mapping of a given SS onto a possible SA is likely to 'explode' for some SSs. This is not so much the case for structures made up according to rules of flectional morphology, which, in general, allow for fully deterministic semantic parsing. Thus, a Turkish morphologically complex sentence such as (6.1) allows for the deterministic mapping onto its underlying semantic form, due to the strict rules of Turkish morphology (the sign '+' stands for bound-morpheme concatenation; note the left-branching scope hierarchy, made possible by the fact that this is a *morphological*, not a *syntactic*, structure; see section 3.7.2.2):

(6.1)   Bu   kitab   yaz   + dır   + a   + ma   + malı   + y   + dı.
        this   book   write + CAUS + POSS + NEG   + NECESS + COP + PAST
        'It should have been impossible to get someone to write this book.'

And the fourfold ambiguity of a German sentence like (6.2) is still easily manageable:

(6.2)   Er ließ den Diktator töten.
        'He made/allowed the dictator (to) kill/He arranged for/allowed the dictator to be killed.'

But an English sentence like (6.3) contains so many lexical and structural ambiguities that a formal parsing procedure is no longer of any practical value:

(6.3)   I had not written to the man I wanted to succeed in 1995 because of his blue eyes.

Here, the speech situation and preceding context (with topic and comment given) are indispensable for a proper real-life interpretation. The Turkish system has the advantage of determinate semantic parsing, but the disadvantage of requiring more machinery and thus of being harder to acquire. The German and English systems are easier to acquire but are more dependent on contextual and situational clues.

What seems to happen in the interpretation or processing of uttered sentences is that listeners first of all identify the lexical items and then jump to a reconstruction of the most relevant scope and predicate-argument relations, largely on the basis of contextual and situational clues and general scenario knowledge (Ritchie 1983; Konieczny et al. 1997; Cutler and Clifton 1999). The process is helped enormously by the contextually given *topic-comment structure*: since the topic has already been processed, all that remains is the comment—a fact not usually taken into account. The projected interpretation is then tested, if necessary, by feeding it back into the productive generator and checking the result for correctness or, in the case of garbled utterances, sufficient and plausible similarity to what should have been the correct output according to the norms that are valid in any linguistic community. Actual real-life semantic parsing is thus to a large extent a matter of *reconstruction-by-hypothesis* or *analysis-by-synthesis* (Townsend and Bever 2001: 160–72).[3] What defines a language is thus *speakers'* competence in producing correct sentences in the intended meaning, not *hearers'* ability to make sense of possibly garbled utterances. Interpretation can cope with a great deal of garbling, but to know what is good English (or any other language) one has to rely on competent speakers whose speech is up to the socially fixed norm in any speech community. For this reason we consider grammars to be primarily *generative*, and not *interpretative*, algorithmic systems.

The output of either a primitive or a non-primitive production algorithm is often called a 'language', especially when it is subject to an interpretation of whatever kind. The empirical question is now (a) whether *natural languages* are recursively enumerable, by means of either a primitive or a non-primitive production algorithm, and (b) if so, whether any production algorithm **A** enumerating all and only the sentences of a natural language is matched by a decision or parsing algorithm deciding whether or not any given string in the vocabulary is or is not generated by **A**.

The assumption underlying almost all current work in formal grammar is that natural languages are at least *recursively enumerable*. But whether natural languages are also *decidable* is considered an open question. In computational linguistics the difficulties are well-known and what one tries to achieve there is statistical approximation rather than deterministic semantic parsing. Linguists tend to demur. My answer is that the question is not relevant, at least not from a theoretical point of view. The only relevant question, in this context, is: what makes natural languages

---

[3] It is perfectly possible, and perhaps even true, that probability measures play a greater role in the interpretation process than hierarchical constituent structure, as is claimed in Frank and Bod (2011). If this is true it is not only unsurprising, since constituent structure is, in principle, not perceptibly manifest and results only from a top-down generation process, but also irrelevant to the theory of grammar, since grammar is of a *generative* and not of an *interpretative* or *processing* nature. The opposition created in Frank and Bod (2011) between probability measures and constituent structure is thus a false one: they are not in competition. These authors suggest further that, *therefore*, hierarchical sentence structure is irrelevant to cognition, thereby implying that sentence/utterance *production* is not part of cognition.

semantically parsable—that is, is there an algorithmic procedure for the reduction of SSs to their underlying SA or, in cases of ambiguity, their underlying SAs? As has just been said, this question will probably have to be answered in the negative. Comprehension of sentences and interpretation of utterances are certainly *guided* by 'reverse' algorithmical processes (clearly so in the case of morphological disentanglement), but they are almost certainly not *determined* by such processes, not in live speech anyway. In comprehension and interpretation, much depends on 'educated guesses', given discourse and situation and perhaps also probability measures (see note 3). These guesses can then, if necessary, be tested according to an analysis-by-synthesis feedback method.

6.3 The Chomsky hierarchy

The Chomsky hierarchy is a typology, or classification, of what are taken to be primitive algorithmic production systems (see Chomsky and Miller 1958; Chomsky 1959, 1963; Chomsky and Schützenberger 1963). In this classification, four types are distinguished, from 0 to 3, each type being characterized by increasingly severe restrictions on its rules. Type 0, called 'transformational' by Chomsky, is totally unrestricted, which means that it accepts as input to its rules not only single symbols (including a start symbol) but also structured strings of symbols. However, the possibility of accepting structured strings of symbols makes algorithms non-primitive, so that they fall outside the hierarchy of primitive production algorithms. Since Chomsky does not make the distinction between primitive and non-primitive algorithmic production systems and since his type-3, type-2 and type-1 grammars are primitive production algorithm types, while type-0 grammars are non-primitive production algorithms, it follows that the Chomsky hierarchy really is a question of primitive algorithmic production systems. Therefore, if the grammars of natural languages turn out to be of type 0—the position taken here—the Chomsky hierarchy loses its significance.[4]

6.3.1 *The primitive generation of tree structures*

The primitive production algorithm types 3, 2 and 1 should be seen as printing machines that act on a single start symbol as initial input and follow a finite set of rewrite rules, in principle (but see section 6.3.2.1) without any memory or other

---

[4] Petersson et al. (2010) argue that the Chomsky hierarchy is likewise irrelevant in the study of how the brain processes incoming linguistic signs—that is, of utterance reception. It should be remembered, however, that the Chomsky hierarchy was set up not with utterance reception but with sentence generation in mind. These two aspects of linguistic processing are radically different from each other.

external source to fall back on.[5] Each rule *rewrites*, or *expands*, a single symbol α into a finite number of *constant* (*non-variable*), normally *serially ordered* symbols, which may include α again. An input symbol or *node* α plus any expansion is the *constituent* α, as shown in Figure 6.1, where one sees the *node* α rewritten as, or expanded into, the *constituent* α containing the symbols β to ζ as a result of the rewrite rule R_i (the sign '+' stands for symbol concatenation):

$$R_i \quad \alpha \rightarrow \beta + \gamma + \delta + \varepsilon + \zeta$$

Thus, if there is a further rule rewriting δ as $\eta + \theta$:

$$R_j \quad \delta \rightarrow \eta + \theta$$

δ, in any tree structure generated, is a constituent containing the string $\eta + \theta$.

The string of symbols thus generated is: $[\beta + \gamma + [\eta + \theta] + \varepsilon + \zeta]$, where the square brackets indicate expanded constituents. The string $[\beta + \gamma + [\eta + \theta] + \varepsilon + \zeta]$ is thus one constituent, consisting of five subconstituents, four of which are mere nodes but one, namely $[\eta + \theta]$, is again an expanded constituent. The symbols α and δ do not occur in the output string because they have been rewritten. Linguists often use the notation of *labelled bracketing*, which shows the names of the expanded constituents concerned by attaching them as subscripts to the left hand side bracket, in the following manner:

$$_\alpha[\beta + \gamma + _\delta[\eta + \theta] + \varepsilon + \zeta]$$

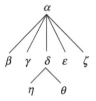

FIGURE 6.1 The hierarchical constituent (tree) structure corresponding to the linestring $_\alpha[\beta + \gamma + _\delta[\eta + \theta] + \varepsilon + \zeta]$ using labelled bracketing

When an input symbol re-appears in the immediate or remote output of a rule R the system is *recursive*, since R may then re-apply. Note that when a symbol α

reappears in the output of a rewrite rule **R**, either α or **R** must be optional: if α or **R** were obligatory, the algorithm would never stop generating strings of symbols and no finite output string would ever come about. Optionality of a symbol γ in the output of a rule is normally indicated by putting round brackets around γ, as in a rule of the form:

$$\alpha \rightarrow \beta \, (+ \, \gamma)$$

This rule is thus really a condensation of two rules, namely:

$$\alpha \rightarrow \beta$$

$$\alpha \rightarrow \beta + \gamma$$

Only a recursive algorithm can produce an infinite set of output strings (structures).

6.3.2 *Type-3 algorithms*

The four types in the Chomsky hierarchy are defined according to the restrictions imposed on their rules. The rules of *type-3 algorithms* (also called *Regular Grammars* or *Markov Systems*; linguists often speak of *Finite State Grammars*) are the most restricted:

Type-3 production algorithms:
Each rule in a type-3 production algorithm has a single-symbol input and an output consisting of either one or two symbols. A one-symbol output is non-rewritable (*terminal*); of a two-symbol output, one symbol is rewritable (*non-terminal*) while the other is not. The rewritable symbol Φ is either always the right hand side or always the left hand side symbol. If Φ is right hand side, the system is monotone right-branching; if left hand side, the system is monotone left-branching. Φ may lead to an immediate or remote output again containing Φ, in which case the output language is infinite.

A type-3 production algorithm is a *Finite State (FS) automaton*, consisting of a finite number of states S_n and transitions from one state to another, starting with S_o, more or less like a railway system. At each transition, a symbol is printed on a ticket, next to the state of arrival. Some states are end states ($S_\emptyset$), in that they do not allow for a transition to any other state. The system has no memory other than what has been printed on the ticket. Simple examples are shown in the Figures 6.2–c and 6.3–d.[6]

---

[6] Cp. Chomsky and Miller (1958: 91):
A finite state language is a finite or infinite set of strings (sentences) of symbols (words) generated by a finite set of rules (the grammar), where each rule specifies the state of the system in which it can be applied, the symbol which is generated, and the state of the system after the rule is applied.

The type-3 *System NN*, for example, generates the set of all and only the digitally written natural numbers:

System NN: **Type-3 production algorithm for digitally written natural numbers**

(a) Initial symbol: N
(b) Vocabulary: {N, 0, 1, 2, 3, 4, 5, 6, 7, 8, 9}
(c) Rules: (1) N → 0 (+ N)
                      (2) N → 1 (+ N)
                      (3) N → 2 (+ N)
                      (4) N → 3 (+ N)
                      (5) N → 4 (+ N)
                      (6) N → 5 (+ N)
                      (7) N → 6 (+ N)
                      (8) N → 7 (+ N)
                      (9) N → 8 (+ N)
                      (10) N → 9 (+ N)

This monotone right-branching system generates, for example, the number 3751, corresponding to the structures shown in Figure 6.2-a, 6.2-b. The corresponding FS automaton is shown in Figure 6.2-c. Here, one starts at state N, from where one has two options. Either one goes to end state $S_\varnothing$, in which case one's ticket is stamped $0,S_\varnothing$ or $1,S_\varnothing$ or $2,S_\varnothing$ or $3,S_\varnothing$, etc. Or else one goes in a circle back to N again, in which case the ticket is stamped $0,N$ or $1,N$ or $2,N$ or $3,N$, etc. In the latter case, one is allowed to start again (the system is recursive). This way any natural number can be printed on the ticket (interrupted by N-symbols, but the last symbol will always be $S_\varnothing$).

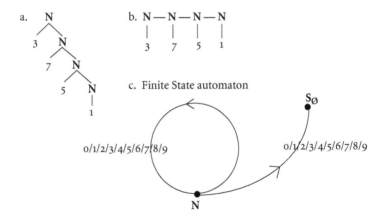

FIGURE **6.2** The number 3751 generated according to *System NN* and the corresponding Finite State automaton

Structure (a) shows a normal constituent tree; (b) is structurally identical to (a) but for the fact that (b) is presented horizontally (turned anticlockwise). The point of the horizontal presentation is to show that all strings generated by a type-3 algorithm have a monotone left- or right-branching serial structure.[7] Clearly, the 'language' produced by System NN is decidable, since any string containing n ($n > 0$) vocabulary elements other than N is generated by it.

The classic algorithms developed by *Al-Ḫuārizmi* can be seen as non-primitive decidable algorithms that take as input any pair of products delivered by *System NN* (any *ordered* pair for subtraction and division) and deliver rational numbers (positive and negative integers plus their fractions) as output. (Thanks to the decimal notation for rational numbers, with o as a position indicator, *System NN* can be reformulated as a system that delivers rational numbers as output, so that the classic algorithms have an input and an output consisting of rational numbers.)

A common toy language used in animal experiments (e.g. Fitch and Hauser 2004) consists of strings of the form *ab, abab, ababab, abababab,* etc. This language is generated by a simple type-3 (FS) algorithm of the following form (the corresponding FS automaton is represented in Figure 6.3–d):

System ABAB:

(a) Initial symbol: S
(b) Vocabulary: {S, S₁, a, b}
(c) Rules: (1)   S   → a + S₁
                       (2)   S1 → b (+ S)

Among the structured strings generated by System ABAB are (a), (b) and (c) in Figure 6.3:[8]

---

[7] The horizontal representation (b) in Figure 6.2 does not show whether the corresponding algorithm is right- or left-branching. By contrast, (a) can only be generated by a monotone right-branching system. Its left-branching counterpart will generate 1 first, then 5 then 7 then 3. To get (b) from the right-monotone (a), (a) must be turned anticlockwise; to get (b) from the left-monotone counterpart of (a), the turning must be clockwise.

[8] The structure assigned to *ababab* in Fitch and Hauser (2004: 378, Figure 1) is erroneous. These authors assign the structure:

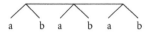

a   b   a   b   a   b

which cannot be generated by a Finite State grammar, as the authors allege, but only by a Context-Free grammar of the right-linear type (Levelt 1974a: 26–7), containing the rule S → a + b (+ S). (Just place an S-symbol above each [a–b] structure in the figure above and tilt the whole structure a little clockwise, and you will see the point.) This *abab* language can thus be generated by different grammars, one a Finite State or regular and one a right-linear Context-Free grammar, each assigning different structures.

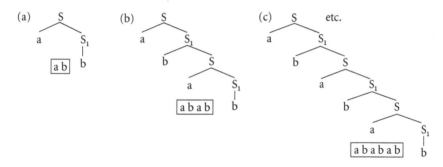

(d) Finite State automaton

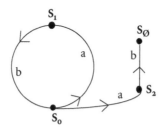

FIGURE **6.3** Some serially structured strings generated by System ABAB and the corresponding Finite State automaton

6.3.2.1 *Nth-order approximations* The question of whether natural languages are generated by type-3 production algorithms would have been quickly answered in the negative, had it not been for the fact that *probability measures* can be attached, as an external device (see section 6.3.1), to each rewriting, given any number of earlier rewritings (Shannon and Weaver 1949; Osgood and Sebeok 1954: 35–49, 93–125). When no probability measure is attached and the system is allowed to generate finite strings at random within the vocabulary, the resulting 'language' is called a *zero-order approximation*. A *first-order approximation* generates strings of symbols (words) according to their frequency of occurrence in the corpus concerned. When, given a representative corpus of English sentences, the preceding word is taken into account, we have a *second-order approximation*. When the two preceding words are taken into account, we have a *third-order approximation*. The following are samples of the first three orders of approximation, as given in Miller and Chomsky (1963: 428–9) (see also Levelt 1974b: 167–8):

ZERO ORDER: *splinter shadow dilapidate turtle pass stress grouse appropriate radio whereof also appropriate gourd keeper clarion wealth possession press blunt canter chancy vindicable corpus*

FIRST ORDER: *representing and speedily is an good apt or came can different natural here he the a in came the to of to expert gray come to furnishes the line message had be these*

SECOND ORDER: *the head and in frontal attack on an English writer that the character of this point is therefore another method for the letters that the time of who even told the problem for an unexpected*

It was expected by many, in those years, that the higher the order of approximation, the more grammatical the output would be. In fact, while the zero- and first-order approximations are hard to read and to remember and, when read, do not receive much of an intonation contour, the second-order approximation is already easier to remember and invites a certain prosody; it sounds like the rambling of a mentally deranged patient.

However, then as now, higher order approximations, given a reasonably sized corpus, would require an astronomically large number of operations, far exceeding the capacity of the computers that were available then and still beyond the practical reach of modern computers. For that reason, a different and less cumbersome method was adopted for approximations beyond the second order, the so-called *projection method*, described as follows in Levelt (1974b: 167–8):

We present speaker *A* with a *pair* of words (chosen at random from a newspaper or from a sentence composed by another speaker), for example, *family was*, and ask him to form a sentence in which the pair occurs. Suppose that the sentence which he produces is *the family was large*. We then present *was large* to speaker *B*, and request that he in turn form a sentence in which the pair occurs. If this sentence is *the forest was large, dark and dangerous* we present *large dark* to speaker *C*, and so forth.

This way, the following strings of words were produced (Miller and Chomsky 1963: 429):

THIRD ORDER: *family was large dark animal came roaring down the middle of my friends love books passionately every kiss is fine*

FOURTH ORDER: *went to movies with a man I used to go toward Harvard Square in Cambridge is mad fun for*

FIFTH ORDER: *road in the country was insane especially in dreary rooms where they have some books to buy for studying Greek*

All this was very exciting, and also amusing, during the 1950s and 1960s, but that does not change the fact that this research was a dead alley.[9]

---

[9] The fact that statistics of usage has been revived in recent times as a method for defining grammars (e.g. Tomasello 2003; Goldberg 1995, 2006) is highly regrettable and difficult to understand in the light of the enormous progress made in the study of syntax since the 1960s (see Seuren 2009a: 26–33 for a more detailed discussion). That frequency measures are an important factor in the process of first and second language acquisition, and probably also in interpretative utterance processing (see note 3), is easily accepted, but the conclusion that, therefore, internalized grammars are made up of frequency measures is entirely unwarranted and obviously false, as anyone acquainted with the syntactic facts that have been observed, and convincingly explained, over the past five decades will confirm.

Miller and Chomsky (1963: 429–30) observe:

Higher-order approximations to the statistical structure of English have been used to manipulate the apparent meaningfulness of letter and word sequences as a variable in psychological experiments. As k [the number of preceding words; PAMS] increases, the sequences of symbols take on a more familiar look and—although they remain nonsensical—the fact seems to be empirically established that they become easier to perceive and to remember correctly.

We know that the sequences produced by k-limited Markov sources cannot converge on the set of grammatical utterances as k increases because there are many grammatical sentences that are never uttered and so could not be represented in any estimation of transitional probabilities. [...]

Even though a k-limited source is not a grammar, it might still be proposed as a model of the user. Granted that the model cannot isolate the set of all grammatical sentences, neither can we; inasmuch as our human limitations often lead us into ungrammatical paths, the real test of this model of the user is whether it exhibits the same limitations that we do.

However, when we examine this model, not as a convenient way to summarize certain statistical parameters of message ensembles, but as a serious proposal for the way people create *and interpret* [italics mine; note that the semantic parameter, left out of account in Chomsky 1963, as shown above, is re-introduced here, but without any consequences for the argument; PAMS] their communicative utterances, it is all too easy to find objections. We shall mention only one, but one that seems particularly serious: the k-limited Markov source has far too many parameters [...]. As we have noted, there can be as many as D^k [D is the number of elements of the vocabulary; PAMS] probabilities to be estimated. By the time k grows large enough to give a reasonable fit to ordinary usage the number of parameters that must be estimated will have exploded; a staggering amount of text would have to be scanned and tabulated in order to make reliable estimates. [...].

The trouble is not merely that the statistician is inconvenienced by an estimation problem. A learner would face an equally difficult task. If we assume that a k-limited automaton must somehow arise during childhood, the amount of raw induction that would be required is almost inconceivable. We cannot seriously propose that a child learns the values of 10^9 parameters in a childhood lasting only 10^8 seconds.

Moreover, Chomsky (1956, 1957) produced arguments to the effect that natural languages could not be finite state (type-3) languages because in natural language one finds dependency relations of unrestricted distance and of unrestricted embeddings (as between *if* and *then* in conditionals or in embedded relative clauses: *The car that the dog that the man saved scratched got away*) that cannot be accounted for in type-3 grammars. It has been pointed out by various authors since then (see Levelt 1974b: 25–6; Seuren 1998: 273; Pullum 2011) that Chomsky's argument was faulty, because a trivial type-3 grammar will produce *all* arbitrary finite strings of English words, just as the trivial type-3 System NN specified above generates all arbitrary finite successions of digits and thus the digital expressions for all natural numbers. If such a trivial type-3 grammar generates all arbitrary finite strings of English words, it must also generate, for example, *The car that the dog that the man saved scratched got away*, or

If if if John left then his wife is sad is true then she doesn't love him is a valid argument then I don't understand your logic and further extensions along these lines. The problem, not addressed by Chomsky, is that such a trivial type-3 grammar fails to filter out ungrammatical sentences, such as **The car that the dog that the man saved scratched* or **If if if John left then his wife is sad is true then*. The argument should, therefore, have been that no regular or type-3 grammar will both produce all grammatical strings and *fail to produce all ungrammatical strings* of English words. Such an argument, however, would require a heavier mathematical machinery than that used by Chomsky at the time.

This erroneous reasoning has given rise to the now widespread, but false, dogma that the presumed property of *unlimited recursion* (nowadays also called 'merge' or 'discrete infinity', though the notional confusion in this domain is almost hilarious) is the main, and according to some the only, feature distinguishing natural human language from other, possibly non-human, systems of communication. This dogma underlies all experimental work recently carried out by Hauser and his associates, and endorsed by Chomsky, on monkeys held in a laboratory at Harvard University. Despite the enormous publicity created around it, this work lacks any relevant relation with natural language or its evolution, as is further argued in section 6.5 below. Unlimited recursion is not an essential property of human languages (a) because there are languages (see Everett 2005 on Pirahã) that have no syntactic recursion at all: in those languages, our subordinated or embedded clauses are independent sentences, the comprehension of the relevant embedding relations being largely discourse- and cognition-driven, and (b) because, as I have argued repeatedly in previous publications, the property of unlimited recursion is to be sought in the human cognitive faculty—that is, in the *thinking*—and not in the syntax, which, as is argued in the Chapters 2 and 3 of the present book, is a mere handmaiden to the mind (see also Pullum and Scholz 2010).

In any case, Chomsky's *conclusion*, though based on a fallacious *argument*, was generally accepted and, it seems, rightly so. Nowadays, no serious linguist can uphold the view that natural language sentences have a monotone right- or left-branching constituent structure of the kind shown in the Figures 6.2 or 6.3 above. We now have overwhelming evidence that the syntactic structures of natural languages far exceed the power of type-3 grammars, which makes this type of grammar irrelevant for the analysis and description of natural languages. No serious linguist can deny the necessity of allowing for complex, hierarchically ordered constituents in surface structures in the sense introduced in Bloomfield (1933). The real debate is about the (in)adequacy of the Bloomfieldian model. FS grammars play no role at all in the theory of grammar.

Then, if grammars of natural languages were type-3 production grammars delivering serially ordered and probability-weighted strings of words, the notion of grammaticality of a string of words (a 'sentence'), which is indispensable in the study of syntax, would be undefinable. This is because there is no nonarbitrary probability limit, other than $p=1$, at or beyond which a generated string of words should be considered part of the language in question and $p = 1$ is not only unattainable for any given sentence in a corpus and for any representative corpus of any natural language, it would also take away all informativity from the sentences generated. The language would thus not even be enumerable, given that the comprehension of the set of strings belonging to it is ill-defined. Finally and most importantly, of course, there is no way this type of grammar can account for the fact that sentences have linguistically defined meanings.

Ironically, Chomsky has always invoked the authority of good old Wilhelm von Humboldt to bolster his claim that the infinity of language is what distinguishes it from other communication systems. Yet, when Humboldt speaks about the fact that 'language makes infinite use of finite means' (Wilhelm von Humboldt in Heath 1988: 91), he places the causal origin of this wondrous property of language in the fact that humans are able to develop unboundedly many different *thoughts*, expressed in linguistic utterances. This becomes clear when one considers Humboldt's phrase of language making 'infinite use of finite means' in its wider context (Heath 1988: 91; italics mine):

But the procedure of language is not simply one whereby a single phenomenon comes about; it must simultaneously open up the possibility of producing an indefinable host of such phenomena, and under all the conditions that thought imposes. For language is quite peculiarly confronted by an unending and truly boundless domain, the totality of all that can be thought. *It must therefore make infinite use of finite means, and is able to do so in virtue of the identity of the force that engenders both thought and language.*

This, however, is not what is asserted with so much emphasis in Chomskyan Autonomous Syntax. For Autonomous Syntax, the source of the, mathematically speaking, infinity of any natural language L lies in the fact that the rules of the *syntax* of L contain certain forms of recursivity so that, as we know from the theory of algorithms, that syntax *generates*, in the technical sense of the term, an infinite number of well-formed structured strings of symbols. Those strings are then, with certain restrictions, taken to be 'projectable' onto certain meanings in ways that do not really capture the interest or the imagination of autonomous syntacticians and are, in fact, left largely unspecified. For them, the syntax of any language L is explicitly 'autonomous', in that it generates sentences regardless of any semantic considerations. This notion of syntax is reminiscent not so much of Humboldt, no matter how often he is quoted by autonomous syntacticians, as of the note scribbled by a bored medieval monk in his breviary, which he was required to read every day for a certain number of hours (see Seuren 1998: 116, note 25):

ABCDEFGHIKLMNOPQRSTUVXYZ: per hoc alphabetum notum componitur breviarium totum. ('from this well-known alphabet is composed the entire breviary').

Of course, the monk was right, just as Humboldt was, but Humboldt's point is that the medieval monks' notion of the 'infinity' of language is derived from, or caused by, the non-linguistic but cognitive fact that humans are always able to produce novel thoughts not produced by anyone ever before. Or, in the words of Gottlob Frege in the opening paragraph of his *Logische Untersuchungen, dritter Teil: Gedankengefüge*, written during the early 1920s and republished in Patzig (1966: 72):

Erstaunlich ist es, was die Sprache leistet, indem sie mit wenigen Silben unübersehbar viele Gedanken ausdrückt, daß sie sogar für einen Gedanken, den nun zum ersten Male ein Erdbürger gefaßt hat, eine Einkleidung findet, in der ihn ein anderer erkennen kann, dem er ganz neu ist. Dies wäre nicht möglich, wenn wir in dem Gedanken nicht Teile unterscheiden könnten, denen Satzteile entsprächen, so daß der Aufbau des Satzes als Bild gelten könnte des Aufbaues des Gedankens. Freilich sprechen wir eigentlich in einem Gleichnisse, wenn wir das Verhältnis von Ganzem und Teil auf den Gedanken übertragen. Doch liegt das Gleichnis so nahe und trifft im Ganzen so zu, daß wir das hie und da vorkommende Hinken kaum als störend empfinden.

(It is remarkable what language does when it expresses an unsurveyable mass of thoughts by means of only a few syllables, so that even for a thought that some citizen of the earth conceives for the first time ever it finds a clothing that allows someone else, for whom the thought is entirely new, to recognize it. This would not be possible unless we could distinguish within the thought as a whole certain parts that correspond with sentence parts, so that the structure of the sentence reflects the structure of the thought. This is, admittedly, a comparison in which we transfer the relation between the whole and its parts to a thought. Yet this comparison is so close and so well applicable that any possible occasional limping will not be felt as being disturbing.)

The autonomous 'infinity' of language is thus just a requirement to be met by any syntactic system of any natural language for it to be able to serve as a vehicle for the expression of a, technically speaking, infinite number of distinct thoughts. (In fact, as mentioned in section 3.8.1 above, syntactic 'recursion' in a language may well be restricted to conjunctive concatenation of simple sentences.)

6.3.2.2 *Entropy as a measure of meaningfulness*   Though it may be evident now that type-3 grammars are not only incapable of accounting for the semantics of sentences but are also totally irrelevant to any kind of semantic theory, this was not evident during the 1950s and 1960s, when the study of meaning was still virally infected with behaviourism and meaning itself was considered to be outside the reach of serious science. True, logically oriented philosophers such as Alfred Tarski and Rudolf Carnap, were already defining 'semantic'—that is, model-theoretic—theories for formal logical languages, but linguists, psychologists and information engineers were, on the whole, unaware of these developments.

The mathematical psychologists, upwardly mobile linguists and information science engineers of the mid-twentieth century, having given up hopes of accounting for meaning as such, took refuge in the notion of *meaningfulness*, which they thought could be quantified or measured in terms of what came to be called *entropy* (Shannon 1948), a measure of the surprise value of a new serially generated symbol. The word was that, using the technique of *n*th-order approximation as described above, it should be possible to measure the meaningfulness of a given symbol α in a serially produced string of symbols on the basis of the probability of the occurrence of α given any number of preceding symbols. The higher the probability of a symbol occurring, the less meaningful it would be and thus the lower the entropy, and vice versa. For example, given the letter *q*, the probability of *u* following it in English texts is close to 100 (the only exceptions I know of are foreign proper names such as *Qatar*, for the well-known Gulf State, or *Qom*, for the holy city in Iran, foreign borrowings such as *qānūn*, an Arabic harp, or acronyms such as *Qantas*, the Australian airline, pronounced ['kʷontǎs]). The *u* after *q* is thus considered to have an entropy measure close to 0, which makes it 'meaningless' or totally uninformative. Or given the string of words *lock + stock + and*, the probability of the next word being *barrel* is again indistinguishable from 100, which gives the occurrence of *barrel* an entropy of (close to) 0, making it 'meaningless'.[10] One should realize also that the addition of a symbol α to a given string of symbols may make the new string ungrammatical, which would assign to α a very high degree of meaningfulness or entropy!

Despite its now obvious deficiencies, this approach enjoyed great prestige at the time, not least because it was backed up by impressive-looking mathematical constructs. We now know, however, that all this is irrelevant for the study of language. In trying to understand what language is and how it works we are not helped at all by the notion of entropy—if only because establishing 'meaningfulness' is a far cry from specifying meanings.[11]

6.3.3 *Context-free and context-sensitive grammars*

One thus sees what Chomsky was up against when he started further developing Zellig Harris's notion of generative grammar during the early 1950s and one can only appreciate the fact that he was able to remove type-3 grammars from the theoretical linguistics agenda. He did so by calling attention to less impoverished algorithmic production systems, in particular type-2 and type-1 grammars and concluded that these were not equal either to the task of generating the set of all and only the

---

[10] This still holds, despite the 1998 British comedy crime movie *Lock, Stock and Two Smoking Barrels*, which occupies a prominent position in the Google search results for 'lock+stock+and'.

[11] This is not to say that the Shannon measure of entropy will never be useful. If you want to decipher a code replacing each letter of the alphabet with an arbitrary other letter, entropy values will quickly reveal (a) the language of the coded document and (b) the true values of the code characters.

sentences of a natural language. His final conclusion was (Chomsky 1957) that grammars for natural languages must be transformational, that is, of type 0. In his model, the output of a type-2 or type-1 primitive base grammar is fed into a non-primitive, transformational algorithm that would in the end deliver all and only the well-formed surface structures of the language under description.

Had he stuck to this valid conclusion, he might well have agreed with those of his followers who, during the mid-1960s, developed the new and exciting theory that the output structures of the base grammar, known as *deep structures*, were at the same time representations of sentence meaning—that is, *semantic analyses* or SAs. These SAs were taken to have the syntactic form of expressions in the language of modern predicate calculus, enriched with a number of operators not used in standard logic. The question of what algorithmic or possibly non-algorithmic process should be taken to produce SAs was considered, in this new approach, to be of less immediate concern: the grammar of a language was now taken to be just the transformational system mapping SAs onto SSs.

The leading figures in this movement, known as *Generative Semantics* (but better named *Semantic Syntax*), were James McCawley (1938–1999), together with John (Haj) Ross, George Lakoff, Paul Postal and perhaps a few others.[12] Chomsky, however, having first gone along with the initial stages of this new theory (Chomsky 1965), made an about-face around 1967 and started a bitter campaign against Generative Semantics, falling back on his earlier view of grammar as a primitive algorithm. The unpleasant and divisive period following this event is known as *the linguistics wars* (see, for example, Harris 1993; Huck and Goldsmith 1995). Its consequences are still deeply felt.

Against this backdrop, let us now see what the less restricted type-2 and type-1 grammars amount to. Type-2 grammars, also called *context-free (CF) grammars*, have, just like type-3 grammars, rewrite rules with one single symbol as input, but the output of a CF rewrite rule is less restricted in that it may consist of any finite number of, possibly optional, linearly ordered (constant, non-variable) symbols, including the zero-symbol $\emptyset$. Rules of the form R_i and R_j generating the schematic tree structure in Figure 6.1 thus illustrate CF rewrite rules. Clearly, CF rewrite rules can generate complex tree structures with (non-crossing) hierarchically ordered constituents. Moreover—a point that has received a great deal of attention in the literature—CF grammars allow for *centre-embedding* of a recursive symbol, something which is strictly disallowed in FS grammars.

For example, a CF grammar can generate all and only those strings in the vocabulary {S, a, b} that consist of n occurrences of a followed by n occurrences of b ($n \geq 1$): *ab, aabb, aaabbb*, etc. Consider System AABB, which is defined as follows:

---

[12] I developed the same theory independently in my Utrecht PhD thesis (Seuren 1969).

System AABB:
(a) Initial symbol: S
(b) Vocabulary: {S, a, b}
(c) Rule: S → a (+ S) + b

System AABB generates, *inter alia,* the following structured strings (Figure 6.4):

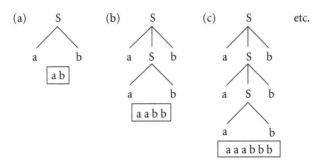

FIGURE 6.4 Some structured strings generated by *System* AABB

Another example of a CF rewrite system is System MIRROR, which generates all and only those strings in the vocabulary {S, a, b} that consist of n ($n \geq 1$) occurrences of a or b in arbitrary order, followed by exactly the same string of a's and b's but in reverse order:

System MIRROR:
(a) Initial symbol: S
(b) Vocabulary: {S, a, b}
(c) Rules: (1) S → a (+ S) + a
                       (2) S → b (+ S) + b

System MIRROR generates, *inter alia,* the following structured strings (Figure 6.5):

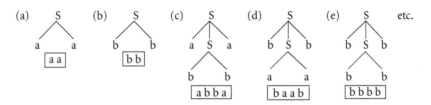

FIGURE 6.5 Some structured strings generated by System MIRROR

Type-1 or *context-sensitive (CS)* grammars are again less restricted in that they allow for context-conditions on the input symbols to rewrite rules. A CS rewrite rule causes (or allows) a symbol a to be rewritten the way a is rewritten by a CF rewrite rule, with the difference that the rewriting is conditional on a being preceded and/or followed by any number of specific symbols taken from the vocabulary given.[13]

CS grammars have a doubtful status, as they are, strictly speaking, already of type o. Consider the toy system MIRROR', which is like MIRROR but has the extra requirement that b immediately followed by a becomes c. The rule system will then look as follows (the notation '/ – a' is normally used for 'when followed by a' and '/ a –' for 'when preceded by a':

System MIRROR':
(a)   Initial symbol: S
(b)   Vocabulary: {S, a, b, c}
(c)   Rules: (1)   S → a (+ S) + a
                         (2)   S → b (+ S) + b
                         (3)   b → c / – a

System MIRROR' generates, *inter alia*, the following structured strings (Figure 6.6):

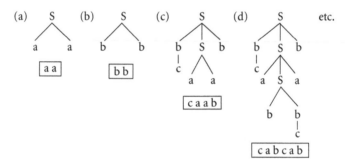

FIGURE 6.6 Some structured strings generated by System MIRROR'

One notes that the context condition on Rule 3 is formulated in linear terms and disregards structure-dependency. This is, of course, formally feasible, but it stretches the limits of a primitive system rewriting one symbol at the time.

These limits are stretched beyond tolerance by the toy language AABBCC. Bach (1964: 31) sets the following problem for his student readers:

Write a grammar for the language in which every string is of the form *abc, aabbcc, aaabbbccc*, i.e. *n a*'s plus *n b*'s plus *n c*'s. Hint: use a rule of the form xy → yx.

---

[13] Bloomfield's (1933) theory of *immediate constituent analysis*, which formed the basis of American structuralist linguistics (Seuren 1998: 190–227), amounts, in principle, to a type-1 grammar consisting of context-sensitive rewrite rules.

The decision procedure is quite simple; it has just been given: just count the number of a's, then check if there is an equal number of b's and c's, in that order. But to formulate a generative algorithm within the bounds of a primitive algorithm of type 1 or type 2 is far from simple. When one follows Bach's suggestion, one gets:

System AABBCC[1]:
(a) Initial symbol: S
(b) Vocabulary: {S, a, b, c}
(c) Rules: (1) S → a + b + c (+ S)
                      (2) c + a → a + c
                      (3) b + a → a + b
                      (4) c + b → b + c

Here, however, the rules (2), (3) and (4) have an input consisting of two serially ordered symbols, which violates the conditions on grammars of type 3, 2 and 1. This grammar no longer allows for simple tree expansions of the type shown in the earlier systems. When the system has generated the tree structure (b1) in Figure 6.7, it cannot go on, unless provisions are made to rewrite two symbols at the same time, which is disallowed for primitive algorithms. Structure (b1), moreover, does not represent a terminal string even though the lowest nodes are all terminal symbols. The terminal string comes about only when all rules have been applied, which is the case in structure (b4). But one should note that the derivation of (b4) as shown in Figure 6.7 is inadmissible in terms of primitive algorithms.

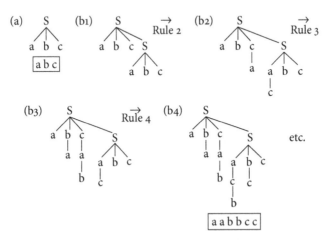

FIGURE 6.7 Some trees generated by System AABBCC[1]

One is, of course, tempted to say that the language generated by *System* AABBCC^1 is much more easily generated by a System AABBCC^2, of the following form ($n \geq 1$):

System AABBCC^2:
(a) Initial symbol: S
(b) Vocabulary: {S, a, b, c, n}
(c) Rule: S → a^n + b^n + c^n

But this is, though formally possible, inadmissible in grammars of type 3, 2 or 1, since these grammars (being simple printing machines) allow only for the writing of *constant* symbols; *variables* are not allowed as they require an additional apparatus for the replacement of variables by constant symbols. System AABBCC^2 thus only generates the one and only tree structure shown in Figure 6.8:

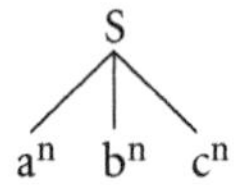

FIGURE 6.8 The only tree structure generated by System AABBCC^2

All we can do, therefore, if we want to avoid the use of variables, is make the system transformational, as in System AABBCC^3 ('T-rule' stands for 'transformation rule'):[14]

System AABBCC^3:
(a) Initial symbol: S
(b) Vocabulary: {S, a, b, c}
(c) CF-rule: (1) S → a + b + c (+ S)
     T-rules: (1) c – a ⇒   a – c
                       (2) b – a ⇒   a – b
                       (3) c – b ⇒   b – c

Here, the concatenation sign '–' differs from '+' in that the latter concatenates symbols in the same (sub)constituent, whereas the former concatenates symbols merely according to left-to-right order, regardless of constituent structure. Moreover,

---

[14] Interestingly, natural languages have many words that function semantically as variables. Looking up *Post Office* in the telephone directory, I may find *See local Post Office*. If I am stupid, I look up *Local Post Office*, interpreting the word *local* as a constant, and will find nothing, but if I use my brains, I first check the value of the variable *local*, say Petersfield, and then look up *Petersfield Post Office*, in which case I will be rewarded. It is not hard to find many words that can function this way as variables in natural languages— though I am not aware of any semantic theory, formal or informal, that deals with such variable use of lexical words. Obviously, however, this kind of semantic variable function has nothing to do with algorithmic production systems, but the example shows that a machinery dealing with variables needs more 'intelligence' than one dealing only with constant symbols.

the new double arrow '$\Rightarrow$' is not an instruction to rewrite a single symbol but an instruction to rewrite a given class of structures. The string *aabbcc* is now generated as in Figure 6.9. (The reader is invited to generate further strings according to System AABBCC[3].)

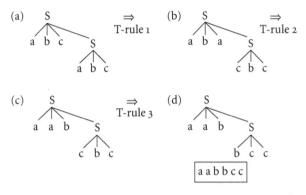

FIGURE **6.9** The string *aabbcc* generated by System AABBCC[3]

There is thus a wide gap between the earlier systems and System AABBCC[3], which is classified as belonging to type 0 of transformational grammars. Since CS grammars fudge the issue a little by allowing for context-sensitive rewritings, many researchers have preferred to leave out type-1 systems from the hierarchy.

6.4 The rise and fall, and then the rise again, of transformational grammar

During the 1950s, Chomsky's teacher Zellig Harris and Chomsky himself concluded, on the strength of various arguments, that natural languages are not generated by CS and even less by CF grammars and require a type-0 transformational grammar. One important argument, raised by Zellig Harris and often quoted during the early years of transformational grammar, was that there are regular correspondences between sentence types, such as active transitive sentences and their passive counterparts, or between assertions and questions, etc. This makes it uneconomical to generate such corresponding pairs as if they were not related. It is preferable to make use of such empirical generalizations by letting a primitive base grammar generate the simplest sentence types and adding a transformational component turning certain output sentence types of the base grammar into derived sentence types: actives would thus be transformed into passives, assertions into questions, etc.

In later years, the transformational turn was confirmed, corrected and enriched by successful analyses in terms of transformational rules such as LOWER-SUBJECT DELE-TION (*John wants [John go] $\Rightarrow$ John wants to go*), or LOWER-SUBJECT RAISING (*John wants [I go] $\Rightarrow$ John wants me to go*) (see, for example, Ross 1967, Postal 1974, but there was a plethora of publications at the time), or, for French, German, Dutch and many other languages, LOWER-PREDICATE RAISING (French: *Je ferai* [*Robert voir la lettre*] (I will make Robert see the letter) ⇒ *Je* [*ferai voir*] *la lettre à Robert*) (Seuren 1996).

Yet despite the obvious successes of transformational grammar, Chomsky has constantly tried, since the late 1960s, to weaken the role of the transformational component and to strengthen the primitive base grammar. By pointed contrast, Generative Semantics (Semantic Syntax) considers the base grammar, which generates well-formed structures in the language of predicate calculus, marginal to grammar as such, taking the non-primitive transformational system to constitute the grammar of a language.

Chomsky's tendency to revert to primitive algorithms as models for natural language grammars was supported by a few rather technical, yet highly influential papers by Stanley Peters and Robert Ritchie published in the early 1970s (Peters and Ritchie 1971; Peters 1973). In these papers, the authors showed that the generative grammar models current during the late 1960s were so licentious as regards the restrictions they imposed on type-0 grammars in general that further and more systematically formulated restrictions were necessary if they were to escape the charge of being too powerful and unrestricted for a sensible theory of human language. Existing grammatical analyses would allow for totally unrestricted languages subject only to the general condition of being recursively enumerable, whereas it is obvious that human languages are not unrestricted but are subject to certain universal constraints. One will, for example, never find a language whose grammar contains a rule saying that a certain symbol σ must be inserted after every, say, seven symbols other than σ and only then. Yet linguistic theory as it was around 1970 contained no formal provision that would ban such a rule. The articles by Peters and Ritchie provoked a run on presumed non-mathematical and possibly arbitrary language universals, whereby it was hoped that a robust theory of language universals would save type-0 grammars by restricting them in a way that would narrow the theory down to a definition of precisely the set of natural human languages.

Chomsky's attitude in this respect was extreme, in that he wanted to reduce the transformational element to a minimum of only one transformational operation ('move α' in some versions of his ever changing theory). This meant a minimization of the transformational component and a maximization of the stricter primitive algorithms. This gradual process of shifting the weight of explanation back to primitive algorithms, especially CF or CS rewrite systems, went hand-in-hand with Chomsky's insistence on the view that natural grammars are autonomous and not dependent on semantic input. Such a reversal would have been impossible had he adhered to the theory of Semantic Syntax or any variety thereof taking grammars to be algorithms mediating between SAs and SSs, since any such theory, if formal, involves by definition non-primitive algorithms. Meanwhile, the empirical adequacy of the theory was, to a large extent, sacrificed on the ideological altar of Autonomous Syntax.[15]

In Semantic Syntax, a different strategy is followed. Here, maximally unified generalizations and corresponding transformational analyses were sought within the bounds of 'transformational space', in the hope of arriving at grammatical descriptions that are seen as crucially correct given a continued absence of counter-examples and a great similarity across languages. Any possible tentative language universals can then be drawn inductively or by hypothesis from the available successful descriptions.

6.5 Autonomous Syntax and the evolution of language

It thus appears that experimental work in the area of language evolution, investigating the parsing capabilities of apes, monkeys, birds or other animals with regard to meaningless strings of symbols in toy *abc*-languages generated by extremely simple finite state or CF-rewrite grammars, as mentioned or reported in, notably, Hauser et al. (2002), Fitch and Hauser (2004), or Fitch (2010), must be judged misguided and indeed irrelevant. Apart from the fact that this work is based on the false premiss that unlimited recursion is the central feature distinguishing human language from non-human communication systems (see section 6.3.2.1 above), such experiments, at best, test the presence of a *decision* algorithm, whereas what counts is a, perhaps undecidable, *productive* algorithm. And if the processing performed by the monkeys in question were in any sense 'semantic' in nature, the results would still not be relevant, since, as is argued in section 6.2 above, grammars define *production competence*, not interpretation capabilities at the receiving end. Even if it were shown, as is claimed, that monkeys or other animals really do react to deviations from the *abab* pattern, the conclusion that these animals have internalized an FS grammar such as *System* ABAB discussed above is unwarranted, since the monkeys may simply react to an uncomplicated repetitive diagrammatic pattern that may be *formally defined* in terms of an FS grammar but has nothing to do with their cognitive machinery to recognize such a pattern. No matter what level of proficiency the animals concerned, or indeed

---

[15] Outside the school of Chomskyan 'generativists', other attempts have been made at developing non-primitive but well-restricted algorithmical grammars. The most notable such attempt is the theory of *Tree Adjoining Grammar* (TAG), developed in the school of Aravind Joshi (see, for example, Joshi and Schabes 1997; Levelt 2008 postscript: 1–5). Here, primitive algorithms generate subtrees that can be joined together (merged or unified) by a non-primitive algorithm to form sentences. TAG-theory, in various guises, has been elaborated to a high degree of mathematical and computational precision and has, for that reason, acquired a prominent position in computational linguistics (the world of theoretical linguistics has, unjustly, paid relatively little attention to it). TAG clearly instantiates a type-0 grammar that heavily constrains the unlimited freedom of a Turing machine. To what extent it can be regarded as relevant for (psycho)linguistics, in particular for the process of mapping propositional structures (SAs) onto surface structures and vice versa, remains to be seen.

humans, may achieve in this respect, the test results, if reliable,[16] tell us nothing about any *linguistic* or *syntactic* capabilities. After all, the poor animals have never been seen to *produce* the strings in question. All these tests tell us is to do with the animals' prowess in detecting deviations from extremely simple patterns in symbol strings—a capacity that, if real, may well be due to other factors than an internalized type-3 FS 'grammar'. In any case, what these experiments were about is not sensibly represented in terms of FS or CF grammars, whose capacity far exceeds the simple material these researchers worked with.

The research referred to above still clings to Autonomous Syntax, as it tests monkeys on tasks defined in terms of type-3 and type-2 algorithmic production grammars. An obvious object of critique, in this respect, is Fitch (2010), an insightful and generally well-balanced study, which, however, begins to limp when it touches on the theory of grammar and stumbles when it speaks about meaning. Fitch, who is not a linguist, defends Autonomous Syntax as follows (Fitch 2010: 106–7):

Formalist theories attempt to treat linguistic syntax like the rules of mathematics or computer programming: as symbols with little intrinsic meaning, following explicit rules of combination and permutation. From the formal perspective, a syntactician's goal is to come up with an explicit, mechanical algorithm that can generate all of the 'well-formed' or 'grammatical' sentences of a language and no others (or, given an input, to determine whether or not the sentence is part of this set). […]

The formal approach to syntax attempts, as far as possible, to leave meaning out of the picture. One good reason is practical: the state of the art in dealing with formal syntax at an explicit, mathematical level is well-developed while our capacity to deal explicitly with questions of meaning remains rudimentary (illustrated by the lack of computer programs that can deal even vaguely intelligently with meaning). But there are other compelling reasons as well. The most prominent is that we are able to make syntactic judgments about grammaticality even when we can't understand the meaning. It is easy to see that a nonsense sentence like *The snar truffed several snarps into the twale* is syntactically well-formed in English, even if we can form no clear semantic picture of its meaning. Chomsky's famous sentence *Colorless green ideas sleep furiously* provides a classic example: even though each of these words is familiar, and the sentence is fully correct syntactically, it defies ordinary semantic interpretation in some obvious ways. The sentence is *syntactically* well-formed but semantically ill-formed. For these reasons, and despite the obvious fact that any complete model of language will have eventually to grapple with meaning and all its complexities, the formalist gambit regarding syntax [i.e. Autonomous Syntax; PAMS] has appealed to several generations of theoretical linguists.

---

[16] The reliability of the experiments concerned has been called into serious doubt now that Marc Hauser, a main player in the evolutionary study of animal psychology, has been found guilty of scientific misconduct consisting in repeated tampering with test data, specifically those that relate to experiments on pattern recognition with cotton-top tamarin monkeys. The alleged ability of these monkeys to detect deviations from the *abab* pattern (Fitch and Hauser 2004) is therefore at best uncertain but more probably a fable. Even so, however, it remains worth our while to discuss the question of the *relevance* of these experiments.

This passage is in many ways revealing. It shows, first, that Fitch's preference for Autonomous Syntax is partly based on mere convenience: a great deal is known about syntax but very little about meaning, or so he says; therefore, let us, for now at least, forget about meaning. He refers to formal model-theoretic semantics (Fitch 2010: 120) but doesn't really buy it (and rightly so; see Chapter 9), mainly because it leaves cognition out of account and is not open to a realist interpretation. A hesitant account is given of 'propositional' and 'mentalist' semantics (Fitch 2010: 120–5), but there is no organic link with syntax.

Then, as regards quasi-sentences like *The snar truffed several snarps into the twale*, all such sentences show is that they contain some unknown nouns or verbs—a common situation in language learning. But they don't show why Autonomous Syntax should be preferred, since Semantic Syntax has no problem with them either: lexical meanings can, to some extent, be replaced with variables without the propositional structure being affected. Chomsky's *Colorless green ideas sleep furiously* is even less telling: all it requires for full interpretation is a suitable context. That this sentence is *syntactically* well-formed is beyond doubt, but what does it mean to say that it is *semantically* ill-formed? What are the criteria for *semantic wellformedness*? Despite the voluminous (mainly philosophical) literature on this subject, no clear criteria have so far emerged. Finally, Fitch falls for the classic fallacy of *argument from authority*: so many linguists believe in Autonomous Syntax that it must be right! One is thus, unfortunately, left with the impression that there are precious few real arguments in favour of Autonomous Syntax.

The following pages bring no succour. Speaking about the Chomsky hierarchy, Fitch says (2010: 108–9):

This hierarchy also provided a foundation for some early psycholinguistics work [...]. However, after some initial contributions [...], Chomsky and many other theoretical linguists lost interest in this approach when it became apparent that the remaining open questions addressable within this formal framework had little relevance to the details of natural language and its implementation in human brains [...]. The core difficulty is related to the structure-dependence of syntax discussed above: traditional formal language theory concerns sets of strings but *not* their structures. Today, a student of computer science is far more likely than a linguist to be well versed in formal language theory. Nonetheless, this approach remains of considerable interest in formulating computational questions about how the human brain implements language, and for comparing human capabilities with those of other species. [...] The utility of the Chomsky hierarchy is that it provides a formally defined, widely accepted, and well-understood classification for computational systems less powerful than Turing machines (including, presumably, actual brains).

Here again eyebrows are raised. Having first said that Chomsky lost interest in his hierarchy 'when it became apparent that [it] had little relevance to the details of natural language and its implementation in human brains' (implying that Chomsky was right in doing so), Fitch continues to say that '*nonetheless*, this approach remains of considerable interest', giving as the only motivation for his 'nonetheless' that the Chomsky hierarchy 'provides a starting point for a more detailed exploration of the capabilities and limitations of rule-governed systems—including brains—that can generate and recognize discrete strings' (Fitch 2010: 109).

There are at least two hidden assumptions. One is that the evolution of animal to human brains follows the mathematically defined Chomsky hierarchy step by step, from type 3 to type 0. Given the importance of exaptation in evolution, this is highly unlikely. Specialization is the hallmark of nature and is, in most cases, not definable in terms of mathematical hierarchies. The other hidden assumption is that any signalling system or any form of potential language in subhuman species is of the Autonomous Syntax and not of the Semantic Syntax type, so that the vervet monkeys' alarm calls would arise from the activation of an algorithmic start button and not from the urge to warn conspecifics of imminent danger. This is not impossible, especially in cases where such animal signals are finite in number and, apparently, triggered by a limited class of specific situation types. But then it is highly questionable if such signalling systems (apart from the organs involved in their use) are indeed sensibly considered to be precursors of human languages, each of which allows for the generation, through a finite machinery, of a mathematically speaking infinite number of strings endowed with speech-act and propositional meanings. If, as I claim is the case, natural language grammars mediate between SAs and SSs, the capability to 'generate and recognize discrete strings' is nothing to do with the capability to produce and interpret linguistic utterances. All that matters then is the capability to map SAs onto SSs and to reduce (often not well-formed) SSs to their proper corresponding SAs.

Even in the unlikely event that Chomskyan Autonomous Syntax is formally viable as a technique for the formal characterization of well-formed surface structures, the conclusion that the Chomsky hierarchy is irrelevant to the study of language evolution will still stand. For Autonomous Syntax is incompatible with a *realist* interpretation of the theory and compatible only with an *instrumentalist* interpretation. But what the evolutionary studies of human language are after is precisely a realist, and not at all an instrumentalist, theory.

Chomsky has always hedged on the issue of realism (see Seuren 2004a: 61–71), but in Hauser et al. (2002) he suddenly goes for realism in a big way while still holding on to his Autonomous Syntax, thereby entering the realm of 'absurdity' in the sense described above. A realist interpretation of Chomskyan Autonomous Syntax implies that one begins constructing one's utterances by mentally pushing a start button regardless of *what* one intends to say. This makes syntax a *random sentence generator* (Seuren 2004a: 16, 24–8), which is absurd in any realist perspective. Autonomous Syntax is thus disqualified as a realist model for the grammars internalized by speakers. Given that the experimental work referred to above is predicated on a strong realist interpetation, it has no choice but to keep all theorizing in terms of primitive algorithms, and thus of Autonomous Syntax, at arm's length.

A strictly formal or mathematical characterization of output structures need not say anything about the actual mechanisms in nature that produce the output in question. The *Fibonacci sequence* of natural numbers, for example, is mathematically defined in terms of a simple recursive algorithm ('start with the sequence 0,1; any following number in the sequence is the sum of the two preceding ones'), but this does not mean that nature, when it produces arrangements that display regularities corresponding to the Fibonacci sequence (as, for example, the arrangement of seeds in a sunflower, or of petals in a flower), has 'internalized' that mathematical function. All we can say with regard to biological instantiations of the Fibonacci sequence is that the mathematical function is *epiphenomenal* on an underlying mechanism, whose nature may as yet be unclear.

One may go further and think of procedurally more plausible algorithms that stand a better chance of approximating physical reality. Fibonacci, in his *Liber Abaci* of 1202, tells the tale of rabbit pairs, each pair producing a new pair every month starting from the second month after birth. This tale models the sequence in that, if one starts with one rabbit pair, the total number of elements (rabbit pairs) in the model is always the corresponding Fibonacci number, as is shown in Figure 6.10-a (where the circles represent successive months). A different model, producing the Fibonacci numbers as the total number of elements in each successive cycle starting from one element in the innermost cycle (the cycles representing successive states of growth), is shown in Figure 6.10-b, where each element reproduces itself twice: once on the subsequent cycle and once on the cycle after that (Seuren 2004a: 66; 2009a: 10–12). Which of these two models corresponds better, if at all, with the physical reality they model is a question biologists will have to decide on.

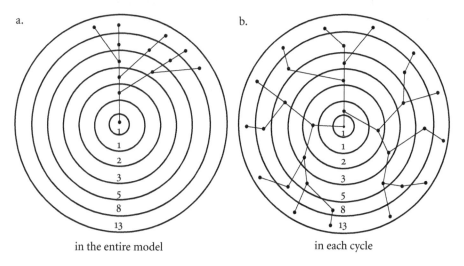

a.   b.

in the entire model   in each cycle

FIGURE 6.10 The Fibonacci sequence produced by two potentially realist algorithms

This just shows that there is much more to the question of 'internalization' of algorithmical production systems than meets the eye. The same output is often generated by different algorithms (see also note 8 above), which may stand different chances of reflecting the actually underlying physical reality. Even if the results of output experiments such as have been reported on by Hauser, Fitch and others on monkeys, birds or other animals were reliable, they would tell us little or nothing about the internal systems producing the output.

6.6 Conclusion

The overall conclusion is that if natural languages belong to the mathematically defined category of type-0 languages, that is, transformational languages, produced by mathematically unrestricted rewrite systems, then the Chomsky hierarchy is irrelevant to the study of language. It was relevant as long as it was thought that all that grammars have to do is generate surface constituent structures from an initial start symbol. But this notion of autonomous grammar is untenable, in fact absurd, from a realist point of view and unnecessary and undesirable, in fact perverse, from an instrumentalist standpoint. When it is accepted that there is no other way to define a grammar than as a transformational or mediational system mapping intents—that is, propositional structures under speech act operators—onto surface structures, type-3, type-2 and type-1 'grammars' vanish from the linguistic horizon. The interest is then no longer focused on the mathematical properties of grammars but on any non-mathematical, empirically definable properties which, when taken together, uniquely characterize the class of grammars of natural languages. The idea that the natural evolution of language should have followed the Chomsky hierarchy in that the most primitive form of language would have been of type 3, followed by type 2, then by type 1 and finally by type 0, is totally unfounded and, in fact, hilarious.

7

Reflexivity and identity in language and cognition

7.1 The overall programme*

The present chapter is, like the others, part of my wall-to-wall programme in semantics and grammar, aimed at an adequate fit between the ecological data of natural language on the one hand and a unified theory of language on the other. Part of this programme is the replacement of the Gricean maxims by a more precise treatment of the data. While the possible world semantics (PWS) paradigm is rejected in its entirety because of its overformalization, its conceptual untenability and its ignoring of well-known, basic empirical obstacles (see Chapter 9), the Gricean paradigm is rejected on account of its underformalization, its conceptual unclarity and, again, its inadequate empirical coverage. A central element in this programme, which was started by the present author in the 1960s, has been the development of an empirical theory of the natural logic that is part of the human innate endowment. This logic takes away all explanatory power from the Gricean maxims.

In this chapter I launch an explicit attack at the Gricean maxims. The weapon used is the notion of semantic reflexivity. First, the True Binarity Principle (TBP) is argued for: in language, binary predicates are always truly binary, in that they require distinct mental entity representations (addresses). When a binary relation is taken to hold between an entity and itself, lexicon and grammar require reflexivization of the predicate. A fully reflexivized predicate is a different predicate from its non-reflexive counterpart. Halfway reflexivization retains binarity in a weakened form. TBP solves a number of paradoxes, for example, the paradox that the sentence *All girls envy the girl Trisha* does not entail that Trisha envies herself, even though she is herself a girl. Next it is argued that the so-called identity predicate *be*, as in *The morning star is the evening star*, or *Zeus is Jupiter*, is not a counterexample to TBP, since it does not

* This chapter is to a large extent based on Seuren (1989), which I felt needed a wider audience as well as an updating. I am grateful to Daniel Casasanto of the Max Planck Institute for Psycholinguistics at Nijmegen for help and inspiration, to Vasilikí Folia and Salomi Asaridou for help with the Greek and to Beyza Sümer for help with the Turkish example sentences.

express a binary relation but is an instruction to the effect that, in order to obtain truth, two so far distinct mental addresses are to be merged into one. Finally, it is argued that cognitive models in general are not just information stores as found in data bases but are structured as possible situations and that situational knowledge directs access to, and use of, information retrieved from available world knowledge. Cognitive models are thus driven by a general design feature that makes them respect situational features, including the denotational non-identity of the terms of a binary relation. This direction of research looks more promising when one wishes to explain the facts of natural language than the paradigm of the Gricean maxims.

One central feature of my approach is that it steers a middle course between formalization and non-formalization: formalize as much as possible, but admit that we have to stop and fall back on more traditional forms of science when formaliza- tion becomes artificial and starts losing touch with reality—which is generally the case when we deal with cognition as a whole, because cognition is still too vast, too complex and too mysterious to be caught entirely in terms of formal analyses. Grammar is an exception in that it has proved to be fully formalizable, at least topdown—that is, as a transformation system from *semantic analyses* (SAs) to *surface structures* (SSs) (Seuren 1996). Topdown grammar is a *module* in the sense that it is an autonomous, fully algorithmic processing unit in cognition, which takes a token input and delivers a token output, while classifying the token input in terms of types and unclassifying the type output again as tokens. (This is what *processing* means: token in, token out, but in between a treatment in terms of types which are subject to rules.) Bottom-up grammar, or *parsing*, is obviously not fully algorithmic but needs frequent appeals to both general encyclopaedic and contextual knowledge for it to arrive at the SA intended. It is argued in the present chapter that such appeals to cognition are guided by available general knowledge about types of situation. Both the type-level comprehension of sentences and the token-level interpretation of utterances are strongly dependent on what we know about situations generally.

A second central aspect of my work is my dissatisfaction with the Gricean maxims, which were introduced primarily to bridge the gap between established logic and natural logical intuitions. It seems to me that natural logical intuitions are just one kind of semantic intuition and are thus to be accounted for by a *semantic* theory, not by a pragmatic surrogate. Semantics, however, is in a sorry state, owing to the overall destructive effects of twentieth-century positivism, with behaviourism as one par- ticularly damaging manifestation. The most obvious, and most embarrassing, fact about semantics is that no serious, generally accepted notion or definition of meaning exists.[1] Nor are any viable formalization techniques available as yet to analyse and

---

[1] For me, *linguistic meaning is primarily the system-driven property of a sentence S as a linguistic type- level unit, in virtue of which a linguistically competent hearer is able to reconstruct speaker's intent (that is, a speech act operator over a proposition) from any utterance token of S, given proper values for contextual and*

describe lexical meanings. With one great exception: the meanings of those lexical items that represent logical operators are formalizable, at least in great part, with the means available today. If they were not, they would not form a logical system. The logic concerned is the *natural logic* of language and cognition, not the 'official' or 'standard' logic or logics developed by mathematicians. Most of my work over the past ten years has been dedicated to the development of a theory of natural logic in this sense (see Seuren 2010). It has been found that the assumption of a proper natural logic makes the Gricean maxims otiose.

A third central aspect in my work is my dissatisfaction with the framework of possible world semantics (PWS), which, in my view (see Chapter 9) must be denied a place in the study of language, not only because it runs in the face of well-known empirical obstacles, notably the unsolved problem of *propositional attitudes* (Dowty et al. 1981: 175), but also because it is constitutionally unable to establish a link with the study of cognition—despite vacuous claims to the contrary. It may perhaps be considered to be a branch of mathematics, but it fails to satisfy the conditions for good empirical science: an adequate coverage of the facts, valid generalizations and proper predictivity or retrodictivity. Its ontological assumptions are, furthermore, incoherent and its methodology nebulous.

Finally, I have, over the past forty years, developed a theory of *presupposition* within the wider framework of *discourse semantics*. This theory claims that every new utterance in a coherent discourse requires *incrementation* of its interpretative content to a cognitively real discourse domain (DD). Since logic can be defined as the theory of coherence through texts, presupposition theory is part of the study of the natural logic of language. Moreover, since presuppositions are responsible for the fact that sentences, as type-level units, are, in principle, tailored to be anchored to certain DDs while being unfit for others, presupposition theory is considered part of a *cognitive* theory of semantics.

The semantic theory I envisage is thus much more cognitively oriented and covers a much wider range of topics than PWS. It deals *inter alia* with speech acts, with presuppositions, with topic-comment (or 'information') structure (which has been shown to be of a strictly semantic, and not a pragmatic nature; see Seuren 2010, Ch. 11), with the way thoughts crystallize into SAs, which are, when the decision is taken to express them linguistically, automatically transduced by the topdown grammar into surface structures and, ultimately, into sound or writing. But here I will, for your entertainment and instruction, focus on one specific topic, the notion of *semantic reflexivity*, which shows perhaps better than anything else the inadequacy of the Gricean approach and the power and promise contained in my approach,

---

situational parameters. (see also section 9.2.1). This definition may still be in need of further refinement, but it has served me well over the years. See also Seuren (2009a: 280–92).

which combines a logico-semantic, a grammatical, a discourse-semantic and a cognitive orientation into one large integrated whole.

7.2 Semantic reflexivity

The grammars of many languages have a special category of reflexivity, in that special, mostly obligatory, markings are provided for cases where, roughly speaking, the referent of one (mostly the subject) term is identical to the referent of another term under the same predicate. Thus, given the binary predicate *love*, expressing a relation that usually holds between two *different* entities, if one wants to say in English that this relation holds between, say, *John* and himself, one has to say *John loves himself*, and not *John loves John*.

There is a sizeable and highly informative literature on how different languages express, or fail to express, different forms of reflexivity, but this is not what I want to go into now. The point I want to make here is of a more abstract and general nature, namely that all natural languages appear to share the condition that an *n*-ary predicate must be *truly n*-ary in that the terms of an *n*-ary predicate must not be codenotational. When they are, semantic reflexivization occurs, often marked by overt grammatical means. The term *codenotational* is to be understood in a cognitive sense: what is at issue is not *referential* identity but identity of *cognitive entity representations*, or else reflexivization would not work in counterfactuals such as (7.3a,b) below, to mention just one argument.

Semantic reflexivization of an *n*-ary predicate P implies that a different, though related, predicate P^{refl}, with n-1 terms, has come about. The term that is lost is always an oblique (that is, non-subject) term, usually the direct object, owing to the fact that subjects are primary in the argument hierarchy (see, for example, Keenan and Comrie 1977). For a binary predicate like *love* this means that, when its two terms are codenotational, a new, unary, predicate arises that can be rendered as something like 'self-love'. This is what I have called (Seuren 1989) the *True Binary Principle* (recently also known as the *Presumption of Disjoint Reference*):

True Binarity Principle (TBP):
For all binary predicates P, aPb is uninterpretable when a and b are codenotational. In that case, a new unary predicate P^{refl} is created, meaning 'self-P'.

I speak of *semantic* reflexivity because the transition from P to P^{refl} takes place in the semantics of the language in question or, to be precise, even before the semantics, in cognition, as is shown below. It is semantic reflexivity that determines semantic intuitions of the kind discussed below. The linguistic expression of TBP in the surface sentences of any language, appears to be slow, at least that is what one gathers from the data. It looks as if languages first develop sets of 'strong' reflexive pronouns for the oblique cases, such as German *sich selbst*, Dutch *zichzelf*, French *soi-même*, Italian *se stesso*, Greek *eaftó*, Turkish *kendi* and, of course, the so-called *body-reflexives* known from many, especially Creole, languages.[2] Predicates with these strong reflexives still retain grammatical vestiges of binarity, as is shown below, but they are subject to certain, largely unexplored, grammatical restrictions with regard to ordinary binary predicates. For example, they do not allow for passivization.

A second stage then consists in fully grammaticalized reflexivization, expressed by reflexive verb morphology, as in Turkish, Greek, Latin and many other languages, or by 'weak' reflexive pronouns, such as German *sich*, Dutch *zich*, Latin *se*, French *se*, etc. From a grammatical point of view, English appears to have stopped at the 'halfway' stage, expressing semantic reflexivity only through its strong reflexives *himself* etc., not having developed any weak reflexive pronouns. The picture is far from clear at the moment and much further research is required to clear up the uncertainties. But as far as can be seen at present, it would seem that both 'halfway' and fully grammaticalized reflexivization express semantic reflexivization, perhaps with some difference regarding emphasis.

TBP should be seen as a constraint on the semantics and logic of natural language predicates. For logic as practised by professional logicians it makes no difference whether two terms under a given predicate are codenotational, but for cognition and for the semantics of natural language it does, as I will now attempt to show.

7.3 Why do we need the True Binarity Principle?

Why do we need a principle like TBP for language and presumably also for cognition? The reason is that it solves a number of seemingly unrelated so-called 'paradoxes' (*paradox* in the sense of a strident clash between, on the one hand, a 'standard' logical analysis and natural language on the other).

Let me give a few examples. Consider first the general fact that natural language predicates that are both transitive and symmetrical are not reflexive.[3] What I mean is this. A *transitive predicate* P_{tr}, like *be older than*, is one that induces the entailment that if $aP_{tr}b$ is true and $bP_{tr}c$ is also true, then necessarily—that is, in virtue of the meaning of P_{tr}—$aP_{tr}c$ is true. Thus, if John is older than Harry and Harry is older than Roy, then necessarily, as a semantic entailment, John is older than Roy. We also have *symmetrical predicates*, such as *hold hands with*. A predicate P_{sym} is symmetrical just in case if $aP_{sym}b$ is true, then, necessarily, $bP_{sym}a$ is also true. Thus, if John is

---

[2] As is well-known, some languages, and especially Creole languages, have so-called *body reflexives*. Mauritian Creole, for example, says *Li pe lav so lecor* (literally 'he washes his body') for 'he is washing himself'. The Surinamese Creole Sranan says *A e wasi en skin* (literally 'he washes his skin'). As long as such body reflexives have not been fully grammaticalized for all predicates and are still to some extent semantically transparent, one best assumes that they do not (yet) grammatically represent full reflexivity and are still in a 'halfway' stage.

[3] The term *transitive* in the sense intended has nothing to do with what grammarians call a *transitive verb*, namely a verb with a subject and a direct object, but with transitivity as a property of relations in the logic of relations.

holding hands with Harry, then, necessarily, Harry is holding hands with John.[4] Finally, a predicate P_{refl} is *reflexive* just in case if $aP_{refl}b$ is true, then, necessarily, both $aP_{refl}a$ and $bP_{refl}b$ are true. Given these definitions, it follows that if a predicate P is both symmetrical and transitive, P must be reflexive. This is easily shown. Let P be both symmetrical and transitive. Suppose aPb is true. Then, since P is symmetrical, bPa is also true. Since P is transitive, it now follows that both aPa and bPb are true.

Here, however, natural language does not follow the logic of relations. Consider predicates like *be a colleague of* or *be a sibling of*. These are both symmetrical and transitive, as is easily checked. Yet they are not reflexive, because I can never be a colleague, or a sibling, of myself. And if I am one of seven children in a family and am asked how many siblings I have, then the correct answer is six, not seven, because I do not have myself as a sibling. Worse, if language followed logic in this respect, I would be a sibling but not a brother (and even less a sister) of myself, even though a sibling is semantically defined as 'either brother or sister of'.

Does this mean that language is unlogical? Not at all, and if it did mean that, there would still be the question of why language has chosen to be 'unlogical' in precisely this way. The answer is, it seems to me, that language is perfectly logical but it has a constraint in the form of TBP, which immediately explains these apparently aberrant data. In fact, TBP ensures that no binary reflexive predicates will occur in language at all: any would-be expression aPa will automatically be reflexivized into aP^{refl}.

Then, there are cases involving reflexive pronouns:

(7.1)   a. Larry kicked himself but Jake didn't. (McCawley 1982: 137)
      b. Fred broke his legs, and so did Leo.

In (7.1a), *Jake didn't* can only mean 'Jake didn't kick himself'. And in (7.1b), if *his* is used reflexively, i.e. as 'his own', then *so did Leo* can only mean 'Leo broke his (own) legs'. The same phenomenon is observed in cases like:

(7.2)   a. If you are not ashamed of yourself, I will be.
      b. It is hard for Gary to understand himself, as it is for everybody.

The first of these can be understood as saying that I will be ashamed of *myself* if you are not ashamed of *yourself*. The deletion of 'ashamed of myself' in the consequent clause can be accounted for only if, at some level of analysis, 'be ashamed of yourself' (with the subject *you*) and 'be ashamed of myself' (with the subject *I*) are identical. They are if we analyse both as a reflexivized 'be self-ashamed'. And (7.2b) can only be read as implying that *understanding oneself* is hard for everyone, not that *understanding Gary* is hard for everyone.

---

[4] Note that *hold hands with* and similar symmetrical predicates, such as *conspire with*, are not transitive, because if Harry is holding hands (or conspiring) with John and John is holding hands (or conspiring) with Roy, then it is not necessarily so that Harry is holding hands (or conspiring) with Roy.

The difference between referring pronouns and reflexives is clearly illustrated in the following sentences:

(7.3)   a. If I were you, I would fall in love with myself.
       b. If I were you, I would fall in love with me.
       c. It would be nice to meet myself some time, to see if I would like me.

Clearly, (7.3a) is an exhortation to indulge in narcissism, whereas (7.3b) is one way, out of a multitude of ways, of making a pass at someone. Similarly for (7.3c), which evokes a virtual situation where the speaker has been split up into two different persons. In (7.3b–c), the non-reflexive pronoun *me* is referential, and significantly not reflexive, even though the words *I* and *me* are necessarily coreferential. The point is, to be sure, that in these sentences the antecedent and the referring pronoun are no longer *codenotational*: after they have been disidentified in a cognitive construction, there are two cognitively distinct elements ('addresses') precluding reflexivity. (Although it is easy to see the point of this analysis in an intuitive way, the technical elaboration of the mechanism involved is far from trivial. But it cannot be my purpose here to go into such technical details.)

Geach (1962: 132) has the famous example (taken from the fourteenth-century philosophical literature on *Exponibles*; see Seuren 2010: 314–15):

(7.4)   a. Only Satan pities himself.
       b. Only Satan pities Satan.

He concludes 'that here at least the reflexive pronoun is not a referring word at all'. One may generalize this to the statement that reflexive pronouns are *never* referring words. One needs an analysis in terms of an underlying Semantic Analysis (SA) to distinguish the two meanings. The following will do as an approximation:

(7.5)   a. 'the class of x such that x pities x comprises only Satan'
       b. 'the class of x such that x pities Satan comprises only Satan'

Here one sees that (7.5a) contains the reflexivized predicate 'x pities x' ('x self-pities'), whereas (7.5b) does not. Any theory, such as those that circulate in so-called cognitivist linguistics, that prohibits the assumption of such an 'abstract' underlying semantic form will be basically unable to account for facts such as (7.4a,b) above, or (7.6a,b) below.

The following example is of a similar nature. We have here a little dialogue (taken from real life) between a father and his young son who is crying because he has just hurt himself:

(7.6)   a. Father: Well-educated boys don't cry.
       b. Son: Í didn't educate me!

If the boy had said:

(7.7)   Í didn't educate myself!

his answer would not have made sense and the effect would have been lost. Current but inadequate theory will provide the following logico-semantic analysis of (7.6b):

(7.8)   not [Educate (I,I)]

with a discourse-driven contrastive accent overlay on the subject term *I*, considered to be of a pragmatic nature. But, given the grammatical process of reflexivizing an object term that is co-denotational with the subject term, (7.8) would give (7.7), not (7.6b), and (7.6b) will remain unexplained, both grammatically and semantically. The answer is found in different underlying SA-structures. (7.6b) is to be analysed as (7.9a), without any reflexivization, whereas (7.7) is derived from (7.9b), with the reflexivized predicate *self-educate*:

(7.9)   a. not [the x such that x educated me] be **I**
         b. not [the x such that x educated x] be **I**

Or consider Russell's famous *Barber Paradox*:

(7.10)   Jones, who is a prisoner, shaves all the prisoners who do not shave them-
         selves, and only those.

The question is: does or does not Jones shave himself? In terms of standard logic, this question cannot be answered because if he does, he does not and if he does not, he does. Therefore, for standard logic, Jones cannot exist, having contrary properties. Yet we, natural speakers, find this sentence perfectly understandable and we see no problem with it.

Or take the sentence:

(7.11)   All girls envy the girl Trisha.

This sentence is not naturally understood as entailing that Trisha envies herself (if that were possible at all), though 'logically' it does have that entailment because Trisha is a girl and should, therefore, according to (7.11), envy Trisha. A logician will say that if Trisha does not envy herself, (7.11) is false, but a natural speaker will not deem it false for that reason, even though Trisha does not envy herself. TBP helps out: it says that the complex unary predicate *envy the girl Trisha* is applicable to all girls except to Trisha herself, because, if applied to Trisha, the original binary predicate will violate TBP and must be reflexivized. This way, the phrase *all girls* automatically excludes Trisha in a sentence like (7.11).

It has been observed (Smullyan 1981: 224) that in standard predicate logic, the following argument is valid:

(7.12)   a. Everyone fears Dracula.
       b. Dracula fears only me.
       c. *Ergo*: I am Dracula.

In terms of standard logic this is correct (assuming that Dracula is a person and hence falls in the range of *everyone*). In standard logic (7.12a) entails that Dracula is one of those who fear Dracula, or *dFd*. (7.12b) says that *dFme* and for no $x \neq me$, *dFx*. Thus, the only constant individual-denoting terms that will yield truth for the function *dFx* are those that refer to the individual referred to by *d*, i.e. Dracula. We now see why this argument, no matter how correct in classical calculus, fails to convince: a crucial step in it is the entailment *dFd*, which follows from (7.12a). But under TBP this entailment fails to follow.

The naturalness of established logic is again under attack in the following case:

(7.13)   a. Frank is Jacob's son.
       b. Jacob is Frank's father.
       c. *Ergo*: Frank is his father's son.

Logically, the argument is correct: (7.13a) is equivalent with (7.13b) (given that both Frank and Jacob are human males). The substitution of *his father* for *Jacob* in (7.13c) should thus be legitimate according to the age-old principle of *substitution salva veritate* of co-referring terms. But (7.13c) is a tautologous platitude while (7.13a) and (7.13b) are normal informative statements that can be true or false. Put differently, a question like *Are you your father's son?* is silly in a way that *Are you Jacob's son?* is not. The difference is due to the fact that *his* in (7.13c) is a covert reflexive third-person possessive (Latin *sui*, not *eius*, or Swedish *sin*, not *hans*; see section 5.2.1), whereas there is no sign of any reflexivity in either (7.13a) or (7.13b).

Sometimes there is an ambiguity. The second conjunct of the following sentence:

(7.14)   Helga thinks that she will win, and so do I.

can imply either that I think that Helga will win, in which case *she* is used referentially, or that I think that I will win, in which case *she* is used reflexively. English has no morphological marking for reflexive pronouns in dependent clauses (indirect reflexivity). Some languages do, however.[5]

Reflexivity is a far-reaching phenomenon that goes beyond language and originates in cognition. This is tellingly illustrated by a quote from the Dutch daily newspaper *NRC-Handelsblad* of 7 January 1987, which contained a feature on the

---

[5] A reliable test for semantic reflexivity is replacement with a so-called *epithet pronoun*, such as *the bastard* or *the bitch* (see section 5.2.1). When *she* in (7.14) is replaced with, for example, *the bitch*, the indirect reflexive relation between *Helga* and *she* disappears.

Swedish firm Electrolux, comparing it with the Dutch firm Philips. There the following sentence occurred (translated here into English):[6]

(7.15)   Moreover, Philips always sends Dutch management to its foreign branches; Electrolux *does so* only in exceptional cases.

The context leaves no doubt that what was meant is that Electrolux sends Swedish, not Dutch, management to its foreign branches only in exceptional cases. Background knowledge is thus brought to bear to ensure the correct, reflexive, interpretation. I will not now attempt to gauge the depths of the system underlying these phenomena. All we need here is the observation that an *n*-ary predicate $(n > 1)$ is reflexivized, in a very wide sense that includes an appeal to background knowledge, to become an *n*-1-ary predicate when the term that is eliminated is codenotational with some other term (usually the subject) or contains an attributive adjunct that is codenotational with some other term (usually the subject). This reflexivization need not be grammatically overt in all cases, yet it is semantically and cognitively real.

The Gricean maxims provide no satisfactory answer. Levinson (2000: 181, 277–80) gives the example (taken from Geach; see example (7.4) above) *Only Felix voted for him* versus *Only Felix voted for himself*. To explain the contrast, he posits a scale whereby a reflexive pronoun (*himself*) is more informative than a nonreflexive pronoun (*him*). The Gricean *Maxim of Quantity* ('make your contribution as informative as is required, not more') would then predict that the use of *him* 'implicates' that the more informative *himself* is not intended by the speaker. However, the examples given above show that this appeal to the Gricean maxims lacks generality and is thus *ad hoc*, and therefore inadequate. It fails to apply to the Barber paradox presented in (7.10), which does not allow for the 'less informative' *them* instead of *themselves*. It fails to apply to (7.11), which does not even contain a pronoun that could compete with a reflexive, and also to (7.4b), where the double occurrence of *Satan* imposes denotational identity, just as the *himself* of (7.4a) is supposed to do. Yet Levinson's principle fails to show up the semantic difference. Likewise for the difference between (7.6b) and (7.7). Since no other pragmatic attempts are known to solve the predicament of semantic reflexivity, one has to conclude that the answer is to be sought elsewhere.

Against the background of data such as those presented above, it will be clear that one has little choice but to accept that a principle such as TBP is at work in cognition and in language. That being so, the question arises: *why* should such a principle be operative in cognition and language? It seems to me that a reasonable answer is found

---

[6] The Dutch daily *NRC-Handelsblad* seems to have a predilection for reflexivity when discussing Philips, especially on the seventh of the month. In the same newspaper's issue of 7 August 1992, the following sentence appeared (translated here into English): 'Jan Timmer defends himself against criticisms of Philips'. (Jan Timmer was CEO of Philips from 1990 till 1996.)

in the fact that binary predicates are prototypically used to render situations where the two arguments of the relation expressed by a binary predicate have distinct and not identical cognitive denotations. Situations characterized by the relation LOVE, for example, prototypically involve (at least) two entities, not one single entity. For the marked cases where LOVE involves one single individual, language and cognition have invented cognitive-semantic reflexivization.

7.4 The predicate of identity, or rather, identification

One might object that the identity predicate *be* violates TBP in identity statements, such as (7.16a–c), because one would expect some form of reflexivization:

(7.16) a. Zeus is Jupiter.
   b. The Morning Star is the Evening Star.
   c. The Matterhorn is the Cervino.

One might say that the identity predicate is a binary predicate that expresses the identity relation and thus requires for truth that its two terms refer to the same entity. Identity statements should thus be intrinsically reflexive. This, however, is not so. For one thing, as has been noted above, what is at issue in cases of reflexivization is not *referential* identity but identity of *cognitive entity representations*, which are supposedly different when sentences like (7.16a–c) are uttered. This is why Frege (1892) introduced his distinction between *sense* (Sinn) and *reference* (Bedeutung): the two terms of a nontrivial identity statement have different senses but the same referent. If 'sense' is taken as standing for the 'search procedure' that helps speaker and hearer to 'get at' the reference object (Dummett 1981: 44–6), it becomes understandable why sentences like those in (7.16) are not necessarily true platitudes, given the factual identity of the two term referents.

But there are many other complicating factors. As a preliminary, I must mention that there is great confusion in the existing philosophical and linguistic literature regarding the identity predicate. The American philosopher Willard Van Orman Quine made a fatal mistake, leading philosophers and semanticists astray, when he took the *is* in sentence (7.17) to be the *is* of identity (Quine 1953: 143–4):

(7.17) The number of planets *is* nine.

This sentence is not an identity statement at all but expresses the assignment of the *value* NINE to the *parameter* THE NUMBER OF PLANETS. This is not the *be* of identity but the *be* of value assignment (see Seuren 2009a: 188–94). Curiously, this value-assigning *be* has never been identified as such in logic, semantics or philosophy. Consequently, there is no logic, no semantics and no grammar of value-assignments to parameters—which, among other things, has prevented a proper analysis of topic-comment structures to get off the ground. In general, answers to WH-questions are value-assignment statements:

(7.18)   a. What is your name? My name is Pieter.
          b. What is the temperature? The temperature is 90 degrees.
          c. Who is the author of this book? The author of this book is Frege.

Here *name, temperature* and *author* are parameters waiting for a value to be assigned when applied to the arguments *you, here-and-now* and *this book*, respectively.

But let us limit ourselves to true identity statements, such as (7.16a–c), and try to be as precise as we can manage regarding their nature. We say that an identity statement of the form *A is B* can be paraphrased as:

'The definite NPs *A* and *B* refer to the same entity'.

The use of proper names is typically highly frequent in identity statements.

Almost four decades ago, the Oxford philosopher Peter Strawson wrote the following inspired text (Strawson 1974: 54–5):

I offer, then, a model or a picture of a man's knowledge of, or belief about, all those particular items of which he has some identifying as well as some non-identifying knowledge. We are to picture a map, as it were, of his identifying historical and geographical knowledge—in an extended sense of these words. On the knowledge map we represent the unity of every cluster of identifying knowledge […] by a filled-in circle or dot. […] From each dot radiate lines bearing one-or-more-place predicate expressions; and these lines, with their inscriptions, represent the various propositions which the man is able to affirm, from his own knowledge, regarding the items. […] These lines are of different kinds. Some join one dot to another. These are relational propositions like 'Caesar loved Brutus'. Some curl back on their dot of origin. They are reflexively relational propositions like 'Caesar loved himself'. Some are joined to a dot only at one end. These are non-relational propositions like 'Caesar was bald'. Now when a man equipped with such a knowledge map receives what is for him new information, … he incorporates such new information in his stock of knowledge. [… W]hen [the statement] is an identity statement […], he adds no further lines. [… W]hat he does is to eliminate one dot of two, at the same time transferring to the remaining one of the two all those lines and names which attach to the eliminated dot. […]

We might improve this model, perhaps. Instead of thinking of the man as operating on his knowledge-map, when his knowledge-state is changed, we may think simply of the knowledge-map as becoming changed. When he learns something from an ordinary predication, new lines inscribe themselves on his map, attached to the appropriate dot or joining two different dots. When he learns from an identity-statement, the two appropriate dots approach each other and merge, or coalesce, into one, any duplicating lines merging or coalescing at the same time.

This passage presages the development of discourse semantics, which started immediately after Strawson's (1974). In terms of discourse semantics, the identity predicate *be* does indeed merge two thus far distinct mental entity addresses in the discourse domain (DD) into one address, pooling all the information specified for the two previously distinct addresses (Seuren 1985: 427). In Seuren (2009a: 189), the identity predicate is defined as follows:

> We define the identity predicate as an intensional binary predicate that merges two object representations (addresses) into one, so that one single new virtual object comes about, to be instantiated by one single actual object, if any. It would be more appropriate, therefore, not to speak of the 'identity' but of the 'identification' predicate.

The point is thus that an identity statement is not an ordinary binary predicate expressing a relation between two entities and adding that information to two distinct entity addresses in the existing DD, but takes two thus far distinct addresses, d_1 and d_2, in the existing DD and produces a new, updated, DD where d_1 and d_2 have been merged into a new address d_3 which unites, or pools, all information associated with the old d_1 and d_2. In this perspective, it is better to speak of the *identification predicate*, rather than of the *identity predicate*.

7.5 Is identity-*be* a counterexample to TBP?

Since the identity (identification) predicate does not express a binary relation, it is to be expected that it is not open to semantic reflexivization of the kind described in section 7.2. Yet, as so often, language is deceptive. English, like many other languages, does have sentences like (7.19), which look as if they would constitute a counter-example to the analysis presented here:

(7.19)   He is not himself anymore.

But the counterexample is only apparent. First, sentence (7.19) does not contain the *be* that establishes denotational identy, as it does not allow for the rendering 'the NPs *he* and *himself* do not refer to the same entity anymore'. Rather, the *be* in sentence (7.19) is the copula *be* of attribution, as in *He is a carpenter*, or *He is a good man*. The sentence is then seen as a conventionalized, slightly metaphorical, expression paraphrasable as something like 'he is no longer what we have always known him to be'.

Grammatically, (7.19) cannot be an ordinary reflexive sentence. This appears straight away from the fact that in case-marking languages that use a direct equivalent for (7.19) and not, for example, a locative, as in the Turkish sentence (7.21), whatever reflexive nominal is used to express *himself* always occurs in the nominative, never in the accusative. Thus, the Modern Greek equivalent of (7.19) is (7.20), where the phrase *o eaftós tou* is in the nominative, not in the accusative:

(7.20) Den íne   piá   o   eaftós tou.
        not he-is more the self his
        'He is not his self any more.'

Moreover, in many languages (7.19) is not rendered by a seemingly 'reflexive' verb copula. In Turkish, for example, (7.19) reads as (7.21), with a locative phrase:

(7.21) Artık (o)   kendi-n-de değil.[7]
        more (he) himself-in not-is
        'He is not *in* himself any more.'

As has been said, in many languages, including Greek, Turkish, Italian, German, Dutch (but not in English), reflexivization occurs in two forms, as full and as halfway reflexivization. Greek and Turkish realize the former as part of verb morphology, as in (7.22b) and (7.23b), respectively, and the latter, as the adjectival noun *eaftós* (self) for Greek, as in (7.22c), and for Turkish as the adjective *kendi* (own), as in (7.23c).

(7.22) a. Plén-i   ta roúcha tou.
           wash-3sgPres the clothes his
           'He washes his clothes.'

        b. Plén-ete.
           wash-3sgPresRefl
           'He washes himself. (he self-washes)'

        c. Plén-i   ton   eaftó tou.
           wash-3sgPres the-Acc self-Acc his
           'He washes himself. (he washes his own person)'

(7.23) a. (O)   çocuğ-u   yık-ıyor.
           (he-Nom) child-Acc   wash-3sgPres
           'He washes the child.'

        b. (O)   yıka-n-ıyor.
           (he-Nom) wash-Refl-3sgPres
           'He washes himself. (he self-washes)'

        c. (O)   kendi-ni   yık-ıyor.
           (he-Nom) self-Acc   wash-3sgPres
           'He washes himself. (he washes his own person)'

But (7.22c) and (7.23c) do not instantiate full grammatical reflexivization, as one can see, for example, from the grammaticality of (7.24a,b) and the ungrammaticality of (7.25a,b). These examples show that the Greek *eaftó*-reflexive and the Turkish *kendi*-reflexive are only 'halfway' on the road to full grammatical expression of reflexivization. Their predicates are still of a binary character even though they are

---

[7] The *-n-* in *kendi-n-de* is a grammaticalized linking consonant.

subject to certain restrictions, such as the lack of a passive. Whatever semantic difference exists between fully and halfway grammatically expressed reflexivization seems to have to do with an effect of greater emphasis or contrast of the latter compared with the former. Sentences like (7.22c) or (7.23c) are not simply understood as 'he washes himself' but rather as 'he washes his own person'. Perhaps what is at issue is a different topic–comment structure: 'whom he washes is himself'. We do not know: a great deal is still to be investigated. In any case, we observe that (7.24a,b) are grammatical, while (7.25a,b) are not:

(7.24) a. Plén-i   ton   eaftó tou   ke   eséna.
           wash-3sgPres   the-Acc   self-Acc his   and   you
           'He washes himself and you.'

        b. (O)   kendi-ni   ve   sen-i   yık-ıyor.
           (he-Nom)   self-Acc   and   you-Acc   wash-3sgPres
           'He washes himself and you.'

(7.25) a. *Plén-ete   ke   eséna.
           wash-3sgPresRefl   and   you
           '*He self-washes and you.'

        b. *(O)   ve   sen-i   yıka-n-ıyor.
           (he-Nom)   and   you-Acc   wash-Refl-3sgPres
           '*He self-washes and you.'

One might object that the ungrammaticality of (7.25a) and (7.25b) is due to the trivial fact that in both cases there is no fully fledged conjunctive *and*-phrase since one leg of the phrase is missing, but this objection is answered by the Dutch–German example (7.28a) below, which is ungrammatical even though the surface structure contains a fully fledged *and*-phrase with two parallel constituents.

Since English allows for (7.26), one may conclude that English *self*-reflexives grammatically manifest halfway reflexivization, though they express semantic reflexivity:

(7.26) He washes himself and you.

Dutch or German are different in that they distinguish between a full *zich* or *sich* reflexive and a halfway *zichzelf* or *sichselbst*-reflexive:

		Dutch:	*German*:
(7.27)	a.	Hij wast zich.	Er wäscht sich.
		he washes himself	he washes himself
		(he self-washes)	(he self-washes)
	b.	Hij wast zichzelf.	Er wäscht sichselbst.
		he washes himself	he washes himself
		'He washes himself.'	'He washes himself.'

(7.28) a. *Hij wast   zich   en   jou.   *Er wäscht sich   und dich.
            he   washes himself and you   he   washes himself and you
            '*He self-washes and you.'   '*He self-washes and you.'

        b. Hij wast   zichzelf en jou.   Er wäscht sichselbst und dich.
           he   washes himself   and you   he   washes himself   and you
           'He washes himself and you.'   'He washes himself and you.'

It is thus clear that the apparent 'reflexivization' of the verb *be* in the English sentence (7.19) and its equivalents in other languages is not ordinary semantic reflexivization, even though it looks as if it were. We may, therefore, conclude that sentences like (7.19) do not constitute counterexamples to TBP.

7.6 Dynamic sentence meaning: discourse incrementation

We may also conclude that the *be* of identification, which has caused so much trouble in modern formal semantics, can only be adequately described in terms of its dynamic function in discourse semantics, since its semantic effect consists in the merging of what were two distinct addresses into one, as Strawson proposed. This analysis of the identification predicate *be* thus supports the general insight that what is required is a *dynamic view* of sentence meaning, in that the meaning of a given sentence S is now seen as a determining factor in the transition from an existing DD to an updated DD—what is now normally called the *incrementation* of an uttered sentence to a given discourse domain.

In my more naïve days (Seuren 1975), I still thought that sentence meaning fully determines the change from an existing to an updated DD—a view taken over as such, and still held, in incremental versions of PWS, such as Kamp's Discourse Representation Theory or DRT (Kamp 1981; Kamp and Reyle 1993). In fact, however, sentence meaning, though a strong determining factor, *underdetermines actual incrementation*—a point duly stressed in the pragmatics literature of the past few decades.

What is needed, as a matter of principle, for a full interpretation—that is, a full integration of newly uttered sentences into a given DD—is an *appeal to situational and background knowledge* taken by the speaker to be available to the audience. Thus, the linguistically unambiguous sentence:

(7.29) Lorenzo was holding Adriana's hand.

is interpreted in different ways according to the DD at hand. The most normal or prototypical interpretation is that Lorenzo stood in a relation of tenderness with regard to Adriana, of either an amorous or a caring or a comforting nature, with all the attendant expectations thereof. A less typical situation would be one in which the hand Lorenzo was holding was severed from the rest of Adriana's body. Such an interpretation is possible but needs unequivocal contextual clues for it to come about.

In general, there always is some wider situation in which the utterance is positioned. It is not so that a sentence like (7.29) is interpreted merely as expressing a hand-holding relation between Lorenzo and Adriana: there always is a further positioning of the sentence in terms of some known situation type. If that is lacking, as in:

(7.30)   The issue was flying for a broomstick over some light on happiness.

uttered without any preceding explanation, the utterance is uninterpretable or incomprehensible. For it to be comprehensible a specific context is required explaining what an issue is doing flying for a broomstick over some light on happiness. In the absence of any further explanation, one cannot even disambiguate the word *issue*: is it the issue of a journal or the issue up for discussion?

This goes to show that the appeal that must be made to an available knowledge base for the precise selection of the lexical (polysemous) meaning variety intended and for the suppletion of missing antecedents, as in (7.31a), is driven by speaker and hearer's situational knowledge. (7.31b) is immediately interpretable because we know that parties normally mean a great deal of noise. (7.31c) is immediately interpretable in those cultures where funerals normally involve loud noise. But in other cultures, where funerals are supposed to be very quiet, (7.31c) will provoke surprise and puzzlement:

(7.31)   a. There was a wedding going on. *She* was lovely.
            b. There was a party going on. *The noise* was terrible.
            c. There was a funeral going on. *The noise* was terrible.

It is not so that a DD merely lists all entities referred to in the discourse and all relations between them—as in Strawson's map metaphor quoted above. A DD is not just an information store of the kind found in computerized data bases. On the contrary, DDs are structured as possible situations of known types. It is widely accepted that a full interpretation of utterances is underdetermined by the linguistically defined meanings of the corresponding sentences and that full interpretation requires access to, and use of, information retrieved from available world knowledge. What is not widely recognized is that this access to available world knowledge is, unless overridden by specific information supplied, to a large extent driven by knowledge of prototypical *situations*. It is in terms of *known situation types* that utterances seek an interpretation.

The relevance of the discourse-dependency for reflexivity phenomena is that the antecedent of a reflexive pronoun is also sometimes to be sought in cognition, rather than in the sentence itself. This is shown in (7.32a), where the antecedent for the reflexive *myself* is not overtly present. In (7.32b) it is overtly present (*Jack*), but not in the canonical subject position:

(7.32)   a. Thanks for your advice not to get myself involved.
        b. Thanks for your advice to Jack not to get himself involved.

In (7.32a) it is the implication that the advice has been given to the speaker which enables the use of the reflexive *myself*. By contrast, (7.32b) says explicitly that the advice has been given to Jack, which prohibits the use of *myself* and enables the use of *himself*, even though *Jack* is not the subject term of a main verb.

This takes us back to our starting point. Having defended and, I hope, established the validity of the True Binarity Principle as a restriction on binary transitive predicates, we may now ask for the motivation behind this principle. This motivation is not hard to find: it lies in the *situatedness* of utterance interpretation. A prototypical *love*-situation involves two entities, a lover and a lovee, the one being distinct from the other.

Situatedness is a typical feature of utterance interpretation (Zwaan 1999; Zwaan and Radvansky 1998). The force of situatedness is such that it is often (presuppositionally) encoded in the meanings of lexical predicates, which frequently require a particular setting or situation type to be properly used (one *commits* a crime but one *makes* a mistake or a donation). It is also, as I argue, encoded in certain general principles of cognition and language, such as the True Binarity Principle. We have here a viewpoint that has not so far been investigated systematically and on a wide scale. It would seem that research along these lines is more promising than a further fruitless hanging on to Gricean principles that have been shown to be too weak.

7.7 Conclusion

We thus conclude our trek from the True Binarity Principle, through reflexivization and the identity (or identification) predicate, through incremental discourse semantics and the situatedness hypothesis, back to the True Binarity Principle—all in the interest of explaining otherwise unexplained facts of language and language use. The explanation provided involves semantics, syntax and cognition, but no appeal to the Gricean maxims. These maxims, which were set up primarily to account for the discrepancies between standard logic and natural language, seem to lose any significance when *cognitive* principles are allowed to interact with logical systems (in a proper definition of what logic amounts to). Principles of *language use* or *linguistic interaction* do not seem to play a role. Seuren (2010) constitutes an argument for this view in general. The present chapter adds to this by concentrating specifically on reflexivity. My contention is that the Gricean maxims had better be totally dispensed with, even though what they say is a true enough reflection of speakers' behaviour when they are sufficiently cooperative and of hearers' expectations when they are good judges of the situation. But they have nothing to do with the (discourse-) semantic, grammatical and cognitive mechanisms and principles underlying the system of language and guiding its use.

8

The generalized logic hierarchy
and its cognitive implications

8.1 Introduction*

This chapter is an exercise in elementary logic, with important implications for the study of meaning in natural language and for the study of cognition in general. Its main result is that the overall condition of a non-null extension of the Restrictor predicate R—the condition that $[[R]] \neq \emptyset$—in sentences of the type 'All R is M' (the classic type **A**, as *All Romans are mortal*), far from bringing about the logical fault known as *undue existential import* or UEI, is the main reason why natural predicate logic, in its various forms, is maximally powerful and functional. It is also a central criterion in the hierarchy of logical systems presented here, the *generalized logic hierarchy* (GLH). It is shown that the triadic predicate logic, defined by relations of contrariety and presented in Hamilton (1866) and Jespersen (1917), henceforth called *basic-natural predicate logic* or BNPL, when extended to a hexadic (or bi-triadic) system by the addition of subcontraries, forms the basis of GLH and that the tetradic classic Boethian Square of Opposition, henceforth called *the Square*, is a (termino-logically confusing) subpart of BNPL. Both these systems leave the null class, in particular as the extension of the Restrictor predicate R, out of account—a sure sign not of nature's logical incompetence, as has been thought for the past century, but of its inbuilt wisdom. For if we follow modern logic and admit the null set, the maximally powerful system of BNPL which comprises the Square, begins to fray. The crucial criterion here is whether sentences of type **A** are considered true or false when $[[R]] = \emptyset$. When they are declared false, the damage done to the full bi-triadic BNPL system is minimal, but when they are declared true, as in modern logic, the damage is massive. GLH thus quantifies the intuitive unnaturalness of standard modern logic. Natural language, through its presupposition mechanism, has the

---

* This chapter would not have come about without the challenge posed, and the inspiration generated, by Dany Jaspers' work on what he playfully calls the 'logic' of colours. Our many stimulating discussions on this topic have not only been very enlightening in a general sense but also sparked the discovery that this chapter is about. I am also grateful to Larry Horn for help and suggestions.

best of both worlds: it maintains the full logical power of both BNPL and the Square and solves the UEI problem by means of its presuppositional machinery.

The point is actually quite simple, as long as the extensions of the predicates R and M, written as [[R]] and [[M]], are kept down to what I call 'natural sets'—that is, not equal to either $\emptyset$ or to the set **Ent** of all entities under consideration.[1] Under this condition, there are only seven possible configurations of [[R]] and [[M]], represented as 1 to 7 in Figure 8.3 below. Now take the triadic Hamiltonian system BNPL with three mutually contrary sentence types, **A** (All R is M), **Y** (Some but not all R is M) and **N** (No R is M), jointly covering the set **Un** of situations 1 to 7. Let **A** be true in the situations 1 and 3, **Y** in 2, 4 and 6, and **N** in 5 and 7 of Figure 8.3. Then any pair formed from **A**, **Y** or **N** is a pair of contraries, in that they can never be true together in **Un** at the same time. But then also, any pair formed from **A** ∨ **Y** (say **I**), **N** ∨ **Y** (say **O**) and **A** ∨ **N** (say **U**) is a pair of subcontraries, in that they can never be false together in **Un** at the same time. Moreover, it now follows that **A** entails **I** (**A** ⊢ **I**), **N** entails **O** (**N** ⊢ **O**), **A** entails **U** (**A** ⊢ **U**), **N** entails **U** (**N** ⊢ **U**), **Y** entails **O** (**Y** ⊢ **O**) and **Y** entails **I** (**Y** ⊢ **I**). Finally, **A** and **O**, **I** and **N**, and **Y** and **U** are contradictories. All of which means that a hexagon of logical relations can be drawn, in which each vertex stands in some logical relation to each other vertex, as shown in Figure 8.10 below.

An analogous result is obtained when one takes three mutually disjoint sets, call them A, Y and N, together constituting **Ent**, plus their unions A ∪ Y (or I), A ∪ N (or U) and Y ∪ N (or O). Now, obviously, A ⊂ I, A ⊂ U, Y ⊂ I, Y ⊂ O, N ⊂ U and N ⊂ O, while A = Ō, Y = Ū and N = Ī. Moreover, I ∪ O = **Ent**, U ∪ O = **Ent** and I ∪ U = **Ent**, which makes I, O and U the set-theoretic counterparts of the subcontraries in the logical system. The analogy consists in the fact that, while the mutually disjoint sets A, Y and N jointly constitute **Ent**, the analogous mutually contrary, but contingent, sentence types **A**, **Y** and **N** are defined in, or by, human cognition in such a way that they jointly cover **Un**, the set of all possible situations (but without ∅, the null set of possible situations, true for necessarily false sentences, and without **Un**, the set of all possible situations, true for necessarily true sentences).

The BNPL hexagon works fine as long as **A**, **Y** and **N** are mutually contrary and **I**, **O** and **U** are mutually subcontrary, but it begins to fray when the human intellect infringes upon human nature by allowing [[R]] to be null. When A-type sentences are declared false when [[R]] = ∅, the damage is limited, but when they are declared true when [[R]] = ∅, as in standard modern logic, the hexagonal BNLP system disintegrates, as has been said. *Apparently, natural human cognition does not count the null set as a factor in the relations between sets and hence in defining possible situations.* It goes without saying that this fact is of prime interest to the study of how

---

[1] In fact, what I consider to be a *natural set* (Seuren 2010: 75) is unequal to ∅ or **Ent** and is not a singleton. The latter condition is needed for the distinction between singularity and plurality. Since this distinction plays no role in the present context, it is disregarded here.

cognition, language and logic relate to each other. Yet it is unknown to most logicians, even to those who occupy themselves explicitly with the logic and semantics of natural language. And when it is pointed out to them, it fails to awaken their interest. At least, that is what I have found so far.

The reason why natural-language logicians and formal semanticists take little interest in such matters seems to be, simply, that they consider the restriction that [[R]] and [[M]] be natural sets, and in particular that [[R]] be non-null, to be an infraction of the laws of logic and hence anathema. In their view, predicate logic, in the form of the traditional Square, had suffered for so long under this logical 'error' of UEI and the logical world is now so proud of having eliminated this 'error' by the adoption of modern Russellian logic, that one would be seriously compromised if one looked back to reconsider the whole question. Yet in not doing so one throws the baby out with the bathwater, missing the chance to discover the rich supply of logical insights obtained when one looks at what happens in the hierarchy when this restriction is lifted. Moreover, one misses the chance to see different ways in which this restriction can be lifted, with different degrees of damage to the basic system, and with no damage at all if presuppositions are taken into account. In fact, it is shown below that the condition that $[[R]] \neq \varnothing$ does *not* make the logic inconsistent: it only does so when the Conversions ('not all' is equivalent with 'some not' and 'not some' with 'all not') are maintained. When the Conversions are given up in favour of one-way entailments, the system is sound. BNPL is a precious good, not only because it is so rich and powerful but also because it fits natural logical intuitions much better than standard modern logic and is thus a good starting point for the study of natural predicate logic. The 'fault' of UEI vanishes in the process.

The present chapter analyses in detail the logical effects on the various systems of logic discussed of the condition placed on the universal quantifier that [[R]] should be non-null. In doing so we reject the contention that this condition makes the logic faulty: it only does so if the Conversions are maintained. To conduct the analysis in a proper way, it is useful to develop the technique of *valuation space (VS) modelling*, which is explained in the sections 8.2 and 8.3 and is seen to provide an effective method for testing the soundness of logical systems. VS-modelling is the main instrument in the laying out of the differences and similarities between the various logical systems considered. It is applied to the (bi-)triadic logic of Hamilton (1866) and Jespersen (1917) (our BNPL), to the classic Square, to Aristotelian-Abelardian predicate logic (AAPL) (Aristotle's original system, rediscovered and reconstructed by the medieval French philosopher Peter Abelard) and to standard modern predicate logic (SMPL). It is then shown that the Hamiltonian triadic system, with external and internal negation, amounts to the bi-triadic system of BNPL, that the Square is merely a subpart of BNPL, and that in AAPL and SMPL, which accept $\varnothing$ as a possible predicate extension, BNPL begins to fall apart.

The logical systems considered differ according to (a) which of the six vertices are selected as terms for the logical relations, (b) whether or not they accept a null Restrictor domain [[R]], and if they do, (c) whether universally quantified sentences are deemed true or false when [[R]] = ∅. When a null [[R]] is left out of account, the system has maximal power in that all pairs of vertices are logically related. When a null [[R]] is taken into account, some relations are lost so that the hexagon is partly undone. And, as has been said, when universally quantified sentences are deemed false when [[R]] = ∅, as in AAPL, the damage is limited, but when they are taken to be true, as in SMPL, the damage is such that BNPL collapses.

The Hamilton-Jespersen bi-triadic system, though treated with a certain disdain in logical circles, is thus seen to be 'basic' in a hitherto unknown general and profound sense. The recent history of this insight is now gradually being unravelled by researchers like Larry Horn, Alessio Moretti and Dany Jaspers, to whom I owe much of the information that follows. Horn (1990) points out that the first author known to have spotted the presence of the Hamilton-Jespersen system in the traditional Square was the still obscure figure of Paul Joseph Jacoby (1915–1993) in Jacoby (1950), quickly followed by the French physicist and logician Augustin Sesmat (1885–1957) in Sesmat (1951), and by the French philosopher Robert Blanché (1898–1975) in Blanché (1952, 1953, 1966), but Horn's references remained unnoticed till quite recently, when a renewed interest arose in the logical and cognitive nature and the history of the Square. The authors from the 1950s were (re)discovered in reverse order. Blanché was unearthed first, then Sesmat, who was brought to my attention by Alessio Moretti, and finally Jacoby, whose (1950) paper was recently sent to me by Larry Horn. I will henceforth speak of the Blanché hexagon, as it occurs for the first time, in the form used here, in Blanché (1952, 1953). Sesmat (1951) does have the hexagon but in a slightly different nomenclature; Jacoby (1950) does not yet have the hexagon (though Jacoby 1960 does).[2]

---

[2] Although it is widely assumed that the advent of modern Russellian logic in the early 1900s put an immediate end to the Square, this is not quite the way things went. The classic Square kept being taught in Catholic seminaries and in philosophy courses for priests in a religious order until at least the 1970s. In these circles, attempts were made to save the Square from the onslaught caused by modern mathematical logic. Authors like Jacoby, Sesmat and Blanché should be seen in this light (Jacoby taught in the Catholic Seton Hill University and only published in the Catholic journal *The New Scholasticism*; Sesmat, a priest, taught in the Catholic Institute of Paris; Blanché was a devout Catholic. From about 1930 till the 1960s, Catholicism went through a period of intellectual, literary and artistic prominence, especially in France but also to a considerable extent in the United States. This provided an ideal context for a revival of the time-honoured logic system that had been so suddenly and so cruelly removed from its position of primacy in the early years of the century. Very much the same applied to Catholic Poland and the ecclesiastical background of the revival of medieval philosophical studies in that country during and after the 1930s (see Blanché 1970: 133). One thinks of the Polish Dominican priest Józef Maria Bocheński (1902–1995) or the Catholic Polish logician Jan Łukasiewicz (1878–1956), who both pioneered medieval logical studies. In America, the initiator of medieval logical studies, Ernest Addison Moody (1903–1975), was again a Roman Catholic. The Englishman Peter Thomas Geach (born 1916), whose references to medieval logic stimulated research into medieval logic in Great Britain, is an unusually staunch Roman Catholic.

Yet, though early harbingers, Jacoby, Sesmat and Blanché fell short of seeing the full logical implications of the hexadic system. None of them considered the question of a null extension for [[R]] and the ensuing problem of UEI, simply taking the Square as the point of departure for their hexagon of logical relations. Sesmat defined the Y-vertex (which he called U) as the conjunction of I and O ('some yes and some no') and introduced the U-vertex ('all or none') (which he called Y), as a disjunction of A and N (traditional E), to make the system complete. (I have taken over Blanché's denominations Y (for $I \wedge I^*$) and U (for $A \vee N$).)

The perspective held by Blanché was also different from mine. For him, the hexagon of logical relations was the hypothetical basis for a more general theory of relations between lexical items forming a closed lexical field and thus for cognition as a whole (see Figure 8.14 below). He proposed that human cognition is especially prone to world construal in terms of the hexagon of logico-cognitive relations he developed. When Blanché speaks of a 'generalized logic' (Blanché 1966: 21–34), what he has in mind is a generalization to lexical relations in cognitive structures, not a general theory of logical systems. In this spirit he writes (Blanché 1966: 23): 'Unfortunately, the classic Aristotelian theory is applied to propositions, not to concepts.' My analysis is thus less far-reaching than Blanché's, but the more precise and the more detailed for it. Blanché's perspective is shared by Dany Jaspers, who, in his thought-provoking works (Jaspers 2010, 2011), applies the Blanché hexadic system to colour perception (see section 8.5.2).

8.2 The notion of valuation space

Before I can broach the central issue of the present paper, the construction of a generalized logic hierarchy providing a frame for all varieties of bivalent extensional predicate logic, I need to develop the notion of VALUATION SPACE (VS), first presented, but left underexploited, in Van Fraassen (1971). It was further developed in Seuren (2002, 2006, 2007, 2010) as a means for a compact representation of logical systems and as an instrument for testing logical soundness. Here, I present, for the first time, a *formal construction procedure* for VS-models.

> The notion of valuation space is defined as follows (see also section 9.8):
> VALUATION SPACE: The valuation space /S/ of a sentence S is the set of possible (admissible) situations in which S is true.

We posit a universe **Un** of all situations in which sentences of a logical language L are true or false. **Un** is a matrix of *sentences* and *valuations*, each valuation being an assignment of truth or falsity to all sentences of L. Each valuation is a description of a situation sit_n. Situations differ from possible worlds in that they are defined for the sentences of L, not language-independently. The terms *situation* and *valuation* are thus interchangeable. If L has n semantically independent sentences and the system is bivalent, **Un** for L will contain 2^n possible valuations/situations. The number of valuations quickly explodes: for 25 sentences, there are already $2^{25} = 33,554,432$ valuations.

Consider a toy model where L consists of three semantically (and thus logically) independent sentences A, B and C. This gives a VS-model of eight (2^3) valuations, as shown in Figure 8.1 ('T' stands for 'true'; 'F' for 'false'). Each valuation is an assignment of truth values to A, B and C.

valuations(= **Un**):	1	2	3	4	5	6	7	8
A	T	F	T	F	T	F	T	F
B	T	T	F	F	T	T	F	F
C	T	T	T	T	F	F	F	F

FIGURE 8.1 Bivalent VS-model for the semantically independent sentences A, B and C

The VSs for A, B and C—that is, /A/, /B/ and /C/, respectively—are thus as follows:

$$/A/ = \{1,3,5,7\}$$
$$/B/ = \{1,2,5,6\}$$
$$/C/ = \{1,2,3,4\}$$

When a sentence S is logically necessary, /S/ = **Un**; when S is logically impossible, /S/ = ∅.

As regards the logical compositions, /¬A/, /¬B/ and /¬C/ are simply the complements in **Un** of /A/, /B and /C/, respectively; /A ∧ B/ = /A/ ∩ /B/; /A ∨ B/ = /A/ ∪ /B/:

$$/¬A/ = \{2,4,6,8\}$$
$$/¬B/ = \{3,4,7,8\}$$
$$/¬C/ = \{5,6,7,8\}$$
$$/A ∧ B/ = \{1,5\}$$
$$/A ∨ B/ = \{1,2,3,5,6,7\}$$

When two sentences are such that the truth or falsity of the one makes the truth or falsity of the other impossible for *semantic* reasons (not for physical, social or whatever other reasons), they are not semantically independent. In that case, some valuations become *inadmissible*. Thus, when A ⊢ B (A entails B), the situations 3 and 7 in Figure 8.1 are inadmissible, as they represent impossible situations. When A >< B (A and B are contraries), the valuations 1 and 5, where both A and B are simultaneously true, are inadmissible. When A ≡ B, /A/ = /B/. Equivalence of A and B leaves only 1, 4, 5 and 8 as admissible valuations, cutting out 2, 3, 6 and 7.

The logical relations are thus definable in the set-theoretic terms of valuation spaces as follows (contradictoriness is the combination of contrariety and subcontrariety):

(8.1) a. Entailment: $A \vdash B$ if and only if $/A/ \subseteq /B/$
       b. Equivalence: $A \equiv B$ if and only if $/A/ = /B/$
       c. Contrariety: $A >< B$ if and only if $/A/ \cap /B/ = \emptyset$
       d. Subcontrariety: $A >< B$ if and only if $/A/ \cup /B/ = \mathbf{Un}$
       e. Contradictoriness: $A >|< B$ if and only if $/A/ \cap /B/ = \emptyset$ and $/A/ \cup /B/ = \mathbf{Un}$

We can, if we wish, designate one specific valuation from the valuation field $\mathbf{Un}$ as the situation sit_{des}, where the assigned values all correspond with what has been stipulated to be the case in a model. This is useful for the definition of truth in a model: a proposition S is true in a model, just in case the situation sit_{des} is an element in /S/. If sit_{des} equals what is considered to be the actual world, we may speak of sit_{act}. In sit_{act} all assigned values will then correspond with what is actually the case in our world. In the present analysis, however, the notions of sit_{des} or sit_{act} are uncalled for. In other words, we do not need the notion 'truth in a (designated) model'; all we need is the notion 'truth in a valuation'.

VS-models are conveniently represented in the form of Euler diagrams. Figure 8.2–a shows a two-dimensional representation of the mutually partially intersecting VSs of two contingent—that is, semantically, and thus logically, independent—sentences, say A and B. This means that a situation *s* in $\mathbf{Un}$ can be just in /A/, just in /B/, in both /A/ and /B/, and in neither /A/ nor /B/. A and B can thus be both true or both false or one can be true while the other is false—which is what *semantic independence* means. The pairs <A,B>, <A,C> and <B,C> in Figure 8.1 are logically independent, since the VSs of the members of each pair mutually partially intersect, without their union being equal to $\mathbf{Un}$.

The sentences A and B in Figure 8.2 are all *contingent* in that their truth value depends on what happens to be the case: for a sentence S to be noncontingent, /S/ must be either $\emptyset$ (S is necessarily false) or $\mathbf{Un}$ (S is necessarily true). In all cases in Figure 8.2, both A and B are contingent sentences, as neither /A/ nor /B/ equals $\mathbf{Un}$ or $\emptyset$.

8.3 How to construct a VS-model for a logical system

We now consider VS-models for systems of predicate logic such as standard modern predicate logic (SMPL) or the classic Aristotelian-Boethian Square of Opposition, using a simple symbolic language consisting of the sentence types **A** (All R is M) and **I** (Some perhaps all R is M), with the external (sentential) negation ¬ preceding the type name and the internal (predicate) negation * following the type name. This gives the following eight sentence types, where R ranges over predicates in R (=Restrictor)

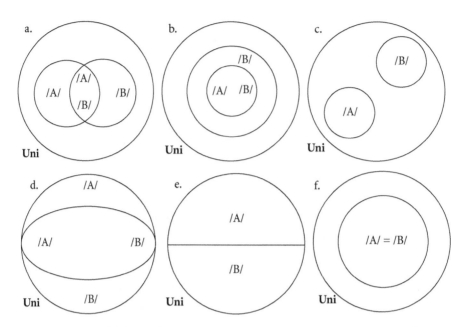

FIGURE 8.2 VS-models (Euler diagrams) for (a) logical independence, (b) entailment (A ⊢ B), (c) contrariety (A >< B), (d) subcontrariety (A >< B), (e) contradictoriness (A >|< B), and (f) equivalence (A ≡ B)

position and M over predicates in M (=Matrix) position.[3] (Below, the further sentence types **N** (No R is M), **Y** (Some but not all R is M) and **U** (All or no R is M) will be introduced.)

(i)	**A**	All R is M	(All Romans are mortal)
(ii)	**I**	Some R is M	(Some Roman(s) is (are) mortal)
(iii)	**¬A**	Not all R is M	(Not all Romans are mortal)
(iv)	**¬I**	Not some R is M	(Not some Roman(s) is (are) mortal)
(v)	**A***	All R is not M	(All Romans are not mortal)
(vi)	**I***	Some R is not M	(Some Roman(s) is (are) not mortal)
(vii)	**¬A***	Not all R is not M	(Not all Romans are not mortal)
(viii)	**¬I***	Not some R is not M	(Not some Roman(s) is (are) not mortal)

---

[3] The Restrictor and Matrix positions are elegantly defined by the property of *conservativity* of all natural language quantifiers (Keenan and Stavi 1986). A quantifier Φ is conservative just in case, in the notation of generalized quantifiers specified in note 5 below, $\Phi(R(x),M(x)) \equiv \Phi(R(x),(R(x) \wedge M(x)))$. This condition, which is fulfilled by all natural language quantifiers, distinguishes the *Restrictor predicate* R from the *Matrix predicate* M, since natural language quantifiers do not generally fulfill the condition $\Phi(R(x), M(x)) \equiv \Phi((R(x) \wedge M(x)),M(x))$. Other than this, conservativity is not relevant in the present context.

Note that ¬I stands for the traditional Boethian **E** and **I*** for traditional **O**. The advantage of this new nomenclature is that we can now distinguish between ¬I and **A***, and between ¬A and **I*** in logics where these are not equivalent pairs.

We can, if we wish, extend this notation with the *inverted types* (*inversions*), where the Restrictor and the Matrix predicate are interchanged. For this, the sign ! (exclamation mark) is placed immediately after any of the bare sentence type symbols **A** or **I**. Then, in addition to the postposed asterisk we can introduce the preposed asterisk for the *negation of the Restrictor predicate* (preposed internal negation). This gives the further types:

A!	All M is R	***A***	All not-R is not M	**A*!**	All not-M is R
I!	Some M is R	***I***	Some not-R is not M	**I*!**	Some not-M is R
***A**	All not-R is M	**A!***	All M is not R	**A*!***	All not-M is not R
***I**	Some not-R is M	**I!***	Some M is not R	**I*!***	Some not-M is not R

In order to set up a VS-model for a predicate logic, we lay out the system in terms of situation classes forming the VSs for the sentence types in question. Figure 8.3 shows all possible relations between the Restrictor predicate extension [[R]] and the Matrix predicate extension [[M]] (the double square brackets are left out in Figure 8.3 for the sake of readability). The surrounding squares in the situation classes 1–15 of Figure 8.3 stand for the non-null domain **Ent** of all entities. Case 16 lacks a surrounding square, as it represents the case where **Ent** = ∅. $\overline{X}$ is the complement of a set X in **Ent**. When [[R]] or [[M]] equals neither **Ent** nor ∅, they are considered *natural sets* (mostly printed as circles). When [[R]] or [[M]] equals **Ent** or ∅, or when **Ent** = ∅, that condition is specified as such.

The distinction between *natural* and the *non-natural* sets ∅ and **Ent** is relevant for a variety of reasons, one of which being that there is at least one theorem that is valid in SMPL but only holds in the Square and other systems that have the subaltern entailment **A** ⊢ **I** if ∅ and **Ent** are left out of account. The theorem in question states the equivalence of 'All R is M' and 'All not-M is not R', or **A** ≡ **A*!*** (*contraposition*). It is shown below that, although this holds in SMPL, it does not in the Square or similar intuitively more acceptable logical systems, unless they are restricted to natural sets.

In Table 8.1 below all VSs are listed for all sentence types defined in SMPL and the Square. To do this, one has to know whether any given sentence type is true or false for any of the situation classes 1–16 of Figure 8.3. This is decided on the basis of the semantic definitions of the quantifiers in the systems concerned. At least three definition styles are possible. The standard *syncategorematic* definitions of the quantifiers in SMPL are given in (8.2), where $\forall_x[R(x) \rightarrow M(x)]$ stands for **A** and $\exists_x[R(x) \wedge M(x)]$ stands for **I**:

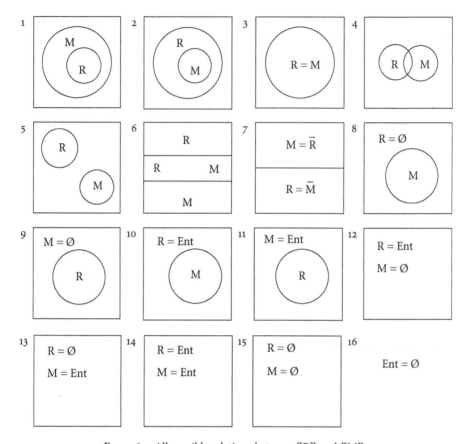

FIGURE 8.3 All possible relations between [[R]] and [[M]]

(8.2)   a. $\forall_x[R(x) \rightarrow M(x)]$ is true iff for all substitutions *a* for *x*, *a* being the name of some entity e $\in$ **Ent**, $R(a) \rightarrow M(a)$ is true.

   b. $\exists_x[R(x) \wedge M(x)]$ is true iff for at least one substitution *a* for *x*, *a* being the name of some entity e $\in$ **Ent**, $R(a) \wedge M(a)$ is true.

In (8.3), $\forall$ and $\exists$ are defined as *unary (higher-order) predicates over sets* (cp. Löbner 1990: 68):

(8.3)   a. $[[\forall]] = \{[[R(x) \rightarrow M(x)]] \mid [[R(x) \rightarrow M(x)]] = \textbf{Ent}\}$
   b. $[[\exists]] = \{[[R(x) \wedge M(x)]] \mid [[R(x) \wedge M(x)]] \neq \varnothing\}$

Both $[[R(x) \rightarrow M(x)]]$ and $[[R(x) \wedge M(x)]]$ denote a set of entities, given a state of affairs: $R(x) \rightarrow M(x)$ and $R(x) \wedge M(x)$ are thus, logically speaking, predicates. When $[[R(x) \rightarrow M(x)]]$ equals **Ent**, $\forall$ delivers truth; when $[[R(x) \wedge M(x)]]$ is nonnull, $\exists$ delivers truth. This is how Russell defined $\forall$ and $\exists$.

In both (8.2) and (8.3), the quantifiers are undefined for the case that Ent = Ø (case 16) for lack of possible substitutions. All one can do is stipulate that **A** is true but **I** false when Ent = Ø. This stipulation may be adopted here, in accordance with the definitions given in (8.4).

Then, since the definition styles (8.2) and (8.3) are possible only for quantifiers that are expressible in terms of truth functions, while most quantifiers other than ∀ and ∃ are not, a third alternative is preferable, consisting in defining ∀ and ∃ as *generalized quantifiers*.[4] In this alternative, the quantifiers are *binary higher-order predicates*, expressing a relation between the Restrictor set and the Matrix set. **A** and **I** are now written as $\forall_x(M(x),R(x))$ and $\exists_x(M(x),R(x))$, respectively.[5] Now the problem of a null Ent does not arise, since [[M]] and [[R]] denote sets, no matter whether they are arrived at by substitution rotating over Ent or as Ø given in advance because Ent = Ø.

As generalized quantifiers, ∀ and ∃ are defined as in (8.4):[6]

---

[4] This does not mean that I follow the theory of generalized quantifiers as it has existed in the literature since Barwise and Cooper (1981). My approach differs in essential respects from that theory, in particular in that I reject the notion of the subject term as a bundle of properties to which the predicate is added. I agree with Löbner (1990) that the primary function of definite terms is to establish reference and that a predicate P is a function that creates truth just in case the (n-tuple of) referent(s) is an element in the extension [[P]] of P (see also note 6 below).

[5] Most logicians (and myself also in footnote 3 above) place M(x) and R(x) in the opposite order, writing $\forall_x(R(x),M(x))$ for **A** and $\exists_x(R(x),M(x))$ for **I**. In the light of my grammatical theory (Seuren 1996) and of the arguments presented in section 4.4, I prefer to place M(x) in subject position and R(x) in direct object position, thus uniting the grammatical treatment of quantifiers with that of prepositional operators. Both first incorporate their object term, forming a composite prepositional or quantifying predicate, which is then lowered into the position reserved for it in the Matrix structure as it is at that stage of the cyclic treatment (see Figure 9.6 in section 9.10.2). Logically speaking, there is no difference. One notes, moreover, that OBJECT INCORPORATION is a very common, if not universal, grammatical process (as in English *take-care-of* or the verb *hammer* for 'use-a-hammer', or in nominalizations such as *cooking the meal*), whereas SUBJECT INCORPORATION is extremely rare. It occurs, for example, in the Paleosiberian language Chukchee (Muravyova 1992), which has impersonal composite verbs for meanings like 'grass-grow', so that 'it is grass-growing' means 'grass is growing'.

[6] My notion of generalized quantifier differs from the notion found in the bulk of the literature in that, in my analysis, definite determiners, such as *the*, do not count as quantifiers but form a linguistic category in their own right whose main use is to establish reference (see Löbner 1990: 10, 46, 66). In my theory, generalized quantifiers are binary higher-order predicates in logico-semantic structure, establishing a set-theoretic relation between two sets. The rationale for the generally accepted notion of generalized quantifiers is the overall demand for model-theoretic compositionality, which makes formal semanticists treat individuals as sets of properties, in stark contrast to the way they are treated in language and cognition. My main reason for rejecting that theory is that it does not agree with the linguistic facts. To take just two simple arguments from many that could be adduced, the unmarked, noncontrastive negation of *Many boys laughed*, with the existential quantifier *many*, is *Not many boys laughed*. *Many boys did not laugh*, with the internal negation, is not the negation of *Many boys laughed*. By contrast, the negation of *The boy laughed* is *The boy did not laugh*, and not **Not the boy laughed*. No distinction between the external (sentential) and the internal (predicate) negation is available here (as already noted by Aristotle). Then, propositional operators, such as *possibly* naturally go with a grade-1, non-contrastive rising accent on the highest predicate of the S-structure forming their scope in logico-semantic structure. For example, we have *Possibly* ALL *boys laughed, Possibly* SOME *boy(s) laughed, Possibly,* MOST *boys laughed*, but not **Possibly* THE *boy(s) laughed* (for further comment, see Seuren 2010: 386–95).

(8.4) a. $[[\forall]] = \{<[[R]],[[M]]> \mid [[R]] \subseteq [[M]]\}$
       b. $[[\exists]] = \{<[[R]],[[M]]> \mid [[R]] \cap [[M]] \neq \emptyset\}$

To define the Square the help is needed of the definitions given in (8.2), (8.3) or (8.4) but these definitions do not suffice since what they define is SMPL, not the Square. Contrary to what is commonly taken for granted (for example Parsons 2006, 2008), the Square is not defined by simply adding the condition that $[[R]] \neq \emptyset$ to the definitions of (8.2a), (8.3a) or (8.4a). As is shown in section 8.4.1, the Conversions ($A \equiv \neg I^*$ and $I \equiv \neg A^*$) are no longer valid when this condition is added, but are reduced to one-way entailments from I^* to $\neg A$ and from I to $\neg A^*$, as A is now false when $[[R]] = \emptyset$. To retain the Square, complete with the Conversions, we have no choice but to leave out of account the situations 8, 13, 15 and 16, where $[[R]] = \emptyset$. This keeps the system consistent but restricted to situations where $[[R]] \neq \emptyset$, thus causing what is generally seen as the logical defect of *undue existential import* (UEI). Given the overall restriction that $[[R]] \neq \emptyset$ (and thus $\mathbf{Ent} \neq \emptyset$), the definitions given in (8.2), (8.3) and (8.4) carry over to the logical system known as the Square.

We now know when and how to assign truth or falsity to all sentence types defined above with regard to the situation classes of Figure 8.3, no matter which style of quantifier definition is used. The result is shown in Table 8.1. The second column, for the Square, leaves out all situation classes where the Restrictor predicate extension is null, because, as we have seen, the Square is undefined for such cases.

Table 8.1 shows that the extension of the Square with inversion and/or preposed internal negation brings little news. The main result is that $I \equiv I!$ and $I^* \equiv I^*!$. As Aristotle said (*Prior Analytics* 25a10–11), in existentially quantified sentences, Restrictor and Matrix terms can be interchanged *salva veritate*. Both /I/ and /I!/ equal {1,2,3,4,6,10,11,14}, in both the Square and SMPL. For the rest, the logical relations valid in the Square are simply transferred from this system to its inverted analog.

Although, in SMPL, 'All R is M' ≡ 'All not-M is not R' ($A \equiv A^*!^*$), this does not hold in the Square. In the Square, /A/ = {1,3,11,14} but /A*!*/ = {1,3,8,15}. The equivalence can be maintained only if the non-natural sets $\emptyset$ and $\mathbf{Ent}$ (situations 8–16) are left out of account and the logic is restricted to natural sets only. Yet in SMPL the equivalence $A \equiv A^*!^*$ does hold, since, in SMPL, both /A/ and /A*!*/ equal {1,3,8,11,13,14,15,16}.

Likewise, in the Square, $A^* \not\equiv A!^*$, as /A*/ = {5,7,9,12} but /A!*/ = {5,7,8,13}, again due to the extreme values $\emptyset$ and $\mathbf{Ent}$. But in SMPL, the equivalence $A^* \equiv A!^*$ does hold: both /A*/ and /A!*/ equal {5,7,8,9,12,13,15,16}. The same holds, of course, for *A and *A! ($\equiv A^*!$): they are equivalent only within the limits of natural sets, since both then have the VS {6,7}.

TABLE 8.1 The VSs for all sentence types in SMPL and the Square

SMPL	Square (minus 8,13,15,16)
/A/ = {1,3,8,11,13,14,15,16}	/A/ = {1,3,11,14}
/¬A/ = {2,4,5,6,7,9,10,12}	/¬A/ = {2,4,5,6,7,9,10,12}
/I/ = {1,2,3,4,6,10,11,14}	/I/ = {1,2,3,4,6,10,11,14}
/¬I/ = {5,7,8,9,12,13,15,16}	/¬I/ = {5,7,9,12}
/A*/ = {5,7,8,9,12,13,15,16}	/A*/ = {5,7,9,12}
/¬A*/ = {1,2,3,4,6,10,11,14}	/¬A*/ = {1,2,3,4,6,7,10,11,14}
/I*/ = {2,4,5,6,7,9,10,12}	/I*/ = {2,4,5,6,7,9,10,12}
/¬I*/ = {1,3,8,11,13,14,15,16}	/¬I*/ = {1,3,11,14}

SMPL	Square (minus 9,12,15,16)
/A!/ = {2,3,9,10,12,14,15,16}	/A!/ = {2,3,10,14}
/¬A!/ = {1,4,5,6,7,8,11,13}	/¬A!/ = {1,4,5,6,7,8,11,13}
/I!/ = {1,2,3,4,6,10,11,14}	/I!/ = {1,2,3,4,6,10,11,14}
/¬I!/ = {5,7,8,9,12,13,15,16}	/¬I!/ = {5,7,8,13}
/A!*/ = {5,7,8,9,12,13,15,16}	/A!*/ = {5,7,8,13}
/¬A!*/ = {1,2,3,4,6,10,11,14}	/¬A!*/ = {1,2,3,4,6,10,11,14)
/I!*/ = {1,4,5,6,7,8,11,13}	/I!*/ = {1,4,5,6,7,8,11,13)
/¬I!*/ = {2,3,9,10,12,14,15,16}	/¬I!*/ = {2,3,10,14}

SMPL	Square (minus 10,12,14,16)
/*A/ = {6,7,10,11,12,13,14,16}	/*A/ = {6,7,11,13}
/¬*A/ = {1,2,3,4,5,8,9,15}	/¬*A/ = {1,2,3,4,5,8,9,15}
/*I/ = {1,4,5,6,7,8,11,13}	/*I/ = {1,4,5,6,7,8,11,13}
/¬*I/ = {2,3,9,10,12,14,15,16}	/¬*I/ = {2,3,9,15}
/*A*/ = {2,3,9,10,12,14,15,16}	/*A*/ = {2,3,9,15}
/¬*A*/ = {1,4,5,6,7,8,11,13}	/¬*A*/ = {1,4,5,6,7,8,11,13}
/*I*/ = {1,2,3,4,5,8,9,15}	/*I*/ = {1,2,3,4,5,8,9,15}
/¬*I*/ = {6,7,10,11,12,13,14,16}	/¬*I*/ = {6,7,11,13}

SMPL	Square (minus 11,13,14,16)
/A*!/ = {6,7,10,11,12,13,14,16}	/A*!/ = {6,7,10,12}
/¬A*!/ = {1,2,3,4,5,8,9,15}	/¬A*!/ = {1,2,3,4,5,8,9,15}
/I*!/ = {2,4,5,6,7,9,10,12}	/I*!/ = {2,4,5,6,7,9,10,12}
/¬I*!/ = {1,3,8,11,13,14,15,16}	/¬I*!/ = {1,3,8,15}
/A*!*/ = {1,3,8,11,13,14,15,16}	/A*!*/ = {1,3,8,15}
/¬A*!*/ = {2,4,5,6,7,9,10,12}	/¬A*!*/ = {2,4,5,6,7,9,10,12}
/I*!*/ = {1,2,3,4,5,8,9,15}	/I*!*/ = {1,2,3,4,5,8,9,15}
/¬I*!*/ = {6,7,10,11,12,13,14,16}	/¬I*!*/ = {6,7,10,12}

The question is now: how do we construct VS-models for the logics concerned? Cutting out the inverted sentence types and the preposed internal negation and thus restricting ourselves to the sentence types that have been constitutive for logical systems from the Aristotelian beginnings onward, we compile Table 8.2, which lists the sentence types that are true in each situation class.

This allows us to reduce the sixteen situation classes to four *pooled superclasses*, for both SMPL and the Square, each superclass being a truth-maker for a specific set of sentence types and for a specific set of truth conditions. For SMPL, the situation classes in $\{1,3,8,11,13,14,15,16\}$ are truth-makers for both A and $\neg I^*$, those in $\{2,4,5,6,7,9,10,12\}$ for both $\neg A$ and I^*, those in $\{1,2,3,4,6,10,11,14\}$ for both I and $\neg A^*$ and those in $\{5,7,8,9,12,13,15,16\}$ for both $\neg I$ and A^*. The same holds for the Square, except that the situation classes 8, 13, 15 and 16 are to be disregarded since here $[[R]] = \emptyset$.

There are thus four new (super)spaces. (Super)space 1 is reserved for cases where $[[R]] \neq \emptyset$ and $[[R]] \subseteq [[M]]$, (super)space 2 for those where $[[R]] \cap [[M]] \neq \emptyset$ but $[[R]] \nsubseteq [[M]]$ (cases where $[[M]] \subset [[R]]$ are included), and (super)space 3 for situations where $[[R]] \cap [[M]] = \emptyset$ but $[[R]] \neq \emptyset$. (Super)space 4, inoperative in the Square, is reserved for cases where $[[R]] = \emptyset$.

TABLE 8.2 **Standard sentence types listed for each situation class**

Situation class:	truth for sentence types:	pooled superclass:
1	A, I, $\neg A^*$, $\neg I^*$	1
2	$\neg A$, I, $\neg A^*$, I^*	2
3	A, I, $\neg A^*$, $\neg I^*$	1
4	$\neg A$, I, $\neg A^*$, I^*	2
5	$\neg A$, $\neg I$, A^*, I^*	3
6	$\neg A$, I, $\neg A^*$, I^*	2
7	$\neg A$, $\neg I$, A^*, I^*	3
8	A, $\neg I$, A^*, $\neg I^*$	4 (not in Square)
9	$\neg A$, $\neg I$, A^*, I^*	3
10	$\neg A$, I, $\neg A^*$, I^*	2
11	A, I, $\neg A^*$, $\neg I^*$	1
12	$\neg A$, $\neg I$, A^*, I^*	3
13	A, $\neg I$, A^*, $\neg I^*$	4 (not in Square)
14	A, I, $\neg A^*$, $\neg I^*$	1
15	A, $\neg I$, A^*, $\neg I^*$	4 (not in Square)
16	A, $\neg I$, A^*, $\neg I^*$	4 (not in Square)

This can be graphically represented as in Figure 8.4–a, representing SMPL, where each ring represents a pooled superclass, numbered from 1 to 4. Space 4 is reserved for the situation classes 8, 13, 15, 16, where [[R]] = Ø. The same is done for the Square in Figure 8.4–b, where space 4 (pooling the situation classes 8, 13, 15, 16) must be left blank, because the Square is unable to cater for cases where [[R]] = Ø.

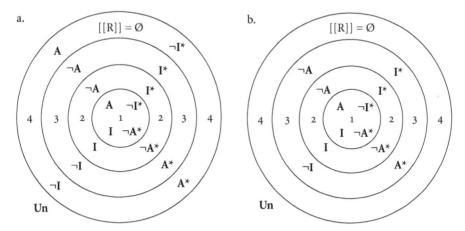

FIGURE 8.4 The VS-models for (a) SMPL and (b) the Square

VS-models of the kind shown in Figure 8.4 allow one to list the VSs (in terms of pooled superclasses) for each of the eight sentence types in question in the manner of Table 8.3.

TABLE 8.3 **The pooled VSs for the eight standard sentence types**

SMPL	Square (minus space 4):
/A/ = {1,4}	/A/ = {1}
/¬A/ = {2,3}	/¬A/ = {2,3}
/I/ = {1,2}	/I/ = {1,2}
/¬I/ = {3,4}	/¬I/ = {3}
/A*/ = {3,4}	/A*/ = {3}
/¬A*/ = {1,2}	/¬A*/ = {1,2}
/I*/ = {2,3}	/I*/ = {2,3}
/¬I*/ = {1,4}	/¬I*/ = {1}

This again makes it possible to read off the logical relations that hold for any pair of sentence types in the language given, following the VS-definitions of the logical relations specified in (8.1) above. These relations can then be visualized as an *octagonal figure*, where each of the eight vertices stands for a sentence type and each pair of vertices is either characterized by some logical relation or left uncharacterized, in which case the two vertices in question are logically independent. Figure 8.5 shows the resulting octagons for SMPL (a) and the Square (b). The VS corresponding to each vertex is specified, so that the logical relations are easily read off the octagonal representation (= stands for equivalence, CD for contradictoriness, C for contrariety, SC for subcontrariety, > for entailment).

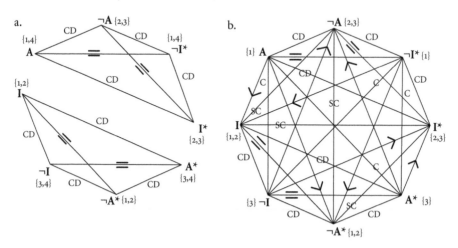

FIGURE 8.5 The octagons for (a) SMPL and (b) the Square

The octagonal representation is a further extension of the Square notation, assigning a vertex to each sentence type. The classic Square notation, given in Figure 8.6–a, results from a reduction of all equivalent pairs of vertices to single vertices. The equivalent Figure 8.6–b reveals that the Square really is a composition of the two logically isomorphic triads <A,I,¬I> and <A*,I*,¬I*>—which shows that the internal negation of the M-predicate makes no logical difference, as the logic is defined by the meanings of the operators (see the MODULO-*-PRINCIPLE and the ISOMORPHY PRINCIPLE in Seuren 2010: 33–6). Compared with the Square, SMPL is so impoverished that a Square representation no longer makes any sense.

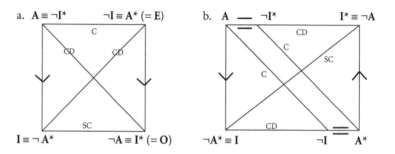

FIGURE 8.6 The classic Square (a), represented as two isomorphic triangles (b)

Representations such as those in Figure 8.5–a,b or in Figure 8.6–a,b allow one to see at a glance which logical relation, if any, holds between any two sentence types. One also notes that the octagon for the Square is, technically speaking, *complete*, in that some logical relation exists between any pair of sentence types, whereas the octagon for SMPL, shown in Figure 8.5–a, is highly incomplete, as most pairs of sentence types are logically independent. The difference resides only in the fact that, when $[[R]] = \emptyset$, A- and A*-type sentences are declared true in SMPL, while in the Square they are undefined.

8.4 Valuation spaces and polygons for other logical systems

8.4.1 *Aristotelian-Abelardian predicate logic (AAPL)*

Aristotle's original logic never suffered from undue existential import (UEI) the way the traditional Square does. Abelard saw that and restored Aristotle's predicate logic to its original, exceptionless, form (Seuren 2010: Ch. 5). Yet this fact seems to have escaped the notice of the logical world.[7]

For both Aristotle and Abelard, A- and A*-type sentences are false when $[[R]] = \emptyset$. VS-modelling makes one see the result at a glance. Figure 8.4 shows that SMPL and the Square are identical but for space 4, left blank in the Square but giving truth for A- and A*-sentences in SMPL. What happens when they are declared false in space 4 is shown in Figure 8.7, which gives the resulting VS-model and octagon. This is the logic originally developed by Aristotle and made explicit by Peter Abelard around 1125, without the overlay created by Aristotle's commentators Apuleius, Ammonius and Boethius (Seuren 2010: 136–8). We speak accordingly of *Aristotelian-Abelardian predicate logic* or AAPL.

Other than the Square, AAPL is not open to the criticism that the system collapses when $[[R]] = \emptyset$, as it caters for all admissible situations, including those that involve the null set. It is less powerful than the Square, in that it contains fewer logical relations, but it is a great deal more powerful than SMPL. Notably, the subaltern entailment schema holds in AAPL, since $/A/ = \{1\}$ is included in $/I/ = \{1,2\}$.

Interestingly, contraposition of the A-type does not hold in AAPL, and in general in all systems where A* is false or undefined when $[[R]] = \emptyset$, since a sentence like *All men are beings* is true in this world but its contraposition *All non-beings are non-men* is false, the class of non-beings being necessarily empty. Contraposition of the A-type only holds in those systems where A* is true when $[[R]] = \emptyset$.

---

[7] William and Martha Kneale did notice (Kneale and Kneale 1962: 57) that Aristotle (*On Interpretation* 17b16–26 and 20a16–23) only stated the one-way entailment from A* to ¬I and rejected the converse, thus steering clear of the Conversions, but they seem to have missed the importance of this fact for the logical system concerned. On page 210 of the same book they write that Aristotle, apparently, 'did not intend [. . .] anything different from the doctrine later attributed to him by Boethius'. The Kneales might not have committed this error if they had had the system of VS-modelling at their disposal.

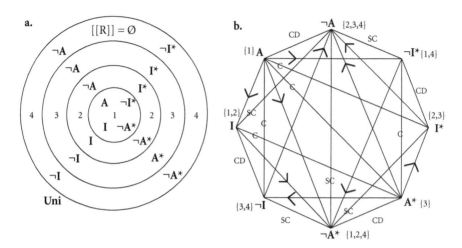

FIGURE 8.7 The VS-model and octagon for AAPL

The quantifiers are defined as in (8.4) above, except that the universal quantifier has the extra condition that $[[R]] \neq \emptyset$, as in (8.4a'):

(8.4)   a'. $[[\forall]] = \{<[[R]],[[M]]> \mid [[R]] \subseteq [[M]] \text{ and } [[R]] \neq \emptyset\}$

The added condition that $[[R]] \neq \emptyset$ does not save the Square, as is often maintained, as it changes the Conversions into one-way entailments. In fact, the two quantifiers cannot be defined in set-theoretical terms, in the manner of (8.4a'), in such a way that they yield the logic of the Square. An extra condition must be stipulated to the effect that the Conversions hold. It is precisely this extra condition that makes the Square unsound: in a sound logic, the operators must be fully definable in strictly set-theoretical terms. The Square, therefore, cannot be kept intact other than by presuppositional means.

8.4.2 'Leaking' the O-corner

Not all logicians, in the course of the post-Abelardian history of logic, have accepted this conclusion. Some have tried to save the traditional Square by stipulating that the old E- and O-corners (that is, the A*- and I*-vertices, and their respective equivalents ¬I and ¬A, of Figure 8.5–b) lack existential import, letting only the A- and I-corners, and their equivalents, retain it. This answer to the UEI-problem of the Square is often irreverently called the 'leaking O-corner analysis', which I abbreviate to the hopefully more respectable LOCA.

LOCA was adopted, or in any case tried out, by some fourteenth-century nominalist philosophers, in particular by Buridan and Ockham, and a bevy of fifteenth-century philosophers (see Ashworth 1973), and then again, surprisingly, by some twentieth-century American philosophers, notably Moody (1953), Thompson (1953), Klima (1988) and Parsons (2006, 2008). On the face of it, this solution has a great deal going for it, since on the stipulation that only the A- and I-corners and their equivalents have existential import, the Square remains entirely intact, as is shown in Figure 8.8.

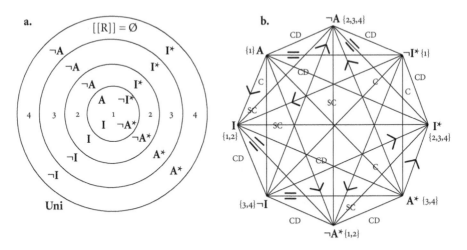

FIGURE 8.8 The predicate logic resulting from LOCA

This analysis, however, does not stand up to scrutiny. One problem is that LOCA makes it impossible to provide unitary meaning descriptions for the natural language quantifiers. Both SOME and ALL will have to be defined as inducing existential import—that is, requiring that $[[R]] \neq \emptyset$—when the Matrix predicate M(x) is non-negated, but as losing existential import when M(x) is negated. Yet both M(x) and ¬M(x) are sentential functions and thus take sets as their denotations. This would mean that SOME and ALL have existential import with positively defined Matrix sets, but lack existential import with negatively defined Matrix sets. Not only is this intuitively repugnant, as it would assign existential import to (8.5a), which is of type I, but take it away from (8.5b), which is of type I*:

(8.5)   a. Some men are unmarried.
        b. Some men are not married.

It is also logically repugnant, as it requires different meaning descriptions for the quantifiers according to whether the Matrix clause M(x) is negated or non-negated, which goes against the MODULO-*-PRINCIPLE (see Figure 8.6-b above and Seuren 2010: 33–6).[8]

---

[8] An analogous result is obtained when one lets the I-corner leak, so that (absurdly) the A- and I-corners do not have existential import while the A*- and I*-corners do. On that assumption the Square is likewise saved, as is easily checked, but analogous objections are raised. In particular, the existential quantifier can no longer be given one single definition.

To avoid this difficulty, Klima (1988) and Parsons (2006, 2008), using a late-medieval device to justify the assignment of falsity to sentences like *This unicorn is a mammal*, introduced an ontological zero element ø, defined as being devoid of an extension (referent) but as having the property of being allowed as a substitution for variables in a sentential function P(x) generally when [[P]] = Ø and otherwise when the logical system allows for substitution, though it does not produce truth but falsity when thus used.[9] This is taken to hold for all extensional predicates—that is, for predicates that require actual existence for their subject term referent. Intensional predicates, which lack this condition, such as *be imaginary* or *be talked about*, are not included in this analysis.

Stripped of the unnecessary formal complexities in Klima and, especially, Parsons,[10] the use of ø is seen to require so-called *restricted quantification* (Geach 1962), where the range of the variables is restricted to the Restrictor predicate extension [[R]] and **A** is read as 'for all x such that x ∈ [[R]], M(x)' is true, or ∀x:R(x) | M(x) (where the part between the colon and the upright stroke is, if you like, the *range* of the restricted quantifier ∀x or ∃x and the part after the upright stroke is the *argument*). Likewise, **I** is read as 'for some such that x ∈ [[S]], M(x)', or ∃x:R(x) | M(x). In the same vein, **A*** is read as 'for all x ∈ [[R]], ¬Mx', or ∀x:R(x) | ¬M(x), and **I*** as 'for at least one x ∈ [[R]], ¬Mx', or ∃x:R(x) | ¬M(x).

Given that, in restricted quantification, a *legitimate substitution is a substitution of a name for any element e yielding truth for the range*, we get the following truth conditions for **A** and **I**:

(8.6) a. ∀x:R(x) | M(x) is true iff for all legitimate substitutions *a* for *x* in M(x), M(a) is true.

   b. ∃x:R(x) | M(x) is true iff for at least one legitimate substitution *a* for *x* in M(x), M(a) is true.

---

[9] Klima and Parsons may well have been inspired, besides the medieval sources, by the wayward but sharp British philosopher Hugh MacColl (see Astroh et al. 2001 for his biography), too easily dismissed in Russell's famous 'On denoting' (1905: 491). MacColl (1905a, 1905b) defined the null class Ø as consisting of all non-actual, virtual entities, so that the phrase *the present king of France* would denote any member of Ø and produce falsity. Russell's rejection of MacColl's analysis, though justified in itself, is based on the false contention that this is what Alexius Meinong held, that position having been rejected earlier on in the article on the again false grounds that this would violate the Law of Contradiction. It is ironical that such a uniquely influential article as Russell (1905) should be so replete with errors and false attributions.

[10] Parsons' formalism is unduly complex, but reduces, in the end, to Geach-style restricted quantification. Besides, Parsons does not use the symbol ø but a hyphen, calling hyphen substitution 'substitution of nothing', which is misleading because when nothing is substituted, the variable simply stays in place. (This amounts to the ploy used by Odysseus in Homer's *Odyssey*, when Odysseus escaped from the Cyclops Polyphemus, whose single eye he had just pierced with a red-hot club, by telling the Cyclops that his name was 'No-one'. When the blinded Polyphemus called on his fellow Cyclopes for help and revenge, he told them that No-one had pierced his eye, which made the other Cyclopes think that it must have been the Gods punishing Polyphemus.) In an epilogue called 'Epicycle', Parsons discusses the philosophical question of the reification of 'nothing', quoting various ancient, medieval and modern authors. But he does not come to any clear conclusion.

The problem here is that when [[R]] = Ø, there is no legitimate substitution for *x* in M (x), so that no truth value can be established. This perennial problem of restricted quantification is why this system has not had a career in logic. But apart from that, with ø added, following Klima and Parsons, as a (or, rather, the only) legitimate substitution when [[R]] = Ø, M(ø) is false and hence ¬M(ø) true. This makes ∀x:R(x) | M(x) false but ∀x:R(x) | ¬M(x) true when [[R]] = Ø, and likewise for ∃x:R(x) | M(x) and ∃x:R(x) | ¬M(x).

Though ingenious, this answer runs foul of a variety of problems. First, the introduction of ø leads to paradox, as shown by sentence (8.7):

(8.7)   ø is the zero element.

Here, against the instruction for the substitution of ø, ø has been taken as a value for the variable *x* in the sentential function *Be the zero element(x)* even though [[Be the zero element]] ≠ Ø since it contains ø as its only element. Moreover, although (8.7) is obviously true because ø is, in fact, the zero element, it should be false because ø stands in for the variable *x* in the sentential function *Be the zero element(x)*. Likewise paradoxical is the answer to the question whether ø does or does not belong to any predicate extension [[P]], when [[P]] = Ø. If it does, then why does it produce falsity? If it does not, then why is it a legitimate substitution for *x* in P(x)? All this shows ø to be an ontological monstrosity.

Another drawback is the unnaturalness of having to say that *All flags are not green* and *Some flags are not green* are true in the absence of any flags. This unnaturalness stands out most clearly for **I***-sentences: when I say *Some flags are not green*, I may justifiably be expected to be able to produce a specific flag that is not green—the standard procedure of *existential instantiation*. When there are no flags at all and I produce the zero element as an instance of a flag that is not green, my interlocutor will have good reason to consider me a crook. This means that the introduction of ø blocks the procedure of existential instantiation, widely used in logical proof theory, which allows one to posit an arbitrary entity *a* for *x* in any true proposition headed by the existential quantifier so as to see what happens to *a* in the rest of the logical derivation. This again leads up straight to the point that the notion 'extension of a predicate *P*' now becomes problematic: if ø ∈ [[P]], why does it produce falsity for P (x)? If ø ∉ [[P]], why is it an admissible substitution within the range of [[P]] ? All this seems to me to be sufficient grounds for saying that ø is logically and ontologically vicious, and that, in any case, LOCA is a non-candidate for the position of Logic of Language.

But does it save the Square and is it still a good logic? My answer is that it does not save the Square and is not a good logic. I will first show that it does not save the Square. According to Aristotle (*Prior Analytics* 25a8–14), I and I! (Some M is R) are equivalent. That this is so, is easily seen: I is true just in case [[R]] ∩ [[M]] ≠ Ø; I! is true just in case $[[M]] \cap [[R]] \neq \varnothing$; $[[M]] \cap [[R]] = [[R]] \cap [[M]]$; hence, **I!** is true just in case $[[R]] \cap [[M]] \neq \varnothing$. Likewise for the equivalence of **I*** (Some R is not-M) and **I*!** (Some not-M is R): **I*** is true just in case $[[R]] \cap [[\overline{M}]] \neq \varnothing$; **I*!** is true just in case $[[\overline{M}]] \cap [[R]] \neq \varnothing$; $[[R]] \cap [[\overline{M}]] = [[\overline{M}]] \cap [[R]]$; hence, **I*!** is true just in case $[[R]] \cap [[\overline{M}]] \neq \varnothing$. In Aristotelian-Boethian and Aristotelian-Abelardian logic, as well as in standard modern logic, all of which have a symmetrical existential quantifier, both **I** and **I*** are thus equivalent with their inversions **I!** and **I*!**, respectively. In these logics, the following principle, derived from their set-theoretical foundations, holds:

Under the existential quantifier, the Restrictor term and the Matrix term (range and argument) are freely interchangeable *salva veritate*.

In the ø-variant of LOCA, however, which is claimed by its authors to be the proper analysis of the Square, this does not hold—unless the function ¬M(x) is banned and only lexically negative predicates like non-M(x) are allowed. This is shown as follows. Take a situation Σ where $[[R]] = \{a,b,c\}$ $(a,b,c \in \mathbf{Ent})$ and $[[M]] = \varnothing$. 'Some R is not M' (**I***), analysed as $\exists x{:}R(x) \mid \neg M(x)$, is true in Σ, since a, b and c are the legitimate substitutions for x in M(x) and ¬M(a), ¬M(b) and ¬M(c) are all true, which satisfies the truth condition for **I*** as formulated above. However, 'Some not-M is R' (**I*!**), analysed as $\exists x{:}\neg M(x) \mid R(x)$, is false in Σ, since, given that $[[M]] = \varnothing$, the only legitimate substitution for x in R(x) is the zero element ø yielding falsity for R(x).

One could propose to modify the substitution conditions for ø in such a way that all elements e in **Ent** are admitted in M(x), since all e in **Ent** satisfy the range ¬M(x), which would make the range of the formula $\exists x{:}\neg M(x) \mid R(x)$ equal to **Ent**. This would make **I*!** true, just like **I***. But now the problem reappears for a situation Σ', in which, again, $[[R]] = \{a,b,c\}$ but $[[M]] = \mathbf{Ent}$. Now **I*** is false but **I*!** is undecidable since now all elements in **Ent** yield falsity for the range ¬M(x) of $\exists x{:}\neg M(x) \mid R(x)$, which leaves this formula without any legitimate substitution for x in R(x) and hence with its truth value undecided. LOCA thus fails to save the Square.

That it is also at least doubtful as a logic appears from the fact that it undermines the set-theoretic foundations of the system, in that the Restrictor term and the Matrix term of existentially quantified propositions are no longer freely interchangeable *salva veritate* although they should be according to their semantic definition, which is based on set-theoretical necessity.

This argument against the ø-variant of LOCA hinges on the assumption that there is no logical difference between a negative predicate *not-P*, as a predicate in its own right, and the negated function ¬[P(x)]. This question is much debated in the literature, especially by Locists, but, as far as I can see, it is a mere red herring. The answer is actually quite simple. Under the standard axiom of bivalence, the two sentences *The flag is not green* and *The flag is not-green*, both with a definite (singular) subject term, are logically equivalent. Any difference there may be has to do with different *presuppositions*. As Aristotle already observed, the only generalization that can be made for a predicate *P* and its negative counterpart *not-P* (or *un-P*, or whatever morphological or lexical means the language has available for creating negative predicates) is that they make for *contrary* sentences, which cannot both be true, but can both be false. A sentence like *The unicorn is not polite* is reckoned to be true in standard bivalent logic, given the absence of real unicorns in this world. But *The unicorn is not-polite*, or rather *The unicorn is impolite*, is false, as it is subject to the presupposition, induced by the predicate *(im)polite*, to the effect that the subject term referent must be an animate being taking part in social life.[11]

In standard bivalent logic, however, whether of the Aristotelian or of the Russellian kind, there is no truth-conditional difference. *The flag is not green* has the proposition underlying *The flag is green* under the sentential negation operator ¬ and says that the flag does not belong to the set of green things. *The flag is not-green* has the same operator ¬, but now internally, over the propositional function Green(x), which, as has been known since Frege, is also a predicate. It says that the flag belongs to the set of things that are not green, which, on the standard assumption that the universe of entities **Ent** is divided into those entities that are green and those that are not green, is the same as saying that the flag does not belong to the set of green things. The two are thus truth-conditionally equivalent.[12]

For sentences with a quantified subject term, the same conclusion follows. In *No flag is green*, the negation has large scope and stands over the embedded proposition *Some flag is green*. In *Some flag is not green*, *some*, or $\exists x$, has large scope and stands over the embedded propositional function ¬(Green(x)), which, as has just been shown, is equivalent with Not-green(x). It follows that this last sentence is logically equivalent with *Some flag is not-green*. Since only singular and quantified sentences figure in the logics at issue, it follows that in all cases, whether the sentence has a definite ('singular') or a quantified subject term, *not P* equals *not-P*. The conclusion is thus that, for the systems concerned (which means that presuppositions are not involved), there is no logical difference between *not P* and *not-P*.

Locists who rely on ∅ will reply that, if [[M]] = ∅, the single predicate extension [[not-M]] is the complement of [[M]] in **Ent**, so that each element in **Ent** qualifies as

---

[11] In Strawson's (1950) presupposition theory *The unicorn is not polite* is taken to lack a truth value due to presupposition failure. In my theory of trivalent presuppositonal logic, detailed in many publications since 1985 and recapitulated again in Seuren (2010: 311–77), the sentence is ambiguous, according to whether the negation is *minimal* (presupposition-preserving), in which case the sentence is radically false due to presupposition failure, or *radical* (presupposition-cancelling), in which case the sentence is true. By contrast, the internal predicate negation in *The unicorn is not-polite* can only be minimal (the radical negation cannot occur internally) making this sentence radically false. But when presuppositions are left out of account, the hyphen makes no logical difference.

[12] I disregard here the analysis, current in most forms of present-day formal semantics but abhorrent to me (see notes 4 and 6 above), in which the definite article is analysed as a quantifier. Even in that analysis, however, the argument that there is no truth-conditional difference between *not P* and *not-P* in sentences with a definite noun phrase as subject term stands.

an admissible substitution, in *Some not-M is R*, for *x* in the range of the existential quantifier. This will make I*! true in the situation *Σ* described above, just like I*, because [[not-M]] = **Ent** and {a,b,c}—the extension of *R*—is included in **Ent**. This is correct, as far as I can see, but it implies that functions of the form ¬(P(x)) are banned from the logical language of the ø-variant of LOCA, on pain of inconsistency of the logic concerned, and that only functions of the form 'not-P(x)', or 'un-P(x)', are allowed, because it is only with the latter that the ø-variant of LOCA avoids logical disaster. Such a restriction, however, is entirely *ad hoc* and not supported by any independent logical principle or metaprinciple. No logical system can have its soundness depend on such an arbitrary stipulation. The introduction of the zero element into predicate logic thus looks very much like tinkering undertaken with the sole purpose of rescuing the Square as a valid logical system. And, incidentally, it is historically unthinkable that Aristotle would have envisaged anything like LOCA, with or without ø. It seems to me that this should put paid to this analysis.

8.4.3 *Basic-natural predicate logic (BNPL)*

8.4.3.1 *The inadequacy of the Gricean solution*   Much has been written about the question of whether natural language *some* should be taken to mean 'some perhaps all' ('not null'), as in standard logic, or 'some but not all' ('only some'). The accepted view nowadays is that *some* 'really' means 'some perhaps all', and that the meaning 'some but not all', which strikes us as being the most natural meaning, is the result of pragmatic factors operative in language use, in particular the Gricean maxim 'Make your contribution as informative as is required' (Grice 1975: 45).

The Gricean maxims are practical principles meant to 'correct' or restrict literal meanings based on (established) logic. Their application is taken to produce the Gricean *implicatures*—non-cogent inferences drawn by the listener on the basis of the maxims. Thus, when a speaker says *Some children got hurt*, there will be an implicature that not all children got hurt, provided it is assumed that the speaker (a) has full knowledge of the discussion domain and (b) observes the maxims. This is probably correct, but it is too weak to explain the mismatch between natural logical intuitions and standard logic.

In general, the maxims are too weak. For example, they fail to account for the fact that self-entailment (A⊢A), though valid, is counterintuitive, that subcontrariety is almost impossible to grasp intuitively, whereas contrariety is simple, that some logical equivalences are intuitively obvious whereas others are not. For example, logically naïve speakers immediately understand that *He liked neither planes nor trains* is equivalent with *He didn't like planes and he didn't like trains*. Yet *He didn't like planes and trains* is not immediately understood as *He didn't like planes or he didn't like trains*; in fact, a great deal of intellectual effort is required to establish the latter equivalence. Yet in standard logic the equivalences have equal status, due to De

Morgan's Conversion Laws. Finally, and perhaps most stringently, if the literal meaning of *some X* is 'not null'—that is, either all X or a part of X—there is no way the Gricean maxims can account for the unequivocal meanings of the expressions *only some* or *no more than some*. The only answer left is to say that at least one literal meaning of *some X* is 'part of X', which, when extended with a preposed *at least,* gives the 'not null' meaning of standard logic.

Logic is not to be tampered with. It is like traffic: you have to follow the rules and respect the meanings of the road signs. While politeness and an understanding of each other's intentions is useful and desirable, a *flouting* of the traffic rules or the road signs because you trust that the other driver, or the pedestrian, will guess your intention may cost lives. When you arrive in another, perhaps less developed, country, with different traffic rules and different meanings for the road signs, you had better not simply take it for granted that the traffic system you have in your safe home country is universally or necessarily valid in all other countries, ascribing the deviant behaviour of traffic participants to their informal understanding of each other's intentions, required because of the bad road conditions and the great variety of rickety vehicles. Such an attitude may land you in serious trouble. To avoid trouble, you are best advised to try and find out precisely what the traffic system in that foreign land amounts to.

For the logician, natural language is a foreign country, which, on the face of it, looks badly organized and unruly. Many logicians commit the error of assuming—condescendingly—that the place has no proper traffic code and that people avoid accidents on the basis of an intuitive mutual understanding of their intentions. One (not very good) logician who made this mistake then tried to capture these intentions in the format of a set of 'maxims', non-cogent principles that he hoped would allow him to get by—only to find out in the end that the country in question does have a proper traffic code after all and that his 'maxims' have landed him with a hefty fine or in jail.

This is the situation in natural language. It may look unruly and badly organized, but in fact it is highly organized and it has its own very well worked-out logical code, which is a great deal more functional than the streamlined and *a priori* logical code in the Olympian world of the logicians. Flouting or bending the rules and meanings of natural language because you trust the hearer will grasp your intention may go well for a while, but it may cause serious damage when it comes to the crunch and your listener takes you up on your meanings. And because the 'crunch' is usually about matters of logic, this applies especially to *logical meanings*—that is, the meanings of the logical operators, which define the logical system that is at work.

8.4.3.2 *The logical system of BNPL*

So let us take some distance from the logic of the professional logicians and try out a logical system where *some* means just 'part of', without the added 'perhaps all', and let us see if we can propose such a logic as the natural predicate logic that humans are endowed with at birth (not, of course, as an explicit calculus present in the conscious brain, but in the form of naturally given lexical meanings for the quantifiers and the negation, on the basis of which we, analysts, can formulate the logical system following from those meanings). This would make the Gricean maxims not false but otiose as an explanatory factor.

This hypothetical *basic-natural predicate logic* (BNPL) was first formulated by William Hamilton in his posthumous (1866) and later also by Otto Jespersen (1917: 86; 1924: 324), who was, admittedly, not a good logician but an excellent linguist. The central feature of BNPL is that *some* is taken to mean 'some but not all'—the so-called *exclusive some*. In this logic, there are three mutually contrary basic operators: *all*, exclusive *some*, and *no*, corresponding to the sentence types A, Y, and N, respectively. (Of course, N ≡ ¬I, but since, in this logic, *No R is M* is a basic sentence type, N is used instead of ¬I.) These types are distributed over the VS-model as in Figure 8.9–a. The resulting dodecagon is shown in Figure 8.9–b.

In Figure 8.9, Y stands for *Only some R is M*, with VS {2}. Space 4 is inoperative, as BNPL is predicated on the assumption that $[[R]] \neq \emptyset$. When space 4 is made operative in the sense that A, A*, Y and Y* are false while N is true, the dodecagon of Figure 8.9–b loses a few relations on the right hand side, while all but two equivalences are reduced to one-way entailments, as shown in Figure 8.11 (Seuren 2010: 96).

When the six equivalences of Figure 8.9–b are united into single vertices, as in Figure 8.10, the dodecagon of Figure 8.9–b is reduced to a hexagon—in fact, the Blanché hexagon shown in Figure 8.14 below. *The Square and BNPL are thus seen to form one generalized system GLH, based on a triad of mutually contrary sentence types.* The triad of contraries {1}, {2} and {3} can be extended with a corresponding triad of subcontraries {1,2}, {2,3} and {1,3}, each being the union of two contraries. The remaining logical relations follow automatically.

This conclusion fails to follow when space 4, containing the situations where $[[R]] = \emptyset$, is taken into account. Then the VSs of the six sentence types no longer form a system with three contrary and three subcontrary pairs. In BNPL with space 4 added and A declared false, as in Figure 8.11, /N/ equals {3,4}, no longer {3}, as in BNPL without space 4, so that N (= ¬I) no longer entails I* (see Figure 8.10 below). In the Square with space 4 added and A declared false (as in AAPL), I, with VS {1,2}, and I*, with VS {2,3}, no longer form a subcontrary pair, with the result that, again, ¬I, with VS {3,4}, no longer entails I*, which has VS {2,3}. In SMPL, A (with VS {1,4}) and ¬I (with VS {3,4}) are no longer contraries and I (with VS {1,2}) and I* (with VS {2,3}) are no longer subcontraries. Now A no longer entails I and A (with VS {1,4}), which makes the whole system collapse.

The systems in question are now seen to differ only in (a) the selection of the vertices, (b) whether or not they take space 4 for $[[R]] = \emptyset$ into account, and (c) when they do, whether they declare A and A* true or false in space 4. When space 4 is left idle, the system is maximally powerful. When space 4 plays its part, BNPL is weakened in that it loses a number of logical relations. AAPL loses some logical relations but SMPL loses more—so many that the system hardly maintains itself.[13]

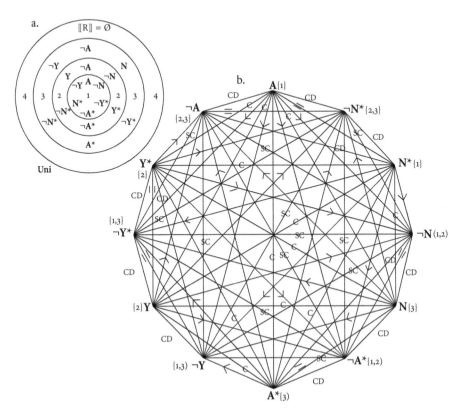

FIGURE 8.9 The VS-model and complete dodecagon for BNPL without space 4

In the logic of Figure 8.11, **A** and **A*** are declared *false* (as in AAPL). The resulting dodecagon is Figure 8.11–b. This dodecagon is not reducible to a hexagon like that of Figure 8.10, as only two equivalences have been left (**Y ≡ Y*** and **¬Y ≡ ¬Y***). The result would be a not very interesting decagon. Yet when **A**, **Y**, and **N** are taken as vertices, extended with vertices for **A ∨ Y** (= **I**), **A ∨ N** (= **U**) and **N ∨ Y** (= **I***), a hexagon like that shown in Figure 8.10 comes about, but now the equivalence relations between **A** and **N***, **I** and **¬A***, **N** and **A***, and **¬A** and **¬N*** no longer hold, which means that this variety of BNPL occupies a lower position in GLH.

---

[13] Smessaert (2011) points out that, besides the classic Square <A, I, A*, I*>, there are also, in the hexagon of Figure 8.10, the Squares <Y, I*, A, U> and <Y, I, A*, U*> with precisely the same constellation of logical relations. The reason why these 'Squares' did not make it in history, or in the human mind, is probably their lack of cognitive functionality.

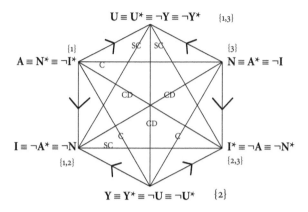

FIGURE 8.10 GLH resulting from condensing the dodecagon of BNPL without space 4

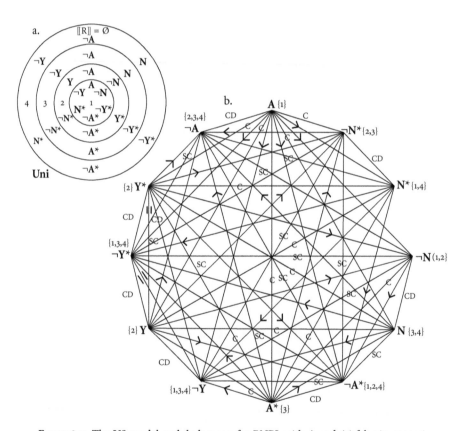

FIGURE 8.11 The VS-model and dodecagon for BNPL with A and A* false in space 4

However, when space 4 is made operative and **A** and **A*** are declared *true* when
[[R]] = Ø, as in SMPL, the result is Figure 8.12, where the dodecagon of Figure 8.9 has
been further undone. Yet the six equivalences make it possible to reduce the
dodecagon to a hexagon, which is shown in Figure 8.13. Here, however, there is
only one single-space VS left, {2}, reserved for **Y** (≡ **Y***). This destroys the hexagon
as defined by three mutually contrary plus three mutually subcontrary vertices. The
hexagonal structure in Figure 8.13 is thus only apparently a subpart of BNPL, as
BNPL is defined as a bi-triadic system of three mutually contrary sentence types plus
their three subcontrary disjunctions. Therefore, when space 4 is taken into account
and **A** and **A*** are taken to be true in space 4, BNPL is undone, even though there is a
hexagonal representation.

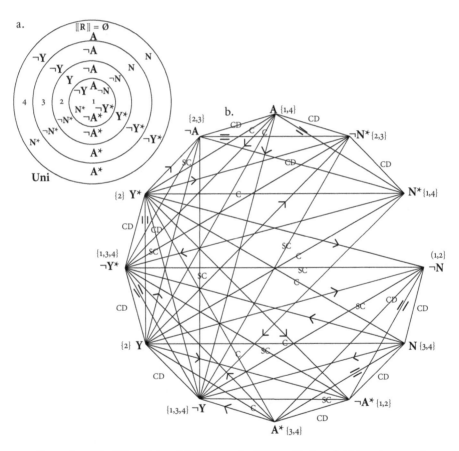

FIGURE 8.12 The VS-model and dodecagon for BNPL with **A** and **A*** true in space 4

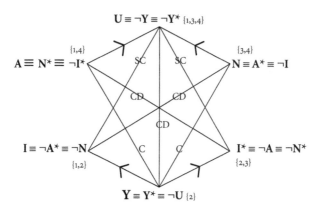

FIGURE 8.13 Weakened BNPL resulting from condensing the dodecagon of Figure 8.12

8.4.3.3 *Unilateral and bilateral* some: *some tentative thoughts*   What follows, in this section, is less a strictly argued position—based on convincing evidence and strict faultless reasoning—than a flight of speculation of the kind that either leads to nothing or, if we are lucky, is the starting point of a train of thought that will, in the end, give rise to new insights and discoveries. I present these thoughts on the off chance that the latter will prove to be the case, keeping in mind what the anthropologist Gregory Bateson wrote (1972: 75; courtesy of Haj Ross, p.c.):

[…] the advances in scientific thought come from a combination of loose and strict thinking, and this combination is the most precious tool of science.

Following this maxim, I now let, for only a little moment, my thoughts run loose.

Natural language appears to waver between the basic-natural triad of contraries <A,Y,N> on the one hand and, on the other, the Square, which is composed of the two isomorphic triads <A,I,¬I> and <A*,I*,¬I*>, connected by the equivalences ¬I ≡ A* and A ≡ ¬I*, as shown in Figure 8.6–b above. This 'wavering' becomes visible in that *some* and its existential cognates (including *most, many, few* and the numerals) are sometimes used in a *unilateral* or *inclusive* sense, setting only a (sometimes vague) lower boundary—in which use *some* lexicalizes the I-vertex— and sometimes in a *bilateral* or *exclusive* sense setting both a lower and an upper boundary (less than all)—in which use *some* lexicalizes the Y-vertex. Does this mean that *some* and its existential cognates are systematically ambiguous across the languages of the world? Strictly speaking the answer must be 'yes', but then the question arises why human languages should exhibit this systematic ambiguity.

In Seuren (1993) it was pointed out that numerals automatically acquire the bilateral 'precisely' reading when used as the comment predicate in a topic-comment structure. A sentence like (8.8a) is automatically interpreted as 'John has exactly two children', when it is considered the surface manifestation of the underlying topic-comment structure (8.8b), where 'the x such that x is the number of John's children' is a *parameter* and TWO is the *value* of the parameter, grammatically expressed as a predicate:

(8.8)   a. John has two children.
   b. the x such that x is the number of John's children is TWO

The topic-comment structure (8.8b) typically occurs as an answer to the question (8.9a), with the underlying topic-comment structure (8.9b), where 'the x such that x is the number of John's children' is the same parameter and WHAT? is a request for its value:

(8.9)   a. How many children does John have?
   b. the x such that x is the number of John's children is WHAT?

The underlying structure (8.8b) of the answer (8.8a) is thus identical to the underlying structure (8.9b) of the question (8.9a), but for the fact that the question word WHAT? has been replaced with the answer word TWO (with raised accent, maintained in surface structure). Such a question-answer pair makes sense only when the questioner presumes that the respondent has full relevant knowledge of the subject matter the question is about.

I still consider this analysis correct, but it needs further generalization. The topic-comment solution that seems to work for numerals does not work for *some*. Yet the two share the property (also shared by the quantifier *most*) of vacillating between a unilateral ('at least') interpretation and a bilateral interpretation with a lower limit as well as an upper limit that excludes *all*. The crucial common factor seems to be a *hearer's presumption of speaker's complete relevant situational knowledge*. When that presumption is there, the exclusive or bilateral interpretation of *some* and its partners (including *most* and the numerals) prevails. When it is not there or it is not relevant, *some* and its partners are preferably interpreted unilaterally—that is, with a lexically determined lower limit and *all* as the upper limit. This means that the crucial factor deciding between a unilateral or a bilateral interpretation is not the presence or absence of an underlying topic-comment structure but rather the question of *whether there is a presumption on the part of the hearer of speaker's full relevant situational knowledge*.

The common (cognitive) satisfaction condition shared by the two *some*'s is the experience of the 'presence of something of a certain category'—arguably a primary, if not primordial, experience going back to each person's earliest childhood. The 'something of a certain category' will, in this primordial sense, not cover the entire scene or situation at hand but will be experienced as present precisely because it distinguishes itself from the situation as a whole. This provides the psychological basis for a tripartition with respect to a given category C of entities in a situation S, in that either all entities in S are of category C or (only) some are or none are. This tripartition generates the triadic logic of BNPL. The presumption of complete knowledge will have been the norm in primitive communities, where talk will have been mostly about *hic et nunc* topics and situations—and likewise for children in the process of acquiring their first language. When a speaker expresses this primitive experience of 'some' in a linguistic form, the hearer will take this as a report on what the speaker has actually experienced or is experiencing, and since, in simple cases, a situation is confined by what is experienced, the hearer will automatically assume that the speaker has complete relevant knowledge of the situation and will thus, unwittingly, apply BNPL in his or her reasoning.

In less simple cases, however, the presumption of complete relevant knowledge will no longer hold, as the speaker may report on a situation that has not (yet) been completely searched or inspected, so that the speaker's experience will cover only part of the entire situation. In such a case a report on the 'presence of something of a certain category' must leave open the possibility of the 'some' experience turning into an 'all' experience when the inspection is completed or when a universal hypothesis is formed. In that, more highly developed, type of interaction, *some* is automatically interpreted unilaterally and thus occupies the I-corner in the hexagon.

In this perspective, it is easier to understand why and how the same word *some* has come to be used for what are in fact two distinct logical operators. It is fascinating to see how the same 'some' experience takes on different logical roles according to whether the word reporting on the experience is used in an interactional situation with or without the presumption of complete relevant knowledge. The logical analysis shows that *some* really is ambiguous, whereby the ambiguity is *caused by* factors to do with the interactional situation. Normally, the interactional situation helps to disambiguate, or resolve, an existing, truth-conditional, ambiguity in actual token interpretation. Here, however, the ambiguity appears to be *created by* the interactional situation, which, at the same time, resolves it. The interactional situation is thus part of the satisfaction conditions of *some*—an absolute novelty in semantics, whose consequences will take some time to think through.

Suppose I use *some* in a situation where my hearer is entitled to expect that I have complete relevant knowledge but I ignore that justified presumption and speak as if that presumption does not hold, without telling my interlocutor so. For example, I report on an accident I have witnessed in which all four passengers of a car have died, yet I say *Some of the passengers were killed*. Is this a question of not being cooperative in the Gricean sense? In a way yes, but the lack of cooperativeness consists in giving information (in terms of a unilateral existential quantifier) that would be adequate in a situation where I did not have complete relevant knowledge, while letting the other person believe that I do have complete relevant knowledge, so that he or she will take my *some* in its bilateral meaning. One may call this 'abuse of ambiguity', but one may also say that I have not told the truth—that is, I have misled the listener or lied to him/her. In general, when a person A uses an ambiguous expression *e* in a meaning α, knowing that a person B will interpret *e* in a meaning β, incompatible with α, A has certainly misled B and may even, in a sense, be said to have lied to B. The literature on speech acts and also the philosophical literature on truth and falsity hardly deals with this particular aspect of uttering falsehoods, but the question would seem to deserve some serious attention.

The use of *some* for the unilateral I-vertex will then be the result of a higher degree of cultural development, accelerated by literacy and school training. It has the distinct advantage over the more primitive bilateral or exclusive *some* of allowing for a true existential proposition before a complete check has been carried out (or a universal hypothesis has been formed). Bilateral *some* cannot be used in such a case, because it implies 'not all' and would thus risk becoming false the moment *all* has been ascertained (or posited) to be true. In this perspective, bilateral *some* is an obstacle to inductive theorizing.

One may still ask why the same word *some* is used for the logically distinct operators in Y-type and I-type sentences and why not two different words? The answer may well be that, in general, at the more advanced level of cultural development at which logical thinking begins to take place and, among other things, I-type sentences begin to be required, the introduction of *new* single-morpheme lexical items for such abstract concepts as logical operators, which are totally inaccessible to awareness or conscious introspection, must be taken to be highly unlikely. Instead, it seems more reasonable to surmise that, when a name is needed for a new logical operator, one will resort to the name of the operator that is cognitively and psychologically closest, making the existing term ambiguous. For the existential quantifier in the new I-type this is the bilateral *some* of the basic sentence type Y (just as for the new inclusive *or* it is its basic exclusive cousin of the same name).

From a slightly different perspective it may be observed that bilateral *some* is *prototypical* in the sense that this is what infants grow up with, while its extension to unilateral *some* is the product of culture and education. A similar extension from a prototypical to a stricter analytical meaning is found in, for example, the word *animal*, which is prototypically a non-human animal but in a more analytical sense it covers humans as well. Likewise for the geographical name *America*. Prototypically, *America* stands for the United States of America, but in more critical discourse, the term covers South, Central and North America. It would seem that the case of prototypical bilateral *some* as against the more analytical unilateral *some* may fruitfully be thought to fall into the same category.

All this is, of course, speculative and would have to be investigated more closely by specialists in 'primitive' or 'elementary' thought in conjunction with child psychologists—something that cannot be undertaken here, for obvious reasons. All I can do here is point to the ontogenic and phylogenic developmental dimension of the problem area at hand as a potential quarry for explanations.

Apart, however, from the developmental aspect, we observe that English, as an instance of natural language, operates with three monomorphemic expressions for the standard quantifiers, reflecting the three primary quantifiers of BNPL: *all*, (bilateral) *some*, and *no* (whereby it is assumed that the use of *some* is extended to its unilateral or inclusive cousin). The internal negation is used without restrictions but is never morphologically incorporated into the quantifier (often, of course, into the Matrix predicate). The external negation is allowed to occur sentence-initially before *all* and *every*. In this position, in English and many other European languages, the negation is somehow lexically united with, but not lexically incorporated into, the universal quantifier: *not-all, not-every*.[14] This is not possible for *each* (**not-each* is ungrammatical), for unknown reasons. Nor does it occur with *some*: **not-some* does not occur as a semi-lexical unit. It is usually said that this is because *not-some* is lexicalized as *no*, but we have seen that *not some* and *no* are not equivalent in BNPL, which has bilateral *some*, so that *not some* should mean 'either all or no'. The reason is more likely to be that *not some* is an unlikely candidate for lexicalization, even in a weakened semi-lexicalized form, because 'all' and 'no' do not form a cognitive continuum.[15] A semi-lexical unit *not-no* is relatively rare in the languages of the world, but Latin, for example, has the understatement or *litotes* forms *nonnulli* (lit. 'not none', used for 'quite a few'), *nonnusquam* (lit. 'not nowhere', used for 'in quite a few places'), *nonnumquam* (lit. 'not never', used for 'quite often'). Dutch has the colloquial idiom *niet-niks* (lit. 'not nothing'), used for 'quite something'.

8.4.3.4 *The presuppositional solution*   The question remains of how natural language copes with UEI. In language, the problem of UEI has been solved not by simply adding space 4 to the calculus and thus weakening the logical system, but, much more ingeniously, by incorporating UEI into the general mechanism of presupposition.

---

[14] There is a problem with the meaning of *not-all* (*not-every*), which naturally means 'only some', and not 'only some or none', although that is what it should mean according to BNPL. Jespersen (1917: 86–91) and Horn (1972, 1989) assume a pragmatic principle of *scalarity*, according to which the negation, when applied to a quantifiable scale, cuts off only the higher part of the scale, leaving the lower part intact. In Seuren (2010: 100) it is observed that the narrowing of 'only some or none' to just 'only some' follows automatically when the sentence has a topic-comment structure with *all* in comment position: if *all* in a sentence like *Ben didn't eat all of his meal* is comment, the underlying structure is 'what Ben ate of his meal is not all', which presupposes, and hence entails, that Ben ate at least some of his meal, excluding the reading 'Ben ate none of his meal'. Yet the cases where *all* is not in comment position then remain unexplained. If it turns out that in those cases the meaning 'only some or none' prevails, it may be assumed that the answer given in Seuren (2020: 100) is correct and sufficient. If not, all that is left, as far as I can see at the moment, is the scalarity answer given by Jespersen and Horn.

[15] The question of why natural language does not have, or hardly has, a lexicalization **nall* for 'not-all' (or **nand* for 'not-and') (Zwicky 1973; Horn 1972, 1989: 252–67; Levinson 2000: 69–71) thus does not arise. Such a lexicalization would only be expected if *no* is taken to be a lexicalization of 'not-some', which, for logically naïve speakers, it is not. Moreover, *not-all* is already semi-lexicalized. For a challenging alternative explanation, which I cannot go into here, of the universal absence of a single-word lexicalization corresponding to **nall* and **nand* in the languages of the world, one is referred to Jaspers (2005: 219–27).

Language deals with UEI by marking its predicates for intensional term positions. Most predicates are extensional with regard to their argument terms, in the sense that they presuppositionally require actual existence of the argument-term referent for truth. A violation of this satisfaction condition leads to presupposition failure and thus to radical falsity. Some predicates, however, allow for intensional objects as reference value for some argument-term position. Thus, a sentence like (8.10a) is true in the full sense of the term, while (8.10b) is false, even though neither Apollo nor Poseidon have ever existed. This is possible because *be worshipped* is nonextensional with regard to its subject term:

(8.10)   a. Apollo was worshipped in the island of Delos.
         b. Poseidon was worshipped in the island of Delos.

Besides existential presuppositions, there are categorial presuppositions, such as the presupposition of sentence (8.11) that John has been away. If John has not been away, (8.11) suffers from presupposition failure:[16]

(8.11)   John has come back.

Ample research by the present author over the past forty years (summarized in Seuren 2010, Chs 7, 10) has established that presuppositions are entailments doing their work as semantically fixed conditions, laid down in the meanings of the predicates used, on the coherence of preceding discourse and that the default way of building up discourse domains is without presupposition failure.

That presupposition is a form of entailment follows from the standard definition of entailment, which says that a sentence P entails a sentence Q just in case whenever P is true, Q must also be true in virtue of the meanings of P and Q. This means that when P entails Q, P and *not-Q* are semantically or analytically incompatible (contraries). Given that *John has come back* presupposes *John has been away*, one sees that whenever it is true to say that John has come back, it is, by semantic necessity, also true that John has been away. Yet presuppositional entailments form a special category in that, as is widely known, in most cases, the negation seems not to behave 'properly' with presuppositions. Normally, when P entails Q, *not-P* loses that entailment. Presuppositions, however, are, in most cases, preserved as strong suggestions, so strong that they have often been mistaken for entailments of negated carrier sentences. When it is true that John has *not* come back, there is still a strong intuition that John did go away, which is not the case with 'standard' or classical entailments.

---

[16] Some categorial presuppositions are analytical or anchored in the semantics of the predicate concerned and are thus independent of the actual state of affairs. Their violations are immediately spotted, without any world knowledge, by any competent speaker of the language. Thus, a sentence like *The wind fell asleep* suffers from presupposition failure no matter the way the world happens to be, simply because the predicate *fall asleep* requires an animate being as subject-term referent, which the wind is not. Such presupposition failures often function as literary metaphors (Seuren 2001b).

In standard logic, it is possible for both P and *not-P* to share an entailment, but in such a case the entailed sentence is a 'necessary' truth—that is, true in all valuations— in the running universe of discourse. (The usual term *necessary truth* reflects the fact that standard logic operates in a metaphysically conceived universe of all possible situations, without taking the possibility of restricted universes into account.)

This is precisely the point. The fact that both P and *not-P* share a presupposition Q implies that Q defines the universe of discourse: presuppositions restrict the universe of discourse to exactly the set of situations in which they are true. Natural language negation primarily selects a complement within a universe of discourse that is restricted by a variety of factors, in particular by the presuppositions carried by any given sentence. It is only as a result of metalinguistic reflection that the negation can reach back into a less restricted universe of discourse. When used for that purpose, it needs emphatic accent and is subject to certain grammatical constraints (Seuren 2010: 334–42).[17]

In general, presupposition failure is corrected by a special, emphatically stressed, discourse-correcting *radical negation*, which produces a marked echo-effect in that it rejects or corrects an earlier utterance by a previous speaker that needs to be removed from the discourse domain. An example is (8.12), which evokes a previous speaker who has just said *John has come back*. The speaker of (8.12) corrects that utterance on account of presupposition failure and in doing so, he lifts the restriction on the current universe of discourse imposed by the faulty presupposition:

(8.12)   John has NÓT come back. He has never been away!

It is not necessary, in the present context, to review the whole of presupposition theory (for an extensive survey, see Seuren 2010, Ch. 10). Let it suffice to point out that the default remit of natural predicate logic is restricted to default discourses without any presupposition failure. Within this area, all presuppositions are always satisfied, including existential presuppositions. As long as intensional predicates such as *be worshipped* are disregarded, there is no need for space 4 in default natural predicate logic. Space 4 is brought in only in marked cases of presupposition failure.

---

[17] Cruse (2006: 138) writes: 'Presupposition is not the same as entailment', giving as his reason that both P and *not-P* may have the same presupposition. Yet presuppositions must be entailments because they fulfill all the requirements: if *John has come back* is true, then *John has been away* is, by semantic necessity, also true. And *John has come back* is incompatible with *John has not been away*. To say that presuppositions are not entailments thus runs counter to the standard definition of entailment. What led Cruse astray is the fact that when both P and *not-P* entail Q, Q must be a 'necessary' truth—that is, true in all valuations—in the universe of discourse defined by Q. Presuppositions are a special kind of entailment because they define the universe of discourse for the sentences that carry them, and their negations, to function in. Clearly, standard logic is unable to deal with such universe restrictions. Cruse then decides to treat presupposition as a 'pragmatic' phenomenon, implying that this exonerates the theoretician from giving a formally precise analysis. This demonstrates again that 'pragmatic' answers are but a stopgap for failing formal insight.

BNPL is thus applicable in full force, its range of application being protected by a coating of presupposition satisfaction. When that coating falls away, a third truth value, *radical falsity*, is needed, turned into truth by the metalinguistically flavoured (Horn 1985) radical negation mentioned above.

8.5 The Blanché hexagon

8.5.1 *The logical aspects*

Sesmat (1951) and Blanché (1966) are early harbingers of natural predicate logic. Blanché in particular attempted to extrapolate from the logical relations of the Square to conceptual relations in general (both Sesmat and Blanché completely disregarded cases where $[[R]] = \emptyset$, and hence the UEI problem). In principle, these two authors extended the Square with two extra vertices, U for $A \vee E$ and Y for $I \wedge O$—in Blanché's notation. (In order to do justice to the authors in question, I am falling back on the old E- and O-notation for what I have so far called N and I*). The result is shown in Figure 8.14-a (Blanché 1966: 56). As conceptual analogs, Blanché cites, *inter alia*, the hexagon of the artithmetical operators =, $\neq$, >, $\geq$, < and $\leq$, as in Figure 8.14-b (Blanché 1966: 64, replicating Sesmat 1951: 412) and the hexagon of what Blanché calls 'alethic' operators, as in Figure 8.14-c (Blanché 1966: 89).[18]

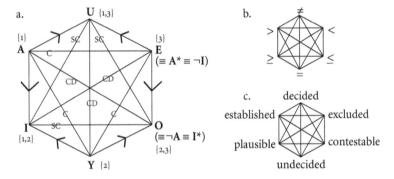

FIGURE **8.14** Blanché's hexagon, applied to arithmetical and 'alethic' operators

---

[18] One notes that, while the arithmetical analog of Figure 8.14-b is entirely convincing, the lexical analog of Figure 8.14-c is not, since not all entailment relations of Figure 8.14-a carry over to Figure 8.14-c. When the truth or falsity of a proposition is merely undecided, it does not follow that it is plausible: it may be both implausible and undecided, which again calls into question the relation of subcontrariety posited between *plausible* and *decided*. Blanché does not comment on this problem. The general research programme, however, may well turn out to be of great importance to the theory of the lexicon.

Leaving the conceptual extrapolations aside and concentrating on the purely logical aspect, we notice that all logical relations defined for the Square remain intact, but the VSs of U and Y and their compositions with the external and internal negations, as specified in Table 8.4, are to be added.

TABLE 8.4 **The pooled VSs for Blanché's operators U and Y and their negative compositions (space 4 is inoperative)**

/U/ = {1,3}	/Y/ = {2}
/¬U/ = {2}	/¬Y/ = {1,3}
/U*/ = {1,3}	/Y*/ = {2}
/¬U*/ = {2}	/¬Y*/ = {1,3}

The internal negation thus makes no logical difference for U and Y: $/U/ = /U^*/ = \{1,3\}$ and $/Y/ = /Y^*/ = \{2\}$. U/U* and Y/Y* are contradictories: $\neg U \equiv \neg U^* \equiv Y \equiv Y^*$. Moreover, U and Y are duals: $U \equiv \neg Y^*$ and $Y \equiv \neg U^*$. It is, therefore, superfluous to draw a 16-vertex polygon for all logical relations in Blanché's logic: the vertices that would have to be added to the Square reduce to two, which gives the hexagon of Figure 8.14–a.

The mutually contrary vertices A, Y, and E, forming the contrary triangle <A,Y,E> in Figure 8.14–a, are the only vertices characterized by a singleton valuation space, while the vertices of the triangle <I,O,U> of subcontraries all have VSs consisting of two classes, each VS forming the union of the singleton VSs of the two adjacent vertices. On the assumption that cognition does not deviate from mathematical simplicity without good reason, this suggests that the three vertices A, Y, and E are cognitively basic, while the vertices I, O, and U are cognitively derived, as is maintained in Seuren (2010: Ch. 3). This again suggests that the primordial meanings of the natural language quantifiers *all*, *some*, and *no* correspond to the vertices A, Y, and E, respectively.

8.5.2 *Applications to conceptual fields and colours*

How general is the logical Blanché hexagon? It is well-known that the same hexagonal arrangement fits the binary propositional connectives, with the operators *and*, *(inclusive) or*, *(exclusive) or*, *not and*, *neither... nor* and *neither-or-both*. Deontic logic is a further obvious application (Lenk 1974; Beller 2008, 2010), with the operators *obligatory*, *permitted*, *optional*, *not obligatory*, *forbidden* and *categorical* (that is, *obligatory or forbidden*). Likewise for epistemic modal logic with the operators *necessary*, *possible*, *contingent*, *not necessary*, *impossible* and *non-contingent* ('necessary or impossible'). We may also think of the hexagon formed by *cause* (*make*), *allow* (*let*), *non-determined, allow that not* (*let not*), *prevent* (*disallow, stop*) and *determined*. But how far does this go? We have already seen Sesmat's (and Blanché's) faultless application to the arithmetical operators >, ≥, =, ≤, < and ≠, shown in Figure 8.14–b. Yet, as they stand, Blanché's further conceptual and lexical extrapolations may seem a little too adventurous (see note 18), though they are thought-provoking.

Lexical gaps complicate a hexagonal mapping of the relations involved. This problem is manifest in the examples given above. It also turns up, for example, in the contrary triad <*cooked, raw, rotten*> for eating meat across the world, which lacks terms for the corresponding subcontrary triad. The quadruple <*stationary, forward, moving, backward*>, corresponding to <Y,A,U,E>, lacks terms for the I- and O-vertices. The triads <*luck, lot, misfortune*> or <*look forward to, expect, fear*>, corresponding to <A,U,E>, have no items for the other three vertices. And so forth. It thus seems rash to posit that, as a rule, lexical items are grouped in six-tuples *à la* Blanché—though Blanché's hypothesis may be read as saying that predicates forming a closed lexical field can be located in a hexadic structure of the kind discussed. Yet the thought underlying Blanché's effort is not to be dismissed too lightly. A more systematic and more cautious effort might well reveal an interesting and possibly explanatory system of logic-like relations in certain well-defined lexical fields in the languages of the world.

Dany Jaspers (2010, 2011) has presented a specific application of the Blanché hexagon to the lexical field of colour terms. Putting colours for sentence types, he presents the hexagon for colours of Figure 8.15.

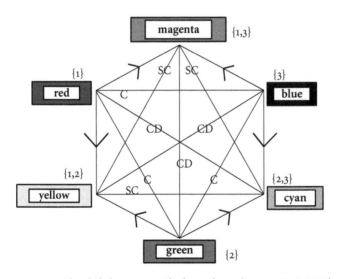

Figure 8.15 Blanché's hexagon applied to colours (Jaspers 2010, 2011)

The Blanché triad of contraries <A,Y,E> has been mapped onto the triad of primary colours <red, green, blue> and the Blanché triad of subcontraries <I,O,U> onto the triad of secondary colours <yellow, cyan, magenta>. The spaces {1}, {2} and {3} correspond to the unmixed wavelength ranges of red, green and blue, respectively. A VS {m,n} is the *additive* mixing of {m} and {n}—that is, the superimposition of pure *m* and pure *n* lightwaves in a light-emitting source. 'Entailment', as in 'red "entails" yellow', is thus interpreted as 'red is an additive component of yellow'. The colour white is the result of the addition of the three primary colours. *Subtractive* colour mixing (as in the mixing of paints) is based on the absorption of light waves by a coloured object in white light. Thus, when an object is yellow, its surface absorbs blue, leaving yellow, the additive result of red and green. The secondary colours yellow, cyan and magenta thus result from the absorption of blue, red and green, respectively, while black results from the absorption of at least two secondary colours. The parallel with subcontrariety is obvious: the addition of any two secondary colours yields white, the 'universe' of all colours. Contradictoriness (known as *complementarity* for colours) is reflected in terms of minimal pairs of colours additively giving white, which corresponds to {1,2,3}. Table 8.5 shows the simple algebra of this system, where white is the analog of **Un**, the disjunction (union) of all non-negated sentence types in the logic and hence necessarily true, and black is the analog of Ø, the conjunction (intersection) of all non-negated sentence types in the logic and hence necessarily false.

TABLE 8.5 **The algebra of additive and subtractive colour mixing**

primary and secondary colours:
Red + Green = Yellow
Green + Blue = Cyan
Red + Blue = Magenta

White and Black:
Red + Green + Blue = White
White – Red = Green + Blue = Cyan
White – Green = Red + Blue = Magenta
White – Blue = Red + Green = Yellow
White – (Red + Green + Blue) = Black

complementary colours:
Red + Cyan = White
Green + Magenta = White
Blue + Yellow = White

Since the colours white and black are missing from Figure 8.15, just as **Un** and Ø are missing from its logical counterparts, Jaspers resorts to a three-dimensional representation of the hexagon, developed by Hans Smessaert for logical purposes and presented in Smessaert (2009), reproduced here in Figure 8.16. In logical terms, the vertex marked {1,2,3} designates the necessarily true sentence type, call it Ω (/Ω/ = Un), while the vertex marked Ø designates the necessarily false sentence type, call it Ψ (/Ψ/ = Ø). In colour terms, Ψ, with VS Ø (black), is the absence of chromaticity, while Ω, with VS {1,2,3} (white), is the addition of all colours of the spectrum. All internal diagonals between the top and the bottom of the box in Figure 8.16 stand for 'contradictories' (complementary colours). The first vertex reached from the vertex *black* via an outer edge is always a primary colour; the second vertex reached along an outer edge (the first from any primary colour) is always a secondary colour; the third vertex so reached (the first from any secondary colour) is always the tertiary colour white.

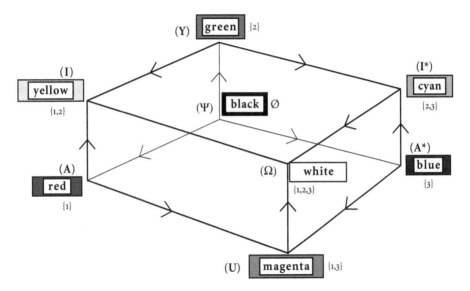

FIGURE 8.16 3D-representation of the hexagon for colours, with black and white added

What to make of this remarkable isomorphy is not entirely clear, given the present state of our knowledge. We may have to do with a feature of human cognition driving not only natural predicate logic but also other areas of cognitive processing. There may also be systematic consequences for lexicalization processes. We do not know. But it is certainly worth our while to be on the lookout for further parallels of this nature.[19]

---

[19] The literature on the perception, neurophysiology, classification and naming of colours is enormous and, as is to be expected, there are many different camps sometimes bitterly combating each other. For a survey, see Saunders and Van Brakel (1997); see also section 2.4.1.1 in the present book. It cannot be my purpose here to enter that fray here, as I have too many frays to cope with already. Like Jaspers, I stay with what is perceived as the common middle ground.

With the help of two friendly phonetician colleagues I have tried out if there is an analog for the three cardinal vowels [i], [a] and [u], supplemented with the three secondary vowels [é], [ó] and [ü]. So far, however, our (their) investigations have not yielded any tangible results. It should be noted, however, that the groundwork needed for such an analogy has not been done (yet) in phonetics. Although the problem has been known for over half a century, it is still not known what mechanism explains the phonological identity of phonetic vowel perception in the vowels produced by different speakers: the phonologically same vowels produced by different speakers (males, females, young, old, etc.) have very different physical qualities, yet we interpret them as 'the same' on the phonological level. One has some ideas of the factors involved, but the mechanism as such has never been disclosed in detail, let alone mechanically simulated. Present-day automated speech perception does not work at all well and to the extent that it does it is largely based on global measurements and statistical frequency measures. Nor has one been able to synthesize speech utterances from parametrically controlled sound generators to any degree of acceptability. Early attempts to do that, dating back to the 1960s, were on the whole unsatisfactory, but even now purely physical speech synthesis fails to yield a sound that, for example, is convincingly perceived as the vowel [i]: all one hears is a nondistinct high-pitched electrical bell sound. As a result, purely physical speech synthesis was given up in favour of techniques that manipulate sounds produced by human speakers: this is what one hears in elevators or when listening to a GPS navigator in one's car. But the connection with purely physical parameters of sound has not been made: phonetics has become speech technology and the link between physical data and perceptive results is still missing. Little wonder that it is not possible, given our present knowledge, to find auditory analogs for the logical notions of entailment, contrariety, subcontrariety and contradiction, or for the colour perception notions of addition, mutual exclusion, subtraction and complementarity. I thus consider the question of a possible vowel analog to the bi-triadic perception of colours still open.

8.5.3 *The bi-triadic nature of the Blanché hexagon and, who knows, of cognition*

Now back to logic. The Blanché logical hexagon is a mathematically necessary consequence of any system that works with three mutually exclusive sets jointly constituting the universe **Ent** of all entities considered. To see this, take an **Ent** divided into three mutually exclusive areas A, B and C (Figure 8.17–a), corresponding to the triad <A,B,C> in Figure 8.17–b. When **Ent** is interpreted as the set of all possible situations and A, B, C as sentence types, the three vertices A, B, C in Figure 8.17–b form a triad of contraries. From this it follows that the complements, $\overline{A}, \overline{B}, \overline{C}$ of A, B, C, form a second triad <$\overline{A}, \overline{B}, \overline{C}$> of subcontraries such that $\overline{A} = B \cup C$, $\overline{B} = A \cup C$ and $\overline{C} = A \cup B$. This gives rise to the Blanché hexagon of Figure 8.17–b, which is the generalized logic hexagon discussed above. All one needs, therefore, to obtain this hexagon, is an **Ent** consisting of three mutually exclusive sets jointly making up **Ent**. (Yet, as we have seen, the same bi-triadic hexagon can be set up for areas that are not, or not obviously, reducible to sets, such as colour perception.)

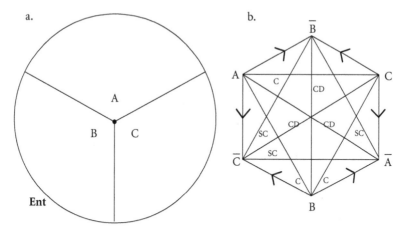

FIGURE **8.17** The hexagon (b) derived from three mutually exclusive sets forming **Ent** (a)

No such set-theoretic construction is possible with **Ent** consisting of *two* mutually exclusive sets A and B, because the complement of the one equals the other. But with *four* mutually exclusive sets forming **Ent** the interesting construction shown in Figure 8.18–b comes about. Here the two dimensions of Figure 8.17–b do not suffice; we need a three-dimensional box-like representation, as in Figure 8.18–b.

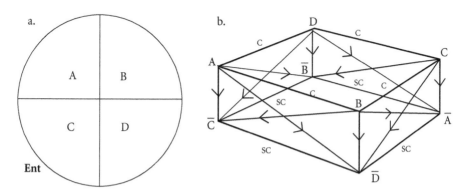

FIGURE **8.18** The box (b) derived from four mutually exclusive sets forming **Ent** (a)

What we now see is that the basic-natural Hamiltonian system of BNPL and the still natural system of the Square, both derivable from, and expressible in terms of, the Blanché hexagon reflecting GLH, are based on the *triadic* division of **Ent** and not on the *tetradic* division of Figure 8.18. It is obviously possible to develop a logical system based on the tetradic division, although it remains to be seen how interesting any such logic would be. One could, for example, define a GLH with four mutually exclusive basic quantifiers *All*, *Some₁*, *Some₂* and *No*, where *Some₁* requires that [[R]] and [[M]] mutually partially intersect and *Some₂* that [[M]] $\subset$ [[R]]—two conditions that are covered by the one basic-natural *some* in the Y-type sentence of BNPL. Such a system would then no longer fit the pattern of GLH. But no logician has so far elaborated this possibility.[20]

In the light of this analysis, we may read Blanché as suggesting that human cognition is generally programmed for triadic, and not for tetradic or even higher-order, divisions and the systems derived from them. If this turns out to be correct, we will have an important universal of human cognition, so far unsuspected in cognitive psychology, linguistics or any other discipline dealing with human cognition. It would also show that standard modern logic is a great deal more subservient to cognition and a great deal less metaphysically necessary than is currently thought (albeit mostly implicitly) by professional logicians.

Admittedly, some elements in the above analysis are uncertain and even speculative, but the analysis given surely helps to get a clearer idea of what the uncertainty is about. It shows, in particular, how all extensional bivalent systems of predicate logic are, in one way or another, either derived from or positioned in terms of GLH, which is based on a triadic division of **Ent**. For the rest, there still is a vast expanse of unexplored terrain before us.

---

[20] A rare exception is Gottschalk (1953), who presented a generalized tetradic analysis of predicate logic based on the four vertices of the classic Square of Opposition. Apparently, however, Gottschalk failed to see (a) that the Square is in fact a combination of two isomorphic triadic structures differing only in the fact that the one has no internal negation whereas the other does (see Seuren 2010: 28–37), and (b) that the classic Square is merely a part of the bi-triadic structure consisting of Hamilton's primary triangle of contraries plus the resulting secondary triangle of subcontraries.

9

The intensionalization of extensions

9.1 Introduction

This chapter is a study in the foundations of natural language semantics. It aims at replacing the paradigm of *possible world semantics* (PWS) in all its varieties with a more realist, cognitively oriented research programme. Yet even if I advocate a wholesale rejection of PWS, I must admit here, as I have done on other occasions, that PWS has given rise to a new blossoming of semantics, which would not have occurred had it not been for the mathematicization of logic as it took place from the 1850s onward. Much as I oppose PWS, I owe it, and the tradition behind it, a great debt.

The chapter has a dual purpose. First, it revives and confirms known arguments for the rejection of PWS as a valid paradigm. Then, it presents an alternative theory that allows for a cognitive-realist interpretation (to the extent that cognitive theories allow for a realist interpretation). This new paradigm for semantics makes semantics cognitive and thus per se intensional. It requires a theory of reality—an ontology—that reflects the way humans naturally construe the world. Natural ontology is a construal of sensory inputs in terms of a pre-established system of forming categories and relations resulting in a picture of the world that is, on the one hand, caught in its own terms but, on the other, verifiable and falsifiable on empirical grounds. The world as thus construed is seen as full of entities and properties. The entities may be taken to be concrete objects or matter, or abstract entities of all kinds, whereby the limits and methods of abstraction are the perennial object of ontological classifications in philosophy. Besides *actual* reality, the human mind constructs all kinds of *virtual* reality in the form of what could or might or cannot be or happens not to be actual reality. All virtual reality is *created* by the imaginative mind, individually or collectively. This essentially Kantian perspective requires that extensions count only insofar as they are mentally represented and projected onto what is construed as the actual or a virtual world.

The point of view just formulated shakes the foundations of established formal semantics, with its non-human and purportedly 'objective' ontology, and will, therefore, provoke adverse reactions. Yet one should realize that this new perspective finally, after so many years of frustration, creates the terms for a solution to the problems that have so far stood in the way of an adequate theory of meaning—besides many other advantages. We now see our way towards a principled solution of the otherwise unsolvable problems of *partiscience* (propositional attitudes) and of the ontological dilemma of *Boolean 1 and 0 as sentence extensions* (truth values). Some will consider it a disadvantage that the new cognitive perspective precludes full formalization. But this is to be expected, since there can be no proper semantic theory without an input from cognition, and cognition has so far escaped full formalization.

9.2 Some basic notions

9.2.1 *Language as a system of conventional signs: what is meaning?*

Formal and natural languages are not of a kind. The former have been designed by mathematicians or computer scientists; the latter are lodged in human cognition as products of evolution and learning. To follow Montague, who felt he should 'reject the contention that an important theoretical difference exists between formal and natural languages' (Montague 1974: 188), is to overestimate the power of mathematics and to underestimate the human mind.

This requires some comment. To begin with, I defend the *causal theory of signs*, according to which meanings are properties of perceptible form-types (signs) revealing the cause of their occurrence. More precisely, meaning in the general sense of *meaning of a sign S* is defined as follows (Seuren 2009a: 280–4):

The meaning of a form-type S is the systematic property of tokens of S to bring about in an informed perceiver the certain and consciously accessible knowledge of the present or past occurrence of their necessary but unperceived cause C.

Meanings thus require a cognizing subject that has conscious knowledge of causal relations. This knowledge must be learned beyond the learning involved in mere perception. Smoke is thus a sign of combustion going on. The meaning of smoke is its systematic property of making the informed perceiver know for certain that there is combustion causing the smoke.

Beyond such *natural signs*, there are *conventional signs*, which differ in that the cause *C* is not a natural but a cognitive cause convened between sender and perceiver. Thus, a red traffic light is a conventional sign manifesting an order put out by authorities for traffic to stop. *Linguistic* meaning is of the conventional kind and is primarily a property of the grammatico-semantic units known as sentences, which function semantically in the context of discourse and situation and in virtue of the lexical meanings in their structural positions in the sentences involved (for extensive discussion, see Chapter 8 in Seuren 2009a):

Linguistic meaning is primarily the system-driven property of a sentence *S* as a linguistic type-level unit, in virtue of which a linguistically competent hearer is able to reconstruct speaker's intent (that is, a speech act operator over a proposition) from any utterance token of S, given proper values for contextual and situational parameters. In a secondary and derived sense, linguistic meaning is a property of type-level lexical elements and of grammatical constructions.

A sentence is thus a coded message, not a direct expression, such as a cry when pain is felt.

It follows that the meanings of conventional signs must be learned or acquired before the signs in question can be used. This is an important fact, since, as will become clear, the semantics of a language has to be acquired (learned): whatever, in the interpretation of utterances, is not subject to a learning process but is provided by already present cognitive powers, such as the determination of reference objects, is—unless it is a consequence of an innate principle—not part of the semantics of a language.

This analysis applies to *natural* language, as it has come about as a product of evolution and is used universally and without any formal training by all mentally unimpaired human beings, regardless of their level of education. It does not apply to artificial formal languages that have been consciously constructed by sophisticated mathematicians. The latter are not the object of empirical study as they harbour no mysteries beyond possible mathematical properties that may not have been foreseen during their construction. Natural languages, by contrast, have not been constructed by humans but are highly complex objects of empirical study presented by nature, full of mysteries yet to be discovered. The thought that we as individual humans, no matter how sophisticated, can sit down and think up systems bred into the human mind during hundreds of thousands of years of evolutionary development on the basis of mere *a priori* projection and without profound prior empirical research has no place in science and deserves the name of fanciful hubris. Modelling is fine, but it requires careful preliminary analysis. This is precisely what is lacking in PWS, which is based on no knowledge of language at all.

9.2.2 *Propositions, intents, and L-propositions*

A *proposition* is taken to be the token mental act of assigning a property to an entity or *n*-tuple of entities (henceforth simply *entity*). A proposition is thus, among other things, *the primary bearer of a truth value*, since the entity in question will or will not actually possess that property. Being the primary bearer of a truth value is what unites all definitions of the notion of proposition through the ages (Nuchelmans 1973, 1980, 1983)—the only exception being the definition 'set of possible worlds' current in PWS. In linguistic interaction, a proposition *p* is always commanded by a socially binding operator that commits the speaker and/or appeals to or obliges the listener as regards *p*. A sentence never expresses just a proposition ('Mary now baking pies'; Lewis 1946: 48) but must contain a speech act operator specifying the speaker's socially binding commitment with regard to the proposition expressed (Seuren 2009a: Ch. 4).

I call the combined cognitive structure consisting of a socially committing speech act operator and a proposition an *intent*. All utterances express speakers' intents. The object of semantics is speakers' intents, not just propositions. PWS deals only with the propositional element in intents. It is true that the complexities of semantics derive mostly from the propositional part of intents, but that cannot be a reason to pay no attention at all to the speech act component. Since the present chapter is directed at PWS, it concentrates on the propositional aspect, leaving the social commitment or speech act factor underexposed.

An intent enters the language module as a *Semantic Analysis* (SA), which underlies the surface form of the corresponding sentence. The proposition cast into the language-specific form of an SA is an *L-proposition*. L-propositions are type-level predicate logic formulae with lexical items taken from the lexicon of the language L. The grammar of L processes SAs into well-formed type-level surface sentences. The phonology-cum-phonetics of L converts surface sentences into a form that is ready for realization as a token utterance.

In this set-up, *L-propositional meaning* is defined as follows:

The meaning of an L-proposition *P* underlying a sentence *S* is the system-driven, type-level property of *P* to reveal to the competent hearer the underlying token mental proposition *p* as part of a necessary cause of any token occurrence of *S*, given pre-established reference and indexing relations.

At the L-propositional level, all lexical items, including the logical operators, are assumed to be predicates, regardless of their surface category: *all lexical meanings, including those of the logical operators (see Chapter 8), are predicate meanings.* The grammar of L determines the surface category (see Seuren 1996).

9.2.3 *Semantic questionnaires*

A proposition, as a token mental act of assigning a property to an entity, forms a rich cognitive ensemble incorporating all sorts of collateral detail. When you tell me that your wife walked out of a lecture on illegal immigration yesterday, your underlying proposition will normally be embedded in a cognitive ecology containing a wide gamut of information specifying, for example, the source of your information, the time of her leaving, the contextual function of your message, possibly her reasons for leaving or her manner of leaving, and so on. Not all this information is, or need be, expressed in the final utterance, but what you, the speaker, have decided what the core message will be—that she walked out of a lecture on illegal immigration—is the minimum that must be conveyed.

Interestingly, languages differ in the requirements they impose on how intents crystallize into SAs. Each language has, as part of what Slobin (1987) has called 'thinking-for-speaking', corresponding with the concept of 'microplanning' (Levelt 1989), what may be called a *semantic questionnaire* that must be 'filled in' before the message can be processed. Some languages require a specification of the kind of source of information the speaker relies on (expressed in the grammatical category of evidentiality), or of the position of the event on the time axis relative to the time of speaking (expressed as tense), or of the manner of presentation of the event (expressed as aspect), and so on, while other languages do not or leave it to the speaker to specify such details. Such cross-linguistic differences are naturally reducible to differences in each language's 'semantic questionnaire'. The cognitive embedding of propositions has to be rich enough to provide the information required on such questionnaires, which are like immigration forms. Some states require that you specify the purpose of your visit ('business', 'vacation', 'study', 'other'), but others do not or in terms of different categories. Expressing a proposition p in a language L involves a processing of p in the administrative terms of the lexicon and the grammar of L—one of the many obstacles in the way of good quality machine translation.

The cognitive perspective in semantics thus provides a basis for an explanation of the fact that languages differ in their expression of semantic categories, so that translation from one language into another, always and as a matter of principle, requires an appeal to the cognitive embeddings of the propositions that are to be translated: translation is a rethinking and re-expression of the original text in another language.

It should be understood that this notion of a different semantic questionnaire for each language conflicts in no way with the theory that each sentence in any language has an underlying, semantically analytic form, its Semantic Analysis or SA, cast in the structural terms of a universal logical language—a variety of the language of modern predicate calculus—explicitly expressing semantic scope and variable binding relations, as well as predicate-argument structure, and with universal meanings for the logical operators. This theory, in so far as it is formulated here, allows for non-logical lexical items/predicates to vary indiscriminately from language to language, provided they are allocated to specific positions in SA-trees (as in Seuren 1996). (It may well be that the theory is too liberal in this regard, in that lexical predicates are subject to universal constraints, but no general theory of universal lexical constraints has so far seen the light.) What is universal about the logical language of SAs is not the lexical predicates selected from the lexicon of each language but the fact that whatever predicate is selected must fit into the scope-determining structural format of that logical language. Thus, proposition-modifying predicates of tense, aspect, modality, evidentiality or other possible general categories that have a bearing on propositions as a whole will often, but by no means always, be assigned a position in the auxiliary component of SA-trees, between two tenses, for example, whereas predicates assigning a property to individuals will normally be placed in the matrix part of the SA-structure (see Seuren 1996 for a full discussion). Such differences do not affect the overall structural principles of the language of SAs.

9.2.4 *Grammar, meaning, and cognition*

Natural language semantics is the study of the *type-level*, systematic aspects of linguistic meaning, not of the *token-level* application to specific entities and situations. The well-known distinction between type-level *comprehension* and token-level *interpretation* is thus upheld and carried through systematically in the present chapter.

Semantics is part of the machinery of each specific language L and has to be acquired by anyone aiming at command of, or competence in, L. The language machinery operates at type level. It is a processing machine that mediates between token entities at either end: actual speech sounds (or script) at one end and intents with propositions at the other. As with any processing machinery, it is token in, token out. The token inputs need to be fitted into the categories of the machinery (phonemes, lexical items, tense, aspect, grammatical structures, etc.).

The language machinery makes ample use of naturally given, pre-existing cognitive categories—a matter of cognitive economy—but the natural and the linguistic categorization systems are not identical, as appears from the fact that lexical conceptualizations differ considerably from language to language, often without corresponding culturally determined conceptual differences.

A few examples of this general phenomenon should suffice. *Prima facie* one would say that English *bald* corresponds with German *kahl*, but where German has *ein kahler Baum*, English speaks of *a bare tree*. English *teacher* corresponds with Italian *insegnante*, but the English sentence *Salieri was Beethoven's teacher* cannot be translated into Italian by using the word *insegnante*; the word *maestro* is appropriate in this context. German *Abstand* and *Entfernung* both translate into English as *distance*. But *Abstand* (literally 'stand-off') is appropriate in contexts where there is an opposition between two parties; it consequently has a connotation of staying apart or even hostility. *Entfernung* evokes a perspective in which one thinks of bridging the distance by travel or otherwise. This last example is instructive in that it shows that an account of lexical meaning in terms of PWS is bound to fail, precisely because the cognitive dimension is missing. Particularly instructive, in this respect, is the case of English *threshold* and its German counterpart *Schwelle*. Although the two words denote the same class of objects, the use of *Schwelle* has been extended to cover what are known as speedbumps, but it is unthinkable that *threshold* could be used in that sense. The reason lies in different cognitive perspectives. *Schwelle* is understood as a (shallow) elevation in the ground surface, whereas *threshold* has the cognitive connotation of a separation between two spaces. Yet the extensions of *threshold* and *Schwelle*, in their non-extended uses, are identical. Hardly anything is known in an analytical way about such phenomena. Yet they are real and they require an appeal to cognition.

Grammar is not 'autonomous and independent of meaning' (Chomsky 1957: 17), as Chomskyan generativists still hold, nor is grammar fully explained by requirements of cognition, design and use, as is maintained by functionalists and cognitivist linguists in the face of crucial counterevidence and at the expense of conceptual clarity (Seuren 2004b; Seuren and Hamans 2010). Instead, grammar, as a type-level coding system, is *in the service of meaning.* In doing its service, grammar enjoys a certain amount of freedom as regards lexical form and in many other ways. Hence the diversity of languages, dialects and sociolects. But it has to stay within the terms of its remit, which is the mediation of meaning between thought and sound.

9.2.5 *Virtual and actual facts*

Consider a token utterance of the type-level sentence *The pope fell off his horse*, where the past tense takes us to—is *keyed* to—some moment in the year 1750 and the noun phrase *the pope* is keyed (refers) to the person charged with that office at that time.[1] Whether the uttered sentence is true or false is of no concern to the semanticist, though it may be of concern to the historian. The semanticist's concern is the *type-level meaning* of that sentence, which is the sentence's property of being usable to enable perceivers of its token utterances to reconstruct the token proposition conceived by its producer.

Its type-level linguistic meaning is the fact that it describes the *type-virtual fact* of a, no matter which, pope falling off his horse at some definite time previous to the time of speaking, whatever that time is. Given proper keying to a historical situation, we get a *token-virtual fact* of that pope falling off his horse at the past moment contextually or otherwise specified by the past tense. This token-virtual fact becomes a *token-actual fact* if and only if it is true that that pope fell off his horse at that moment. If it is false that that pope fell off his horse at that moment, the token-virtual fact remains a token-virtual fact, as it lacks actuality.[2]

Token-virtual facts are created by cognition and are thus the product of a proposition as defined above (the token mental act of assigning a property to one or more entities). Type-virtual facts are abstractions of token-virtual facts. They are what remains when all specific entities, events and other world-elements that an actually uttered L-proposition is about, or is keyed to, are left unspecified. What are called 'referring expressions' in a type-level L-proposition are thus only *potentially* referring expressions. They are, if one wishes, variables ranging over *actually* referring expressions in token utterances. Type-actual facts and type-actual entities are not

---

[1] I use the term *keying* for the mental, or intentional, focusing on the particular entity or setting an utterance is about. The term is taken from French *roman à clef* or German *Schlüsselroman*, which is a novel that may be read as being applicable to real persons and situations. See also section 9.8 below.

[2] On the nature of facts, see Seuren 2009a: 220–4 and section 9.7 below.

included in this analysis; they require a Platonic universe, which I am not prepared to argue for. (More is said about virtual facts below, in the sections 9.7 to 9.10.)

We can thus set up Figure 9.1, which describes in schematic terms the processing stages leading up to the uttering of true or false propositions and the corresponding ontological elements (facts). It should be noted that what I call 'ontology' here is an attempt not at constructing any 'objective' ontology, which is an activity pursued by certain metaphysicians, but at reconstructing the natural ontology that humans operate with, something that ought to be done in cognitive science. This 'cognitive' ontology must involve virtual besides actual entities, because utterances that are not about actual entities or actual facts are as meaningful as those that are. False utterances, for example, are not about actual facts, yet they are blamelessly meaningful, which means that they must be about something. I say that they are about virtual facts. All virtual elements in the ontology humans operate with are *creations* of the mind; they have no mind-independent 'existence' or 'subsistence'.

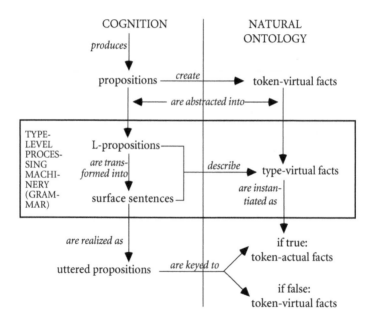

FIGURE 9.1 How propositional meaning relates to facts in natural ontology

9.2.6 *Truth conditions and use conditions: 'settling' phenomena*

Truth conditions of sentences are a by-product of semantics: the thesis that truth conditions *define* sentence meanings is too strong. The sentences *The bottle is half full* and *The bottle is half empty* have the same truth conditions but different meanings.

Being half full and being half empty are different, though related, properties, as becomes apparent when one considers the sentences *The bottle is not yet half full* and *The bottle is not yet half empty* or *John hoped that the bottle was half full* versus *John hoped that the bottle was half empty*. Likewise for *John bought a car from Harry* and *Harry sold a car to John*, which are truth-conditionally but not semantically equivalent (try embedding them under *I resent that…*). Meaning, especially lexical meaning, is defined in part by truth conditions, but also by positive, negative or neutral evaluations (as in *clever* versus *sly*; *hope* versus *fear* and the neutral *expect*, or as in the negative *brat* versus the neutral *child*), perspective takings (as in *come* versus *go*, *sell* versus *buy*, *here* versus *there*), associations (*ajar*, typically said of a door or a hinged window, but not of, say, an eyelid or a curtain or a lid on a pan), and further non-truth-conditional parameters.

Every language has, besides *truth conditions* for the definition of its meanings, also a wide variety of *use conditions*. As is argued in Chapter 1, all natural languages, being part of the *social reality* in the communities where they are spoken, are subject to a continuous process of what I have called 'settling'. This means that, as a result of social spreading processes within a speech community, speakers tacitly agree on certain grammatical patterns, on certain specializations, extrapolations or transfers of lexical meanings, on certain fixed, idiomatic word combinations in special meanings—all, of course, within any universal boundaries for variability set for all languages. Thus we say in English that there is a fly *on* the ceiling, not *at* the ceiling, though if one says *at the ceiling* one does not utter a falsehood (if there is indeed a fly on the ceiling), but one only expresses oneself inadequately, given the socially valid norms for correct usage. And if Dan and Liz are a married couple, Dan is married *to*, not *with* Liz, and vice versa, but they may be married *with* three children. And when you say that Kharim is a *hairtrimmer*, rather than using the more common *barber*, what you say is not false, when Kharim is indeed a barber, but true, only deviantly formulated. Such non-truth-conditional use conditions are very much part of what we take to be linguistic competence and they should all be properly recorded in dictionaries and grammars. Needless to say, PWS has so far maintained a total silence on such matters. The real natural-language semanticist should investigate to what extent such 'settling' phenomena are subject to, perhaps very subtle, cognitive criteria or whether they are cognitively neutral and merely consist in idiosyncrasies of linguistic form, to be stored in linguistic memory.

9.2.7 *Comprehension is part of semantics; interpretation is not*
We remember from section 9.2.1 that linguistic meaning is defined as follows:

Linguistic meaning is primarily the system-driven property of a sentence *S* as a linguistic type-level unit, in virtue of which a linguistically competent hearer is able to reconstruct speaker's intent (that is, a speech act operator over a proposition) from any utterance token of S, given proper values for contextual and situational parameters. In a secondary and derived sense, linguistic meaning is a property of type-level lexical elements and of grammatical constructions.

It follows from this definition that the assignment of 'proper values for contextual and situational parameters' is not a question of the study of meaning as part of the language system, but rather belongs to the pragmatic study of the myriad of ways in which language is used. Semantics as an academic discipline is part of the study of the language *system*, not of language *use*. Semantics studies the processing machine, not the processing itself. It is a *type-level*, not a *token-level*, activity, though it must localize and define the places where the machinery needs token input from use conditions.

This type-token distinction is standardly ignored in PWS, where it is often said that the semantics of a language links the expressions of that language with the reality they are about. This, however, is not correct, at least not for natural languages. One of the core differences between a natural and a formal language (as used in logic or in computers) is that natural languages are semantically mediated by the minds of their speakers, whereas formal languages are semantically mediated by an inbuilt model theory, and model theories differ essentially from human minds. The semantics of a natural language L does not link the expressions of L with the external world, but with the mental representations needed and used for dealing cognitively with the external world. The mind first 'processes' the external world in terms of categories, viewpoints, evaluations and other parameters. Language then links up linguistic forms with mental 'forms'. There is no direct link between language and the world, as was already seen by Ogden and Richards, who speak of 'an imputed relation' (Ogden and Richards 1923: 11; for more comment see Seuren 2009a: 230–2). The real, causal, relations with the world in the use of language go via the mind, which does the primary job of categorizing and processing.

This has far-reaching consequences. One is that a distinction must be made between, on the one hand, *type-level*, or *sentence-level*, *comprehension*—the hearer's reconstruction of the speaker's intent without any values for contextual and situational parameters—and, on the other, *token-level*, or *utterance-level*, *interpretation*—the hearer's reconstruction of the speaker's intent complete with the required values for contextual and situational parameters. The terms I have used in Seuren (2009a) and (2010) are *anchoring* and *keying*: for adequate utterance interpretation, a sentence must be *anchored* to an ongoing discourse and *keyed* to a specific situation, so that the deictic and definite expressions can *refer* to specific entities or parameter values.

From this it follows that the semantics of a natural language L does not link the expressions of L with the external world but is instrumental in establishing the link between the expressions of L and mental representations of the external (or any thought-up internal) world. The final link with the actual world is not established by language but by the so far not very well understood cognitive machinery of *intentionality* (with *t*) enabling a cognizing subject to focus on, or attend to, specific situations and specific elements in situations.

Interpretation and its subdivision reference, being part of language use, are thus not a matter of semantics, but comprehension is, being a matter of linguistic competence, not of linguistic practice. When I say, here and now, *That man is buying a newspaper*, the question of who the phrase *that man* refers to, if it refers to anyone at all, is as immaterial for the semantic as it is for the grammatical study of language. What the semanticist needs to know is that the phrase *that man* is in need of a proper reference value for the sentence as a whole to have a truth value. This is in itself uncontroversial, yet semanticists keep insisting that semantics links language with the world, whereas a modicum of reflection will tell them that it does not.

Comprehension has to be learned, in contrast to the assignment of reference values. Once comprehension has been acquired as part of the language acquisition process, the ability to *interpret* utterances is taken for granted. Comprehension is studied in semantics; interpretation has not found a true home so far. Perhaps cognitive psychology should take it under its wing.

9.2.8 *Software realism and weak instrumentalism*

The theory I propose is, in principle, of a *causal realist* nature. In practice, however, given (a) the inaccessibility of the neural hardware and (b) the question of its direct causality with regard to the facts of language, the realism aimed at is best restricted to a *software realism*, the brain software forming a more plausible level at which causal relations with regard to natural language are to be sought than the brain hardware. The heart of this problem is that *consciousness* has not so far been formally modelled. We have no idea of how physical processes give rise to conscious experiences or vice versa. All we have is a restricted set of correspondences between experiential and neural data. This obstacle is fatal for any attempt at full formal modelling of cognitive faculties, including those that causally underlie the use of language. Even so, the ultimate aim remains a theory that lays bare the causes of the observable phenomena, at whatever level of explanation.

The data for the theory are problematic as they are of a phenomenological nature and consist of intuitive native judgements on whether or not a given string of words *R* is a proper expression of an intended meaning in the language at hand. When it is not, we have, in principle, ungrammaticality on a reading—though many 'ungrammatical' or 'unidiomatic' strings of words are easily repaired. (When there is no meaning at all for which *R* is a proper expression, one may speak of ungrammaticality in an absolute sense.) It is well known that data of this nature are tricky and that, for other than really clear cases, batteries of proper empirical criteria should be developed to ensure more reliable results (Levelt 1974c: 14–21).

Despite these obstacles, we have reached a stage where it has proved possible to formalize some *modular* (algorithmically organized) parts of the language system, in particular the *grammar algorithm* converting SAs into surface structures. But the ways in which the language system links up with cognition have so far escaped formal analysis and are still largely unclear. For example, the chameleonic nature of lexical meaning (polysemy etc.), or the way in which mental intents crystallize into SAs for subsequent lexical, grammatical and phonological processing have so far resisted formalization. It will be clear that PWS is of no help in these respects, as it has nothing to say about the cognitive aspects of semantics.

Philosophers of science make a distinction between *realism* and *instrumentalism*. A realist theory aims at the reconstruction of the causal reality underlying the observable phenomena, claiming direct or indirect reference relations of certain crucial elements in the theory to elements in the hypothesized reality, which causally explains the data.[3] When the underlying physical reality is inaccessible, or insufficiently explanatory, a software realism is the next option.

Instrumentalism aims at capturing the observed data in terms of a formal system that may or may not model a causally underlying reality, about which it is in principle agnostic. The instrumentalism that denies any causally underlying reality or is indifferent in this regard may be called *strong instrumentalism*. Strong instrumentalist theories can only be said to describe, and hopefully also to predict, the data. When there is a chance of an instrumentalist formal system describing or approximating the causally underlying reality, we speak of *weak instrumentalism*. Although weak instrumentalism in semantics still lacks, strictly speaking, an interpretation onto an *actual* cognitive machinery, it has an interpretation onto a *virtual* cognitive machinery, defined by what that machinery would be like if the formalism were to correspond to reality. In semantics, weak instrumentalism and software realism are thus not too far apart.

Montague was a strong instrumentalist, but many or most of his followers tend to weak instrumentalism, as appears from the numerous attempts to make PWS palatable to cognitive scientists (see section 9.3.1 below). My argument in section 9.3 is that they will be forced back to strong instrumentalism unless they give up the possible worlds framework, since there is no chance that this framework will ever even approximate the reality causally underlying the semantic phenomena of natural language.

---

[3] The correspondences between elements in the theory and ontological reality constitute a research area in its own right (Levelt 1974a: 6). As regards natural language, Levelt (1974b: 27–65) presents a method for measuring the degree to which theories of grammar correspond to structural intuitions reported by native speakers. This method has not, unfortunately, taken root in linguistics, and even less in semantics—though Osgood et al. (1957) presented a method for the measuring of semantic relatedness of lexical meanings.

9.2.9 *Formal explicitation of natural cognitive systems*

Beyond these distinctions, there is a point of view not discussed in the philosophy of science literature and relevant only for disciplines concerned with cognitive computing systems such as arithmetic, grammars, natural logic or semantics. In these disciplines, one may take a theory to be a *formal automaton*, providing a *formal explicitation* of the full consequences of a computing system that is assumed to be present in embryonic or restricted form in the mind or brain. The neural machinery allows humans to perform operations up to a limited level of proficiency or capacity, but gives up when more is required (cultural development and scholastic training help to crank up the level of performance). This makes it an interesting and relevant exercise to figure out where these faculties would end up if they were not subjected to any limitations of working space and memory capacity.

Generative theories of grammar have been looked at from this perspective, in that a generative grammar is describable as an algorithm producing an infinite set of sentences of finite but unrestricted length, though any practical implementation will be restricted by memory and working space capacity. Such a view implies that the theory is not looked at from a *modelling* point of view but as a *formal explicitation* of what is, in some form, somehow, present in the mind. The logical systems discussed in Chapter 8 and the logico-semantic system expounded in section 9.8 are to be seen as exercises in formal explicitation as described here.

9.3 Critique of PWS

9.3.1 *Foundations and methodology*

PWS, in all its varieties, fails methodologically, empirically and philosophically. This has been known for three or four decades, yet, paradoxically, PWS practitioners carry on as if nothing were amiss. Methodologically, there is the 'exceedingly vexed question' (Dowty et al. 1981: 13) of the *psychological reality* of PWS. While the literature on the *ontological status* of possible worlds contains rather outspoken views, ranging from realism to mathematical abstraction, there is great uncertainty regarding the *modelling aspects* of PWS (Chapter 8 in Dowty 1979, though interesting, sensible and well written, yields little in the way of principled conclusions). Is PWS a realist or an instrumentalist theory? If realist, how does it map onto mental reality (*software realism*) or neural reality (*hardware realism*)? If instrumentalist, is it indifferent with regard to any underlying reality (*strong instrumentalism*), or does it still reckon with a system actually present in the mind or brain and responsible for the data but agnostically left out of account (*weak instrumentalism*)?

Thomason, in his introduction to Montague (1974), implies correctly that Montague was a strong instrumentalist (Thomason in Montague 1974: 2):

According to Montague the syntax, semantics, and pragmatics of natural languages are branches of mathematics, not of psychology. The syntax of English, for example, is just as much part of mathematics as is number theory or geometry.

All Montague intended to achieve was to describe in mathematical terms what must be the case in a model when an assertive sentence is true—an exercise that is no doubt challenging and useful in many ways, but of ancillary value to a theoretical linguist, who tries to find out how language works in the brain or mind, in the world and in the society of humans. But Montague was not a theoretical linguist, at most an external technical expert called upon for a certain purpose.[4]

David Lewis deserves to be classified as a weak instrumentalist (Lewis 1972: 170):

I distinguish two topics: the description of possible languages or grammars as abstract semantic systems whereby symbols are associated with aspects of the world; and second, the description of the psychological or sociological facts whereby a particular one of these abstract systems is the one used by a person or population. Only confusion comes of mixing these two topics.

This tallies with the view expressed by Barbara Partee (Partee 1979: 2):

The fact that some logician is not interested in psychology does not preclude the possibility that he or she may develop a theory which can be taken as a serious candidate for a psychological theory.

Most other writers on the subject are likewise weak instrumentalists. They still reckon with a system that is implemented in the mind or brain and causally responsible for the data but is, for the moment, agnostically left out of account. They are, however, also overconfident in that they skip any preliminary enquiry of what kind of possible 'abstract system' will do the job, implicitly assuming that the programme of extensionalization of intensions in terms of possible worlds will be a candidate—even when it is *a priori* clear that it must end in empirical deadlock. Weak instrumentalist PWS suffers from its strong instrumentalist Montagovian origin and is, in the end, forced back to that origin.

---

[4] I thus disagree with Montague:

Like Donald Davidson, I regard the construction of a theory of truth—or rather, of the more general notion of truth under an arbitrary interpretation—as the basic goal of serious syntax and semantics; and the developments emanating from the Massachusetts Institute of Technology offer little promise towards that end. (Montague 1974: 188)

This corresponds in no way to what the established discipline of linguistics is about. The sneer directed at the MIT linguistics of the day may be justified to the extent that that specific brand of linguistics indeed offers little promise as regards semantics, but to generalize from there to the whole two-millennia-old tradition of the discipline by denying it the predicate 'serious' is perhaps a little over the top. It certainly offends the linguists, who do not wish to see the subject matter of their discipline prescribed by philosophers who have very little knowledge of matters of language.

9.3.2 *Empirical inadequacy of PWS*

Besides many other empirical shortcomings (such as the neglect of scope differences; see the sections 3.7.2.2 and 9.11), one, well-known, irremediable fault of PWS is its failure to account for the fact that logically equivalent L-propositions embedded under certain, commonly called *intensional*, predicates are often not mutually substitutable *salva veritate*, while PWS has no choice but to say that they always are. This problem comes to a head, empirically speaking, in cases of necessarily true and necessarily false L-propositions. Let John, who has an ancestral shrine in his garden, hold the necessarily false belief that his ancestors are both dead and alive. Then PWS makes it follow that John believes any necessary falsity, for example that alligators do and do not have emotions, or that the square root of 4096 is 266—even when John holds no beliefs at all with regard to alligator emotions or square roots. And analogously for necessarily true sentences. The reason is that PWS takes the extension of an L-proposition T embedded under a partiscient ('intensional') predicate to be the set of possible worlds in which T is true. Since that set equals $\emptyset$ for necessarily false L-propositions and W (the set of all possible worlds) for necessarily true L-propositions, one necessary truth or falsity is worth another.

This problem is known as *the problem of propositional attitude sentences*, but a better name is perhaps *the happy extensionalist problem*, as it stems solely from the happy but naïve illusion that language users deal directly with an actually existing, extensional world and not with what they construe as being 'out there' on the basis of their experiences and perceptions (see the sections 9.2.7 and 9.5). No amount of theoretical rethinking has so far produced a solution.[5] Most authors ignore the issue, letting the time bomb tick.

9.3.3 *Truth values as extensions and as Boolean 1 and 0*

A further problem resides in the widespread convention of taking the truth value of an (interpreted) L-proposition as its extension and treat the values *True* and *False* as Boolean 1 and 0, respectively. This is convenient because the Boolean functions of

---

[5] The seriousness of this problem is recognized by Dowty et al., who write (1981: 175):

We must acknowledge that the problem of propositional attitude sentences is a fundamental one for possible world semantics, and for all we know, could eventually turn out to be a reason for rejecting or drastically modifying the whole possible worlds framework.

As one would expect, quite a few attempts have been made to solve this well-known problem within the terms of PWS. The most notable example is Cresswell (1985), where the author replaces the notion that propositions are sets of possible worlds with a more finely grained notion implying that propositions are propositional functions with the values of the free variables specified under the λ-operator. This proposal was discussed in detail by Von Stechow (1985), but, despite his obvious sympathy for this approach, Von Stechow had to conclude that Cresswell's attempt was, in the end, unsuccessful. Other, later, attempts never reached the degree of sophistication of Cresswell (1985) and will be left unmentioned here. It is, anyway, commonly accepted among PWS practitioners (a) that the problem is basic and threatening, and (b) that it has not been solved.

product, union and complement now compute the classic truth functions $\vee$, $\wedge$ and $\neg$, respectively. The idea goes back to Frege, who proposed it in his epochal paper 'Ueber Sinn und Bedeutung' ('On sense and reference') of 1892. Although calling out for protest, the decision to take the truth value of an L-proposition as its extension is hardly ever discussed in the literature, and when it is (e.g. Shramko and Wansing 2010), the authors steer clear of the problem of ontological anomaly. The only author who expressed his doubts in this regard is Michael Dummett (1973: 412–13):

> But the idea that truth-values are constituents of an independent reality does not play any comparable [to the nominal reference function; PAMS] role in Frege's philosophy. Whether a given thought is true or false is, of course, an objective matter; but that the truth-value of the thought is itself an entity which is one of the components of reality is a conception which is held merely in order to complete the analogy according to which the referents of all expressions are extra-linguistic correlates of those expressions, belonging to the real world, and does not appear to be a thesis which has any significance on its own.

Dummett's doubt is justified (for discussion, see Seuren 2009a: 207; 2010: 46). The extension of a linguistic expression is by definition part of the (or a) world. Extensions populate worlds, regardless of what is said or thought about them, and their 'being there' makes, or helps make, propositions true or false. If truth values are the extensions of sentences, they must be part of the world and make the underlying propositions true or false, which is absurd. Truth values are not denizens of worlds regardless of whether that world contains individuals forming mental propositions and expressing them linguistically. Moreover, there is no principled reason why such abstract denizens of those worlds in which cognizers form propositions should figure in Boolean algebra. It is at least remarkable that the literature, with the exception of Dummett, has so far kept a firm silence on this ontological anomaly of PWS theory.

Montague himself was likewise, at least sometimes, distrustful of the notion that sentences denote truth values. In his 1968 paper 'English as a formal language', the Fregean distinction between an *extension* (Bedeutung) and an *intension* (Sinn) for L-propositions is given up for the position that sentences merely have a 'denotation', which, for him, is a proposition—that is, a set of possible worlds (Montague 1974: 217):

> It is wrong to maintain—as Frege possibly did in [Frege 1892]—that an analysis of ordinary English (or German) requires a notion of *sense* as well as one of *denotation*. The fact that we have been able to do with denotation alone depends on [...] our decision to regard sentences as denoting propositions rather than truth values.

This way the truth-functional operators are reduced to set theoretical functors, which justifies a Boolean derivation of the truth tables. However, besides the artificiality and, for many, the absurdity of seeing a proposition as a set of possible worlds, this answer falls again foul of the happy extensionalist problem, since any truth-functional composition that is necessarily true or false will then denote, in Montague's sense, the set *W* of all possible worlds or the null set, respectively, so that in a partiscient context any necessarily true or false truth-functional composition will be replaceable *salva veritate* with any other necessarily true or false L-proposition. Quod non.

In sum, the entire framework of PWS suffers from at least two related irreparable foundational defects. This in itself legitimizes a total revision: PWS has apparently met its Boojum.

9.4 Intensions and the blocking of substitutivity

9.4.1 *Frege's system of extensions and intensions*

While the term *extension* is used for whatever it is in the world that makes or helps make sentences true, the term *intension* has nothing better to show for it than a loosely knit family of uses ranging from introspective psychology to mathematical functions. What once was a unified notion began to fall apart when, after 1950, mathematical logic invaded the semantics of natural language.

Traditionally, intensions were assigned to predicates only. The *intension* of a predicate *F* used to be the analysis of the concept underlying *F* in terms of the conditions to be satisfied by any entity for it to deserve the predicate *F*. Nowadays we speak of the *satisfaction conditions* of *F*. The *extension* of *F* in any given world *w* is then the set [[F]] of entities *x* such that F(x) delivers truth in *w*.

Frege generalized the extension-intension distinction to definite referring terms and sentences (L-propositions, Frege's *Sätze*). His reason for doing so was his discovery[6] of the unsettling fact that co-referring terms are not substitutable *salva veritate* in certain contexts known as *intensional contexts* but here called *partiscient contexts*.[7] Partiscient contexts block substitution *salva veritate* (SSV) of co-referring terms. For example, when *Harry believes that John loves Mary* is true, it does not follow automatically that *Harry believes that the burglar loves Mary* is also true, even though John and the burglar are one and the same person. This fact is alarming because it poses a serious threat to the Aristotelian theory of truth as correspondence— a threat Frege intended to remove.

The intuitive answer is, of course, that SSV is blocked because Harry need not *know* that John and the burglar are the same person and because a person's belief is restricted by the extent of their knowledge. This answer, though correct in principle (hence the term *partiscient*), is in need of greater precision and integration into a general semantic framework. Frege sought to fulfill this need by distinguishing

---

[6] Or rather, *rediscovery*, since the problem had already been spotted by Eubulides (fourth century BCE) in his *Electra paradox*, used to attack Aristotle's theory of truth as correspondence (see Seuren 2005).

[7] The neologism *partiscient* was introduced in Dever (2008: 185), in a not too dissimilar context, as a counterpart to *omniscient*.

between the *extension* and the *intension* of an L-proposition, the *extension* being, in his vision, its truth value and the *intension* being the underlying thought. Since he took the predicate *believe* to select the *intension* of its object clause as input, and since the thought underlying *John loves Mary* differs from the thought underlying *The burglar loves Mary*, the two embedded L-propositions are not mutually substitutable *salva veritate* under *believe*, so that, *a fortiori*, the terms *John* and *the burglar* are not that way substitutable either.

As regards the extension and the intension of *predicates*, Frege took the extension of a predicate *F* to be a concept (*Begriff*), taken as a mental entity in its own right. When this notion of concept is translated into current set-theoretic terms, in the spirit of Carnap or Montague, we may say, somewhat bending Frege's original intention, that the extension of a predicate *F* is what has been defined above as [[F]]. The intension of *F* he took to be the conceptual content, specifiable in terms of the satisfaction conditions of *F*—that is, the conditions to be satisfied by any entity for it to qualify for *F*.

For Frege, as for PWS, the extension of a *definite referring term* a is its actually existing reference value: the unique entity *e* in the world cognitively or intentionally focused on by the speaker and, if all goes well, also by the listener. Clearly, this fails to account for reference to non-existent entities in true sentences, such as *Apollo was worshipped on the island Delos*.[8]

On the intension of a definite term, Frege is less clear. He speaks (Frege 1892: 26) of the 'mode of presentation' ('Art des Gegebenseins'), but not even the Frege specialist Dummett (1981: 44–46), comes to a firm conclusion about what Frege might have meant, though he is inclined to read Frege as saying that the intension of a definite referring term is the cognitive search procedure followed by speaker and hearer to 'get at' the reference object. I follow Dummett in this interpretation (Seuren 1998: 373–4, 2009a: 204), though I do not follow Frege in his doctrine.

Frege thus posited a distinction between extensions and intensions for (a) referring expressions (definite terms), (b) predicates, (c) full L-propositions and (d) L-propositions in partiscient (intensional) contexts. His analysis is represented in Figure 9.2.[9]

---

[8] Frege implicitly answers this objection by relegating virtual entities to contexts created by intensional operators such as *in the story*. Yet this answer is unsatisfactory, because Apollo was *really* worshipped on Delos, not 'in the story'. One should note also that the distinction made by authors like Kripke (1972) between definite descriptions on the one hand and proper names on the other is rejected here. Proper names are definite descriptions of the form 'the *x* such that *x* is called "N"', where "N" stands for a quoted name (see Seuren 1998: 378–81; 2009a: 130). No problems arise with this account and no further assumptions need be made.

[9] Frege failed to specify the *intension* of an L-proposition in a partiscient term position. Perhaps we should be generous and assume that, for him, the thought underlying a partisciently embedded L-proposition is both its extension and its intension.

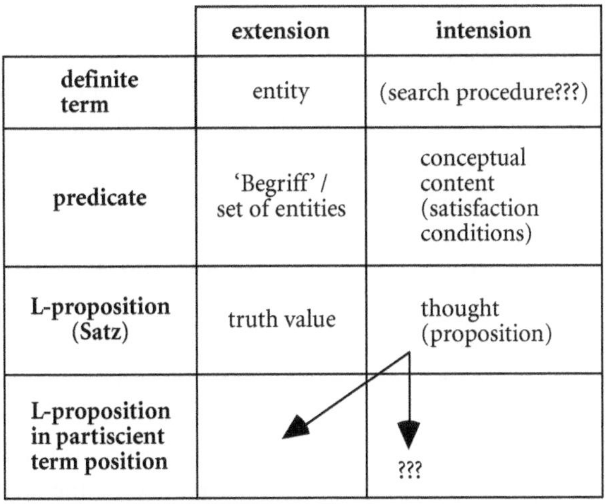

	extension	intension
definite term	entity	(search procedure???)
predicate	'Begriff' / set of entities	conceptual content (satisfaction conditions)
L-proposition (Satz)	truth value	thought (proposition)
L-proposition in partiscient term position		???

FIGURE 9.2 Frege's position with regard to extensions and intensions

Frege's (re)discovery of the blocking of SSV in partiscient contexts and his proposed solution made for a historic breakthrough in natural language semantics. But is his solution adequate? It implies that an L-propositional object term that is input to a predicate like *cause*, which does not block SSV in its object clause, should be the *extension*—that is, the truth value—of the embedded L-proposition. But then any other L-proposition with the same truth value should be substitutable *salva veritate*, which is absurd, because if it is true that the fire caused the roof to collapse it is not necessarily also true that the fire caused Copenhagen to be the capital of Denmark, even though it is true both that the roof collapsed and that Copenhagen is the capital of Denmark.[10]

---

[10] Some may object that *cause* expresses a three-place relation between a causer, an object and a property describing what happens to the object. This view seems less tenable in the light of sentences like (i) or (ii)—to give just two from a host of possible examples all pointing to the same conclusion (see Postal 1974 for extensive discussion):

(i) The depression caused it to rain for hours on end / made it rain for hours on end.
(ii) His answer caused the penny to drop / made the penny drop.

In (i), *it* can hardly be taken to refer to an object. In (ii), there is no penny at all to be affected by the property of dropping. Rather, *the penny* is the non-referring subject term of the idiom *The penny dropped* and the grammar algorithm has mechanically raised this subject term to the position of (quasi-)object term of *cause* or its synonym *make*, according to the rule of SUBJECT-TO-OBJECT RAISING. Note that in *He let the penny drop*, which does have an SA-form in which *let* is a three-place predicate expressing a relation between the *he*, a penny and the property of dropping, the idiomatic sense has disappeared, so that the sentence, if true, must be about an actual penny. This means that, semantically speaking, *cause* and *make* are best taken to be two-term predicates expressing a relation between a causer and a token-virtual fact, expressed by an embedded proposition, possibly in the shape of a nominalization. Semantically, this appears to make more sense than a treatment of *cause* as a three-term predicate.

This problem is hardly discussed in the PWS literature—not surprisingly, given the problems it creates for PWS. When it is (e.g. Lewis 1973; Dowty 1979: 99–110; McCawley 1981: 316–18), *cause* is not treated as a predicate taking a clause or nominalization as object term, but, curiously, as a material implication or counter-factual, considered accountable for in terms of possible worlds (Dowty 1979: 103–8). Dowty rightly points at a number of problems in this regard, to which may be added the mystery of how any reasonable grammar could reduce a material implication or counterfactual to the verb *cause*, as well as the non-truth-functional character of *cause* in nongeneric uses (as in the example above). Causation is better seen as an ontological category in its own right, not reducible to, or describable in terms of, an *if–then* relation. How that ontological category should be defined is not germane to the present study.

The only solution in Fregean terms seems to be to let *cause* also take the intension ('thought') as input from its embedded object clause and let the meaning of *cause* require the truth of this thought. But this is counterintuitive since what is caused is not a thought but a fact (whether state of affairs or event). Moreover, if this solution is adopted, the reason for assigning truth values as extensions to L-propositions evaporates, because then even the truth-functional operators of propositional logic can be said to accept L-propositional intensions as input and to regulate the output entailments in virtue of their meaning description in the form of truth tables. In fact, something along these lines seems implicit in Montague's proposal (1974: 217), mentioned above, to drop the distinction between *extension* and *intension* for sentences and speak only of their *denotation*, which he takes to be a proposition—that is, a set of possible worlds.

A related problem for Frege's analysis concerns SSV of *referring terms* as object terms of partiscient predicates. John may have great faith in Mr Snow, who is a local magistrate, but have no faith at all in the drunkard he met in the pub last night, although, unbeknownst to John, the magistrate and the drunkard are the same person. Supplanting intensions for extensions here does not work, first because Frege is unclear about the intension of referring phrases and secondly because if we take that to be the referential search procedure, as suggested above, we get the counterintuitive result that John has (or hasn't) great faith in something that is in fact a search procedure. It makes more sense to say, as we do, that John's faith, or lack of it, extends to his virtual entities Mr Snow and the drunkard, whose identification in the actual world is not registered in his knowledge.

9.4.2 *The cognitive view of intensions*

Intensions are thus placed squarely in the cognitive domain and extensions in the world domain. Frege still grew up in that tradition but, given the incipient positivism of his day and the rising tide of mathematicization, he wished to avoid what he saw as the complications brought about by the cognitive factor. To this end he sought refuge in some form of Platonism, the philosophical paradigm that sees ontological reality as consisting primarily of *Ideas* (concepts). In this context, Frege wrote his 1918 paper 'Der Gedanke' ('The thought'), in which he reduces thoughts to ontologically highly doubtful Platonic Ideas.

This was unwelcome to later generations of possible-world semanticists, whose cultural climate was defined not only by anticognitivism (one thinks of the enormously influential movement of behaviourism, which for decades declared anything to do with the mind anathema), but also by anti-Platonism, given that the dominant trend in Anglo-Saxon philosophy since the early 1900s has been nominalist and definitely not realist or, worse, Platonist. It was, therefore, incumbent on the new developers of PWS to redefine intensions not only in non-cognitive but also in non-Platonist terms. So they defined intensions as functions from possible worlds to entities (for definite terms), to sets of entities (for predicates), and to truth values (for propositions), not realizing, apparently, that in doing so they were letting in ontological entities that were at least as doubtful as Plato's Ideas. The result has been the, bluntly speaking, absurd notion that a proposition is a set of possible worlds.

I wish to reinstate the cognitive view of intensionality. *Intensionality is the defining property of conceptual content.* Anything resulting from the human cognitive processing machinery is intensional. Concepts, propositions, L-propositions, meanings, and even the mental representations of actual reality, are intensional. Intensions are to be distinguished from *virtual extensions*, which are virtual entities of any level of abstraction or reification: properties, situations, processes, facts (see Seuren 2009a: Ch. 2 for extensive arguments that human ontology comprises virtual reality). Token-virtual entities, properties, situations, processes or facts are creations of the mind which, in the natural ontology of humans, are taken to have some sort of 'being', as witnessed by the fact that we naturally refer to and quantify over them, but which are taken to lack actuality as long as it has not been established, through the methods that have been developed for this test, that they must be taken to be actual. The cognizing mind is, in non-hallucinating subjects, fully aware of the distinction between what is or should be taken to be merely virtual and what, in addition, is or should be taken to be actual. Virtual reality is two-sided: it is intensional in virtue of its being a creation of the mind and extensional in virtue of the fact that it may help in establishing truth or falsity. It may, moreover, be as Platonic or undisciplined as it likes to be, as long as it is not actual.

9.5 The Kantian paradox of knowledge and virtual reality

This lands us inevitably in the *Kantian paradox of knowledge.* In trying to determine the nature of reality, the first principle is that the real, knowledge-independent, nature of the outside world is unknowable and unprovable. This is what made

Descartes posit his principle *Cogito ergo sum*: all I know with certainty is that I exist, because I am undeniably conscious of my own experiences; the rest is conjecture. Kant followed suit by arguing that what is taken to be the outside world cannot but come to us via our perceptual and cognitive machineries and not 'directly' in the form of what it is 'an und für sich' (in and for itself). Our view of the outside world is, therefore, necessarily the product of a *cognitive construal* carried out in each individual's mind. To think that we can grasp the world as it *really* is ('an und für sich'), is naïve and unwarranted. An ontology can only be a systematic account of the best possible construal of the world as it presents itself to us, in the light not only of human experiences, impressions, sensations, perceptions and predictions, but also of logical reflection on them and of the insights afforded by science. Creating an 'objective' ontology on *a priori* grounds is hubris.

All we can do, no less in philosophy than in ordinary life, is go by the most reliable and most coherent construal, as Leibniz taught us, and take the great *inductive leap*, which allows us to lead our lives on the basic and to some extent naïve assumption that the world is as it presents itself to us, complete with other people and thus other minds like our own, whom we recognize as being in the same predicament and venturing the same inductive leap. And, if we are to trust our experiences that have been built up during our lifetimes and are undeniable, as stated in the Cartesian *cogito*-argument, this construal proves to be not only sufficiently uniform among the members of the human race (*pace* magical and religious construals in many societies), but also sufficiently reliable for us to get by in relative safety for ourselves and in a relatively good communion with what we have decided are our fellow humans— a good indication that basic world-construal procedures are innate and innately expected by each of us to be innate in others.[11]

Thus, the experience of certainty we have in relation to what we call our 'knowledge' is based on an innate world-construal procedure, which is naïve and uncritical in unsophisticated individuals and societies but open to refinement and purification by rational thought and systematic testing by means of scientific experiments. This conclusion is called the *paradox of knowledge*: we think that we know with certainty, only to find out on reflection that we cannot be certain, while we still go on behaving with the certainty we had before we started to reflect and consider this behaviour rational. It follows that extensions are only 'extensions' in terms of our world construal and thus much more 'intensional' than is currently acknowledged. It also follows that a proper semantics for natural language should start with intensions and should accept the reality, though not the actual existence, of virtual entities, properties, events, situations, facts etc. Unfortunately, this great Cartesian-Kantian reservation regarding certainty and knowledge, though it pervaded the whole of philosophy

---

[11] When the inductive-leap mechanism does not work properly in an individual, the result is a condition generally diagnosed as autism.

from Descartes till the early twentieth century, has all but disappeared from the agenda of Anglo-Saxon philosophy and hence from the agenda of logic and model-theoretic semantics.

One thus has no choice but to accept that a theory of natural ontology must allow for virtual reality. It would be a disaster if we, humans, did not have it. We would be unable to plan ahead of actual events, to form a hypothesis about an entity still not proven to exist, etc., since we would be unable in principle to think about the future or about possible situations other than the actual one. In short, the human race would be unable to survive.

For Quine, an entity cannot be an entity unless it has a precisely defined identity: 'No entity without identity', was his slogan in the famous and highly rhetorical first chapter 'On what there is' in his 1953 book. His argument there is that I can imagine a host of 'possible men' in a doorway, without being able to distinguish one from another, making the notion of possible men ontologically unmanageable. Therefore, he argues, one should avoid the 'slum of possibles', which is nothing but a 'breeding ground for disorderly elements'. In fact, however, this argument is a sleight-of-hand, because it applies a criterion for *actually existing* entities to *virtual* entities (Seuren 2009a: 80–4). All this argument shows, when deprived of its rhetoric, is that actually existing entities are not virtual entities—hardly world news. What Quine failed to mention is that virtual entities are *per se* the product of human imagination and thought, and that it is precisely that faculty of imagination and thought which determines the identity of any given thought-up entity. In disciplined thinking, as in scientific hypotheses or in police investigations, virtual entities are kept properly apart from each other and from actual entities, whereby what were thought to be different entities can be identified and single virtual entities can be split up, without such thought processes leading to incoherence or confusion. In dreams or fantasies, by contrast, such mergings and splittings-up often occur in uncontrolled ways, without any clear identity criterion.

9.6 The new game of extensions and intensions

We give up Frege's extension–intension parallelism for all expression types. A definite referring term has an 'extension', if you like, but this 'extension' is often a virtual entity, as in the true sentence *Apollo was worshipped on the island of Delos* (Seuren 1985: 252).[12] Therefore, rather than speak of the 'extension' of a definite

---

[12] Possible-world philosophers have great difficulty with the fact that humans assign proper names to non-existent entities as easily and naturally as they do with regard to actually existing entities. This fact is *per se* unaccountable for in Kripke's 'causal' theory of proper names (Kripke 1972), which is sufficient reason for rejecting that theory. Menzel (1990) goes further, saying that humans cannot name nonexistent entities: 'it seems reasonable that we cannot name objects that do not exist' (Menzel 1990: 386, note 12). It is a good thing that freedom of speech is protected by law.

referring term, I will speak of its *reference value*, or ρ-value (Seuren 1985: 248), which is, in principle, a token-virtual entity that is endowed with extensional or actual being when found out to have actual existence and *requires* actuality when its commanding predicate requires for truth that it be extensional. The notation ρ(a) is thus used for the token reference value of the term *a*, which is in principle virtual (intensional) and becomes extensional only when it finds its real-world actual instantiation as a result of extra-semantic, cognitive interpretation processes.

Consider the definite noun phrase (NP) *the farmer*, represented in L-propositional structure as in Figure 9.3 and read as 'the x such that x is a farmer':

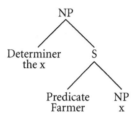

FIGURE 9.3 The SA-structure of the NP *the farmer*

Standard model-theoretic semantics requires an extensional reference function associated with the Determiner, which should select, without any external help, the unique reference object of the NP *the farmer* from the set of those entities that satisfy its semantic description. But this is impossible unless this set contains just one member. Small wonder that this reference function has never been formalized in any theory. Nor need it be, not in semantics anyway, because, as has been said (section 9.2.7), reference to actually existing entities, just like the determination of truth values, is not a matter of semantics but of cognitive psychology, called upon in the interpretation of utterance tokens. Cognitive psychology finds this reference function hard to define and to formalize, because of its crucial dependence on context, situation and world knowledge. In this respect, the reference function does not differ from so many other cognitive functions that prove to be hard to formalize or define for similar reasons.[13]

---

[13] I do not wish to discount serious attempts at formalizing referent search procedures, such as *Centering Theory* (see, for example, Walker 1997). In fact, the more successful such attempts, the better our understanding of language *use*. What we are concerned with here, however, is the language *system*. The point is that semantic theory does not require a referent search procedure, as reference is not part of semantics, while PWS does require such a procedure, since it fails to make the necessary distinction between type and token (sentence and utterance), but cannot provide one, since it is incapable of taking the wider cognitive context of uttering sentences into account. Little wonder that Russell was so keen on getting rid of definite descriptions.

At least for fully lexical referring phrases such as *the farmer*, the ρ-function is *guided* by the semantic content of the nominal predicate (*farmer*), but it is not *determined* by it, unless the nominal predicate denotes a set consisting of just one element. When I say to my colleague at work *Let's meet in the pub at six*, then the particular pub referred to is likely to be one of many pubs in town. Yet my colleague and I know exactly which pub is meant. Extensional reference requires a wider cognitive context for it to be successful. Since this wider context has so far resisted formalization, so has the ρ-function.

The situation is different with regard to predicates. Here it does make sense to distinguish their extension from their intension in the traditional way. The extension $[[F]]$ of a predicate F is, again, the set of entities to which F is truthfully applicable and the intension of F is the set of (world, cognitive, social, experiential, or emotive) satisfaction conditions to be fulfilled by any entity to qualify for F. This differs from Frege-inspired doctrine in that predicates are no longer functions from entities to truth values, but from (type or token) virtual entities to (type or token) virtual facts—facts being a specific kind of entity—regardless of any specific 'world'.

Since L-propositions can be re-used as argument terms under a higher embedding predicate, they likewise need a ρ-value, which is likewise a token-virtual extension (type-virtual when unkeyed). L-propositional ρ-values are virtual facts which are turned into actual facts when the L-proposition in question is true. The ultimate value of an L-proposition S is thus not a truth value but in all cases a virtual fact: type-virtual when unkeyed; token-virtual when keyed; then token-actual when true, token-virtual when false, as shown in Figure 9.1. The ρ-values of both terms and L-propositions are thus virtual entities that seek extensional counterparts as their sentences strive for the attainment of truth. Virtual, mind-created entities seek actual values in each 'world' to the extent that this is necessary to help L-propositions to the value True. Falsity is established only when truth is unattainable.[14]

---

[14] Truth seems to be the preferred value in interpreting utterances. In Seuren (1985: 318–19, 2009a: 126) the example is given of a department with two professors of English, one Dutch and one British:

(i) There is a professor of English in this department. *He* is British.

The second sentence, *He is British*, clearly counts as true in this situation. But this requires that *he* refers to the Brit, not to the Dutchman, which means that the reference function optimizes truth, not falsity. Another example is given in Clark (1992: 94), where a situation is described of two men seen to be walking down the street, one very fat, one very thin. Now both (ii) and (iii) are true, but with different referents for *that man*; (iv) cannot be given a truth value because it fails to provide a clue for determining the reference value needed for truth:

(ii) That man weighs too much for his own good.
(iii) That man weighs too little for his own good.
(iv) That man is my neighbour.

Interpretation thus goes for truth to begin with. It goes for falsity when the utterance is well-keyed but truth is unattainable. It gives up on truth or falsity when the utterance cannot be properly keyed, as in (iv).

9.7 The nature of facts

Facts are a hybrid sort of thing. They are part of the world but only in so far as they make propositions true: *no propositions, no facts* (Seuren 1985: 250). One cannot isolate or identify actual facts as such. A question like 'How many actual facts are there in this room?' hardly makes sense. The only sensible answer to such a question would be: infinitely many, in fact as many as the number of true propositions that can be conceived and possibly expressed about this room. And that number has no finite upper bound. Actual facts emerge from the world as *truth-makers* for propositions. They are not independent 'things', nor are they the same as 'states of affairs'. An actual fact is whatever it is that makes a given proposition true. It is circular to say, as Wittgenstein did in his *Tractatus Logico-Philosophicus*, that the world is the totality of all facts. If this were correct, there would be no world if there were no propositions—an implausible view, given our construal of the world as something that exists independently of minds forming propositions about it.

Given a true L-proposition of the form $F(a)$, the corresponding actual fact may be described as $\rho(a) \in [[F]]$. However, in order to specify the *meaning* of an L-proposition we need virtual facts, as actual truth or falsity makes no semantic difference. The virtual fact corresponding to $F(a)$ may be written as $*\rho(a) \in [[F]]^*$. Semantically different sentences correspond to different virtual facts, even when they are truth-conditionally equivalent (see section 9.2.5 above).

Token-virtual facts are the ontological counterpart of the well-keyed L-propositions describing them. But an L-proposition may be unkeyed, as when I say, here and now and without any further clarification, *The man was right after all.* This is just a type-level sentence of English, which may be written on a board, commented upon, analysed or described grammatically or semantically. Without a key, it does not describe a token fact and thus cannot be true or false. All it does is provide a type-virtual fact, a mould for a token-virtual fact—like a form that has not been filled out but has a structure. This type-virtual fact becomes a token-virtual fact when the corresponding sentence is properly anchored and keyed and it becomes a token-actual fact when it is true, in any given 'world' or situation.

9.8 Valuation spaces

In this context, it is useful to introduce the notion of *valuation space* (VS), originally presented in Van Fraassen (1971), but left underdeveloped by that author. A valuation space is defined as follows (see section 9.2):

The VALUATION SPACE /S/ of an L-proposition *S* is the set of possible (admissible) valuations (situations) in which *S* is true (modulo key).

Given a set of L-propositions forming a language L, the *valuation field* Un (Universe) of L is the matrix of the L-propositions in question and truth valuations. A truth valuation is a *situation description* or simply a *situation*. A situation (valuation) sit_n is an assignment of truth or falsity to the L-propositions of L and is thus a partial description of, if you like, a 'possible world' *w*—but since a full specification of *w* would require an unattainable degree of detail, *w* is not a possible world in the current sense. A sit_n is a description that goes as far as there are L-propositions available in any given discourse to describe *w*.

Situation descriptions are not possible world descriptions and situations are not possible worlds. They differ in that a valuation field Un is constructed on the basis of given sentences of a language L, whereas possible worlds are conceived as language-independent entities in ontological space. A situation sit_n is not a possible world because sit_n is restricted by the sentences L has available or by any subset of sentences of L one wishes to consider. A valuation field Un only provides possible virtual ontologies, according to its being keyed to virtual entities, some of which may be actual. As such it is mind-internal. The Kantian paradox of knowledge (section 9.5) thus pervades the semantics of natural language.

A further difference between a Un and a set of possible worlds is the fact that Un can be seen as being gradually built up through discourse. Any Un as realized at some point in time *t* is then a representation of a discourse built up till *t*. This is basic to presupposition theory: a presupposition *P* of a sentence *S* is a condition on *S* that *P* has been valued True prior to *S* in the discourse (Heim 1990; Seuren 1985, 1988, 2000, 2010).This aspect is not further elaborated here, yet it will be clear that it has considerable explanatory potential for the formal theory of presuppositions and discourse.

Un will thus contain all admissible combinations of truth and falsity for the sentences of L. Given a bivalent semantics, if L has *n* logically and semantically independent sentences, there are 2^n situations. Situations that are inadmissible on grounds of semantic or logical inconsistency are scrapped. For example, if in a sit_n a sentence *S* is valued True and a sentence *T* is valued False while *S* logically or semantically entails *T*, sit_n is inadmissible and gets scrapped. Logical compositions of L-propositions by means of the truth-functional *truth predicates*—the operators of propositional logic and the predicates *true* and *false*—are valued automatically in any given sit_n, given the truth values in sit_n of their component L-propositions.

For the sake of clarity, a toy model may be useful (see section 8.2). Consider a toy model where L consists of three logically and semantically independent sentences *A*, *B* and *C*. This gives a VS-model of eight (2^3) valuations/situations, as shown in Figure 9.4 ('T' stands for 'true'; 'F' for 'false'). Each valuation (situation) is an assignment of truth values to *A*, *B* and *C*.

valuations (=**Un**):	1	2	3	4	5	6	7	8
A	T	F	T	F	T	F	T	F
B	T	T	F	F	T	T	F	F
C	T	T	T	T	F	F	F	F

FIGURE 9.4 VS-model for the semantically independent sentences *A, B* and *C*

The VSs for *A, B* and *C*—that is, /A/, /B/ and /C/, respectively—are thus as follows:

$$/A/ = \{1,3,5,7\}$$
$$/B/ = \{1,2,5,6\}$$
$$/C/ = \{1,2,3,4\}$$

When a sentence *S* is logically necessary, /S/ = **Un**; when S is logically impossible, /S/ = Ø.
    As regards the logical compositions, /¬A/, /¬B/ and /¬C/ are simply the comple-ments in U of /A/, /B/ and /C/, respectively; /A ∧ B/ = /A/ ∩ /B/; /A ∨ B/ = /A/ ∪ /B/:

$$/¬A/ = \{2,4,6,8\}$$
$$/¬B/ = \{3,4,7,8\}$$
$$/¬C/ = \{5,6,7,8\}$$
$$/A ∧ B/ = \{1,5\}$$
$$/A ∨ B/ = \{1,2,3,5,6,7\}$$

When two sentences stand in some logical relation to each other and are thus not semantically independent, some valuations become *inadmissible*. Thus, when A ⊢ B (*A* entails *B*), the situations 3 and 7 in Figure 9.4 are inadmissible, as they represent impossible situations. When A >< B (*A* and *B* are contraries), the valuations 1 and 5, where both *A* and *B* are simultaneously true, are inadmissible. When A ≡ B, /A/ = /B/. Equivalence of *A* and *B* leaves only 1, 4, 5 and 8 as admissible valuations, cutting out 2, 3, 6 and 7.
    The logical relations are thus definable in terms of valuation spaces as follows (contradictoriness is the combination of contrariety and subcontrariety):

a. Entailment: S ⊢ T   if and only if /S/ ⊆ /T/
b. Equivalence: S ≡ T   if and only if /S/ = /T/
c. Contrariety: S >< T   if and only if /S/ ∩ /T/ = Ø
d. Subcontrariety: S ⋈ T   if and only if /S/ ∪ /T/ = U
e. Contradictoriness: S >|< T   if and only if /S/ ∩ /T/ = Ø and /S/ ∪ /T/ = U

One specific sit_n in **Un** may be designated as the *actually obtaining* situation sit_{act}. In semantics, however, the notion of truth is better associated with a specific sit_n, regardless of whether or not sit_n equals sit_{act}. This is the well-known notion of 'truth in a model'.

A **Un** may be *indexed* to a specific *key* (see note 1 above) consisting of reference relations between the referring terms in L and a set of entities **Ent**. For **Un** as a whole, reference is rigid for any given key, in that terms always refer to the same entity, but not vice versa: the same entity may be referred to by different terms. This is the *modulo key* condition mentioned above in the definition of Valuation Space. The *modulo key* condition is necessary because a semantic system is constant under varying reference values. The ontology of **Un** thus varies according to its key. But for **Un** itself, such indexical variation makes no difference, just as a *roman à clef* will remain the same novel under a different 'key'. An unkeyed **Un**, whose sentences describe type-virtual facts, is thus a function from specific keyings to token-virtual facts. The token-virtual fact $*\rho(a) \in [[F]]*$ described by the L-proposition $F(a)$ extends over the whole of **Un**, modulo key. When $F(a)$ is valued True in any given sit_n, $*\rho(a) \in [[F]]*$ becomes the actual fact $\rho(a) \in [[F]]$ in sit_n. When $F(a)$ is valued False, $*\rho(a) \in [[F]]*$ remains virtual.

Formally, one may keep **Ent** restricted to extensional entities—though that would be empirically inadequate. But the moment L includes existence predicates such as *exist* or *imaginary*, all entities in **Ent** will be *intensional* or *virtual* entities to begin with. An entity $e \in$ **Ent** will then become the *actual* entity e in those situations (valuations) where the L-proposition *Exist(a)* (where $\rho(a) = e$) is valued True and *Imaginary(a)* False. Moreover, as I have argued in many publications (e.g. Seuren 1985, 1988, 2000, 2010), when the predicate F in an L-proposition $F(a)$ is extensional with regard to its argument term and thus induces the presupposition that $\rho(a)$ exists, but $\rho(a)$ is denied existence in the sit_n at hand, $F(a)$ is valued Radically False, a third truth value next to True and Minimally False. And likewise for all other presuppositions. I will, however, leave this aspect out of consideration here and stay strictly bivalent.

9.9 The truth predicates

The truth predicates (*true, false, not* (¬), *and* (∧), *or* (∨)) are part not only of language but also of logic, in particular propositional logic. The system outlined above is a semantic system—a method for the specification of meanings—and is thus not a subject matter for logic, which is more coarse-grained and is not interested in the specification of individual sentence meanings but only in logical relations of entailment, contrariety, contradiction, and the like. Yet logic does intrude on a semantic specification method, because logical relations hold in virtue of the *meanings* of the logical operators, which are treated as predicates at the L-propositional level (Seuren 2010: 37–59). That being so, the logic emerging from a language L is part of the semantics of L. The truth predicates are operators in propositional logic.

Therefore, their meanings determine the propositional logic associated with natural language (assuming that all languages are logically equivalent). At the L-propositional level, *true, false, not, and, or* are predicates that take L-propositions as argument terms, which thus need p-values. With type-virtual facts as L-propositional p-values, the question is: how does this work?

It helps to look first at non-logical complement-taking predicates. The claim is that for all L-propositions S, embedded or not, $p(S)$ is a virtual fact. The higher complement-taking predicate then assigns a property to the virtual fact in question, just as all predicates assign properties to the p-values of their argument terms. Many complement-taking predicates, such as *believe, want, hope, probable, possible*, leave the virtual character of the input fact intact. Other predicates, however, require the input virtual fact to be an actual fact: they require truth of the embedded L-proposition T for the truth of the overarching L-proposition S, which thus entails T. Categories of entailing complement-taking predicates are *aspectual, factive, causative* or *resultative* predicates.[15] *Aspectual* predicates are, e.g. *begin* (+ *to*–inf or + *-ing*), *stop* (+ *-ing*), *continue* (+ *to*–inf or + *-ing*) or *tend* (+ *to*–inf). A *factive* predicate induces a factive presupposition to the effect that the embedded L-proposition has been established as being true in the ongoing discourse domain or in any intensional (partiscient) subdomain. Examples are *know, realize, have forgotten, be a pity, be regrettable*. *Causative* and *resultative* predicates differ from factives in that the entailment of the embedded L-proposition is not a precondition generating a presupposition, but an update condition generating a simple entailment (see below). Thus, a sentence like *John has forgotten that Rome is in Italy*, with the factive predicate *have forgotten*, presupposes that it has been established as a fact in the current discourse domain that the virtual fact described by *Rome is in Italy* is an actual fact in sit_n. Since the default (minimal) negation preserves presuppositions, the default negative *John hasn't forgotten that Rome is in Italy*, still presupposes that Rome is in Italy. By contrast, a sentence like *The fire caused the roof to collapse*, with the causative predicate *cause*, entails but does not presuppose that the virtual fact described by *the roof collapsed* is an actual fact. Hence, its default negation *The fire didn't cause the roof to collapse* carries no presupposition (under non-contrastive intonation on *the fire* and a normal sentence-final intonation) that the roof collapsed. Analogously for resultative predicates like *manage*: *John managed to escape* entails, but does not presuppose, that John escaped.

We now do the same for the truth predicates, which take virtual facts as input and deliver a virtual fact as output, and whose intensions (meanings, satisfaction conditions) specify entailments regarding the truth or falsity of the embedded

---

[15] Perceptual predicates like *see* or *hear* are best taken not to entail their object clauses. They can be used to provide veridical reports of visual or auditory perception in dreams or hallucinations, as in *I saw the ghost blow out the candle*. How to deal with such cases is a matter for lexicologists.

L-propositions. Thus, the predicate *not* (¬) takes the virtual fact $\rho(T)$ denoted by its argument L-proposition T as input and requires for truth of the overarching L-proposition that $\rho(T)$ remains a virtual fact in sit_n. Likewise, the L-propositional schema (9.1), with the corresponding tree structure in Figure 9.5, requires for truth that both $\rho(S_2)$ and $\rho(S_3)$ are actual facts:

(9.1)   F(a) ∧ G(b)

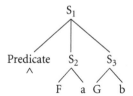

FIGURE 9.5 The SA-structure of F(a) ∧ G(b)

The ρ-values of S_2 and S_3 in Figure 9.5 are as follows:

(9.2)   a. $\rho(S_2) = {}^*\rho(a) \in [[F]]^*$
         b. $\rho(S_3) = {}^*\rho(b) \in [[G]]^*$
         c. Hence: $\rho(S_1) = {}^*<{}^*\rho(a) \in [[F]]^* ,{}^*\rho(b) \in [[G]]^*> \in [[\wedge]]^*$

What counts now is the satisfaction conditions of $[[\wedge]]$ and the other truth predicates (we assume simplistically that their linguistic meanings equal their logical meanings, but see Seuren 2010, Ch. 3 for important qualifications of this view). These are specified in (9.3) (S, T range over L-propositions):

(9.3)   For all sit_n:
         a. $[[\text{True}]]$ = $\{\, \rho(S) \mid sit_n \in /S/ \,\}$
         b. $[[\text{False}]]$ = $\{\, \rho(S) \mid sit_n \notin /S/ \,\}$
         c. $[[¬]]$ = $\{\, \rho(S) \mid sit_n \in \overline{/S/} \,\}$
         d. $[[\wedge]]$ = $\{\, <\rho(S),\rho(T)> \mid sit_n \in /S/ \cap /T/ \,\}$
         e. $[[\vee]]$ = $\{\, <\rho(S),\rho(T)> \mid sit_n \in /S/ \cup /T/ \,\}$

Thus, (9.1) is true if and only if both S_2 and S_3 are true, and false otherwise. The VSs of L-propositions composed with the truth predicates are as defined in (9.4):

(9.4)   a. /True(S)/   =   /S/
         b. /False(S)/ = $\overline{/S/}$
         c. /¬S/   = $\overline{/S/}$
         d. /S ∧ T/   =   /S/ ∩ /T/
         e. /S ∨ T/   =   /S/ ∪ /T/

This avoids the ontological incongruity of taking truth values as extensions of L-propositions, while the Boolean functions still find a natural application in the truth predicates.

9.10 SSV in partiscient contexts

9.10.1 *Under surface predicates*

When an embedded L-proposition T describes a virtual fact produced by a cognizer H in a way that implies possibly restricted knowledge of the sit_n at issue, SSV is blocked in T, as H may not *know* that the terms open to SSV have the same ρ-value. Thus, Harry may *realize* that John loves Mary, but if he does not know that John and the burglar are the same person, he may not realize that the burglar loves Mary. And analogously for all other partiscient predicates. Predicates that have no relation to a partiscient cognizer do not block SSV in their embedded L-propositions. Thus, complements under *begin to, continue to, stop* (+ -*ing*), *tend to, used to, cause* allow for free SSV. But predicates like *realize, forget, assume, be deemed to, be felt to, believe, claim, conclude, consider, obvious, prove, reckon, understand, want* block SSV in their embedded L-propositions.

9.10.2 *Under truth predicates and prepositional operators*

L-propositional embeddings under the *truth predicates* clearly allow for free SSV, since these predicates in no way imply partiscience.

Prepositional operators such as *in the story, on his reckoning, in my view,* etc.—but not *in England, after midnight,* etc.—count as partiscient predicates and thus block SSV—a fact not or hardly noticed in the literature. In the theory of Semantic Syntax (Seuren 1996: 116–28), prepositions are binary predicates at SA-level, with a nominal object term and an embedded S as subject term (their scope). Thus, a sentence like *John is happy in England* is rendered, at SA-level, as in Figure 9.6 (assuming VSO-order):

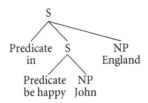

FIGURE **9.6** The SA-structure of *John is happy in England*

The grammar of English and most other languages makes the prepositional predicate *in* incorporate the object term *England* (OBJECT INCORPORATION or OI is a common process in the languages of the world; see note 5 in Chapter 8). The newly formed complex predicate *in-England* is then lowered into a (right- or left-)peripheral position in the subject term Matrix clause, giving (right-peripherally) *John is happy in England*. In cases where the prepositional object-NP denotes a cognitive content (grammatically marked by the fact that it can be followed by a *that*-clause: *the story that...*, but not **England that...*), the complex predicate resulting from OI is partiscient in the sense that encapsulated cognitive content does not *per se* cover omniscient knowledge and will in most cases be very partiscient and often false. It follows that prepositional operators such as *in the story, on his reckoning, in my view* block SSV.

9.10.3 *Under epistemic modals*

In the PWS literature, the *epistemic modalities* of possibility and necessity are stock examples of partiscient context creators and stand as model cases for a treatment in possible world terms. Yet epistemic *may* and *must* are adequately described in terms of partiscience without any appeal to possible worlds. The truth of L-propositions headed by epistemic *may* or *must* is contingent upon the following two conditions: (a) the speaker's relevant though probably restricted knowledge state **K** is correct, as far as it goes, and (b) the embedded L-proposition is *compatible* with **K** (for *may*) or is a *necessary consequence* of **K** (for *must*) (Seuren 2010: 203–6). The speaker's (and hearer's) partiscience is thus built into the semantics of the modal operators. No possible worlds are needed at all.

This description of the epistemic modals implies that they must block SSV in their embedded L-propositions, which they do. (9.5a) may be true while the corresponding form in (9.5b) is false, or vice versa, depending on the speaker's restricted factually correct knowledge state **K**:

(9.5)   a. The Morning Star may/must be inhabited.
        b. The Evening Star may/must be inhabited.

Deontic modals, by contrast, admit of unrestricted SSV in their embedded L-propositions:

(9.6)   a. You may/must now climb Mount Everest.
        b. You may/must now climb Chomolungma.

(9.6a) and (9.6b) are deontically and hence truth-conditionally equivalent, in either form, because the terms *Mount Everest* and *Chomolungma* (the indigenous name for that mountain) refer to the same entity and permissions or obligations presume omniscience.

9.10.4 *Doubtful cases*

For some SA-predicates the question is doubtful. For example, it is not clear whether SSV is blocked in a sentence like (9.7), where John and the burglar are the same person:

(9.7)   It is easy for the police to find John/the burglar.

If one feels that the ease of finding John is related to the knowledge state of the seeker (the police), SSV will be blocked, but if one feels that it is not, SSV will be allowed. Similarly with the predicate *turn out*, as in (9.8):

(9.8)   It turned out that John/the burglar had committed the murder.

Factive subordinating conjunctions like *because* or *although* (which are treated as L-propositional predicates) also give rise to doubt in this respect. Consider the following examples, where Claire is under the illusion that Mr Snow and the vicar are different persons:

(9.9)   a. Claire left because Mr Snow/the vicar had read the wrong passage.
      b. Claire left because Mr Snow/the vicar was using foul language.
      c. Claire fell because she tripped over Mr Snow's/the vicar's dead body.

(9.10) a. Claire left although Mr Snow/the vicar had read the right passage.
      b. Claire left although Mr Snow/the vicar was still speaking.
      c. Claire fell although Mr Snow's/the vicar's car narrowly missed her.

The (a)-sentences seem to resist SSV more strongly than the (b)- or (c)-sentences, owing no doubt to Claire's greater personal involvement with regard to Mr Snow, or the vicar, underwriting the *because*- or *although*-clauses: greater personal involvement implies a greater role of partiscience. If asked why Claire left, someone who knows that the vicar and Mr Snow are the same person may assent to (9.9a) with *the vicar* but not with *Mr Snow*, and likewise for (9.10a), but that person will have no problem with assigning the same truth value to (9.9c) or (9.10c), no matter whether the expression *Mr Snow* or *the vicar* is used. The (b)-sentences seem to be somewhere in the middle. What underwrites the *because*- or *although*-clauses in the (b)-sentences is perhaps less to do with Claire's attitude vis-à-vis Mr Snow, also known to many people (but not to Claire) as the vicar, than with the fact that foul language was being used or that the speech had not yet come to an end, respectively. In the (c)-sentences, SSV is freely allowed, no doubt because Claire's personal involvement, and thus the extent of her world knowledge, plays no part at all in the underwriting of the *because*- or *although*-clauses.

9.10.5 *No happy extensionalist problem*

Does this analysis also steer clear of the happy extensionalist problem? Yes, and trivially so. Since necessary truth or falsity results from all kinds of L-propositions describing different virtual facts, the question of mutual SSV of logically equivalent, and in particular necessarily true or necessarily false, L-propositions does not arise. It is just collateral damage of the fateful decision to consider propositions to be sets of possible worlds. The happy extensionalist problem is not an empirical problem but merely one that is created by the artificiality of the theory of PWS.

This answer to the problem of the blocking of SSV in partiscient contexts poses no threat to the Aristotelian theory of truth as correspondence. All it takes is a proper semantic analysis of partiscient predicates combined with a proper grammar, and a proper ontology of actual and virtual reality. Frege can rest in peace, and so can Aristotle.

9.11 Quantification

A few words must be said about quantification, because no semantic theory deserves that name if it lacks a proper account of quantification (as do intuitive and informal semantic approaches such as are found in cognitivist linguistics; Seuren 2009a: 27–31). Moreover, quantification shows perhaps more clearly than anything else the usefulness of a strict separation of grammar and semantics. The path from sentences to truth conditions consists of two trajectories, the grammar and the semantics. The grammar connects sentences with their underlying L-propositions (Semantic Analyses; SAs). The semantics takes the L-propositions that underlie sentences as input for the specification of meanings. Going directly from sentences to a specification of meanings (truth-conditions) requires a great deal of unexplanatory mathematical complexity for what is done by the grammar in the much simpler and much more explanatory, non-mathematical terms of tree-structural transformations. This division of labour pays off in that a grammar formulated in terms of tree-structural transformations allows one to state simplifying and explanatory generalizations that will forever be beyond the reach of a semantic theory that skips or incorporates grammar. Semantics should not take over the totally different realm of grammar. The position defended here is closely akin to what used to be known as *Generative Semantics*—the theory that sees grammar as a coding system for meanings (Seuren 1996).

Montague dealt with quantification in his notoriously abstruse paper 'The proper treatment of quantification in ordinary English' (Hintikka et al. 1973: 221–42; Montague 1974: 247–70). Neither the fence of technicality around this article nor the cockiness of its title are justified. Its technical complexity is a consequence of the fact that Montague took English surface sentences as input to his model-theoretic calculus of truth conditions, skipping the grammatical reduction of the surface sentences to their underlying SA or L-propositional form.

Despite its fame in PWS circles, this article shows up a central empirical short-coming of PWS and the theory of grammar (the system relating surface structures to logical structures) that comes with it, namely its intrinsic inability to account for operator scope. Montague-grammar is unable to differentiate between the different meanings of, for example, (9.11a), which is false in most academic meetings, and (9.11b), which is true in most academic meetings, although (9.11b) is merely the passive of (9.11a). Similarly for the German sentences (9.12a) and (9.12b):

(9.11)   a. Nobody here knows two languages.
         b. Two languages are known by nobody here.

(9.12)   a. Ich habe kein Wort lesen können.
            'I couldn't read a word.'

         b. Ich habe ein Wort nicht lesen können.
            'There was one word I couldn't read.'

As is well-known, these semantic differences are a matter of operator scope, imposed by a universal syntactic constraint on the relation of scope with left-to-right order in surface sentences. But since Montague-grammar is crucially based on lambda functions and since lambda functions are insensitive to left-to-right order or to tree structure position, these obvious semantic differences cannot be expressed in it. The answer that has generally been given over the years, even by German-speaking Montagovians, in relation to this obvious problem has always been that such sentences are, in fact, ambiguous as regards the scope of the operators concerned. The untenability of this answer appears most clearly from the German sentence pair in (9.12). English does not allow for a word-by-word equivalent of (9.12b) because, in English, the negation has to go with the auxiliary (*do* if there is none) or else with an existential quantifier, as in *I saw nobody* (Seuren 1996: 111–14, 260–4, 300–9).

The theory defended here does better in this respect. It leaves room for a grammar mapping SA-structures onto surface structures and such a grammar, unlike Montague 'grammar', allows for a condition, the *Scope-Ordering Constraint*, requiring that, in principle, operator scope in SAs be reflected in the left-to-right ordering of the linguistic elements representing the operators in question, with special provisions for peripheral surface constituents, intonational patterns and non-word (affixal) status of the elements concerned (see section 3.7.2.2 above; Seuren 2009a: 28–31).

In the present context, only the universal quantifier *all* (*every*, *each*) and the existential quantifier *some* are considered.[16] In the spirit of the theory of *generalized quantification* (Mostowski 1957; Barwise and Cooper 1981), the universal quantifier ∀ (*all*) and the existential quantifier ∃ (*some*) are taken to be, at SA level, higher-order predicates over pairs of sets. (9.13a) and (9.14a) are thus considered to result from the

---

[16]   See the chapters 2 till 5 and 10 in Seuren (2010) for a detailed analysis of these quantifiers.

underlying L-propositions (9.13b) and (9.14b), respectively (leaving tense out of account):[17]

(9.13)   a. All farmers grumble.

  b. $\forall_x$ (Grumble(x),Farmer(x))

(9.14)   a. Some farmers grumble.

  b. $\exists_x$ (Grumble(x),Farmer(x))

The second (object) argument term in the (b)-structures—Farmer(x)—is the *Restrictor term*, denoting the *Restrictor set*; the first (subject) term— Grumble(x)—is the *Matrix term*, denoting the *Matrix set*. We speak of *Restrictor* and *Matrix* terms because the former restricts the set of entities (farmers) over which the property denoted by the predicate (*grumble*) is distributed (universally or partially), while the latter specifies the main predicate (*grumble*) in the surface Matrix clause. The grammar is again quite simple, at least in main outline (Seuren 1996: 300–9): given the L-propositions (9.13b) and (9.14b), the transformational cycle makes the quantifier first adopt the Restrictor or object term (by OBJECT INCORPORATION or OI); then the new complex quantifier-predicate is lowered on to the position of the variable bound by it in the Matrix term—much like the treatment meted out to prepositional predicates above (see Figure 9.6).

The predicates $\forall$ and $\exists$ in the (b)-sentences are provided with the subscript x for the purpose of variable binding. In (9.13b) and (9.14b) the subscript x can be dispensed with, variable binding being univocal. But in multiply quantified sentences, such as (9.15) or (9.16), variable binding must be disambiguated, which is conveniently done by means of the subscripts x and y:

(9.15)   a. All farmers groom some horse.

  b. $\forall_x(\exists_y(\text{Horse(y)},\text{Groom(x,y)}),\text{Farmer(x)})$

(9.16)   a. Some farmers groom some horse.

  b. $\exists_x(\exists_y(\text{Horse(y)},\text{Groom(x,y)}),\text{Farmer(x)})$

Here, the Restrictor (object) term is again Farmer(x) and the Matrix (subject) term is $\exists_y(\text{Horse(y)},\text{Groom(x,y)})$. (The latter denotes a set because it contains the unbound variable x.) This simple machinery suffices in principle for quantified terms in any position in the sentences of English or any other language, given the regulatory effect of reducing surface sentences to their corresponding L-propositional form.

In extensional terms, the satisfaction conditions of the predicates $\forall$ and $\exists$ are definable as follows:

---

[17] For the order of the Restrictor and the Matrix term, see section 4.4 and note 5 in Chapter 8.

(9.17)   For all predicates M and R and for any sit_n:
  a. $[[\forall]] = \{\ <[[M]],[[R]]>\ |\ [[R]] \subseteq [[M]]$ and $[[R]] \neq \emptyset\}$
  b. $[[\exists]] = \{\ <[[M]],[[R]]>\ |\ [[R]] \cap [[M]] \neq \emptyset\}$

The addition of the condition $[[R]] \neq \emptyset$ in (9.17a) keeps the subaltern entailment from *all* to *some* but reduces the Conversions to one-way entailments: *All F is G* entails *No F is not G* but not vice versa, and *All F is not G* entails *No F is G* but not vice versa (see Chapter 8 above; Seuren 2010: 172–80).

The definitions of (9.17) can be intensionalized—allowing virtual entities as possible ρ-values—by means of presupposition theory. As has been said, most predicates require their terms to denote actually existing entities in the sense that, for an L-proposition P(a) to be true, the L-proposition Exist(a) must first be true, on pain of P(a) being radically false. A predicate like *be a Greek god*, lacks this condition: *Apollo is a Greek god* is true although Apollo never existed. By contrast, the sentence *Hanuman is a Greek god* is false, not because Hanuman never existed but because he is not a Greek god.

This is generalized to all other presuppositions induced by a predicate P. If P presuppositionally requires that ρ(a) be human (as with *be a British national*), then a violation of that condition, as in *The moon is a British national*, will result in radical falsity. The predicate *be a British national* is thus defined as in (9.18). The satisfaction conditions have been split up into two subcategories, the *preconditions* (preceded by the colon) which generate presuppositions, and the *update conditions* (preceded by the upright stroke) which generate classical entailments:

(9.18)   For all actual or virtual entities e and for any sit_n:
  [[Be a British national]] = { e : e actually exists; e is
       human | e satisfies the legal requirements for British citizenship }

Accordingly, the universal quantifier is redefined as in (9.19), though the condition $[[R]] \neq \emptyset$ will be scrapped in a moment (no adaptation is required for the existential quantifier):

(9.19)   For all predicates M and R and for any sit_n:
  $[[\forall]] = \{<[[M]],[[R]]>\ :$ every $e \in [[R]]$ satisfies the preconditions of
    M $|\ [[R]] \subseteq [[M]]$ and $[[R]] \neq \emptyset\}$

The predicate $\forall$ thus has the precondition that for all ρ-values ρ(a) in R(x), ρ(a) satisfies the preconditions of the Matrix predicate M: the preconditions of the Matrix predicate have been transferred from definite terms to universally quantified terms.

Now the unquantified sentence *Apollo is a British national* is radically false because it violates both the existential precondition of the predicate *be a British national* and the precondition of being human (Apollo being rather of a divine nature). The sentence *The Eiffel Tower is a British national* is radically false because it violates the precondition that the subject term referent be human. In the same way, a quantified sentence like *All Greek gods are British nationals* is radically false because the Matrix predicate *be a British national* presuppositionally requires actual existence and human status for its subject term referent, and *All towers are British nationals* is radically false because the Matrix predicate presuppositionally requires its subject term referents to be human.

The null set $\emptyset$ is now no longer on stage. The mere mentioning of an entity 'creates' that entity, since mentioning requires a propositional thought process and thought processes create virtual entities, as has been explained above. This allows us to scrap the condition $[[R]] \neq \emptyset$ from (9.17a) and (9.19), and it reduces the resulting logic, when restricted to truth and minimal falsity, to the classic Square of Opposition. Its fault of undue existential import has now been eliminated owing to the protective coating of radical falsity warding off presupposition failure.

9.12 Conclusion

Our overall conclusion is, first, that PWS has done both good and harm in semantic theory. It has shown that formalization can be of great help in semantics, but it has failed to see where formalization stops being useful and starts being a millstone around the semanticist's neck. By an excess of formalization, it has taken semantics away from the reality of language and cognition, thus alienating more practically oriented linguists as well as cognitive scientists from the theoretical study of meaning and giving them a justification for indulging in non-theoretical common or garden semantics which does not yield the insights that properly moderate formalization delivers. It has forced formalization on the theory where it does not allow for formalization, thus leading to conceptual and empirical tangles that cannot be undone without undoing the theory.

Beyond this critique of PWS, we have presented the outline of a totally new approach to semantics, whereby the concept of meaning has, for the first time ever, been properly defined and semantics is described as the intensional theory of type-level meaning and language comprehension, distinct from a theory of token-level interpretation—all in keeping with the Kantian paradox of knowledge. The semantics of a language has to be learned (acquired); the interpretation of utterances follows naturally and cannot be taught. The extensions of argument terms, whether nominal or sentential, are values in virtual reality, which may acquire actuality as a result of interpretation. It has been indicated how presupposition theory, as a central part of discourse semantics, can be integrated into this system. It has been claimed that grammar and semantics should be strictly separated and some demonstrations have been given of how this separation is to be implemented. Finally, it has been shown in outline how this approach engenders a theory of quantification in natural language. Let anyone who disagrees stand up and be heard.

Bibliography

Akmajian, Adrian and Ray Jackendoff (1970). Coreferentiality and stress. *Linguistic Inquiry* 1.1: 124–6.

Ashworth, E. Jennifer (1973). Existential assumptions in late medieval logic. *American Philosophical Quarterly* 10.2: 141–7.

Astroh, Michael, Ivor Grattan-Guinness and Stephen Read (2001). A survey of the life of Hugh MacColl (1837–1909). *History and Philosophy of Logic* 22: 81–98.

Auer, Peter, Frans Hinskens and Paul Kerswill (eds) (2005). *Dialect Change. Convergence and Divergence in European Languages.* Cambridge: Cambridge University Press.

Auer, Peter and Frans Hinskens (2005). The role of interpersonal accommodation in a theory of language change. In: Auer, Hinskens and Kerswill (eds): 335–57.

Bach, Emmon (1964). *An Introduction to Transformational Grammars.* New York: Holt, Rinehart & Winston.

Barwise, Jon and Robin Cooper (1981). Generalized quantifiers and natural language. *Linguistics and Philosophy* 4.2: 159–219.

Barwise, Jon and John Etchemendy (1999). *Language, Proof and Logic.* CSLI Publications. New York–London: Seven Bridges Press.

Bateson, Gregory (1972). *Steps to an Ecology of Mind. Collected Essays in Anthropology, Psychiatry, Evolution, and Epistemology.* Chicago: The University of Chicago Press.

Beauzée, Nicolas (1767). *Grammaire générale, ou exposition raisonnée des éléments nécessaires du langage, pour servir de fondement à l'étude de toutes les langues.* (2 vols) Paris: J. Barbou. (Modern edition: B.E. Bartlett (ed.), Stuttgart-Bad Cannstatt: Frommann-Holzboog, 1974, 2 vols)

Beller, Sieghart (2008). Deontic reasoning squared. In: B. C. Love, K. McRae and V. M. Sloutsky (eds), *Proceedings of the 30th Annual Conference of the Cognitive Science Society.* Cognitive Science Society, Austin TX: 2103–8.

——(2010). Deontic reasoning reviewed: psychological questions, empirical findings, and current theories. *Cognitive Processing* 11: 123–32.

Berlin, Brent and Paul Kay (1969). *Basic Color Terms: their Universality and Evolution.* Berkeley CA: University of California Press.

Bitterli, Urs (1989). *Cultures in Conflict. Encounters Between European and Non-European Cultures, 1492–1800.* Stanford CA: Stanford University Press.

Blanché, Robert (1952). Quantity, modality, and other kindred systems of categories. *Mind* 61: 369–75.

——(1953). Sur l'opposition des concepts. *Theoria* 19: 89–130.

——(1966). *Structures intellectuelles. Essai sur l'organisation systématique des concepts.* Paris: J. Vrin.

——(1970). *La logique et son histoire: d'Aristote à Russell.* Paris: Colin.

Bloomfield, Leonard (1914). *An Introduction to the Study of Language.* New York: Holt.

Bloomfield, Leonard (1933). *Language*. New York: Holt.

Boas, Franz (1911). Introduction, *Handbook of American Indian Languages. Part I*. Bureau of American Ethnology, Bulletin 40, Part I. Washington D.C.: Government Printing Office: 1–83.

Boroditsky, Lera and Alice Gaby (2010). Remembrances of times east. Absolute spatial representations of time in an Australian Aboriginal community. *Psychological Sciences* 21.11: 1635–9.

Bowerman, Melissa (1988). The 'no negative evidence' problem: how do children avoid constructing an overly general grammar? In: Hawkins (ed.): 73–101.

Bowerman, Melissa and Soonja Choi (2003). Space under construction: language-specific spatial categorization in first language acquisition. In: Dedre Gentner and Susan Goldin-Meadow (eds), *Language in Mind. Advances in the Study of Language and Thought*. Cambridge MA: MIT Press: 387–427.

Breva-Claramonte, Manuel (1983). *Sanctius' Theory of Language. A Contribution to the History of Renaissance Linguistics*. Amsterdam/Philadelphia: Benjamins.

Brown, Roger W. and Eric H. Lenneberg (1954). A study in language and cognition. *Journal of Abnormal and Social Psychology* 49.3: 454–62.

Casasanto, Daniel (2008). Who's afraid of the big bad Whorf? Crosslinguistic differences in temporal language and thought. *Language Learning* 58. Suppl. 1: 63–79.

——(2009). Embodiment of abstract concepts: good and bad in right- and left-handers. *Journal of Experimental Psychology: General* 138.3: 351–67.

——and Kyle Jasmin (2010). Good and bad in the hands of politicians: spontaneous gestures during positive and negative speech. PLoS ONE 5.7: e11805 (pp. 1–5). doi: 10.1371/journal.pone.0011805.

Casasola Marianella and Leslie B. Cohen (2002). Infant categorization of containment, support and tight-fit spatial relationships. *Developmental Science* 5: 247–64.

Chomsky, Noam (1956). Three models for the description of language. *Institute of Radio Engineering Transactions on Information Theory* IT-2: 113–24.

——(1957). *Syntactic Structures*. (= Ianua Linguarum 4). The Hague: Mouton.

——(1959). On certain formal properties of grammars. *Information and Control* 2: 137–67.

——(1963). Formal properties of grammars. In: Luce, Bush and Galanter (eds): 323–418.

——(1964). *Current Issues in Linguistic Theory*. (= Ianua Linguarum, Series Minor 38) The Hague: Mouton.

——(1965). *Aspects of the Theory of Syntax*. Cambridge MA: MIT Press.

——(1972). *Studies on Semantics in Generative Grammar*. (= Ianua Linguarum, Series Minor 107). The Hague: Mouton.

——(1995). *The Minimalist Program*. Cambridge MA: MIT Press.

——(1998). *Linguagem e mente: pensamentos atuais sobre antigos problemas* (=Language and mind: current thoughts on ancient problems. Part I and Part II. Lectures presented at the Universidade de Brasília, 1996). Brasilia: Editora Universidade de Brasília. (Page references are to the English text as sent from MIT.)

Chomsky, Noam and George A. Miller (1958). Finite State languages. *Information and Control* 1: 91–112.

Chomsky, Noam and M.P. Schützenberger (1963). The algebraic theory of context-free languages. In: P. Braffort and D. Hirschberg (eds), *Computer Programming and Formal Systems*. Amsterdam: North-Holland: 118–61.

Clark, Herbert H. (1992). *Arenas of Language Use*. Chicago: The University of Chicago Press.

——(1996). Communities, commonalities, and communication. In: John Gumperz and Stephen C. Levinson (eds), *Rethinking Linguistic Relativity*. Cambridge: Cambridge University Press: 324–55.

Collins Cobuild English Language Dictionary (1987). Collins Birmingham University International Language Database. London–Glasgow: Collins.

Comrie, Bernard (1981). *Language Universals and Linguistic Typology*. Oxford: Blackwell.

——and Edward L. Keenan (1979). Noun Phrase accessibility revisited. *Language* 55.3: 649–64.

Cresswell, Max J. (1985). *Structured Meanings: the Semantics of Propositional Attitudes*. Cambridge MA: MIT Press.

Croft, William (1991). *Syntactic Categories and Grammatical Relations: The Cognitive Organization of Information*. Chicago: The University of Chicago Press.

——(2001). *Radical Construction Grammar*. Oxford: Oxford University Press.

——(2006). *A Glossary of Semantics and Pragmatics*. Edinburgh: Edinburgh University Press.

Cruse, D. Alan (1986). *Lexical Semantics*. Cambridge: Cambridge University Press.

Cutler, Anne and Charles Clifton (1999). Comprehending spoken language: a blueprint of the listener. In: Colin M. Brown and Peter Hagoort (eds), *The Neurocognition of Language*, Oxford: Oxford University Press: 123–166.

Davidson, Donald and Gilbert Harman (eds) (1972). *Semantics of Natural Language*. Dordrecht: Reidel.

De Morgan, Augustus (1847). *Formal Logic: or, The Calculus of Inference, Necessary and Probable*. London: Taylor & Walton.

De Saussure, Ferdinand (1916). *Cours de linguistique générale*. Paris-Lausanne: Payot.

Dever, Josh (2008). The disunity of truth. In: Robert J. Stainton and Christopher Viger (eds), *Compositionality, Context and Semantic Values. Essays in Honour of Ernie Lepore*. Berlin: Springer: 147–92.

Dixon, Robert M. W. (1972). *The Dyirbal Language of North Queensland*. Cambridge: Cambridge University Press.

——(1977). Where have all the adjectives gone? *Studies in Language* 1.1: 19–80.

Dos Anjos Gonçalves da Silva, Zoraide (2011). *Fonología e Gramática Katukina-Kanamari*. PhD thesis, Free University Amsterdam. Utrecht: LOT.

Dowty, David R. (1979). *Word Meaning and Montague Grammar. The Semantics of Verbs and Times in Generative Semantics and in Montague's PTQ*. Dordrecht: Reidel.

——Robert E. Wall and Stanley R. Peters (1981). *Introduction to Montague Semantics*. Dordrecht: Reidel.

Drews, Arthur (1928). *Lehrbuch der Logik*. Berlin: Stilke.

Dryer, Matthew S. (1992). The Greenbergian word order correlations. *Language* 68.1: 81–138.

——(2005a). Relationship between order of object and verb and order of relative clause and noun. In: Haspelmath et al.: 390–3.

——(2005b). Relationship between order of object and verb and order of adjective and noun. In: Haspelmath et al.: 394–7.

——(2009). The branching direction theory of word order correlations revisited. In: Sergio Scalise, Elisabetta Magni and Antonietta Bisetto (eds), *Universals of Language Today*. Berlin: Springer: 185–208.

Dummett, Michael (1973). *Frege. Philosophy of Language*. London: Duckworth.

——(1981). *The Interpretation of Frege's Philosophy*. London: Duckworth.

Eibl-Eibesfeldt, Irenäus (1989). *Human Ethology*. New York: Aldine de Gruyter.

Elffers, Els (2012). Saussurean structuralism and cognitive linguistics. *Histoire Épistémologie Langage* 34.1: 19–40.

Enfield, Nick J. (2000). On linguocentrism. In: Pütz and Verspoor: 125–57.

Evans, Nicholas (2011). Positional verbs in Nen. Unpublished seminar paper Australian National University, 25 February 2011.

——and Stephen C. Levinson (2009). The myth of language universals: Language diversity and its importance for cognitive science. *Behavioral and Brain Sciences* 32: 429–48.

Everett, Daniel L. (2005). Biology and language: a consideration of alternatives. *Journal of Linguistics* 41: 157–75.

Evers, Arnold (1975). *The Transformational Cycle in Dutch and German*. PhD thesis, Utrecht University. [Also: Bloomington IND: Indiana University Linguistics Club (IULC)]

Fitch, W. Tecumseh (2010). *The Evolution of Language*. Cambridge: Cambridge University Press.

——and Marc D. Hauser (2004). Computational constraints on syntactic processing in a nonhuman primate. *Science* 303 (January): 377–80.

Fodor, Jerry A. (1975). *The Language of Thought*. Hassocks, Sussex: The Harvester Press.

——(1983). *The Modularity of Mind. An Essay on Faculty Psychology*. A Bradford Book. Cambridge MA: MIT Press.

——and Jerrold J. Katz (eds) (1964). *The Structure of Language. Readings in the Philosophy of Language*. Englewood Cliffs NJ: Prentice Hall.

Francis, Elaine J. and Laura A. Michaelis (eds) (2003). *Mismatch: Form–Function Incongruity and the Architecture of Grammar*. Stanford: CSLI Publications.

Frank, Stefan L. and Rens Bod (2011). Insensitivity of the human sentence-processing system to hierarchical structure. *Psychological Science* 22.6: 829–34.

Frazer, Sir James George (1906–1915). *The Golden Bough. A Study in Magic and Religion*. London: Macmillan.

Frege, Gottlob (1892). Ueber Sinn und Bedeutung. *Zeitschrift für Philosophie und philosophische Kritik* 100: 25–50.

——(1918). Der Gedanke. *Beiträge zur Philosophie des deutschen Idealismus* I.1: 58–77.

Fuhrman, Orly and Lera Boroditsky (2007). Mental time-lines follow writing direction: comparing English and Hebrew speakers. In: *Proceedings of the 29th Annual Conference of the Cognitive Science Society*, Nashville TN.

Funke, Otto (1924). *Innere Sprachform. Eine Einführung in A. Martys Sprachphilosophie*. Reichenberg: Kraus.

Gaeta, Livio (2010). The invisible hand of grammaticalization. West-Germanic substitutive infinitive and the prefix *ge-**. In: Franz Rainer, Wolfgang U. Dressler, Dieter Kastovsky and Hans Christian Luschützky (eds), *Variation and Change in Morphology*. Selected Papers from the 13th International Morphology Meeting, Vienna, February 2008. Amsterdam/ Philadelphia: Benjamins: 89–105.

Gardiner, Sir Alan H. 1932. *The Theory of Speech and Language*. Oxford: Clarendon Press.

Geach, Peter T. (1962). *Reference and Generality. An Examination of Some Medieval and Modern Theories*. Ithaca NY: Cornell University Press.

Giles, Howard (1973). Accent mobility: a model and some data. *Anthropological Linguistics* 15: 87–105.

——Justine Coupland and Nikolas Coupland (eds) (1991). *Contexts of Accommodation. Developments in Applied Sociolinguistics*. Cambridge: Cambridge University Press and Paris: Éditions de la Maison des Sciences de l'Homme.

Goldberg, Adèle E. (1995). *Constructions. A Construction Grammar Approach to Argument Structure*. Chicago: The University of Chicago Press.

——(2006). *Constructions at Work. The Nature of Generalization in Language*. Oxford: Oxford University Press.

Gottschalk, Walter H. (1953). The theory of quaternality. *The Journal of Symbolic Logic* 18.3: 193–6.

Gould, Stephen J. and Richard C. Lewontin (1979). The spandrels of San Marco and the panglossian paradigm: a critique of the adaptationist programme. *Proceedings of the Royal Society of London*, Series B, Volume 205, No. 1181: 581–98.

——and Elizabeth S. Vrba (1982). Exaptation—a missing term in the science of form. *Paleobiology* 8.1: 4–15.

Green, Georgia (1974). *Semantic and Syntactic Regularity*. Bloomington IND: Indiana University Press.

Greenberg, Joseph H. (1963). Some universals of grammar with particular reference to the order of meaningful elements. In: Joseph H. Greenberg (ed.), *Universals of Language*. Cambridge MA: MIT Press: 73–113.

——(1966). *Language Universals. With Special Reference to Feature Hierarchies*. The Hague: Mouton.

Grice, H. Paul (1975). Logic and conversation. In: Peter Cole and Jerry L. Morgan (eds), *Speech Acts*. (= Syntax and Semantics 3). New York–San Francisco–London: Academic Press: 41–58.

Hallpike, Christopher R. (1979). *The Foundations of Primitive Thought*. Oxford: Clarendon Press.

Hamilton, William (1866). *Lectures on Metaphysics and Logic. Vol. IV (Lectures on Logic. Vol. II*, 2nd edition, revised). Edited by H. L. Mansel and J. Veitch. Edinburgh–London: Blackwood and Sons.

Harbour, Daniel (2009). The universal basis of local linguistic exceptionality. *Behavioral and Brain Sciences* 32: 456–7.

Harris, Randy A. (1993). *The Linguistics Wars*. Oxford–New York: Oxford University Press.

Harris, Zellig S. (1951). *Methods in Structural Linguistics*. Chicago: The University of Chicago Press.

Haspelmath, Martin (1989). From purposive to infinitive: a universal path of grammaticalization. *Folia Linguistica Historica* 10.1/2: 287–310.

——Matthew S. Dryer, David Gil and Bernard Comrie (eds) (2005). *World Atlas of Language Structures*. Oxford: Oxford University Press.

Hauser, Marc D., Noam Chomsky and W. Tecumseh Fitch (2002). The faculty of language: what is it, who has it, and how did it evolve? *Science* 298 (November):1569–79.

Hawkins, John A. (1983). *Word Order Universals.* New York: Academic Press.

——(2004). *Efficiency and Complexity in Grammars.* Oxford–New York: Oxford University Press.

——(ed.) (1988). *Explaining Language Universals.* Oxford: Blackwell.

Hawkins, John A. and Anne Cutler (1988). Psycholinguistic factors in morphological asymmetry. In: Hawkins (ed.): 280–317.

Heath, Peter (1988). *On Language. The Diversity of Human Language-Structure and its Influence on the Mental Development of Mankind.* With an introduction by Hans Aarsleff. (Translation of Von Humboldt 1836). Cambridge: Cambridge University Press.

Heim, Irene R. (1990). On the projection problem for presuppositions. In: Steven Davis (ed.), *Pragmatics. A Reader.* Oxford: Oxford University Press: 397–405.

Herder, Johann Gottfried (1772). *Abhandlung über den Ursprung der Sprache.* Berlin: Voss.

Hinskens, Frans, Peter Auer and Paul Kerswill (2005). The study of dialect convergence and divergence: conceptual and methodological considerations. In: Auer, Hinskens and Kerswill (eds): 1–48.

Hintikka, Jaakko, Julius M. E. Moravcsik and Patrick Suppes (eds) (1973). *Approaches to Natural Language.* Dordrecht: Reidel.

Holm, John (1988/9). *Pidgins and Creoles.* (2 vols) Cambridge: Cambridge University Press.

Horn, Laurence R. (1971). Negative transportation: unsafe at any speed? *Papers from the Seventh Regional Meeting of the Chicago Linguistic Society.* Chicago: Chicago Linguistic Society: 120–33.

——(1972). On the Semantic Properties of Logical Operators in English. Distributed by Indiana University Linguistics Club (IULC) 1976.

——(1978). Remarks on Neg-Raising. In: Peter Cole (ed.), *Pragmatics* (= *Syntax and Semantics 9*). New York–San Francisco–London: Academic Press: 129–220.

——(1985). Metalinguistic negation and pragmatic ambiguity. *Language* 61.1: 121–74.

——(1989). *A Natural History of Negation.* Chicago: The University of Chicago Press.

——(1990). Hamburgers and truth: why Gricean explanation is Gricean. *Berkeley Linguistic Soiety* 16: 454–71.

Huck, Geoffrey J. and John A. Goldsmith (1995). *Ideology and Linguistic Theory. Noam Chomsky and the Deep Structure Debate.* London–New York: Routledge.

Irvine, Judith T. (1992). Ideologies of honorific language. *Pragmatics* 2.3: 251–62.

Jackendoff, Ray (2011). What is the human language faculty? Two views. *Language* 87.3: 586–624.

Jacoby, Paul J. (1950). A triangle of opposites for types of propositions in Aristotelian logic. *The New Scholasticism* 24.1: 32–56.

——(1960). Contrariety and the triangle of opposites in valid inferences. *The New Scholasticism* 34.2: 141–69.

Janssen, Theo A. J. M. (1976). *Hebben-konstrukties en indirekt-objektskonstrukties.* PhD thesis, Radboud University, Nijmegen. Utrecht: HES publishers.

Jaspers, Dany (2005). *Operators in the Lexicon. On the Negative Logic of Natural Language.* PhD thesis, Leiden University. Utrecht: LOT.

——(2010). Logic of colours. The mereological algebra of colours. At: http://www.crissp.be/wp-content/uploads/handoutmitdj.pdf (Accessed: 18 March 2013).

——(2011). *Logic of Colours*. Research paper Hogeschool-Universiteit Brussel.

Jespersen, Otto (1909–1949). *Modern English Grammar on Historical Principles*. (7 vols). Copenhagen: Einar Munksgaard / London: Allen & Unwin.

——(1917). *Negation in English and Other Languages*. Det Kgl. Danske Videnskabernes Selskab. Historisk-filologiske Meddelelser. I,5. Copenhagen: Høst & Søn.

——(1924). *The Philosophy of Grammar*. London: Allen and Unwin.

Joseph, John E. (2012). *Saussure*. Oxford: Oxford University Press.

Joshi, Aravind K. and Yves Schabes (1997). Tree-adjoining grammars. In: G. Rozenberg and A. Salomaa (eds), *Handbook of Formal Languages*, Vol. 3. New York: Springer: 69–124.

Kammacher, Louise, Andreas Stöhr and Jens Normann Jørgensen (2011). Attitudinal and sociostructural factors and their role in dialect change: testing a model of subjective factors. *Language Variation and Change* 23.1: 87–104.

Kamp, Hans (1981). A theory of truth and semantic interpretation. In: Jeroen A. G. Groenendijk, Theo M. V. Janssen and Martin B. J. Stokhof (eds), *Formal Methods in the Study of Language*. Vol. I. Amsterdam: Mathematisch Centrum: 277–322.

——and Uwe Reyle (1993). *From Discourse to Logic. Introduction to Model-Theoretic Semantics of Natural Language, Formal Logic and Discourse Representation Theory*. Dordrecht: Kluwer.

Katz, Jerrold J. and Jerry A. Fodor (1963). The structure of a semantic theory. *Language* 39.2: 170–210. (Also in Fodor and Katz (eds) 1964: 479–518.)

——and Paul M. Postal (1964). *An Integrated Theory of Linguistic Descriptions*. Cambridge MA: MIT Press.

Keenan, Edward L. and Bernard Comrie (1977). Noun phrase accessibility and Universal Grammar. *Linguistic Inquiry* 8.1: 63–99.

——and Jonathan Stavi (1986). A semantic characterization of natural language determiners. *Linguistics and Philosophy* 9: 253–326.

Keesing, Roger M. (1997). Constructing space in Kwaio (Solomon Islands). In: Gunter Senft (ed.), *Referring to Space. Studies in Austronesian and Papuan Languages*. Oxford: Clarendon Press: 127–41.

Klima, Edward S. (1964). Negation in English. In: Fodor and Katz (eds): 246–323.

Klima, Gyula (1988). *Ars Artium. Essays in Philosophical Semantics, Medieval and Modern*. Budapest: Hungarian Academy of Sciences.

Kneale, William and Martha Kneale (1962). *The Development of Logic*. Oxford: Clarendon Press.

Koerner, E. F. Konrad (2000). Towards a 'full pedigree' of the 'Sapir-Whorf hypothesis': From Locke to Lucy. In: Pütz and Verspoor: 1–23.

Konieczny, Lars, Barbara Hemforth, Christoph Scheepers and Gerhard Strube (1997). The role of lexical heads in parsing: evidence from German. *Language and Cognitive Processes* 12.2/3: 307–48.

Köpcke, Klaus-Michael and David Zubin (1996). Prinzipien für die Genuszuweisung im Deutschen. In: Ewald Lang and Gisela Zifonun (eds), *Deutsch—typologisch*. Berlin–New York: De Gruyter: 473–91.

Kripke, Saul (1972). Naming and necessity. In: Davidson and Harman (eds): 253–355.

——(1980). *Naming and Necessity*. Oxford: Blackwell (= Kripke 1972).

Kristiansen, Tore and Jens Normann Jørgensen (2005). Subjective factors in dialect convergence and divergence. In: Auer, Hinskens and Kerswill (eds): 287–302.

Kruisinga, Etsko (1911). *English Accidence and Syntax.* (3 vols). 1st edition. Groningen: Noordhoff.

——(1932). *English Accidence and Syntax.* (3 vols). 5th edition. Groningen: Noordhoff.

Kuteva, Tania (2001). *Auxiliation. An Enquiry into the Nature of Grammaticalization.* Oxford–New York: Oxford University Press.

Labov, William (1966). *The Social Stratification of English in New York City.* Washington D.C.: Center for Applied Linguistics.

Lakoff, George (1987). *Women, Fire, and Dangerous Things. What Categories Reveal about the Mind.* Chicago: The University of Chicago Press.

Lakoff, Robin (1969). A syntactic argument for Negative Transportation. *Papers from the Fifth Regional Meeting of the Chicago Linguistic Society.* Chicago: Chicago Linguistic Society: 140–7.

Langacker, Ronald W. (1987). *Foundations of Cognitive Grammar. Vol. 1: Theoretical Prerequisites.* Stanford CA: Stanford University Press.

——(1991). *Foundations of Cognitive Grammar. Vol. 2: Descriptive Application.* Stanford CA: Stanford University Press.

——(2003). Construction grammars: cognitive, radical, and less so. Plenary paper ICLC 8, Logroño (Spain), June 25, 2003. MS.

Lenk, Hans (1974). Konträrbeziehungen und Operatorengleichungen im deontologischen Sechseck. In: Hans Lenk (ed.), *Normenlogik. Grundprobleme der deontischen Logik.* Pullach bei München: Verlag Dokumentation: 198–206.

Lenneberg, Eric H. (1953). Cognition in ethnolinguistics. *Language* 29.4: 463–71.

Levelt, Willem J. M. (1974a). *Formal Grammars in Linguistics and Psycholinguistics. Vol. 1: An Introduction to the Theory of Formal Languages and Automata.* (= Ianua Linguarum, Series Minor 192/1). The Hague: Mouton.

——(1974b). *Formal Grammars in Linguistics and Psycholinguistics. Vol. 2: Applications in Linguistic Theory.* (= Ianua Linguarum, Series Minor 192/2). The Hague: Mouton.

——(1974c). *Formal Grammars in Linguistics and Psycholinguistics. Vol. 3: Psycholinguistic Applications.* (= Ianua Linguarum, Series Minor 192/3). The Hague: Mouton.

——(1989). *Speaking. From Intention to Articulation.* Cambridge MA: MIT Press.

——(1996). Perspective taking and ellipsis in spatial description. In: Paul Bloom, Mary A. Peterson, Lynn Nadel and Merrill Garrett (eds), *Language and Space.* Cambridge MA: MIT Press: 77–108.

——(2008). *Formal Grammars in Linguistics and Psycholinguistics.* Anastatic reprint of Levelt (1974a, b, c) plus Postscript. Amsterdam/Philadelphia: Benjamins.

Levinson, Stephen C. (2000). *Presumptive Meanings. The Theory of Generalized Conversational Implicature.* Cambridge MA: MIT Press.

——(2001). Yélî Dnye and the theory of basic color terms. *Journal of Linguistic Anthropology* 10.1: 3–55.

——(2003). *Space in Language and Cognition. Explorations in Cognitive Diversity.* Cambridge: Cambridge University Press.

Lewis, Clarence I. (1946). *An Analysis of Knowledge and Valuation.* La Salle IL: Open Court.

Lewis, David (1969). *Convention: A Philosophical Study*. Cambridge MA: Harvard University Press.

——(1972). General semantics. In: Davidson and Harman (eds): 169–218.

——(1973). Causation. *The Journal of Philosophy* 70.17: 556–67.

Li, Peggy and Lila Gleitman (2002). Turning the tables. Language and spatial reasoning. *Cognition* 83.3: 265–94.

Löbner, Sebastian (1990). *Wahr neben Falsch. Duale Operatoren als die Quantoren natürlicher Sprache*. Tübingen: Niemeyer.

Luce, R. Duncan, Robert R. Bush and Eugene Galanter (eds) (1963). *Handbook of Mathematical Psychology*. Vol. II. New York: John Wiley & Sons.

Lucy, John A. (1996). The scope of linguistic relativity: an analysis and review of empirical research. In: John J. Gumperz and Stephen C. Levinson (eds), *Rethinking Linguistic Relativity*. Cambridge: Cambridge University Press: 37–69.

Lyons, John (1977). *Semantics. Vol. I*. Cambridge: Cambridge University Press.

MacColl, Hugh (1905a). Symbolical reasoning VII. *Mind*, New Series Vol.14, No 54: 390–7.

——(1905b). The existential import of propositions. A reply to Bertrand Russell. *Mind*, New Series Vol.14, No 55: 401–2.

Malotki, Ekkehart (1983). *Hopi Time. A Linguistic Analysis of the Temporal Concepts in the Hopi Language*. Berlin: Mouton.

Marty, Anton (1908). *Untersuchungen zur Grundlegung der allgemeinen Grammatik und Sprachphilosophie*. Halle: Niemeyer.

McCawley, James D. (1970). English as a VSO-language. *Language* 46.2: 286–99.

——(1973). *Grammar and Meaning. Papers on Syntactic and Semantic Topics*. Tokyo: Taishukan.

——(1981). *Everything that Linguists Have Always Wanted to Know about Logic* *but were ashamed to ask*. Oxford: Blackwell.

——(1982). *Thirty Million Theories of Grammar*. Chicago: The University of Chicago Press.

McDonough, Laraine, Soonja Choi and Jean M. Mandler (2003). Understanding spatial relations: flexible infants, lexical adults. *Cognitive Psychology* 46.3: 229–59.

Menzel, Christopher (1990). Actualism, ontological commitment, and possible world semantics. *Synthese* 85.3: 355–89.

Miller, George A. and Noam Chomsky (1963). Finitary models of language users. In: Luce, Bush and Galanter (eds): 419–91.

——and Philip N. Johnson-Laird (1976). *Language and Perception*. Cambridge MA: Belknap Press/Harvard University Press.

Montague, Richard (1970). English as a formal language. In: Bruno Visentini et al. (eds), *Linguaggi nella società e nella tecnica*. Milan: Edizioni di Comunità: 189–224. (reprinted in Montague 1974: 188–221).

——(1974). *Formal Philosophy. Selected Papers of Richard Montague*. Edited with an introduction by Richmond H. Thomason. Princeton: Yale University Press.

Moody, Ernest A. (1953). *Truth and Consequence in Mediæval Logic*. Amsterdam: North-Holland.

Mostowski, Andrzej (1957). On a generalization of quantifiers. *Fundamenta Mathematica* 44: 12–36.

Muravyova, Irina, A. (1992). The Paleosiberian model of incorporation in comparison with the Oceanic one. In: *Pan-Asiatic Linguistics. Proceedings of the Third International Symposium on Language and Linguistics.* Chukalongkorn University, Bangkok, January 8–10, 1992. Vol. I: 205–15.

Niedzielsky, Nancy and Howard Giles (1996). Linguistic accommodation. In: H. Goebl, P. Nelde, H. and S. Zdenek and W. Wölck (eds), *Contact Linguistics: An International Handbook of Contemporary Research.* Berlin/New York: Walter de Gruyter: 332–42.

Nuchelmans, Gabriel (1973). *Theories of the Proposition. Ancient and Medieval Conceptions of the Bearers of Truth and Falsity.* Amsterdam: North-Holland.

——(1980). *Late-Scholastic and Humanist Theories of the Proposition.* Amsterdam: North-Holland.

——(1983). *Judgment and Proposition. From Descartes to Kant.* Amsterdam: North-Holland.

Núñez, Rafael E. and Eve Sweetser (2006). With the future behind them: convergent evidence from Aymara language and gesture in the crosslinguistic comparison of spatial construals of time. *Cognitive Science* 30.3: 401–50.

Ogden, C. K. and I. A. Richards (1923). *The Meaning of Meaning: A Study of the Influence of Language upon Thought and of the Science of Symbolism.* London: Routledge & Kegan Paul.

Osgood, Charles E. and Thomas A. Sebeok (eds) (1954). *Psycholinguistics. A Survey of Theory and Research Problems.* Report of the 1953 Summer Seminar Sponsored by the Committee on Linguistics and Psychology of the Social Science Research Council. (= Indiana University Publications in Anthropology and Linguistics, Memoir 10.) Baltimore: Waverly Press.

——George J. Suci and Percy H. Tannenbaum (1957). *The Measurement of Meaning.* Chicago: The University of Illinois Press.

Overdiep, Gerrit S. (1937). *Stilistische grammatica van het moderne Nederlandsch.* Zwolle: Tjeenk Willink.

Parsons, Terence (2006). The traditional Square of Opposition. In: Ed N. Zalta (ed.), *The Stanford Encyclopedia of Philosophy* (October 1, 2006 revision). At: http://plato.stanford.edu/archives/win2006/entries/square/ (Accessed: 18 March 2013).

——(2008). Things that are right with the traditional Square of Opposition. *Logica Universalis* 2: 3–11.

Partee, Barbara (1979). Semantics—mathematics or psychology? In: Rainer Bäuerle, Urs Egli and Arnim von Stechow (eds), *Semantics from Different Points of View.* Berlin: Springer: 1–14.

Patzig, Günther (ed.) 1966. *Gottlob Frege, Logische Untersuchungen.* Göttingen: Vandenhoeck & Ruprecht.

Peters, P. Stanley and Robert W. Ritchie (1971). On restricting the base component of transformational grammars. *Information and Control* 18.5: 483–501.

——(1973). On the generative power of transformational grammars. *Information Sciences* 6: 49–83.

Petersson, Karl Magnus, Vasiliki Folia and Peter Hagoort (2010). What artificial grammar learning reveals about the neurobiology of syntax. *Brain & Language*, Advance online publication. doi: 10.1016/j.bandl.2010.08.003.

Pinker, Steven A. (1994). *The Language Instinct.* New York: William Morrow.

Post, Emil L. (1944). Recursively enumerable sets of positive integers and their decision problems. *Bulletin of the American Mathematical Society* 50: 284–316.

Postal, Paul M. (1974). *On Raising. One Rule of English Grammar and its Theoretical Implications.* Cambridge MA: MIT Press.

Poutsma, Hendrik (1904–1929). *A Grammar of Late Modern English.* (5 vols). Groningen: Noordhoff.

Pullum, Geoffrey K. (1991). *The Great Eskimo Vocabulary Hoax and Other Irreverent Essays on the Study of Language.* Chicago: The University of Chicago Press.

——(2011) On the mathematical foundations of *Syntactic Structures. Journal of Logic, Language and Information* 20: 277–96.

——and Barbara C. Scholz (2010). Recursion and the infinitude claim. In: Harry van der Hulst (ed.), *Recursion and Human Language.* Berlin: Mouton de Gruyter: 113–38.

Pütz, Martin and Marjolijn H. Verspoor (2000). *Explorations in Linguistic Relativity.* Amsterdam/Philadelphia: Benjamins.

Quine, Willard V. O. (1953). *From a Logical Point of View.* Cambridge MA: Harvard University Press.

Raposo, Eduardo (1987). Case theory and Infl-to-Comp: the inflected infinitive in European Portuguese. *Linguistic Inquiry* 18.1: 85–109.

Ritchie, Graeme (1983). Semantics in parsing. In: M. King (ed.), *Parsing Natural Language.* New York: Academic Press: 199–217.

Romanes, George J. (1888). *Mental Evolution in Man: Origin of Human Faculty.* London: Kegan Paul & Trench.

Rooth, Mats E. (1985). *Association with Focus.* PhD thesis, University of Massachusetts at Amherst.

Rosenbloom, Paul (1950). *The Elements of Mathematical Logic.* New York: Dover.

Ross, John, R. (1967). *Constraints on Variables in Syntax.* PhD thesis MIT. (= Ross 1986)

——(1986). *Infinite Syntax!* Norwood NJ: Ablex.

Russell, Bertrand (1905). On denoting. *Mind,* New Series 14.56: 479–93.

Sandall, Roger (2001). *The Culture Cult. Designer Tribalism and Other Essays.* Boulder CO: The Westview Press.

Sapir, Edward (1921). *Language. An Introduction to the Study of Speech.* New York: Harcourt, Brace & Co.

——(1929). The status of linguistics as a science. *Language* 5: 207–14.

——(1931). Conceptual categories in primitive languages. *Science* 74: 578.

Saunders, Barbara (1998). Revisiting basic colour terms. Paper read at the conference 'Anthropology and Psychology. The Legacy of the Torres Strait Expedition', held at St. John's College, Cambridge, 10–12 August 1998.

——and Jaap van Brakel (1997). Are there nontrivial constraints on colour categorization? *Behavioural and Brain Sciences* 20.2: 167–79.

Schleicher, August (1861/2). *Compendium der vergleichenden Grammatik der indogermanischen Sprachen.* (2 vols). Weimar: Böhlau.

Schmidt, Johannes (1872). *Die Verwandtschaftsverhältnisse der indogermanischen Sprachen.* Weimar: Böhlau.

Schuchardt, Hugo (1885). *Ueber die Lautgesetze. Gegen die Junggrammatiker.* Berlin: Robert Oppenheim.

——(1914). *Die Sprache der Saramakkaneger in Surinam.* Verhandelingen der Koninklijke Akademie van Wetenschappen te Amsterdam, Afdeeling Letterkunde, Nieuwe Reeks, Deel xiv No. 6. Amsterdam: Johannes Müller.

Searle, John (1995). *The Construction of Social Reality.* New York: Free Press.

Senghas, Ann, Sotaro Kita and Aslı Özyürek (2004). Children creating core properties of language: evidence from an emerging sign language in Nicaragua. *Science* 305.5691: 1779–82.

Sesmat, Augustin (1951). *Logique II: les raisonnements, la logistique.* Paris: Hermann.

Seuren, Pieter A. M. (1969). *Operators and Nucleus. A Contribution to the Theory of Grammar.* Cambridge: Cambridge University Press. (re-issued 2010)

——(1972a). *Predicate Raising and Dative in French and Sundry Languages.* Magdalen College, Oxford / Linguistic Agency University Trier (LAUT). (Reprinted in Seuren 2001a: 139–84)

——(1972b). Autonomous versus semantic syntax. *Foundations of Language* 8.2: 237–65. (reprinted in Seuren 2001: 30–54)

——(1972c). Taaluniversalia in de transformationele grammatica. *Leuvense Bijdragen* 61.4: 311–70.

——(1974). Negative's travels. In: Pieter A. M. Seuren (ed.), *Semantic Syntax.* Oxford: Oxford University Press: 183–208.

——(1975). *Tussen taal en denken. Een bijdrage tot de empirische funderingen van de semantiek.* Utrecht: Oosthoek, Scheltema & Holkema.

——(1982). Internal variability in competence. *Linguistische Berichte* 77: 1–31.

——(1985). *Discourse Semantics.* Oxford: Blackwell.

——(1986a). Adjectives as adjectives in Sranan. A reply to Sebba. *Journal of Pidgin and Creole Languages* 1.1: 123–34.

——(1986b). Predicate Raising and semantic transparency in Mauritian Creole. In: Norbert Boretzky, Werner Enninger and Thomas Stolz (eds), *Akten des 2. Essener Kolloquiums über "Kreolsprachen und Sprachkontakte", 29–30 November 1985.* Bochum: Brockmeyer: 203–29.

——(1988). Presupposition and negation. *Journal of Semantics* 6.3/4: 175–226.

——(1989). Notes on reflexivity. In: F. J. Heyvaert and F. Steurs (eds), *Worlds behind Words. Essays in honour of Prof. Dr. F. G. Droste on the occasion of his sixtieth birthday.* Leuven: Leuven University Press.

——(1990). Verb Syncopation and Predicate Raising in Mauritian Creole. *Linguistics* 28.4: 809–44.

——(1991). The definition of serial verbs. In: Francis Byrne and Thom Huebner (eds), *Development and Structures of Creole Languages. Essays in Honor of Derek Bickerton.* Amsterdam/Philadelphia: Benjamins: 193–205.

——(1993). Why does 2 mean '2'? Grist to the anti-Grice mill. In: Eva Hajičová (ed.), *Proceedings of the Conference on Functional Description of Language, Prague November 24–27, 1992.* Prague: Faculty of Mathematics and Physics, Charles University: 225–35.

——(1996). *Semantic Syntax.* Oxford: Blackwell.

——(1998). *Western Linguistics. An Historical Introduction.* Oxford: Blackwell.

——(2000). Presupposition, negation and trivalence. *Journal of Linguistics* 36.2: 261–97.

——(2001a). *A View of Language.* Oxford: Oxford University Press.

——(2001b). Lexical meaning and metaphor. In: E.N. Enikö (ed.) *Cognition in Language Use. Selected Papers from the 7th International Pragmatics Conference, Budapest 2000. Vol. I.* Antwerp, Belgium: International Pragmatics Association (IPrA): 422–31.

——(2002). The logic of thinking. *Koninklijke Nederlandse Akademie van Wetenschappen, Mededelingen van de Afdeling Letterkunde, Nieuwe Reeks* 65.9: 5–35.

——(2003). Verb clusters and branching directionality in German and Dutch. In: Pieter A. M. Seuren and Gerard Kempen (eds): 247–96.

——(2004a). *Chomsky's Minimalism.* Oxford–New York: Oxford University Press.

——(2004b). The importance of being modular. Review article of Croft (2001). *Journal of Linguistics* 40.3: 593–635.

——(2005). Eubulides as a 20th-century semanticist. *Language Sciences* 27.1: 75–95.

——(2006). The natural logic of language and cognition. *Pragmatics* 16.1: 103–38.

——(2007). *The Victorious Square. A Study of Natural Predicate Logic.* Nijmegen: Max Planck Institute for Psycholinguistics. (unpublished)

——(2009a). *Language in Cognition.* (= *Language from Within*, Vol. 1). Oxford: Oxford University Press.

——(2009b). The clitics mechanism in French and Italian. *Probus* 21.1: 83–142.

——(2010). *The Logic of Language.* (= *Language from Within*, Vol. 2). Oxford: Oxford University Press.

——and Camiel Hamans (2010). Antifunctionality in language change. *Folia Linguistica* 44.1: 127–62.

——and Gerard Kempen (eds) (2003). *Verb Constructions in German and Dutch.* Amsterdam/ Philadelphia: Benjamins.

Shannon, Claude E. (1948). A mathematical theory of communication. *Bell System Technical Journal* 27: 379–423; 623–56.

——and Warren Weaver (1949). *The Mathematical Theory of Communication.* Urbana IL: University of Illinois Press.

Sherif, Muzafer and Carolyn W. Sherif (1966). *Groups in Harmony and Tension. An Integration of Studies on Intergroup Relations.* New York: Octagon Books.

Shramko, Yaroslav and Heinrich Wansing (2010). Truth values. In: *Stanford Encyclopedia of Philosophy.* At: http://www.science.uva.nl/~seop/entries/truth-values/ (Accessed: 18 March 2013).

Slobin, Dan (1987). Thinking for speaking. In: Jon Aske, Natasha Beery, Laura A. Michaelis and Hana Filip (eds), *Berkeley Linguistics Society. Proceedings of the Thirteenth Annual Meeting. February 14–16, 1987.* Berkeley CA: Berkeley Linguistics Society: 435–45.

Smessaert, Hans (2009). On the 3D visualisation of logical relations. *Logica Universalis* 3: 303–32.

Smessaert, Hans (2011). Why some hexagons of opposition are fragments: Sesmat-Blanché versus Sherwood-Czezowski. Paper read at LNAT-2, Brussels, 21–22 December 2011.

Smullyan, Raymond (1981). *What is the Name of this Book? The Riddle of Dracula and Other Logical Puzzles.* London: Penguin Books Ltd.

Stassen, Léon (1985). *Comparison and Universal Grammar.* Oxford: Blackwell.

——(1997). *Intransitive Predication.* Oxford: Oxford University Press.

——(2009). *Predicative Possession.* Oxford: Oxford University Press.

Steinthal, Heymann (1855). *Grammatik, Logik und Psychologie. Ihre Prinzipien und ihre Verhältnisse zueinander.* Berlin: Dümmler.

Strawson, Peter F. (1950). On referring. *Mind* 59: 320–44.

——(1974). *Subject and Predicate in Logic and Grammar.* London: Methuen.

Swoyer, Chris (2003). The linguistic relativity hypothesis. *Stanford Encyclopedia of Philosophy.* At: http://plato.stanford.edu/entries/relativism/supplement2.html (Accessed: 18 March 2013).

Tarski, Alfred (1944). The semantic conception of truth and the foundations of semantics. *Philosophy and Phenomenological Research* 4: 1347.

——and Robert Vaught (1956). Arithmetical extensions of relational systems. *Compositio Mathematica* 13: 81–102.

Tervoort, Bernard T. M. (1953). *Structurele analyse van visueel taalgebruik binnen een groep dove kinderen.* (2 vols) Amsterdam: Noord-Holland.

Tesnière, Lucien (1959). *Éléments de syntaxe structurale.* Paris: Klincksieck.

Thompson, Manley H. (1953). On Aristotle's Square of Opposition. *The Philosophical Review* 62.2: 251–65.

Tomasello, Michael (2003). *Constructing a Language. A Usage-Based Theory of Language Acquisition.* Cambridge MA: Harvard University Press.

Torralbo, Ana, Julio Santiago and Juan Lupiáñez (2006). Flexible conceptual projection of time onto spatial frames of reference. *Cognitive Science* 30: 745–57.

Townsend, David J. and Thomas G. Bever (2001). *Sentence Comprehension. The Integration of Habits and Rules.* Cambridge MA: MIT Press.

Trudgill, Peter (2011). *Sociolinguistic Typology. Social determinants of Linguistic Complexity.* Oxford: Oxford University Press.

Tversky, Barbara, Sol Kugelmass and Atalia Winter (1991). Crosscultural and developmental trends in graphic productions. *Cognitive Psychology* 23: 515–57.

Van Cleve, James and Robert E. Frederick (eds) (1991). *The Philosophy of Right and Left: Incongruent Counterparts and the Nature of Space.* Berlin: Springer.

Van Fraassen, Bas (1971). *Formal Semantics and Logic.* New York–London: Macmillan.

Van Kemenade, Ans (1992). The history of English modals. A reanalysis. *Folia Linguistica Historica* 13.1/2: 143–66.

Von Humboldt, Wilhelm (1836). *Ueber die Verschiedenheit des menschlichen Sprachbaues und ihren Einfluß auf die geistige Entwickelung des Menschengeschlechts.* Königliche Akademie der Wissenschaften. Berlin: Dümmler.

Von Stechow, Arnim (1985). Max J. Cresswell, *Structured Meanings: the Semantics of Propositional Attitudes.* Review article. *Journal of Semantics* 4.2: 165–91.

Voorhoeve, Jan and Ursy M. Lichtveld (1975). *Creole Drum. An Anthology of Creole Literature in Surinam.* Caribbean Series 15. New Haven: Yale University Press.

Walker, Marilyn (ed.) (1997). *Centering Theory in Discourse.* Oxford: Oxford University Press.

Weger, Ulrich W. and Jay Pratt (2008). Time flies like an arrow: space-time compatibility effects suggest the use of a mental time-line. *Psychonomic Bulletin & Review* 15: 426–30.

Weisgerber, Leo (1929). *Muttersprache und Geistesbildung.* Göttingen: Vandenhoeck & Ruprecht.

Wetzer, Harrie (1996). *The Typology of Adjectival Predication.* Berlin–New York: Mouton de Gruyter.

Whorf, Benjamin L. (1956). *Language, Thought, and Reality: Selected Writings of Benjamin Lee Whorf.* Edited by John B. Carroll. Cambridge MA: Technology Press of Massachusetts Institute of Technology.

Wundt, Wilhelm (1880). *Logik. Eine Untersuchung der Prinzipien der Erkenntnis und der Methoden Wissenschaftlicher Forschung.* Stuttgart: Enke.

Zwaan, Rolf A. (1999). Situation models: the mental leap into imagined worlds. *Current Directions in Psychological Science* 8.1: 15–18.

——and Gabriel A. Radvansky (1998). Situation models in language comprehension and memory. *Psychological Bulletin* 123.2: 162–85.

Zwicky, Arnold (1973). Linguistics as chemistry: the substance theory of semantic primes. In: Stephen Anderson and Paul Kiparsky (eds), *A Festschrift for Morris Halle.* New York: Holt: 467–85.

Index